CLASSROOM ASSESSMENT

CLASSROOM ASSESSMENT:

Principles and Practice for
Effective Instruction

James H. McMillan
Virginia Commonwealth University

Allyn and Bacon
Boston • London • Toronto • Tokyo • Singapore • Sydney

Senior Vice President and Publisher: Nancy Forsyth
Editorial Assistant: Kate Wagstaffe
Marketing Manager: Kris Farnsworth
Editorial-Production Administrator: Rob Lawson
Editorial-Production Service: Ruttle, Shaw & Wetherill, Inc.
Composition Buyer: Linda Cox
Manufacturing Buyer: Suzanne Lareau
Cover Administrator: Suzanne Harbison

Copyright © 1997 by Allyn & Bacon
A Viacom Company
Needham Heights, MA 02194
Internet: www.abacon.com
American Online: keyword: College Online

Library of Congress Cataloging-in-Publication Data

McMillan, James H.
    Classroom assessment : principles and practice for effective
instruction / James McMillan.
        p. cm.
    Includes bibliographical references.
    ISBN 0–205–16587–7
    1. Educational tests and measurements.   2. Examinations.
3. Examinations—Validity.   4. Examinations—Interpretation.
I. Title.
LB3051.M462498   1997
371.2′6—dc20   96–14657
                                                         CIP

Printed in the United States of America

10 9 8 7 6 5 4   01 00 99 98

*Dedicated to thousands of teachers
who work very hard to improve the lives of their students.*

CONTENTS

1

THE ROLE OF ASSESSMENT IN TEACHING

This book is about how credible assessment information, procedures, and techniques can be used by teachers to improve student learning. In the past twenty years, research on teacher decision making, cognitive learning, student motivation, and other topics has changed what we know about the importance of assessment for effective teaching. For example, one important finding is that good teachers continually assess their students relative to learning goals and adjust their instruction on the basis

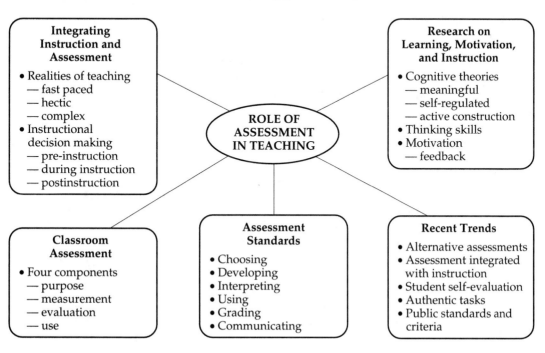

Integrating Instruction and Assessment

- Realities of teaching
  — fast paced
  — hectic
  — complex
- Instructional decision making
  — pre-instruction
  — during instruction
  — postinstruction

Research on Learning, Motivation, and Instruction

- Cognitive theories
  — meaningful
  — self-regulated
  — active construction
- Thinking skills
- Motivation
  — feedback

ROLE OF ASSESSMENT IN TEACHING

Classroom Assessment

- Four components
  — purpose
  — measurement
  — evaluation
  — use

Assessment Standards

- Choosing
- Developing
- Interpreting
- Using
- Grading
- Communicating

Recent Trends

- Alternative assessments
- Assessment integrated with instruction
- Student self-evaluation
- Authentic tasks
- Public standards and criteria

CHAPTER 1   Concept Map

of this information. Another important finding is that assessment of students not only documents what students know and can do, assessment itself influences learning. As a result of this research, new purposes, methods, and approaches to student assessment are being developed. These changes underscore a new understanding of the important role that assessment plays in instruction and learning. This first chapter summarizes the research on teacher decision making to show how assessment is integrated with instruction. The major components of assessment are reviewed, with an emphasis on current conceptualizations that are consistent with recent research related to learning and motivation. Finally, assessment competencies for teachers are summarized to lay the foundation for what is covered in subsequent chapters.

INTEGRATING INSTRUCTION AND ASSESSMENT

The Realities of Teaching

Classroom life is fast paced, hectic, and complex. To illustrate this reality, I have summarized some of what Michelle Barrow does during a typical day in her first-grade classroom. She has ten boys and eleven girls in her class, four of whom are from racial minority groups and six of whom are from single-parent families. As many as four of her students will participate in the gifted/talented program, and four students were retained. See how easy it is for you to get through this list of disparate tasks.

Before school begins in the morning, Michelle:

- reviews what was learned/taught the previous day
- goes over student papers to see who did or did not grasp concepts
- prepares a rough agenda for the day
- has instructional materials ready
- speaks with aide about plans for the day
- puts journals on student desks

As soon as students enter the classroom, Michelle:

- greets students at the door
- reminds students to put away homework
- speaks with Brent about his expected behavior for the day
- reminds Anthony about what he is to do if he becomes bothered or frustrated by others
- gives Colin a morning hug

During the morning, Michelle:

- calls students to the table to go over the reading assignment

- has Dawn read a column of words and then goes back and randomly points to the words to see if Dawn knows them or simply has them memorized
- comments to Lucy that she has really improved since the first day of school
- discusses with Kevin the importance of doing homework every night
- listens as Tim attempts to sound out each word and gradually blends them together
- reminds Maggie that she is to be working in her journal rather than visiting and talking with others
- gives Jason, Kory, and Kristen a vocabulary sheet to do since they have completed their journals
- reviews with all students work to be done in centers, how many students should be in each center, and how to complete the contract
- observes students in learning centers before calling reading groups to tables
- helps Catherine decide which center to go to
- warns Alex and Colin to get to centers rather than playing around
- calls up middle reading level group, asks what an action word is, and has each student give an example of an action word
- verbally reinforces correct answers, gives each student a copy of the week's story, goes through the book and points out action words
- notices that Jenna is not giving answers nor pointing out action words but is instead looking at other students
- calls up the low reading group and focuses on letters *m* and *f*
- asks students to write an *m* on their chalkboards
- notices that Kevin has poor fine-motor skills and makes a mental note to send a message to his parents telling them that he should practice his handwriting
- checks on Anthony to see how many centers he has completed
- reminds students about rewinding the tape player and filmstrip
- notices that students in the writing center are not doing as they were instructed
- gives students a five-minute warning to get ready to go to physical education
- walks beside Anthony down the hall, verbally praising him for following directions
- taps Brent on his shoulder, looks at Maggie
- calls up high reading group, reviews action words
- does gifted/talented curriculum with high group
- notices that Sarah has some difficulty answering higher level thinking questions
- makes a mental note to split gifted group up into two smaller groups

After lunch, Michelle's day continues as she:

- begins math lesson on beginning addition with hippo counter
- walks behind Scott and gives the next problem to the class
- walks to orange table and observes students as they solve a problem
- punches cards of students who have followed directions
- notices that another table immediately stops talking and starts paying attention
- collects hippo counters and has students line up for recess

- sends Jackie to the nurse for a sore throat
- once outside, reminds students of boundaries
- plays "red light green light" with a group of students
- calls Colin and Maggie to sit out for five minutes
- notices Kristen is playing by herself, not with Andrea
- back in classroom, calls students by tables to get a drink and wash hands
- tells students to rewrite sloppy copies
- reminds Kevin and Brent to use guide lines on the paper
- praises and gives punches on cards to Sarah and a few other students for good handwriting and concentration
- assists Dawn with what she is to do
- reaffirms Catherine's question that she is doing the right thing
- notices that Tim is watching others, asks him if he needs help
- gives five-minute warning for music time, notices students working more intensely
- lines up students for music once papers have been collected
- while students are in music, looks over their writing, arranges the papers into groups
- checks in nurse's office for any mail or messages

After students leave for the day, Michelle continues to teach by:

- grading student papers
- making sure materials are ready for the next day
- making notes in her gradebook about notes sent home and how the day went
- checking portfolios to see progress
- calling some parents

Was it difficult to get through the list? If so, you have some empathy for the hectic nature of classrooms and the need to make many decisions quickly about students and instructional activities. What is represented here is just a small sample of Michelle's actions, all of which are based on decisions that in turn depend on how well she has assessed her students. How did she decide to discuss with Kevin the importance of homework? What made her decide to warn Alex and Colin? What evidence did she use to decide that Jenna was not paying attention to the lesson? In each of these cases, Michelle had to conduct some kind of assessment of the student prior to making her decisions. The role of an effective teacher is to reach these decisions reflectively, based on evidence gathered through assessment, reasoning, and experience.

Each decision is based on information that Michelle has gathered through a multitude of student interactions and behavior. Research indicates that a teacher may have as many as 1,000 or even 1,500 interactions with students *each day* (Billups & Rauth, 1987; Jackson, 1968). Often these interactions and decisions occur with incomplete or inaccurate information, making the job of teaching even more difficult.

Consider how the following aspects of Michelle's and other teachers' classrooms affect decision making (Doyle, 1986).

1. Multidimensionality: Choices of teachers are rarely simple. Many different tasks and events occur continuously, and students with different preferences and abilities must receive limited resources for different objectives. Waiting for one student to answer a question may negatively influence the motivation of another student. How can the teacher best assess these multiple demands and student responses to make appropriate decisions?
2. Simultaneity: Many things happen at once in classrooms. Good teachers must monitor several activities at the same time. What does the teacher look for and listen for so that the monitoring and responses to students are appropriate?
3. Immediacy: Because the pace of classrooms is rapid, there is little time for reflection. Decisions are made quickly. What should teachers focus on so that these quick decisions are the right ones that will help students learn?
4. Unpredictability: Classroom events often take unanticipated turns, and distractions are frequent. How do teachers evaluate and respond to these unexpected events?
5. History: After a few weeks, routines and norms are established for behavior. What expectations for assessment does the teacher communicate to students?

It is in these complex environments that teachers must make some of their most important decisions—about what and how much students have learned. Action is based on these decisions. Accurate and appropriate student assessment provides the information to help teachers make better decisions. In the classroom context, then, *assessment* is the gathering, interpretation, and use of information to aid teacher decision making. Assessment, in other words, is an umbrella concept that encompasses different techniques, strategies, and uses.

Instructional Decision Making and Assessment

It is helpful to conceptualize teacher decision making by *when* decisions are made—either before, during, or after instruction. Pre-instructional decisions are needed to set learning goals, select appropriate teaching activities, and prepare learning materials. As instructional activities are implemented, decisions are made about the delivery and pace in presenting information, keeping the students' attention, controlling the students' behavior, and making adjustments in lesson plans. At the end of instruction, teachers evaluate student learning, instructional activities, and themselves to know what to teach next, to grade students, and to improve instruction. Figure 1.1 on page 6 presents examples of the types of questions teachers ask at these different points in the instructional process. The figure also offers examples of the type of assessment information needed to ask these decisions.

Decisions are based on the information provided from the assessments to answer each of the questions. Suppose you want to know how well your students are able to read before you begin formal instruction on the content. You review students'

FIGURE 1.1   Examples of Questions for Decision-Making and Assessment Information

When Decisions Are Made	Questions	Assessment Information
Before Instruction	How much do my students know?	Previous student achievement; test scores; observations of student performance
	Are my students motivated to learn?	Observations of student involvement and willingness to ask questions
	Are there any exceptional students? If so, what should I plan for them?	Student records; conference with a special education teacher
	What instructional activities should I plan? Are these activities realistic for these students?	Overall strengths and needs of students; comments from previous teachers; evaluations of previous teaching
	What homework assignments should I prepare?	Student progress and level of understanding
During Instruction	What type of feedback should I give to students?	Quality of student work; type of student
	What question should I ask?	Observation of student understanding
	How should a student response to a question be answered?	Potential for this student to know the answer
	Which student needs my individual attention?	Performance on homework; observations of work in class
	What response is best to student inattention or disruption?	Effect of the student on others
	When should I stop this lecture?	Observation of student attention
After Instruction	How well have my students mastered the material?	Achievement test results in relation to a specified level
	Are students ready for the next unit?	Analysis of demonstrated knowledge
	What grades should the students receive?	Tests; quizzes; homework; class participation
	What comments should I make to parents?	Improvement; observations of behavior
	How should I change my instruction?	Diagnosis of demonstrated learning; student evaluations

previous grades and performance on standardized tests, and you observe students for a few days to see how well they can read. All of these assessments answer the question: How well do my students read? If the grades, tests, and observations suggest that students have difficulty reading, then you'll decide to use materials that will not be too difficult for them. If, on the other hand, you find that your students are proficient readers, you will decide to use materials that they will find interesting and challenging to read. Think about it from the perspective of being a student. Have you ever been in a class where the instructor failed to find out how much you already knew about the content? You probably were either bored or overwhelmed.

Figure 1.2 illustrates further how assessment is involved in each stage of the instructional process. This figure shows how pre-instructional assessment is used to provide information to transform general learning goals and objectives into specific learning targets. You will usually be provided with general district or school learning goals for a particular grade level or subject. These goals are used as a starting point to develop more specific learning targets that take into account the characteristics and needs of the students and your style and beliefs. Pre-instructional assessment is an absolutely essential step for effective instruction. If you can't identify what specific knowledge, skills, attitudes, and other learning targets are important, it is unlikely that students, parents, or the teacher will know when they have been successful. In other words, you must determine what it is that students should know and be able to do at the end of an instructional unit.

Once clear learning targets are established, the teacher selects instructional strategies and activities to meet the targets. This is often operationalized as a lesson plan or instructional plan. It consists of what teachers will do and what they will have their students do for a specific period of time. During instruction, there is interaction between the teacher and students that constantly involves making assessments about how to respond to students appropriately and keep them on task. During this time, assessment information is used to monitor learning, check for progress, and diagnose learning problems.

After instruction, more formal assessment of learning targets is conducted, which loops back to inform subsequent learning targets, instructional plans, and

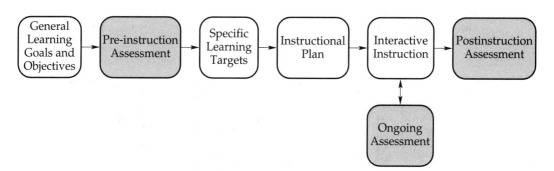

FIGURE 1.2   Relationship between Instruction and Assessment

interactive instruction. Assessment at the end of an instructional unit also provides information for grading students, evaluating teaching, and evaluating curriculum and school programs.

The point is that assessment is not only an *add-on* activity that occurs after instruction is completed. Rather, assessment is integrally related to all aspects of teacher decision making and instruction. Michelle Barrow did assessment *before* instruction by reviewing the performance of students on the previous day's work to see who did and who did not grasp the concepts. She used this information to plan subsequent instruction. *During* instruction Michelle constantly observed student work and responded to provide appropriate feedback and to keep students on task. *After* instruction she graded papers, checked student progress, and made decisions about the focus of instruction for the next day.

With this introduction, we will now consider more specifically what is meant by such terms as *test* and *assessment*, and how current conceptualizations enhance older definitions of *measurement* and *evaluation* to improve teaching and learning.

WHAT IS CLASSROOM ASSESSMENT?

Classroom assessment can be defined as the collection, interpretation, and use of information to help teachers make better decisions. Conceptualized in this way, assessment is more than *testing* or *measurement*, which are familiar terms that have been used extensively in discussing how students are evaluated.

There are four essential components to implementing classroom assessment: purpose, measurement, evaluation, and use. These components are illustrated in Figure 1.3, with questions to ask yourself at each step. The figure shows the sequence of the components, beginning with identification of purpose.

Purpose

Whether done prior to, during, or after instruction, the first step in any assessment is to clarify the specific purpose or purposes of gathering the information. That is, why are you doing the assessment? What will be gained by it? What teacher decision making is enhanced by the information gathered through the assessment

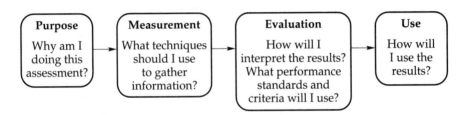

FIGURE 1.3   Components of Classroom Assessment

process? Perhaps most important, how will student learning be enhanced by the assessment? We have traditionally thought about assessment as a way to measure what students have learned, and to grade them. But other reasons for doing assessment need to be considered. For example, will your assessment be designed deliberately to improve student performance, not simply provide an audit of it? Is the nature of the assessment such that it will provide user-friendly feedback to students? Do the results of the assessment make it possible to track student progress in learning, not just current status? Has the assessment motivated students to learn? Do the assessments accurately communicate your expectations to students and what is most valued? Do the assessments provide a realistic estimation of what students are able to do outside of the classroom? Is the purpose to assess breadth or depth of student learning?

You will need to consider these questions to fully integrate assessment with instruction to enhance decision making. Otherwise, your assessments will likely resemble the ones you have probably found least helpful as a student—those that give you little feedback, don't reflect your progress very well, encourage you to study simply to pass the test, and don't match what was taught.

Measurement

The term *measurement* has traditionally been defined as a systematic process of assigning numbers to performance. It is used to determine how much of a trait, attribute, or characteristic an individual possesses. In this book this traditional definition is broadened to include more qualitative ways of defining a trait, behavior, or performance, because much of what teachers do during instruction involves a less than systematic or quantitative process. Thus, *measurement* is the process by which traits, characteristics, or behavior are *differentiated*. The process of differentiation can be very formal and quantitative, such as using a thermometer to measure temperature, or can consist of less formal processes, such as observation ("It's very hot today!"). Typically, measurement is used to assign numbers to describe attributes or characteristics of a person, object, or event, but I want to emphasize that qualitative information can also be used to differentiate. A *test* is a formalized procedure in which students respond to questions.

A variety of techniques can be used to measure a defined trait or learning target, such as tests, ratings, observations, and interviews. As you are well aware, there are different kinds of tests, differing on such characteristics as format (e.g., multiple choice or essay), developer (teacher, school division, or commercial publisher), and form of response (oral or written). As we will see in later chapters, the choice of measurement technique depends on your purpose and learning target. For example, if the purpose is primarily to enhance instruction, the measurement techniques will be designed by the teacher, provide immediate feedback that is meaningful to students, and will be adapted to the local context. On the other hand, if the purpose is primarily to sort students for grading, selected-response techniques will probably be used (e.g., multiple choice) and they will be centrally mandated, with little feedback given to students.

Evaluation

Once measurement is used to gather information you will need to place some degree of value on different numbers and observations. This process is identified in Figure 1.3 (page 8) as *evaluation*, the making of judgments about quality—how good the behavior or performance is. Evaluation involves an *interpretation* of what has been gathered through measurement, in which value judgments are made about performance. For example, measurement consists of the administration and scoring of a test, while evaluation is a judgment about what different test scores mean.

Teachers' professional judgments play a large role in evaluation. What is a "good" student paper to one teacher may be only an "adequate" paper to another teacher. Thus, assessment is more than *correctness*, it is also what is of value.

An important determinant of how you evaluate a performance is the nature of performance standards that you employ. *Performance standards* are what are used to determine whether a performance is "good" or "bad." Increasingly, such standards refer to high, specific, and valued measurable results that indicate a specific level of performance. According to Wiggins (1993), standards should be so high as to be "ideal" and out of reach for all but a few students. For example, in gymnastics the "standard" is defined by performing all skills to perfection and receiving a score of 10. Few ever attain this level of performance, but the standard is clear.

Criteria also play an important part of the evaluation process. *Criteria* are the specific behaviors or dimensions that are evidenced to successfully attain the standard. These criteria may be the most important influences on evaluation. They may be called *scoring criteria*, *scoring guidelines*, or *rubrics*. For example, take as a standard that students know all state capitals in the United States. The criteria are what the teacher uses to conclude that the student does, indeed, know the capitals. For one teacher this may mean giving the students a map and having the students write in the capital for each state; for another teacher it may mean answering twenty multiple-choice questions correctly. Often teachers use criteria for scoring tests and papers without a clear standard. In fact, if only informally, teachers must have some type of criteria to make assessment evaluations.

Both standards and criteria communicate to students the teacher's expectations of them. The nature of questions and feedback, the difficulty of assignments, and the rigor of the criteria tell students what the teacher believes they are capable of achieving. These expectations are important in motivating students and in setting an academic achievement climate in the classroom.

As you can see, setting standards and criteria is a critical component of assessment, one that we will consider in much greater detail in Chapter 2.

Use

The final stage of implementing assessment is how the evaluations are used. The use of test scores and other information is closely tied to the decisions teachers must make to provide effective instruction, and to the needs of students and parents. As indicated in Figure 1.1 on page 6, these decisions depend on *when* they are made; they can also be categorized into three major uses: diagnosis, grading, and instruction.

Diagnosis

Diagnostic decisions are made about individual students as well as group strengths, weaknesses, and needs. Typically, information is gathered that will allow the teacher to diagnose the specific area that needs further attention or where progress is being made. The diagnosis includes an assessment of *why* a student may be having difficulty so that appropriate instructional activities can be prescribed. For example, teachers use homework diagnostically to determine the extent of student understanding and to identify students who do not understand the assignment. A pretest may be used to diagnose specific gaps in student knowledge that need to be targeted. Students are closely monitored to check motivation, understanding, and progress. Standardized test scores may be used diagnostically prior to instruction to plan instructional activities. Such *sizing-up* assessments are done in the beginning of the year to obtain an idea of the abilities and interests of the students.

Grading

Grading decisions are clearly based on measurement-driven information. While most teachers must adhere to grading scales and definitions, there is a great amount of variability in what teachers use to determine grades, how they use the process of grading to motivate students, and the standards they use to judge the quality of student work. Some teachers, for example, use grading to *control* and *motivate* (e.g., "This assignment will be graded"), and often teachers use completed work as a basis for giving privileges and otherwise rewarding students (e.g., "good" papers are posted). Grades and associated written comments also provide *feedback* to students and parents.

Instruction

Teachers constantly make instructional decisions, and good teachers are aware that they must continuously assess how students are doing in order to adjust their instruction appropriately. One type of decision, termed a *process* instructional decision, is made almost instantaneously, such as deciding to end a lecture or ask a different type of question. *Planning* instructional decisions are made with more reflection; they might include changing student seating arrangement or grouping patterns, spending an extra day on a particular topic, or preparing additional worksheets for homework. It is hoped that teachers will use credible measurement information with clear standards to evaluate student behavior accurately.

An important aspect of teaching is *communicating expectations* to students, and assessments are used continuously during instruction to indicate what is expected of students. The teacher's expectations are communicated to students by the nature of the questions the teacher asks (e.g., are the questions easy or hard?), how the teacher acknowledges student answers, the type of feedback teachers give to students as they are completing assignments, and in many more subtle ways of responding to students. The nature of the tests teachers give and how they evaluate student answers communicate standards students are expected to meet.

Finally, assessment processes can be used *as* instruction. Recently developed performance-based and authentic assessments are long term and provide opportunities for student learning. As we will see in later chapters, such assessments are useful as teaching tools as well as methods to document student learning.

RESEARCH ON LEARNING, MOTIVATION, AND INSTRUCTION: IMPLICATIONS FOR ASSESSMENT

As summarized in Figure 1.4, recent research on learning, motivation, and instruction has important implications for the nature and use of classroom assessments. It is becoming increasingly clear that effective instruction usually does much more than present information to students. Rather, good instruction provides an environment that engages the student in active learning that connects new information with existing knowledge. Contemporary cognitive theories have shown that learning is *meaningful* and *self-regulated*. Learning is an ongoing process in which students actively receive, interpret, and relate information to what they already know, understand, and have experienced. Effective assessment, in turn, is designed to be consistent with these findings.

There is a growing awareness that it is essential for students to develop thinking skills (e.g., skills in problem solving and decision making). Students need to be able to apply what they learn to real-world demands and challenges, work with others to solve problems, and be self-regulated learners who have an awareness and willingness to explore new ideas and develop new skills. Instruction and curriculum as well as assessment need to be designed and delivered to enhance these skills.

Recent research on motivation suggests that teachers must constantly assess students and provide feedback that is informative. By providing specific and meaningful feedback to students and encouraging them to regulate their own learning, teachers encourage students to enhance their sense of self-efficacy and self-confidence, important determinants of motivation. Meaningful learning is intrinsically motivating because the content has relevance. The implication here is that assessment does not end with scoring and recording the results. Motivation is highly dependent on the nature of the feedback from the assessment. Thus, in keeping with the integration of assessment with instruction, feedback is an essential component of the assessment process.

The research from cognitive learning theories has laid the foundation for significant changes in classroom assessment. As we discover more about how students learn, we realize that assessment practices, as well as instructional practices, need to change to keep consistent with this research.

FIGURE 1.4   **Linking Instruction and Assessment: Implications from Cognitive Learning Theory**

Theory: Knowledge is constructed. Learning is a process of creating personal meaning from new information and prior knowledge.

Implications for Instruction/Assessment

- Encourage discussion of new ideas.
- Encourage divergent thinking, multiple links and solutions, not just one right answer.
- Encourage multiple modes of expression, for example, role play, simulations, debates, and explanations to others.
- Emphasize critical thinking skills: analyze, compare, generalize, predict, hypothesize.
- Relate new information to personal experience, prior knowledge.
- Apply information to a new situation.

Theory: All ages/abilities can think and solve problems. Learning isn't necessarily a linear progression of discrete skills.

Implications for Instruction/Assessment

- Engage all students in problem solving.
- Don't make problem solving, critical thinking, or discussion of concepts contingent on mastery of routine basic skills.

Theory: There is great variety in learning styles, attention spans, memory, developmental paces, and intelligences.

Implications for Instruction/Assessment:

- Provide choices in tasks (not all reading and writing).
- Provide choices in how to show mastery/competence.
- Provide time to think about and do assignments.
- Don't overuse timed tests.
- Provide opportunity to revise, rethink.
- Include concrete experiences (manipulatives, links to prior personal experience).

Theory: People perform better when they know the goal, see models, know how their performance compares to the standard.

Implications for Instruction/Assessment:

- Discuss goals; let students help define them (personal and class).
- Provide a range of examples of student work; discuss characteristics.
- Provide students with opportunities for self-evaluation and peer review.
- Discuss criteria for judging performance.
- Allow students to have input into standards.

Theory: It's important to know when to use knowledge, how to adapt it, how to manage one's own learning.

Implications for Instruction/Assessment

- Give real-world opportunities (or simulations) to apply/adapt new knowledge.

(continued)

FIGURE 1.4 *(Continued)*

- Have students self-evaluate: think about how they learn well/poorly; set new goals, why they like certain work.

Theory: Motivation, effort, and self-esteem affect learning and performance.

Implications for Instruction/Assessment:

- Motivate students with real-life tasks and connections to personal experiences.
- Encourage students to see connection between effort and results.

Theory: Learning has social components. Group work is valuable.

Implications for Instruction/Assessment:

- Provide group work.
- Incorporate heterogeneous groups.
- Enable students to take on a variety of roles.
- Consider group products and group processes.

Source: Herman, J. L., Aschbacher, P. R., & Winters, L. The National Center for Research on Evaluation, Standards and Student Testing (CRESST). *A Practical Guide to Alternative Assessment.* Alexandria, VA: Association for Supervision and Curriculum Development, pp. 19–20. Copyright © 1992 by The Regents of the University of California.

RECENT TRENDS IN CLASSROOM ASSESSMENT

In the past decade, some clear trends have emerged in classroom assessment. More established traditions of focusing assessment on "objective" testing at the *end* of instruction are being supplemented with, or in some cases replaced by, assessments *during* instruction—to help teachers make moment-by-moment decisions—and with what are called "alternative" assessments. *Alternative assessments* include authentic assessment, performance-based assessment, portfolios, exhibitions, demonstrations, journals, and other forms of assessment that require the active construction of meaning rather than the passive regurgitation of isolated facts. These assessments engage students in learning and require thinking skills, and thus they are consistent with cognitive theories of learning and motivation as well as societal needs to prepare students for an increasingly complex workplace.

Another trend is the recognition that knowledge and skills should not be assessed in isolation. Rather, it is necessary to assess the application and the use of knowledge and skills together. More emphasis is now placed on assessing thinking skills and collaborative skills that are needed to work cooperatively with others. Students are now expected to *self-assess* rather than rely on others for feedback. Newer forms of assessment provide opportunities for many "correct" answers, rather than a single right answer, and rely on multiple sources of information.

FIGURE 1.5   Recent Trends in Classroom Assessment

From	To
Sole emphasis on outcomes	Assessing of process
Isolated skills	Integrated skills
Isolated facts	Application of knowledge
Paper-and-pencil tasks	Authentic tasks
Decontextualized tasks	Contextualized tasks
A single correct answer	Many correct answers
Secret standards	Public standards
Secret criteria	Public criteria
Individuals	Groups
After instruction	During instruction
Little feedback	Considerable feedback
"Objective" tests	Performance-based tests
Standardized tests	Informal tests
External evaluation	Student self-evaluation
Single assessments	Multiple assessments
Sporadic	Continual
Conclusive	Recursive

These and other recent trends in classroom assessment are summarized in Figure 1.5. In presenting these trends, I do not want to suggest that what teachers have been doing for years is inappropriate or should necessarily be changed. Much of what we have learned about evaluating students from previous decades is very important and useful. For example, properly constructed multiple-choice tests are excellent for efficiently and objectively assessing knowledge of a large content domain. What is needed is a *balanced* approach to assessment, in which appropriate techniques are administered and used in a credible way for decision making. Just because the assessment focuses on complex thinking skills or uses portfolios does not mean it is better or more credible. Assessment technique must be matched to purpose and must be conducted according to established quality standards. Some of the recent trends, such as making standards and criteria public, are helpful procedures regardless of the assessment employed, and they will improve traditional as well as newer types of measurement.

On the other hand, some teachers have been profoundly affected by these "new" forms of assessment. This is illustrated quite nicely by Bill Hadley, a mathematics teacher (Stenmark, 1991, p. 12):

After reading the Curriculum and Evaluation Standards (NCTM 1989) last year and taking time to do a thorough self-evaluation of my own assessment practices, I arrived at several startling conclusions. First, I found that the only reason for some of my tests was to produce a number to put in my rollbook. I was receiving very little information about my students' learning or abilities from these exams. Second, it became more and more apparent to me that as I was constructing my tests, I was able to accurately predict which of my students would be able to answer individual questions. Finally, I realized that unless I designed tests that would provide opportunities for students who worked at different paces to demonstrate their abilities, I was testing speed rather than learning.

I decided not to give separate stand-alone tests but to assess my students' growth and understanding of mathematics through the use of performance assessments, observations of students, interviews with students, and oral and written student reports.

The information I received was much more comprehensive and complete, and I found that I was able to give the students grades that I thought very accurately reflected their progress. The students for the most part agreed.

This positive experience with alternative assessment forms and with integrating assessment and instruction will enable me to employ similar methods more often in my other classes. I have discovered that tests do not have to be a primary or necessary type of assessment. Furthermore, traditionally structured tests seem to be an impediment to effective instruction, and their use needs to be carefully examined.

ASSESSMENT STANDARDS FOR TEACHERS

Before leaving this chapter, I want to familiarize you with an important set of newly developed assessment standards for teachers. In 1990, the American Federation of Teachers, the National Council on Measurement in Education, and the National Education Association published a set of standards for teacher competence in educational assessment. This represents an unusual but important collaboration between teaching and measurement professionals.

The standards organize the teacher's professional role and responsibilities into activities occurring prior to, during, and after the appropriate instructional segment. The standards also include responsibilities of the teacher for involvement in school and district decision making and involvement in the wider professional roles of teachers. These roles and responsibilities, which emphasize teacher activities that are directly related to assessment, are outlined in Figure 1.6. You will note that throughout these roles and responsibilities instruction is integrated with assessment. This is consistent with newer trends in assessment, and it forms the basis for the assessment content that is presented in this book.

The standards also indicate specific assessment knowledge or skills that a teacher should possess to perform the roles and responsibilities delineated in Figure 1.6. The standards suggest that teachers should demonstrate skills of selecting, developing, applying, using, communicating, and evaluating assessment information and practices. The standards and corresponding skills are summarized in Figure 1.7 on page 18.

FIGURE 1.6   **The Scope of a Teacher's Professional Role and Responsibilities for Student Assessment**

The scope of a teacher's professional role and responsibilities for student assessment may be described in terms of the following activities. These activities imply that teachers need competence in student assessment and sufficient time and resources to complete them in a professional manner.

Activities Occurring Prior to Instruction

a. Understanding students' cultural backgrounds, interests, skills, and abilities as they apply across a range of learning domains and/or subject areas
b. Understanding students' motivations and their interests in specific class content
c. Clarifying and articulating the performance outcomes expected of pupils
d. Planning instruction for individuals or groups of students

Activities Occurring during Instruction

a. Monitoring pupil progress toward instructional goals
b. Identifying gains and difficulties pupils are experiencing in learning and performing
c. Adjusting instruction
d. Giving contingent, specific, and credible praise and feedback
e. Motivating students to learn
f. Judging the extent of pupil attainment of instructional outcomes

Activities Occurring after the Appropriate Instructional Segment (e.g., lesson, class, semester, grade)

a. Describing the extent to which each pupil has attained both short- and long-term instructional goals
b. Communicating strengths and weaknesses based on assessment results to students and parents or guardians
c. Recording and reporting assessment results for school-level analysis, evaluation, and decision making
d. Analyzing assessment information gathered before and during instruction to understand each student's progress to date and to inform future instructional planning
e. Evaluating the effectiveness of instruction
f. Evaluating the effectiveness of the curriculum and materials in use

Activities Associated with a Teacher's Involvement in School Building and School District Decision Making

a. Serving on a school or district committee examining the school's and district's strengths and weaknesses in the development of its students
b. Working on the development or selection of assessment methods for school building or school district use
c. Evaluating school district curriculum
d. Other related activities

Activities Associated with a Teacher's Involvement in a Wider Community of Educators

a. Serving on a state committee asked to develop learning goals and associated assessment methods
b. Participating in reviews of the appropriateness of district, state, or national student goals and associated assessment methods
c. Interpreting the results of state and national student assessment programs

Source: Standards for Teacher Competence in Educational Assessment of Students (1990). American Federation of Teachers, National Council on Measurement in Education, National Education Association.

FIGURE 1.7   Standards for Teacher Competence in Educational Assessment of Students

Standard	Skills
1. Teachers should be skilled in *choosing* assessment methods appropriate for instructional decisions.	a. Use concepts of assessment error and validity. b. Understand how valid assessment supports instructional activities. c. Understand how invalid information can affect instructional decisions. d. Use and evaluate assessment options considering backgrounds of students. e. Be aware that certain assessment activities are incompatible with certain instructional goals. f. Understand how different assessment approaches affect decision-making. g. Know where to find information about various assessment methods.
2. Teachers should be skilled in *developing* assessment methods appropriate for instructional decisions.	a. Be able to plan the collection of information needed for decision making. b. Know and follow appropriate principles for developing and using different assessment methods. c. Be able to select assessment techniques that are consistent with the intent of the instruction. d. Be able to use student data to analyze the quality of each assessment technique used.
3. The teacher should be skilled in administering, scoring, and interpreting the results of both externally produced and teacher-produced assessment methods.	a. Be skilled in interpreting informal and formal teacher-produced assessment results, including performances in class and on homework. b. Use guides for scoring essay questions, projects, response-choice questions, and performance assessments. c. Administer standardized achievement tests and interpret reported scores. d. Understand summary indexes, including measures of central tendency, dispersion, relationships, and errors of measurement. e. Analyze assessment results to determine student strengths and weaknesses. f. Use results appropriately and not increase students' anxiety levels.
4. Teachers should be skilled in using assessment results when making decisions about individual students, planning teaching, developing curriculum, and making recommendations for school improvement.	a. Use accumulated assessment information to organize a sound instructional plan. b. Interpret results correctly according to established rules of validity. c. Use results from local, regional, state, and national assessments for educational improvement.
5. Teachers should be skilled in developing valid pupil grading procedures that use pupil assessments.	a. Devise, implement, and explain a procedure for developing grades. b. Combine various assignments, projects, in-class activities, quizzes, and tests into a grade. c. Acknowledge that grades reflect their own preferences and judgments.

FIGURE 1.7   *(Continued)*

Standard	Skills
	d. Recognize and avoid faulty grading procedures. e. Evaluate and modify their grading procedures.
6. Teachers should be skilled in communicating assessment results to students, parents, other lay audiences, and other educators.	a. Understand and be able to give appropriate explanations of how to interpret student assessments as moderated by student background factors such as socioeconomic status. b. Explain that assessment results do not imply that background factors limit a student. c. Communicate to parents how they may assess a student's educational progress. d. Explain the importance of taking measurement errors into account when making decisions based on assessment. e. Explain the limitations of different types of assessments. f. Explain printed reports of assessments at the classroom, school district, state, and national levels.
7. Teachers should be skilled in recognizing unethical, illegal, and otherwise inappropriate assessment methods and uses of assessment information.	a. Understand laws and case decisions that affect their classroom, school district, and state assessment programs. b. Understand the harmful consequences of misuse or overuse of various assessment procedures such as embarrassing students or violating a student's right to confidentiality. c. Understand that it is inappropriate to use standardized student achievement test scores to measure teaching effectiveness.

Source: Standards for Teacher Competence in Educational Assessment of Students (1990). American Federation of Teachers, National Council on Measurement in Education, National Education Association.

SUMMARY

This chapter has introduced assessment as an integral part of teacher decision making and instruction. As a systematic method of collecting, interpreting, and using information, good assessment improves student learning. Major points in the chapter include the following:

- Assessment includes four major components: purpose, measurement, evaluation, and use.
- Measurement consists of differentiating behavior or performance.
- Evaluation involves professional judgment of the value or worth of the measured performance.
- Recent research on learning, motivation, and instruction suggests the need to use more alternative forms of measurement, such as performance-based assessments, portfolios, and authentic assessments.
- Professional standards have been developed to provide a framework for what teachers need to know about classroom assessment.

WHAT'S COMING

You have now been introduced to classroom assessment and some of the directions such assessment is taking. I want to give you an overview of the rest of this book—how it is organized, what you can expect, and how you can make the most of the application exercises at the end of each chapter.

The sequence of topics followed in the book reflects the steps teachers take in using assessment as part of instruction. The first three chapters present fundamental principles of any type of assessment. In Chapter 2 we will consider how purpose is clarified through the development of appropriate learning targets. Chapter 3 reviews criteria that will enhance the quality and credibility of assessments. With this background, methods of assessment are presented in the sequence teachers use when planning and delivering instruction. Single chapters are devoted to assessment prior to and during instruction. Separate chapters then present major methods of assessment, based on the different types of learning targets being assessed. These assessments are conducted at the end of a unit of instruction. In this book, the method of assessment follows from what needs to be assessed to emphasize that teachers first determine purpose and learning targets and then select and implement appropriate assessments. The next two chapters examine what teachers do with assessment information in the form of grading and reporting information. There is a chapter on issues concerning the assessment of mainstreamed students, and a final chapter that summarizes important information concerning the administration, interpretation, and use of standardized tests.

SELF-INSTRUCTIONAL REVIEW EXERCISES

In each chapter you will find these self-instructional exercises. They are intended to check your understanding of the content of the chapter. An answer key is provided to give you immediate feedback. Remember that you will learn most if you don't look at the key before you answer the question.

1. What is the relationship between teacher decision making, complex classroom environments, and assessment?

2. What does it mean to say that assessment is not an add-on activity?

3. What is the difference between a *test* and an *assessment*?

4. Refer to Figure 1.1 on page 6. Identify each of the following examples as pre-instructional assessment (pre), ongoing assessment (og), or postinstructional assessment (post).

    a. giving a pop quiz
    b. giving a cumulative final exam
    c. giving students praise for correct answers
    d. using homework to judge student knowledge
    e. reviewing student scores on last year's standardized test
    f. changing the lesson plan because of student inattention
    g. reviewing student files to understand the cultural backgrounds of students

5. Identify each of the following quotes as referring to one of the four components of classroom assessment: purpose (P), measurement (M), evaluation (E), and use (U).

   a. "Last week I determined that my students did not know very much about the Civil War."
   b. "This year I want to see if I could assess student attitudes."
   c. "The test helped me to identify where students were weak."
   d. "I like the idea of using performance-based assessments."
   e. "I intend to combine several different assessments to determine the grade."

6. How do assessments communicate expectations for student learning?

7. Why, according to recent research on learning, is performance-based assessment well suited to effective instruction?

ANSWERS TO SELF-INSTRUCTIONAL REVIEW EXERCISES

1. Complex classroom environments influence the nature of teacher decision making and assessment is needed to make good decisions.

2. "Add-on" means assessment that occurs at the end of an instructional unit, for example, the midterm or final exam. However, in instruction the teacher also assesses students prior to and during instruction. Assessment should not be thought of as only testing at the end of instruction.

3. A test is only one part of assessment. Assessment refers to establishing purpose, measuring something, evaluating what is measured, and then using the information for decision making. A test is one way to measure.

4. a. og, b. post, c. og, d. og, e. pre, f. og, g. pre.

5. a. E, b. P, c. E, d. M, e. U.

6. Expectations are set by the nature of the standards and criteria used in the assessments and the way teachers provide feedback and otherwise respond to students.

7. Recent learning research has shown the importance of connecting new to existing information, of applying knowledge, and of thinking skills. Performance-based assessments foster these behaviors by relating content and processes to problem solving in meaningful contexts.

SUGGESTIONS FOR ACTION RESEARCH

At the end of each chapter, you will also find these suggestions for action research. The intent of these suggestions is to help you apply what you are learning from the book to practical situations. By conducting this type of informal research, the principles and ideas presented will have greater relevance and meaning to you.

1. Investigate the time that is taken for assessment in the classroom by observing some classes. Compare your results to how much time the teacher believes is

devoted to assessment. Also note in your observations the nature of teacher decision making. What kind of decisions are made? How, specifically, does information from assessment contribute to this decision making?

2. Conduct an interview with a teacher or two and ask them some questions about assessment. For example, you could take Figure 1.5 on page 15 and ask the teachers if they believe the so-called recent trends are actually evident. You could also ask about the relationship between assessment and teaching/learning to see the extent to which assessment and teaching are integrated.

3. Interview a school administrator about what teachers need to know about assessment. Ask about the assessment standards to get a perspective on the reasonableness of the standards.

Specific Objectives   Writes correct definitions for 80 percent of the words
Identifies correct antonyms for 50 percent of the words
Identifies correct synonyms for 70 percent of the words
Draws pictures that correctly illustrate 80 percent of the words
Writes sentences that include correct usage of 80 percent of the words

These lists of specific objectives are not exhaustive, because it would be futile to try to identify all possible ways of showing that the general objective has been demonstrated. It would also be overly restrictive to try to specify too much. What I advocate is for teachers to write learning targets that are at an intermediate level of specificity and to not be too concerned about always including all criteria for writing the objectives.

Whether you focus on general or specific objectives, however, the main point is that you need to describe what students will know and will be able to do, and what constitutes sufficient evidence that students have learned, not what you will do as a teacher to help students obtain the knowledge and skills identified. What you plan to do as a teacher may be called a *teaching objective* or *learning activity*, and may include such things as lecturing for a certain amount of time, asking questions, putting students in groups, giving feedback to students individually, conducting experiments, using a map to show where certain countries are located, asking students to solve math problems on the board, having students read orally, and so on. These teaching objectives describe the activities students will be engaged in and what you need to do to be sure that the activities occur as planned. It seems to me that the term *instructional objective* could be used to describe these activities as well, even though to many educators instructional objectives refer to what students will know and do. Regardless of the specific labels, as a teacher you will need to develop lesson plans that will include general learning targets, more specific learning targets, teaching objectives, activities, materials needed, and plans for assessment of student learning. Figure 2.2 on page 28 illustrates a typical lesson plan.

FIGURE 2.1 Specificity of Instructional Objectives

Too Specific	About Right	Too Broad
Given a two-paragraph article from the newspaper, the student will correctly identify ten statements that are facts and five statements that are opinions in less than ten minutes without the aid of any resource materials.	Students will state the difference between facts and opinions.	Students will learn how to think critically.

FIGURE 2.2   Example of a Lesson Plan

Learning Target	Students will differentiate between vertebrate and invertebrate animals by correctly recalling the difference and naming examples of animals in each category.
Materials Needed	Textbook, eight copies of pictures and sketches of the anatomies of vertebrate and invertebrate animals, colored pencils, paper.
Instructional Activities	Set up groups of three or four students. Give each group a set of animal pictures and ask them to classify the pictures into two major groups. Monitor student work for 15 minutes. Ask students to indicate how the animals in each category are the same and how they are different. Emphasize presence of backbone as major differentiating feature. Ask students to further classify vertebrate and invertebrate animals into further categories. Ask students to draw concept maps of different types of animals, using different colored pencils.
Assessment	Without notes, students will be asked to recall the difference between invertebrate and vertebrate animals and give four examples of different types of animals in each category. Give the students a new set of animal pictures and have them apply their rules for group membership to sort the pictures.

Standards-Based Education

It is very likely that you have heard or read about new standards that are being developed in most subject areas. This term, *standards*, is used to describe a recent movement, standards-based education, that is related to reforming which student outcomes should be stressed and how these outcomes are assessed. In 1993 a Technical Planning Group for the National Education Goals Panel published *Promises to Keep: Creating High Standards for American Students*. This paper outlines the approach that the federal government is taking to establish "word-class" academic standards in the United States. Recommendations are made to suggest criteria and processes for two kinds of education standards: content and performance standards. *Content standards* specify "what students should know and be able to do"—the knowledge, skills, ways of thinking, enduring ideas, and issues for an academic discipline. There is significant emphasis on applying knowledge and skills to problems of the real world and on the interdisciplinary nature of different fields. Actually content standards are really no different than what has been called general objectives. In both, the emphasis is on what students can demonstrate after instruction.

Performance standards indicate the degree to which content standards have been attained. Ideally, a performance standard indicates the nature of the evidence (e.g., test, essay, demonstration, project, paper) that is required and the quality of performance that will be deemed appropriate. Inherent in this definition is an important change from earlier discussions of behavioral objectives. Whereas a behavioral objective may have a single criterion and condition (essentially a type of performance standard), performance standards, by indicating the *degree* of attainment, are able to distinguish different levels of accomplishment. In reality, however, performance standards as described in some content areas may look like behavioral objectives and not specify either the nature of the evidence nor the quality of the performance.

Content and performance standards are being developed by national organizations in the arts, citizenship and civics, English and language arts, economics, foreign languages, geography, history, mathematics, physical education, social studies, and science. Standards in several areas are shown in Figure 2.3 on page 30.

Expectations

It is important to distinguish expectations from standards and learning targets. An *expectation* is what you communicate to your students about the level of performance that you think they will be able to demonstrate. This is different from the learning target because it is based on students' previous achievement, aptitude, motivation, and other factors. It may be reasonable to think that most, if not all, of your students will not be able to attain the standard or the highest level of performance. For example, we set a high standard for what constitutes a good play in football, but our expectations for middle school students differ from what we expect of professionals. In school you may have a high standard for a research paper, but your expectations of the students, because of a lack of previous learning, may not meet this high standard. If your expectations are the same as your standards, it is likely that either your standards will drop to accommodate most students, or your expectations will not be consistent with the reality of how students can perform. In either case, you are not doing what is in the best interests of the students. If your standards are lowered, students may attain a false sense of competency; if your expectations are too high, students may be frustrated at what they see as impossible demands. What you need to do is make high standards clear and then teach in a way that is consistent with realistic, yet challenging expectations. You want students to go the extra step, so be explicit with them about why the standards are high.

Criteria

One of the most frustrating experiences of students is not knowing "what the teacher wants" or "how the teacher grades." Perhaps you can recall being in a class in which you did an assignment with little guidance from the teacher about how he or she would grade it. Once your assignment was returned with comments, your reaction might well have been, "If I had only known what the teacher was looking for I could have provided it!" Essentially, this issue is concerned with the criteria the teacher uses for evaluating student work and whether students know, *in advance*, what those criteria are.

Criteria, then, are clearly articulated and public descriptions of facets or dimensions of student performance that are used for judging the level of achievement. As pointed out in Chapter 1, criteria may be called *scoring criteria*, *rubrics*, *scoring rubrics*, or *scoring guidelines*. Although criteria have been promoted most for

FIGURE 2.3   Examples of National Standards

U.S. History[1]

What Students Should Know: The causes of the American Revolution, ideas and interests involved in forging the revolutionary movement, and the reasons for the American victory.

What Students Should Be Able to Do: Demonstrate understanding of the causes of the American Revolution by:

- Explaining the consequences of the Seven Years War and the overhaul of English imperial policy following the Treaty of Paris in 1763, demonstrating the connections between the antecedent and consequent events. (Grades 5–12)
- Comparing the arguments advanced by defenders and opponents of the new imperial policy on the traditional rights of English people and the legitimacy of asking the colonies to pay a share of the costs of empire. (Grades 5–12)
- Reconstructing the chronology of the critical events leading to the outbreak of armed conflict between the American colonies and England. (Grades 5–12)
- Analyzing the connection between political ideas and economic interests and comparing the ideas and interests of different groups. (Grades 7–12)
- Reconstructing the arguments among patriots and loyalists about independence and drawing conclusions about how the decision to declare independence was reached. (Grades 9–12)

Examples of Student Achievement:

- Grades 5–6: Select, chronologically order, and explain the major events leading to the outbreak of conflict at Lexington and Concord.
- Grades 7–8: Marshal historical evidence, including events leading up to the "shot heard 'round the world," and develop a historical argument on such questions as the following: Was the outbreak of conflict at Lexington and Concord probable? Could any action at that point have prevented war with England?
- Grades 9–12: Construct a historical narrative analyzing the factors which explain why a person chose to be a loyalist or a patriot. Why did approximately one-third of the colonists want to remain neutral? Did economic and social differences play a role in how people chose sides? Explain.

Geography[2]

Standard Title: Patterns and Networks of Economic Interdependence on Earth's Surface.

B. Locate and classify economic activities, as exemplified by being able to:

- Classify land in a community by types of economic activity and prepare a map showing the different uses (e.g., industrial, recreational, commercial, residential)
- Use maps to understand the patterns of economic activity in an urban area and suggest reasons for the patterns (e.g., central business districts, industrial areas, shopping malls, places for entertainment and recreation, government service centers)
- Locate economic activities that use natural resources in the local region, state, and nation (e.g., agriculture, mining, fishing, forestry) and describe the importance of the activities to these areas

D. Identify the modes of transportation and communication used to move people, products, and ideas from place to place, as exemplified by being able to:

- Compare the importance of automobile transportation in the United States, relative to

FIGURE 2.3   *(Continued)*

other countries, by preparing graphs and maps that show the number of automobiles per capita in countries in different parts of the world
- List and describe the advantages and disadvantages of different modes of transportation for specific products and purposes (e.g., barges and trains for bulky heavy items; airplanes for high-cost perishables; pipelines for liquids and gases; bicycles, light-rail systems, and cars for urban commuting)

Mathematics[3]

Standard 6: Number Sense and Numeration. In grades K–4, the mathematics curriculum should include whole number concepts and skills so that students can:

- construct number meanings through real-world experiences and the use of physical materials;
- understand our numeration system by relating counting, grouping, and place-value concepts;
- develop number sense;
- interpret the multiple uses of numbers encountered in the real world.

Standard 8: Whole Number Computation. In grades K–4, the mathematics curriculum should develop whole number computation so that students can:

- model, explain, and develop reasonable proficiency with basic facts and algorithms;
- use a variety of mental computation and estimation techniques;
- use calculators in appropriate computational situations;
- select and use computation techniques appropriate to specific problems and determine whether the results are reasonable.

Sources:

1. *National standards for United States history: Exploring the American experience,* Grades 5–12 (1994). Los Angeles, CA: University of California, Los Angeles, National Center for History in the Schools, pp. 72–73.

2. *Geography for life: National geography standards 1994* (1994). Washington, DC: National Geographic Research & Exploration, pp. 126–127. Copyright © 1994 National Geographic Research and Exploration, on behalf of the American Geographical Society, The Association of American Geographers, the National Council for Geographic Education, and the National Geographic Society.

3. *Curriculum and evaluation standards for school mathematics* (1989). Reston, VA: The National Council of Teachers of Mathematics, Inc., pp. 38, 44.

more recent alternative and performance-based assessments, the issue of how student responses will be evaluated lies at the heart of any type of assessment. The key component of criteria is making your professional judgments about student performance clear to others. All methods of assessment involve your professional judgment. If you use multiple-choice testing, judgment is used to prepare the items and decide which alternative is correct. In an essay test, judgment is involved in preparing the question and in reading and scoring answers. Clearly articulated criteria will help you in many ways, including:

- defining what you mean by "excellent," "good," or "average" work
- communicating instructional goals to parents

- communicating to parents, students, and others what constitutes excellence
- providing guidelines for making unbiased and consistent judgments
- documenting how judgments are made
- helping students evaluate their own work

When specifying criteria, it is necessary to summarize the dimensions of performance that are used to assign student work to a given level. The dimensions are what you consider to be essential qualities of the performance. They can be identified by asking yourself some questions: What are the attributes of good performance? How do I know when students have reached different levels of performance? What examples do I have of each level? What do I look for when evaluating student work? Stiggins (1994, p. 186) suggests six steps in devising your own criteria (see Figure 2.4):

Step 1. Begin by reflecting on the meaning of excellence in the performance arena that is of interest to you. Be sure to tap your own professional literature, texts, and curriculum materials for insights, too. And don't overlook the wisdom of your colleagues and associates as a resource. Talk with them! Include students as partners in this step too. Brainstorm your own list of key elements. You don't have to list them all in one sitting. Take some time to let the list grow.

Step 2. Categorize the many elements so that they reflect your highest priorities. Keep the list as short as possible while still capturing the essence of performance.

Step 3. Define each key dimension in clear, simple language.

Step 4. Find some actual performance to watch or examples of products to study. If this step can include the thoughtful analysis of a number of contrasting cases—an outstanding term paper and a very weak one, a flowing and accurate jump shot in basketball and a poor one, a student who functions effectively in a group and one who is repeatedly rejected, and so on—so much the better.

Step 5. Use your clearest language and your very best examples to spell out in words and pictures each point along the various continuums of performance you use to define the important dimensions of the achievement to be assessed.

Step 6. Try your performance criteria to see if they really do capture the essence of performance. Fine-tune them to state as precisely as possible what it means to succeed. Let this fine-tuning go on as needed for as long as you teach.

Once the dimensions have been identified, you can develop a quantitative or qualitative scale to indicate different levels of performance. Label each level as "good," "excellent," "poor," and so on. Examples of criteria for different types of performance are shown in Figure 2.5 on page 33.

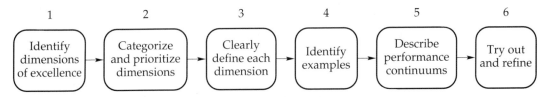

FIGURE 2.4   Steps in Developing Performance Criteria

FIGURE 2.5   Examples of Performance Criteria

Making an Oral Presentation[1]

Excellent:	Pupil consistently faces audience, stands straight, and maintains eye contact; voice projects well and clearly; pacing and tone variation appropriate; well organized, points logically and completely presented; brief summary at end
Good:	Pupil usually faces audience, stands straight, and makes eye contact; voice projection good, but pace and clarity vary during talk; well organized but repetitive; occasional poor choice of words and incomplete summary
Fair:	Pupil fidgety; some eye contact and facial expression change; uneven voice projection, not heard by all in room, some words slurred; loosely organized, repetitive, contains many incomplete thoughts; little summarization.
Poor:	Pupil body movements distracting, little eye contact or voice change; words slurred, speaks in monotone, does not project voice beyond first few rows, no consistent or logical pacing; rambling presentation, little organization with no differentiation between major and minor points; no summary

Knowledge and Use of History[2]

Level V: *Exceptional Achievement*	Offers accurate analysis of the information and issues, provides a variety of facts to explore major and minor issues and concepts involved, extensively uses previous historical knowledge to provide an in-depth understanding of the problem and to relate it to past and possible future situations
Level IV: *Superior Achievement*	Offers accurate analysis of the documents, provides facts to relate to the major issues involved, uses previous general historical knowledge to examine issues involved
Level III: *Commendable Achievement*	Relates only major facts to the basic issues with a fair degree of accuracy, analyzes information to explain at least one issue or concept with substantive support, uses general ideas from previous historical knowledge with fair degree of accuracy
Level II: *Rudimentary Achievement*	Provides only basic facts with only some degree of accuracy, refers to information to explain at least one issue or concept in general terms, limited use of previous historical knowledge without complete accuracy, major reliance on the information provided
Level I: *Minimal Achievement*	Reiterates one or two facts without complete accuracy, deals only briefly and vaguely with concepts or the issues, barely indicates any previous historical knowledge, relies heavily on the information provided

(continued)

FIGURE 2.5   *(Continued)*

Knows the Difference between Statements and Questions

More Than Adequate	Successfully identifies twenty of twenty-five sentences as statements or questions, lists three characteristics of statements and questions, generates four original examples of statements and questions
Adequate	Successfully identifies eighteen of twenty-five sentences as statements or questions, lists two characteristics of statements and questions, generates two examples of statements and questions
Less Than Adequate	Successfully identifies fewer than eighteen of twenty-five sentences as statements or questions, lists one or no characteristics of statements and questions, generates no examples of statements or questions

Estimation[3]

Not Understanding	Makes unrealistic guesses, does not use strategies to refine estimates, cannot model or explain the specified strategy, cannot apply strategy even with prompts
Developing Understanding	Refines guesser estimates by partitioning/comparing, etc., can model, explain, and apply a strategy when asked, has some strategies, others are not yet in place, uses estimation when appropriate
Understanding/ Applying	Makes realistic guesses or estimates, refines estimates to suggest a more exact estimate, uses estimation when appropriate, recognizes and readily uses a variety of strategies

Sources:

1. Airasian, P. W. (1994). *Classroom assessment* (2nd ed.). New York: McGraw-Hill, Inc., pp. 261–262.

2. California Assessment Program 1990 History–Social Science Grade 11 Scoring Guide: Group Performance Task.

3. Beyer, A., & others (1993). *Alternative assessment: Evaluating student performance in elementary mathematics.* Ann Arbor Public Schools. Palo Alto, CA: Dale Seymour Publications, p. 7.

Although it is very helpful for students to know the criteria as communicated in a scoring rubric, it is even more helpful if students can see an example of a finished student product or performance and your evaluation of it. These examples are called *exemplars* or *anchors*. For example, if you have established four levels of performance, an exemplar of work at each level would make the criteria more clear. To emphasize once again, you should share the exemplars with students *before* they begin their work. This will help students internalize the standards and criteria that you use and to know what constitutes excellence. The exemplars could be as simple as giving students examples of the type of math word problems that will be on a test and how their answers will be graded. Of course you don't want to give students something that they will memorize or copy, but you do need to give them a sense of the difficulty of the task.

Learning Targets

What, then, is a learning target? In this book *learning target* is defined as a statement of student performance that includes *both* a description of what students should know or be able to do at the end of a unit of instruction *and* as much as possible and feasible about the criteria for judging the level of performance demonstrated (see Figure 2.6).

The word *learning* is used to convey that targets emphasize the importance of how *students* will *change*. Learning implies a focus on the demonstrated competence of students, not on what you do as a teacher. Change reflects the need to know more than what they know or do at the end of instruction. Change requires knowledge of where students are in relation to the target prior to instruction as well as at the end of instruction.

It is essential that as much as possible about the criteria for judging levels of performance be included in the target. Think for a moment about a target that one would shoot an arrow at. The performance might be stated as "the student will hit the target with an arrow." But you need to communicate more than simply "hit the target." How far away is the target? How large is the target? Does it matter where the arrow hits the target? In other words, you need to indicate something about the dimensions of the performance that translate into qualitatively different levels of performance. Two teachers can state the same learning objective, but if different criteria are used to evaluate the performance, then in reality students in each class are learning something different.

A similar case can be made for learning subjects in school. The target "students will know state capitals in the United States" means something different if the student has to recall all fifty capitals from memory than if the student can correctly match half of the names of capitals with states. You must be able to articulate, as part of the target, the criteria you will use to judge performance, and remember, students should know these criteria *prior* to instruction. This does not need to be done in a single sentence. It is easier, in fact, to think about targets as a description of what will be assessed and how it will be judged. These two aspects of the target can be separated into different sentences. For example, what follows describes what students need to know:

> Students will demonstrate an understanding of the effect of the sun on seasons, length of day, weather, and climate.

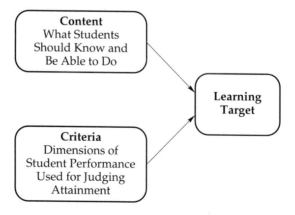

FIGURE 2.6 Components of Learning Targets

Information about criteria could be added with another sentence:

> Students will demonstrate their understanding by correctly answering short-answer questions on each relationship.

If a matching test is used, try this description:

> Students will demonstrate their understanding by correctly matching all effects with the four elements discussed.

In practice, you would not be so wordy in describing the target. It is understood that "students will demonstrate" so you can simply say "understand effect of sun on seasons, length of day, weather, and climate." The information about criteria can be shortened by simply referring to "matching" or "short answer."

Learning targets for units of instruction in Figure 2.7 include both what students should know or be able to do, and some aspects of the criteria. Note that some are written as one sentence and some are more detailed than others in aspects of criteria. The intent is not to worry about including specific aspects of criteria, as was advocated by some for behavioral objectives. Rather, the hope is that you will be aware of the effect of the criteria on the nature of the learning that occurs.

FIGURE 2.7   Examples of Unit Learning Targets

Students will be able to explain how various cultures are different and how cultures influence people's beliefs and lives by answering orally a comprehensive set of questions about cultural differences and their effects.

Students will demonstrate their knowledge of the parts of a plant by filling in words on a diagram for all parts studied.

Students will demonstrate their understanding of citizenship by correctly identifying whether previously unread statements about citizenship are true or false. A large number of items is used to sample most of the content learned.

Students will be able to explain why the American constitution is important by writing an essay that indicates what would happen if we abolished our constitution. The papers will be graded holistically, looking for evidence of reasons, knowledge of the constitution, and organization.

Students will know the difference between components of sentences by correctly identifying verbs, adverbs, adjectives, nouns, and pronouns in seven of eight long, complex sentences.

Students will be able to multiply fractions by correctly computing eight of ten fraction problems. The problems are new to the students; some are similar to "challenge" questions in the book.

Students will be able to use their knowledge of addition, subtraction, division, and multiplication to correctly solve word problems that are similar to those used in the sixth-grade standardized test.

Students will demonstrate their understanding of how visual art conveys ideas and feelings by correctly indicating, orally, how examples of art communicate ideas and feelings. Grades will be based on equal weighing of ideas and feelings.

TYPES OF LEARNING TARGETS

How do you identify appropriate learning targets for your students? It is helpful to begin by realizing that many different kinds of targets are appropriate, because in most classrooms a variety of outcomes are stressed. The challenge is to organize and prioritize your targets to reflect what is most important. To do this, you need to think about a few categories that encompass typical types of learning targets. In this book, categories described by Stiggins and Conklin (1992) are used because these categories are viewed by teachers as important and because each type of target is clearly related to different approaches to assessment. The major categories of targets (see Figure 2.8) are introduced in this chapter and then linked with specific kinds of assessment in subsequent chapters. Note that the categories are not presented as a hierarchy or order. None of the categories is more important than any other. Each simply represents types of targets that can be identified and used for assessment.

Knowledge Learning Targets

Knowledge of subject matter is the foundation upon which all other learning is based. As such, it represents what students need to *know* to solve problems and perform skills. This knowledge may be as simple as mastery of facts and information demonstrated through recall (e.g., remembering dates, events, places, definitions, and principles), or it may involve comprehension and understanding (e.g., summarizing a paragraph, explaining charts, concept learning, drawing conclusions, or giving examples). *Knowing* usually refers to more than simple rote memory, even though some rote memorization may be needed. A student can *know* how to pronounce certain words by memorizing the links between letters and sounds, but it is also necessary to understand the meanings of the words.

FIGURE 2.8   Types of Learning Targets

Knowledge	Student mastery of substantive subject matter
Reasoning	Student ability to use knowledge to reason and solve problems
Skills	Student ability to demonstrate achievement-related skills, such as reading aloud, interpersonal interaction, speaking in a second language, operating equipment correctly and safely, conducting experiments, operating computers, and performing psychomotor behaviors
Products	Student ability to create achievement-related products such as written reports, oral presentations, and art products
Affective	Student attainment of affective states such as attitudes, values, interests, and self-efficacy

Reasoning Learning Targets

Recent advances in cognitive psychology and computer accessibility to information have resulted in increased attention to *thinking skills*. Such capabilities may be described with a number of different terms, including *problem-solving, critical thinking, analysis, synthesis, comparing, intellectual skills, intellectual abilities, higher-order thinking skills,* and *judgment*. Research in cognitive psychology has shown that our ability to use knowledge to think about things is dependent on how we construct the knowledge and the demands that are placed on using the knowledge to reason and solve problems. This research has helped us to classify and understand the different reasoning processes that are used. Several reasoning frameworks will be presented in Chapter 7. The challenge with reasoning targets is defining precisely what is meant by *reasoning, critical thinking, problem-solving,* and so on. The frameworks will help you to formulate definitions that meet your needs.

Skill Learning Targets

A skill is something that the student demonstrates, something that is done. Although, in one sense, recalling information and showing reasoning skills by answering questions is *doing* something, skill learning targets involve a behavior in which the knowledge and reasoning is used in an overt manner. For example, at one level students can demonstrate their knowledge of how a microscope works by recalling correct procedural steps, but skill is needed when the students show the teacher how to do the steps with an actual microscope. It is like the difference between knowing how to manage classrooms by listing seven principles of classroom management, even analyzing case studies of classroom management, and being able to manage students in an actual classroom. Thus, in elementary school, students are expected to demonstrate reading skills and how to hold pencils to write; older students may be required to demonstrate oral presentation skills or speak in a foreign language. Most skills require procedural knowledge and reasoning to use the knowledge in an actual performance.

Product Learning Targets

Products, like skills, are dependent on prior attainment of knowledge and reasoning targets. Products are samples of student work that demonstrate the ability to use knowledge and reasoning in the creation of a tangible product like a term paper, report, artwork, or other project. Thus, products are used to demonstrate knowledge, reasoning, and skills. Performance-based assessments are examples of how product learning targets are measured.

Affective Learning Targets

This final category is broad, complex, and, to a certain extent, controversial. The term *affective* includes emotions, feelings, and beliefs that are different from *cogni-*

tive learning like knowledge, reasoning, and skills. Affect can be described as being positive or negative, and most teachers hope that students will develop positive attitudes toward school subjects and learning, themselves as learners, other students, and school. Affect can also refer to motivational dispositions, values, and morals. Although most teachers believe that positive affect is an important outcome as well as a determinant of cognitive learning, many believe that schools should only be concerned with cognitive learning targets. Because affective learning targets are complex, they are difficult—but not impossible—to assess.

SOURCES OF LEARNING TARGETS

While the categories of learning targets just presented will provide a start to identifying the focus of instruction and assessment (and provides the organizational structure of this book), you will find other existing sources that are more specific about learning targets. Several of these sources are identified in the following sections.

Bloom's Taxonomy of Objectives

Perhaps the best known source for learning targets is the *Taxonomy of Educational Objectives I: Cognitive Domain* (Bloom, 1956). As implied in the title, this initial taxonomy covered cognitive learning objectives. Later publications of the taxonomy focused on the affective and psychomotor areas. Thus, "Bloom's taxonomy," as it has become known, consists of three domains—cognitive, affective, and psychomotor—even though there are three separately published taxonomies.

Bloom's taxonomy of the cognitive domain has received considerable attention and has been used to specify action verbs to accompany different types of cognitive learning (see Figure 2.9 on page 40; other domains will be presented in later chapters). The cognitive domain contains six levels. Each level represents an increasingly complex type of cognition. Although the cognitive domain is often characterized as having "lower" and "higher" levels, only the knowledge level is considered by authors of the taxonomy to be lower; all other levels are higher. The first level, knowledge, describes several different types of knowledge. The remaining five levels are referred to as "intellectual abilities and skills."

Bloom's taxonomy can be very helpful when formulating specific learning targets. However, this categorization of cognitive tasks was done more than thirty years ago, and since that time there have been significant changes in the educational and psychological theories that formed the basis for the taxonomy. Current theories emphasize thinking processes, characterize the learner as an active information processor, and stress domain-specific thinking and learning. The taxonomy, in comparison, was based on a focus on outcomes or objectives, learners as an object and as a reactor in the learning situation, and broad, single organizing principles that cut across different domains (Tittle, Hecht, & Moore, 1993). More contemporary, but less well-known frameworks, such as those by Marzano, Brandt,

FIGURE 2.9   Bloom's Taxonomy of Educational Objectives: Cognitive Domain

Level	Illustrative Verbs
Knowledge: Recalling and remembering previously learned material, including specific facts, events, persons, dates, methods, procedures, concepts, principles, and theories	Names, matches, lists, recalls, selects, retells, states, defines, describes, labels, reproduces
Comprehension: Understanding and grasping the meaning of something; includes translation from one symbolic form to another (e.g., percent into fractions), interpretation, explanation, prediction, inferences, restating, estimation, generalization, and other uses that demonstrate understanding	Explains, converts, interprets, paraphrases, predicts, estimates, rearranges, rephrases, summarizes
Application: Use of abstract ideas, rules, or generalized methods in novel, concrete situations	Changes, demonstrates, modifies, produces, solves, constructs, applies, uses, shows
Analysis: Breaking down a communication into constituent parts or elements and understanding the relationship among different elements	Distinguishes, compares, subdivides, diagrams, differentiates, relates, classifies, categorizes
Synthesis: Arranging and combining elements and parts into novel patterns or structures	Generates, combines, constructs, assembles, formulates, forecasts, projects, proposes, integrates
Evaluation: Judging the quality, worth, or value of something according to established criteria (e.g., determining the adequacy of evidence to support a conclusion)	Justifies, criticizes, decides, judges, argues, concludes, supports, defends, evaluates, verifies, confirms

and Hughes (1988) and Quellmalz (1987), better reflect more recent psychological theories. The taxonomies are still valuable, however, in providing a comprehensive list of possible learning objectives with clear action verbs that operationalize the targets.

Professional Preparation

Throughout your professional preparation you have been exposed to essential principles and methods of different disciplines. As you master each discipline you will be able to identify what is most important for learning. Perhaps you have heard that the best way to learn something is to teach it. Put yourself in the role of a teacher even as you take courses. What specific knowledge is most important?

What do you need to be able to do with the knowledge? What are *you* doing as a student? Do you *really know* the subject, inside and out, so you can do more as a teacher than simply read notes or do exactly what it says in the curriculum guide? You will find that the quality of your assessments will follow from the depth of your understanding of what you teach. The more you understand, the better the assessments.

It is also important to keep current with the professional literature in both the subjects you teach and education in general. This literature will keep you up to date and will give you many ideas about the kind of learning targets that are appropriate.

Textbooks

Most textbooks for students will be accompanied by an instructor guide or a teacher's edition that will provide information to help you plan a lesson, deliver appropriate instruction, and assess student learning. The teacher's edition will typically include "objectives" for each lesson.

Although the objectives in a teacher's edition can be very useful, you should keep in mind that textbook authors emphasize limited, lower-level objectives that are applicable for a wide range of different classes and locations. Furthermore, textbook objectives are neither the *only*, nor necessarily *best*, source for your learning targets. The objectives need to be reviewed in relation to your specific teaching situation and approach.

Three major criteria can be used to evaluate the appropriateness of textbook objectives (Brophy and Alleman, 1991). First, are the objectives stated with clear descriptions of what students will know or be able to do following instruction? Even if the behavior is clearly stated, the textbook probably will not indicate what criteria should be used to complete the learning target. Second, are the objectives appropriate for your students? Have your students learned the prerequisite knowledge and skills? Is the level of learning required appropriate for your students? Third, do the objectives include most of the student outcomes? How complete and comprehensive are the objectives? Are important areas overlooked? Because many textbooks emphasize fundamental knowledge, it is likely that application and more complex thinking skills will not be included. Using these three criteria, you can appraise the appropriateness and completeness of the objectives as a basis for your leaning targets. You will probably need to modify and expand the objectives to meet unique characteristics of both yourself and your students.

Existing Lists of Objectives

You will find it helpful to locate and review lists of objectives that have already been developed. A number of sources can be used to locate these lists. Most methods of teaching textbooks, particularly those in each subject area, will contain illustrative objectives as well as references that can be consulted. Yearbooks and handbooks in different disciplines sometimes contain objectives. Special reports issued by professional groups, such as the National Council of Teachers of Mathematics, the

National Council of Teachers in English, the National Council of Teachers in Social Studies, and the National Science Teachers Association, contain extensive lists of objectives that emphasize thinking skills and applications to real-life problems. For example, the report *Science for All Americans: Project 2061*, prepared by the American Association for the Advancement of Science, recommends four goals for science education: understanding scientific endeavors, developing scientific perspectives about the world, developing historical and social views on science, and developing scientific "habits of mind."

An excellent source is state or local level curriculum guides. Although these guides may present objectives at different levels of specificity, they are very helpful in their comprehensive nature of critical objectives. Some states, such as California, Virginia, and Connecticut, have developed extensive curriculum frameworks. In whatever state you are teaching, it would be worthwhile to contact your state department of education and inquire about existing curriculum guides or frameworks. If you are in a large school or school district, there will probably be a list of instructional objectives for you that you should consult as a starting point. In addition, most states will be responding to the national standards movement by developing a set of state-level core standards for all students. These state-level standards will be reviewed to determine if they are as rigorous as national-level subject-specific standards, feasible, cumulatively adequate, encouraging of students' abilities to integrate and apply knowledge, and reflective of broad consensus building.

National Standards

I have already pointed out that national content and performance standards are being developed in several areas. These standards will be excellent sources for your learning targets because they are being developed with criteria that result in high-quality, complex learning. The national Technical Planning Group (Wurtz, 1993) suggests that standards should be:

- *World Class:* at least as challenging as current standards in other leading industrial countries, though not necessarily the same
- *Important and focused:* parsimonious, while including those elements that represent the most important knowledge and skills within a discipline
- *Useful:* developing what is needed for citizenship, employment, and lifelong learning
- *Reflective of broad consensus building:* resulting from a process of comment, feedback, and revision, including educators and the lay public
- *Balanced:* between the competing requirements for depth and breadth, being definite or specific, and being flexible or adaptable; also balanced between theory or principles and facts or information, formal knowledge and applications, and being forward-looking and traditional
- *Accurate and sound:* reflecting the best scholarship within the discipline
- *Clear and usable:* sufficiently clear so that parents, teachers, and students can understand what the standards mean and what the standards require of them

- *Assessable:* sufficiently specific so their attainment can be measured in terms meaningful to teachers, students, parents, test makers and users, the public, and others
- *Adaptable:* permitting flexibility in implementation needed for local control, state and regional variation, and differing individual interests and cultural traditions
- *Developmentally appropriate:* challenging but, with sustained effort, attainable by all students at elementary, middle, and high school levels (pp. iii–iv)

As you can see, this is a most ambitious set of criteria! Most of the groups working on the standards will have completed their work by the publication of this book. The addresses and phone numbers of the councils and associations working on different subject areas are contained in Appendix A.

The strengths and limitations of these five sources of objectives for establishing learning targets are summarized in Figure 2.10. Initially you may find that textbooks and existing lists of objectives contain ideas that will be most easily translated into practice.

FIGURE 2.10   **Strengths and Limitations of Different Sources for Establishing Learning Targets**

Source	Strengths	Limitations
Bloom's Taxonomy	Established; well known; comprehensive; contains action verbs; hierarchical design	Dated; based on behavioristic learning theories; not consistent with recent cognitive theories of learning
Professional Preparation	Focus on essentials of a discipline; personal experience	Difficult to translate into targets and keep up to date; may be confined to a specific type of target
Textbooks	Directly related to instruction; easily adapted	Tend to emphasize lower-level targets; lacks criteria; need to be modified
Existing Lists of Objectives	Comprehensive; good ideas for targets	May not relate well to a local situation; need to be modified
National Standards	High standards; comprehensive; reflects national expertise; reflects current research on learning; discipline specific	May not relate well to local situation; need to be modified; may not be politically acceptable

CRITERIA FOR SELECTING LEARNING TARGETS

Once you have consulted existing sources of objectives and begun the task of selecting your learning targets, you will need to make some choices about which ones to keep, which need revision, and which are not feasible. The following criteria will help you judge the adequacy of your learning targets. They are summarized in Figure 2.11 in the form of a checklist.

1. *Establish the right number of learning targets.* The actual number of different learning targets will vary, depending on the length of the instructional segment and the complexity of the target. Obviously, the longer the instructional period, the more targets. Also, more complex targets, such as those requiring reasoning, take more time. I have found the following general rules of thumb appropriate: 40–60 targets for a year; 8–12 for a unit; 1–3 for a single lesson. Hundreds of targets for a year are clearly too many.

2. *Establish comprehensive learning targets.* It is essential that the targets represent all types of important learning from the instructional unit. Be careful not to overemphasize knowledge targets. Try to maintain a balance between each of the five areas (knowledge, reasoning, skills, products, and affect). Higher priority may be given to targets that integrate several of these areas. Do not rely too heavily on textbook objectives or teacher's guides.

3. *Establish learning targets that reflect school goals.* Your targets should be clearly related to more general school, district, and state learning goals. Priority may be given to targets that focus on school improvement plans or restructuring efforts.

4. *Establish learning targets that are challenging yet feasible.* It is important to challenge students and seek the highest level of accomplishment for them. You will need to develop targets that will not be too easy nor too hard. It is also important to assess the readiness of your students in order to establish these challenging targets. Do they have necessary perquisite skills and knowledge? Are they developmentally ready for the challenge? Do they have needed motivation and attitudes? Will students see the targets as too easy? As we will see in the next chapter, these are questions that need to be answered through proper assessment prior to your final selection of learning targets, instructional activities, and your assessment of student learning.

5. *Establish learning targets that are consistent with current principles of learning and motivation.* Because learning targets are the basis for learning and instruction, it is

FIGURE 2.11   Checklist for Selecting Learning Targets

1. Are there too many or too few targets?
2. Are all important types of learning included?
3. Do the targets reflect school goals?
4. Will the targets challenge students to do their best work?
5. Are the targets consistent with research on learning and motivation?
6. Are the targets established prior to instruction?

important that what you set as a target will promote learning that is consistent with what we know about how learning occurs and what motivates students. For example, will the targets promote long-term retention in a meaningful way? Do the targets reflect students' intrinsic interests and needs? Do the targets represent learning that will be applicable to life outside the classroom? Will the targets encourage a variety of instructional approaches and activities?

After you identify the targets, it is best to write them out prior to teaching. This will allow a ready reference throughout the lesson and free you to concentrate on the face-paced and complex activities in the classroom. From year to year you will find it necessary to revisit your targets and make appropriate modifications depending on changes in your students, curriculum, textbooks, and state requirements.

SUMMARY

Learning targets—what students should know and be able to do and the criteria for judging student performance—are contrasted in this chapter with more traditional terms such as *goals, objectives,* and *expectations.* The major points include the following:

- Goals are broad statements about student learning.
- Instructional or behavioral objectives are specific statements that indicate what students should know and be able to do at the end of an instructional unit.
- Expectations are the teacher's beliefs about what students are capable of achieving.
- Goals, objectives, and expectations focus on what students do rather than on what the teacher does during instruction.
- Experience has demonstrated that it is not practical to write very specific behavioral objectives that include all aspects of the criteria and testing conditions.
- Learning targets need to contain as much about criteria that is possible and feasible, because criteria are critical in establishing the standards upon which performance toward the learning target is judged.
- Criteria are clearly stated dimensions of student performance that the teacher examines in making judgments about student proficiency. These criteria should be public and explained to students prior to each instructional unit.
- Exemplars and anchors are important examples that help students understand how teacher evaluations will made.
- Five types of learning targets are introduced: knowledge, reasoning, skill, product, and affect.
- Sources for constructing learning targets include Bloom's taxonomy, your professional preparation, textbooks, existing lists of objectives, and national standards.
- Criteria to be used in selecting targets were indicated. You should strive for the right number of comprehensive, challenging targets that will reflect school goals and will be consistent with current principles of learning and motivation.

SELF-INSTRUCTIONAL REVIEW EXERCISES

1. Identify each of the following as a goal (G), behavioral objective (BO), or expectation (E).

   a. My students will pass all their exams.
   b. Students will be familiar with global geography.
   c. It is unlikely that Tom will finish his test.
   d. Students will answer ten of twelve questions about ancient Egypt in fifteen minutes without use of notes.

2. What does the term *criteria* have in common with behavioral objectives? How is it different from what is contained in objectives?

3. Suppose a teacher pulls out a graded paper that was handed in by a student from a previous year's class and distributes it to the class. What would the paper be called in relation to assessment?

   a. Rubric
   b. Anchor
   c. Scoring criteria
   d. Performance criteria

4. Give at least three reasons why using public criteria that are shared with students prior to instruction is an effective teaching/learning tool for evaluating student work?

5. Why is it important to include criteria in learning targets?

6. Identify each of the following as a knowledge (K), reasoning (R), skill (S), product (P), or affect (A) target.

   a. shooting free throws
   b. recalling historical facts from the Revolutionary War
   c. comparing vertebrates to invertebrates
   d. identifying the organs in a dissected frog
   e. working cooperatively with others
   f. building a three-dimensional structure from sticks and glue

7. Why may Bloom's taxonomy of educational objectives not be the best source for identifying classroom learning targets?

8. What are some examples of at least one learning target in each of the five types (Figure 2.8, page 37) that could be stated for you concerning the content of this book?

ANSWERS TO SELF-INSTRUCTIONAL REVIEW EXERCISES

1. a. E, b. G, c. E., d. BO.

2. Criteria are part of what would be included in a behavioral objective. Criteria, in contrast to objectives, contain descriptions of different levels of performance.

3. b.

4. Could have selected from communicating goals and different levels of work to parents, documenting judgments, helping students evaluate their own work, motivating students.

5. Criteria are needed to completely understand the nature of the target and what it takes to achieve different levels of performance. Without criteria, targets are statements similar to simple behavioral objectives (without conditions, criteria, and audience).

6. a. S, b. K, c. R, d. K, e. A, f. P.

7. Bloom's taxonomy is not aligned very well with more recent research on learning and motivation.

8. For example,

Knowledge: Students are able to recall and write accurately 80 percent of the definitions of key terms in the chapter.

Reasoning: Students are able to analyze five examples of learning targets and modify them in writing so that they correspond better to the criteria in the chapter.

Skill: Students will use the library computer system to locate critiques of three published tests.

Product: Students can construct learning targets after receiving an instructional unit on teaching fractions. The targets are judged by the extent to which criteria are included. Or, students can construct a multiple-choice test that corresponds to the criteria in the book.

Affect: Students increase the importance they give to constructing criteria for learning targets.

SUGGESTIONS FOR ACTION RESEARCH

1. Obtain some examples of student work from teachers that will demonstrate different levels of performance on the same assessment. How easy is it to see how the examples are different? See if the criteria you use to differentiate the examples are the same as the criteria the teacher used.

2. In small groups, generate some examples of student performance on the same learning target that would demonstrate qualitatively different levels of achievement concerning the content of this chapter or Chapter 1.

3. Examine textbook objectives and national standards in your area of expertise. How are they similar and how are they different?

4. Interview a teacher and ask about using textbook objectives. How useful are these objectives? What determines whether or not the teacher will use them?

5. In a group of three or four other students, develop a scoring rubric that could be used for judging the performance of a student on an assignment, project, or test that was used in a school setting. Find or generate examples of student work that illustrate different levels of performance.

3

ESTABLISHING HIGH-QUALITY CLASSROOM ASSESSMENTS

Classroom assessment consists of determining purpose and learning targets, systematically obtaining information from students, interpreting the information collected, and using the information. In the previous chapter, establishing learning targets was identified as an essential step in actually conducting assessments. Once you have determined *what* to assess, you will probably be concerned with *how* to

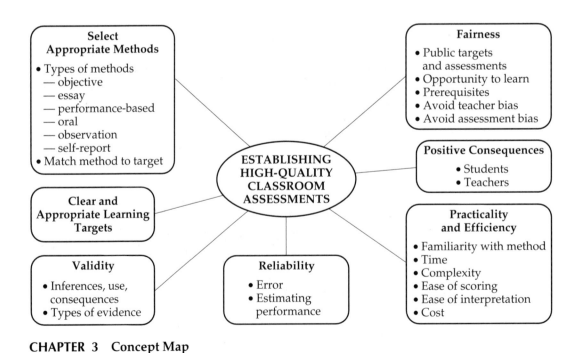

CHAPTER 3   Concept Map

assess it. That is, what methods of data collection will you use to gather the information? At this point it is important to keep in mind several criteria that determine the quality and credibility of the assessment methods you choose. In this chapter, we will review these criteria and provide suggestions for practical steps you can take to keep the quality of your assessments high.

WHAT IS HIGH-QUALITY CLASSROOM ASSESSMENT?

Until recently, the quality of classroom assessment was determined by the extent to which specific psychometric standards of validity, reliability, and efficiency were met. These standards were originally derived for large-scale, published, standardized objective tests, and are still very important, at least conceptually, for most types of assessments. However, for published tests the emphasis is on highly technical, statistically sophisticated standards. Thus, complex statistical procedures, such as correlation, are used to provide estimates of validity, reliability, and measurement error. Different types of validity and reliability are stressed, along with sampling error to estimate efficiency. To interpret standardized tests properly, it is necessary to have a basic understanding of these properties.

But in most classrooms such technical qualities have little relevance because the purpose of the assessment is different. This is not to say that the *ideas* of validity and reliability are not important criteria for classroom assessment. High-quality classroom assessment involves many other criteria as well, substituting technically pleasing types of validity and reliability with concerns about how the assessments influence learning and provide fair and credible reporting of student achievement. For teachers the primary determinant of quality is how the information impacts students. Thus, the focus is on the use and consequences of the results and what the assessments get students to do, rather than on a detailed inspection of the test itself.

High-quality classroom assessments, then, are technically sound and provide results that demonstrate and improve targeted student learning. High quality assessments also inform instructional decision making. As pointed out in Chapter 1, our understanding of learning and motivation, and our realization that much more is demanded of students than demonstrating simple knowledge, has changed how we define high-quality classroom assessments, and because assessment is an

FIGURE 3.1 **Criteria for Ensuring High-Quality Classroom Assessments**

Clear and appropriate learning targets
Appropriateness of assessment methods
Validity
Reliability
Fairness
Positive consequences
Practicality and efficiency

essential part of instruction, high-quality teaching and learning is impossible without sound and credible assessment. The criteria of high-quality classroom assessment are presented in Figure 3.1. Each will be summarized.

CLEAR AND APPROPRIATE LEARNING TARGETS

As pointed out in Chapter 1, sound assessment includes clear and appropriate learning targets. Remember that the learning target includes both what students should know and can do, and the criteria for judging student performance. Are the targets at the right level of difficulty to motivate students? Is there adequate balance with different types of targets? Are the targets consistent with your overall goals and the goals of the school and district? Are the targets comprehensive, covering all major dimensions that you hope to change and need feedback about? Are the criteria for judging student performance clear?

APPROPRIATENESS OF ASSESSMENT METHODS

As you are well aware, a number of different types of assessment methods can be used in the classroom. Some of these methods were introduced in Chapter 1. Although your ultimate choice of an assessment method will depend on how well all of the criteria in Figure 3.1 are met, the match between type of target and method is very important. Even though most targets may be measured by several methods, the reality of teaching is that certain methods measure some types of targets better than other methods do. That is, particular methods are more likely to provide quality assessments for certain types of targets. Thus, one of your first tasks, once you have identified the targets, is to match them with methods.

One way to think about making this match is to place types of targets and methods in the form of a matrix, as illustrated in Figure 3.2. This figure summarizes

FIGURE 3.2   Matching Targets with Methods Scorecard

	Assessment Methods					
	Objective	Essay	Performance-Based	Oral Question	Observation	Self-Report
Targets						
Knowledge	5	4	3	4	3	2
Reasoning	2	5	4	4	2	2
Skills	1	3	5	2	5	3
Products	1	1	5	2	4	4
Affect	1	2	4	4	4	5

Note: Higher numbers indicate better matches (e.g., 5 = high, 1 = low).

the relative strengths of different methods in measuring different targets. Notice that for some targets several methods may be used. This is good in that it provides more flexibility in the assessments you use, but it also means there is no simple formula nor one correct method.

Types of Assessment Methods

To use the matrix, it will be helpful to provide brief descriptions of the different methods, then explain how methods vary in their capability to provide sound assessments to each type of target. In later chapters, the methods will be presented in much more detail. The different types of methods are summarized in Figure 3.3.

> *Objective tests* (also referred to as *selected response* tests or one type of *paper-and-pencil* test) are distinguished by requiring structured student responses and by how they are scored. Typically students either select a response from two or more possibilities, or they supply a one- or two-word answer to a question. The answers are then scored objectively, in the sense that each item is scored correct or incorrect according to preestablished guidelines. If several individuals scored the test, each one would always arrive at the same overall score. Major types of objective tests include *supply type* (short answer and completion), and *selection type* (multiple choice, true/false, and matching).
>
> *Essay tests* are paper-and-pencil assessments that allow students to construct a response that would be several sentences to several pages in length. Essay tests are typically *restricted-response* tests or *extended-response* tests, depending on the degree of freedom provided to the student. Questions that include limits to the content and nature of the answer are restricted-response tests.
>
> *Performance-based* assessments require students to demonstrate a skill or proficiency by asking them to create, produce, or do something, often in a setting that involves real-world applications. Performance-based assessments include paintings, speeches, musical presentations, demonstrations, research papers, investigations, athletic performance, projects, exhibitions, and other products that require students to construct a unique response to a task.

FIGURE 3.3 Different Methods of Assessment

Objective Supply	Objective Selection	Essay	Performance-Based	Oral Question	Observation	Self-Report
Short answer Completion	Multiple choice Matching True/false	Restricted response Extended response	Presentations Papers Projects Athletics Demonstrations Exhibitions	Oral examinations Conferences Interviews	Informal Formal	Attitude survey Sociometric devices Questionnaires Inventories

Assessments can also be made of the process that the student uses to complete the task.

Oral question assessments are used continuously in instruction to monitor student understanding. Teachers ask students questions about the content or process, or they engage students in verbal interaction individually or in groups. Oral questions include oral examinations, interviews, conferences, and other conversations in which information is obtained about student learning.

Observation assessments, like oral questions, are so common in teaching that we often don't think of them as a form of student evaluation. But teachers *constantly* observe students informally to assess student understanding and progress. Teachers watch students as they respond to questions and study, and teachers listen to students as they speak and discuss with others. Often nonverbal communication, such as squinting, inattention, looks of frustration, and other cues, is more helpful than verbal feedback. Observation is used extensively as well in performance-based assessments, and other formal observational techniques are used to assess classroom climate, teacher effectiveness, and other dimensions of the classroom.

Self-report assessments are those in which the students are asked to complete a form or answer questions to reveal how they think about themselves or how they rate themselves. Attitude surveys, sociometric devices, self-concept questionnaires, interest inventories, some aptitude tests, and personality measures are examples of self-report assessments.

Matching Targets with Methods

Figure 3.2 on page 50 presents the Matching Targets with Methods Scorecard. This scorecard has been prepared to give you *general* guidelines about how well particular assessment methods measure each type of target. Remember that the numbers (1=low, 5=high) represent the relative strength of the method to provide a high-quality assessment. Variations to what is presented in the figure should be expected. For example, good objective items *can* provide a high-quality measure of reasoning, but such items are difficult and very time-consuming to prepare. What I have considered in assigning the numbers are both technical strengths and practical limitations. When each method is described in greater detail in later chapters, the variations will become more obvious. For now, however, the scorecard will give you a good overview and provide some preliminary information for selecting methods that are appropriate.

Knowledge

Well-constructed objective tests do a good job of assessing subject matter and procedural knowledge, particularly when students must recognize or remember isolated facts, definitions, spellings, concepts, and principles. Objective questions can be answered and scored quickly, so this type of test is efficient for teachers. Objective tests also allow you to adequately sample from a large amount of knowledge.

Asking students questions orally about what they know is also an effective way to assess knowledge, but this takes much more time and the results are difficult to record. It also takes advanced planning to prepare the questions and a method to record student responses. Thus, assessment by oral questioning is best in situations when you are checking for mastery of a limited number of important facts or when you are doing informal diagnostic assessment. This is usually done during instruction to provide feedback about student progress.

Essays can be used effectively to assess knowledge when your objective is for students to learn large chunks or structures of knowledge that are related. For example, essays would be effective in measuring whether students knew the causes of World War II or the life cycles of different types of animals.

Using performance-based assessments presents some difficulties for determining what students know. Much of the preparation for the performance often takes place out of class, and the final paper or product typically does not provide opportunities for demonstrating that the student has mastered specific facts. If the performance can be successful only if specific requisite skills are required, then an inference of this knowledge can be made. Also, when the performance involves a demonstration of a process or series of steps, knowledge of the process or steps can be assumed when they are demonstrated. Because performance-based assessments are time intensive for teachers and students, they are usually not the best choice for assessing vast amounts of knowledge.

Reasoning

Reasoning skills are demonstrated most efficiently in essays. Usually essays focus directly on specific reasoning skills by asking students to compare, evaluate, critique, provide justification for, organize, integrate, defend, and solve problems. Time is provided to allow students to use reasoning before answering the question. When oral questions require reasoning for an answer they are excellent, but also inefficient, for systematic assessment of all students at the end of a unit.

Performance-based assessments are also quite effective in measuring reasoning skills as long as the product or demonstration clearly illustrates procedures that reveal reasoning or a performance from which we can infer reasoning. For example, by observing students demonstrate how to go about planning a budget for a family of four, you can draw inferences about how the student used all the information provided and balanced different priorities. Science projects illustrate the ability to interpret results and make conclusions.

Objective questions *can* be an excellent method for assessing certain aspects of reasoning. When the item demands more than simply recalling or recognizing a fact, reasoning may be needed. For example, if an item requires the student to interpret a chart, analyze a poem, or apply knowledge to solve a problem, reasoning skills can be measured. However, constructing objective items that assess reasoning is very time-consuming.

Student self-reports of the reasoning they used in answering a question or solving a problem can help you diagnose learning difficulties. Of course students may not even be aware of what they are or are not doing, especially younger students.

Skills

Performance-based assessments are clearly the preferred method to determine systematically whether or not a student has mastered a skill. Whether the student is demonstrating how to shoot a basketball, give a persuasive speech, sing a song, speak in a foreign language, or use a microscope, the skill is best assessed by observing the student perform the task. On a more informal basis, teachers use observation extensively to assess progress in demonstrating skills.

Objective tests and oral questioning can be used to assess student knowledge of the skills, such as knowing the proper sequence of actions or recognizing the important dimensions of the skill. But this represents prerequisite knowledge and is not the same as measuring the extent to which the student can actually *do* it.

Products

It is not difficult to see that the best way to assess student products is to have them complete one through a performance-based assessment. The best test of being able to write persuasively is to write a letter that argues for something; if you want students to be able to act, have them participate in a play.

Like skills, you can use objective items, essay items, and oral questions to determine whether students know the components of the product or to evaluate different products. But there is no substitute for actually creating the product.

Affect

Affective outcomes are best assessed by either observing students or using student self-reports. Remember that affect refers to attitudes, values, feelings, self-concept, interests, and other feelings and beliefs. Because these traits are complex, it is especially important to have clear learning targets.

The most direct and efficient way to assess affect is to ask the students directly through self-report surveys and questionnaires. This method has limitations, but it is still superior to trying to infer affect from behavior. Also, direct oral questioning can be revealing if the right relationship exists between teacher and student and if the atmosphere is conducive to honest sharing of feelings.

Observation can be effective in determining, informally, many affective traits (e.g., motivation and attitudes toward subjects and student self-concept are often apparent when the student shows negative feelings through body posture, a reluctance to interact with others, and withdrawal). Some performance-based assessments provide ample opportunities for teachers to observe affect, though like other observations, this is usually nonsystematic and inferences are required. Because you are both the observer and the one making the inference, you need to be careful to avoid bias. Having clear targets helps to prevent personal opinion or biases from clouding the assessments.

You must make many choices to ensure that you match targets to methods. As you learn about what it takes to do high-quality assessments with each of the methods, your matches will be better. The next two criteria, validity and reliability, are essential to determining this quality.

VALIDITY

What Is a Valid Assessment?

Classroom assessment is a process that includes gathering, interpreting, and using information. This conceptualization has important implications for how we define a familiar concept that is at the heart of any type of high-quality assessment—validity. *Validity* is a characteristic that refers to the appropriateness of the inferences, uses, and consequences that result from the test or other method of gathering information. In other words, is the interpretation made from test results reasonable? Is the information that I have gathered the right kind of evidence for the decision I need to make or the intended use? How sound is the interpretation of the information? Validity is concerned with the inferences, not the test itself. Thus, it is an inference or use that is valid or invalid, not the test, instrument, or procedure that is used to gather information. Often we use the phrase "validity of the test," but it is more accurate to say "the validity of the interpretation, inference, or use of the results."

Validity means a lot more than simply "the extent to which a test measures what it is supposed to measure." Although this notion is important to many decisions and uses, it tends to focus validity on the instrument, as if it were a characteristic that the instrument always possesses. In reality, the same test or instrument can be valid for one purpose and invalid for another. Actually, validity is always a matter of degree, depending on the situation. For example, a social science test may have high validity for inferring that students know the sequence of events leading up to the American Revolution, less validity for inferring that students can reason, even less validity for inferring that students can communicate effectively in writing, and virtually no validity for indicating a student's mathematical ability. A measure is not simply valid or invalid, it is valid to some degree, for example, high or strong, moderate, or low.

How Is Validity Determined?

Validity is always determined by professional judgment. This judgment is made by the user of the information (the teacher for classroom assessment). An analysis is done by accumulating evidence that would suggest that an inference or use is appropriate and whether the consequences of the interpretations and uses are reasonable and fair. Traditionally, the validity of the inference has come from one of three types of evidence: content-related, criterion-related, and construct-related evidence. However, these categories do not adequately address the consequences and uses of the results. Thus, we will consider how classroom teachers can use these three types of evidence, as well as the consequences, to make an overall judgment about the degree of validity. Note that validity is a unitary concept. The idea that there are different types of validity has been replaced with the view that there are different types of evidence to use in determining validity. Figure 3.4 summarizes the major sources of information that can be used to establish validity.

FIGURE 3.4   Sources of Information for Validity

Content-Related Evidence	The extent to which the assessment is representative of the domain of interest.
Criterion-Related Evidence	The relationship between an assessment and another measure of the same trait.
Construct-Related Evidence	The extent to which the assessment is a meaningful measure of an unobservable trait or characteristic.

Content-Related Evidence

One feature of teaching that has important implications for assessment is that often a teacher is unable to assess everything students learn. Suppose you wanted to test for everything sixth-grade students learn in a four-week unit about insects. Can you imagine how long the test would be and how much time students would take to complete the test? What you do in these situations is select a *sample* of content to assess, and then you use student achievement on this sample to make inferences about knowledge of the entire universe or domain of content, reasoning, and other targets. That is, if a student correctly answers 85 percent of the items on your test of a sample of the unit on insects, then you infer that the student knows 85 percent of the content in the entire unit. If your sample is judged to be representative of the universe or domain, then you have content-related evidence for validity. The inference from the results is that the student demonstrates knowledge about the unit.

Adequate sampling of content is determined by *your* professional judgment. This judgment process can be haphazard or very systematic. In a superficial review of the target, objectives, and test items, validity is based only on *appearance*. This is sometimes referred to as face validity. *Face validity* is whether, based on a superficial examination of the test, there seems to be a reasonable measure of the objectives and domain. Does the test, on the face of it, look like an adequate measure? Although it is important to avoid face *in*validity, it is better if the evidence is more structured and systematic.

Once the complete domain of content is specified, the items on the test can be reviewed to be certain that there is a match between the intended inferences and what is on the test. This process begins with clear learning targets. Based on the targets, a *test blueprint* or *table of specifications* is sometimes prepared to further delineate what targets you intend to assess and what is important from the content domain. The table of specifications is a two-way grid that shows the content and types of learning targets represented in your assessment (Figure 3.5 on page 57). Constructing this type of blueprint may seem like an imposing task, and in practice teachers find that the amount of work needed to construct one usually outweighs the benefits. An alternative to the table of specifications is a complete, detailed list of learning targets. Essentially, this list includes all of the cells that would be checked or completed in the table of specifications. At the very least, keep a picture of the table in your mind as a way to check what is being assessed.

FIGURE 3.5 Format for a Table of Specifications.

Major Content Areas	Learning Target					
	Knowledge	Reasoning	Skills	Products	Affect	Totals
1. (Topic)	No./%	No./%	No./%	No./%	No./%	No./%
2. (Topic)	No./%	No./%	No./%	No./%	No./%	No./%
3. (Topic)	No./%	No./%	No./%	No./%	No./%	No./%
4. (Topic)	No./%	No./%	No./%	No./%	No./%	No./%
.	.	.	.	.	.	.
.	.	.	.	.	.	.
.	.	.	.	.	.	.
N (Topic)	.	.	.	.	.	.
Total no. of items/% of test	No./%	No./%	No./%	No./%	No./%	*Total no. of items/100%*

The table is completed by indicating the number of test items (No.) and the percentage of items from each type of learning target for each topic. For example, if the topic was assessment, you might have reliability as one topic. If there were four knowledge items for reliability and this was 8 percent of the test, then 4/8 percent would be included in the table under Knowledge.

I want to emphasize that the goal of a blueprint is to systematize your professional judgment so that you can improve the validity of the assessment. As illustrated in Figure 3.6, your judgment is used to determine what types of learning targets will be assessed (knowledge, reasoning, skills, products, or affect), what areas of the content will be sampled, and how the assessment measures both content and type of learning target. At this point, you are making decisions about the importance of different types of targets, the content assessed, and how much of the assessment is measuring each target and area of content. If the assessment does, in fact, reflect an actual or modified table of specifications, then there is content-related evidence of validity.

Another consideration related to this type of evidence is the extent to which an assessment can be said to have *instructional* validity. *Instructional validity* is concerned with the match between what is taught and what is assessed. How closely does the test correspond to what has been covered in class and in assignments? Have students had the opportunity to learn what has been assessed? This type of ev-

FIGURE 3.6 Professional Judgments in Establishing Content-Related Evidence for Validity

Learning Targets	Content	Instruction	Assessment
What learning targets will be assessed? How much of the assessment will be done on each target area?	What content is most important? What topics will be assessed? How much of the assessment will be done in each topic?	What content and learning targets have been emphasized in instruction?	Are assessments adequate samples of students performance in each topic area and each target?

idence for validity is important for making reasonable inferences about student performance. Again, your professional judgment is needed to assure that, in fact, what is assessed is consistent with what was taught. One way to check this is to examine the table of specifications after teaching a unit and determine whether the emphasis in different areas or on different targets is consistent with what was emphasized in class. For example, if you emphasized knowledge in teaching a unit (e.g., basic facts, definitions of terms, places, dates, names, etc.), it would not be logical to test for reasoning and then make inferences about the knowledge students learned in the class.

Criterion-Related Evidence

Another way to ensure appropriate inferences from test results is to have evidence that a particular assessment is providing the same result as another assessment of the same thing. *Criterion-related* evidence provides such validity by relating an assessment to some other valued measure (criterion) that either provides an estimate of current performance (concurrent criterion-related evidence) or predicts future performance (predictive criterion-related evidence). Test developers and researchers use this approach to establish evidence that a test or other instrument is measuring the same trait, knowledge, or attitude by calculating a correlation coefficient to measure the relationship between the assessment and the criterion.

Classroom teachers do not conduct formal studies to obtain correlation coefficients that will provide evidence of validity, but the principle *is* very important for teachers to employ. The principle is that when you have two or more measures of the same thing, and these measures provide similar results, then you have established, albeit informally, criterion-related evidence. For example, if your assessment of a student's skill in using a microscope through observation coincides with the student's score on a quiz that tests steps in using microscopes, then you have criterion-related evidence that your inference about the skill of this student is valid. Similarly, if you are interested in the extent to which preparation by your students, as indicated by scores on a final exam in mathematics, predicts how well they will do next year, you can examine the grades of previous students and determine informally if students who scored high on your final exam are getting high grades and students who scored low on your final are obtaining low grades. If a correlation is found, then an inference about predicting how your students will perform, based on their final exam, is valid. Based on this logic, an important principle is to conduct several assessments of the learning targets; try not to rely on a single assessment.

Construct-Related Evidence

Psychologists refer to a *construct* as an unobservable trait or characteristic that a person possesses, such as intelligence, reading comprehension, honesty, self-concept, attitude, reasoning ability, learning style, and anxiety. These characteristics are not measured directly, in contrast to performance such as spelling or how many push-ups a person successfully completes. Rather, the characteristic is *constructed* to account for behavior that can be observed. Whenever constructs are assessed, the validity of our interpretations depends on the extent of the *construct-related evidence* that is presented. This evidence can take many forms, any one of which is probably insufficient by itself.

There are three types of construct-related evidence: theoretical, logical, and statistical. One important type of evidence is that derived from beginning with a clear theoretical explanation or definition of the characteristic so that its meaning is clear and not confused with any other characteristic. This is particularly important whenever you emphasize reasoning and affect targets. For example, suppose you want to assess students' attitudes toward reading. What is your definition of *attitude*? Do you mean how much students *enjoy* reading, *value* reading, or *read* in their spare time? Are you interested in their *desire* to read or their perception of *ability* to read? None of these traits is necessarily correct as a measure of attitude, but you need to provide a clear definition that separates your construct from other similar, but different, constructs.

Logical analyses can be one or more of several types. For some reasoning constructs, you can ask students to comment on what they were thinking when they answered the questions. Ideally their thinking reveals an intended reasoning process. Another logical type of evidence comes from comparing the scores of groups who, as determined by other criteria, should respond differently. These groups can be students who have been taught compared to "untaught" students, before being taught and after being taught groups, age groups, or groups that have been identified by other means to be different on the construct.

Statistical procedures can be used to correlate scores from measures of the construct with scores from other measures of the same construct and measures of similar, but different, constructs. For example, self-concept of academic ability scores from one survey should be related to another measure of the same thing but less related to measures of self-concept of physical ability. These statistical approaches are used for many standardized, published surveys and questionnaires. As a teacher, however, it will be most practical to use clear definitions and logical analyses as construct-related evidence.

Figure 3.7 summarizes suggestions for enhancing the validity of classroom assessments.

FIGURE 3.7   Suggestions for Enhancing Validity

- Ask others to judge the clarity of what you are assessing.
- Check to see if different ways of assessing the same thing give the same result.
- Sample a sufficient number of examples of what is being assessed.
- Prepare a detailed table of specifications.
- Ask others to judge the match between the assessment items and the objective of the assessment.
- Compare groups known to differ on what is being assessed.
- Compare scores taken before to those taken after instruction.
- Compare predicted consequences to actual consequences.
- Compare scores on similar but different traits.
- Provide adequate time to complete the assessment.
- Ensure appropriate vocabulary, sentence structure, and item difficulty.
- Ask easy questions first.
- Use different methods to assess the same thing.
- Use *only* for intended purposes.

RELIABILITY

Like validity, the term *reliability* has been used for many years to describe an essential characteristic of sound assessment. *Reliability* is concerned with the consistency, stability, and dependability of the results. In other words, a reliable result is one that shows similar performance at different times or under different conditions. Suppose Mrs. Hambrick is assessing her students' addition and subtraction skills. She decides to give the students a twenty-point quiz to determine their skills. Mrs. Hambrick examines the results but wants to be sure about the level of performance before designing appropriate instruction. So she gives another quiz two days later on the same addition and subtraction skills. The results for some of her students are as follows:

Student	Addition		Subtraction	
	Quiz 1	Quiz 2	Quiz 1	Quiz 2
Rob	18	16	13	20
Carrie	10	12	18	10
Ryann	9	8	8	14
Felix	16	15	17	12

The addition quiz scores are fairly consistent. All four students scored within one or two points on the quizzes; students who scored high on the first quiz also scored high on the second quiz, and students who scored low did so on both quizzes. Consequently, the results for addition are reliable. For subtraction, on the other hand, there is considerable change in performance from the first to the second quiz. Students scoring high on the first quiz score low on the second one, and students scoring low on the first quiz score high on the second. For subtraction, then, the results are unreliable because they are not consistent. The scores contradict one another.

So what does Mrs. Hambrick make of the mathematics scores? Her goal is to use the quiz to accurately determine the defined skill. She cannot know the *exact* level of the skills, but, as in the case of addition, she can get a fairly accurate picture with an assessment that is reliable. For subtraction, on the other hand, she cannot use these results alone to estimate the students' real or actual skill. More assessments are needed before she can be confident that the scores are reliable and thus provide a dependable result. But even the scores in addition are not without some degree of error. In fact, *all* assessments have error; they are never perfect measures of the trait or skill. Let's look at another example to illustrate this point.

Think about the difference between a measure of attitude toward science and time required to run a mile. The measure of attitude will have a relatively high degree of error, but the measure of time will be precise, with little error (highly reliable). This is because there are many more influences on how students answer questions about their attitudes (such as the student's mood that day, the heat in the room, poorly worded items, and fatigue) than there are on a timekeeper's ability to press the stopwatch and read the time elapsed. This is not to say that the measure of time is without any error. It's just that measuring time will have much less error than measuring attitudes.

The concept of error in assessment is critical to our understanding of reliability. Conceptually, whenever we assess something, we get an *observed* score or result. This observed score is a product of what the *true* or *real* ability or skill is *plus* some degree of *error*:

Observed Score = True Score + Error

Reliability is directly related to error. It is not a matter of all or none, as if some results are reliable and others unreliable. Rather, for each assessment there is some *degree* of error. Thus, we think in terms of low, moderate, or high reliability. It is important to remember that the error can be positive or negative. That is, the observed score can be higher or lower than the true score, depending on the nature of the error. Sometimes you will know when a student's score is lower than it should be based on the behavior of the student at the time of the assessment. For example, if the student was sick, tired, in a bad mood, or distracted, the score may have negative error and underestimate the true score. This is obviously a subjective judgment, which is fine for many types of classroom assessment.

Figure 3.8 on page 62, shows how different sources of error influence assessment results. Notice how reliability is influenced by factors within the student (internal sources of error), such as luck, mood, and physical condition, as well as external factors, such as the quality of the test, scoring errors, and test directions. The actual or true knowledge, reasoning, skill, or affect is captured to some extent by the assessment, but the internal and external sources of error also contribute to the assessment. In the end, you get an observed score that is made up of both the actual or true performance, plus some degree of error.

An important practical implication of knowing about error in testing is that small differences between scores of different students should be treated as if they were the same. Your interpretation of a score of 75 should be the same as your interpretation of a score of 77. These observed scores are so close that, when we consider error that can be positive or negative, the true scores of the students should be considered equal (e.g., 75, plus or minus 3, or 77, plus or minus 3).

Standardized tests and some classroom assessments have a statistical estimate of reliability. These estimates are correlations between different times a measure is taken, observations of two or more raters, or the correlation among many test items that purport to measure the same thing. These correlations are used to provide a precise measure of the amount of error called the *standard error of measurement*. We will discuss these techniques in greater detail in Chapter 13. At this point, remember that whenever you obtain a score from an assessment it is only an estimate of the real or true level of knowledge, reasoning, skill, product, or affect.

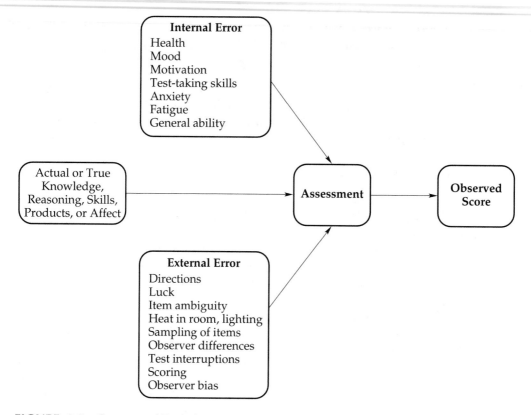

FIGURE 3.8   Sources of Error in Assessment

Figure 3.9 summarizes suggestions for developing and implementing highly reliable classroom assessments. The degree of reliability needed is dependent on the type of decision that will be made on the basis of the results. Higher reliability is needed when the decision has important, lasting consequences for individual students (e.g., placement to receive special education services). When the decision

FIGURE 3.9   Suggestions for Enhancing Reliability

- Use a sufficient number of items or tasks. (Other things being equal, longer tests are more reliable.)
- Use independent raters or observers who provide similar scores to the same performances.
- Construct items and tasks that clearly differentiate students on what is being assessed.
- Make sure the assessment procedures and scoring are as objective as possible.
- Continue assessment until results are consistent.
- Eliminate or reduce the influence of extraneous events or factors.
- Use shorter assessments more frequently than fewer long assessments.

is about groups and is less important, the reliability does not need to be as high (e.g., whether to repeat a part of a unit of instruction).

FAIRNESS

A *fair* assessment is one that provides all students with an equal opportunity to demonstrate achievement. We want to allow students to show us what they have learned from instruction. If some students have an advantage over others because of factors unrelated to what is being taught, then the assessment is not fair. Fair assessments are *unbiased* and *nondiscriminatory*, uninfluenced by irrelevant or subjective factors. That is, neither the assessment task nor scoring is differentially affected by race, gender, ethnic background, handicapping condition, or other factors unrelated to what is being assessed. Fairness is also evident in what students are told about the assessment and whether students have had the opportunity to learn what is being assessed. The following criteria, summarized in Figure 3.10, represent potential influences that determine whether or not an assessment is fair.

Student Knowledge of Learning Targets and Assessments

How often have you taken a test and thought, "Had I only known the teacher was going to test *this* content, I would have studied it"? A fair assessment is one in which it is clear what will and will not be tested. Your objective is not to fool or trick students or to outguess them on the assessment. Rather, you need to be very clear and specific about the learning target—what is to be assessed and how it will be scored. And this is very important: both the content of the assessment and the scoring criteria should be *public*. Being public means that students know the content and scoring criteria prior to the assessment and often prior to instruction. When students know what will be assessed, they know what to study and focus on. By knowing the scoring criteria, students understand much better the qualitative differences the teacher is looking for in student performance. One way to help students understand the assessment is to give them the assessment blueprint, sample questions, and examples of work completed by previous students and graded by the teacher.

FIGURE 3.10   Key Components of Fairness

- Student knowledge of learning targets and assessments
- Opportunity to learn
- Prerequisite knowledge and skills
- Avoiding teacher stereotypes
- Avoiding bias in assessment tasks and procedures

Opportunity to Learn

Is it fair to assess students on things they have not had the opportunity to learn? Opportunity to learn means that students know what to learn and then are provided ample time and appropriate instruction. It is usually not sufficient to simply tell students what will be assessed and then test them. You must plan instruction that focuses specifically on helping students understand, providing students with feedback on their progress, and giving students the time they need to learn.

Prerequisite Knowledge and Skills

It is unfair to assess students on things that require prerequisite knowledge or skills that they do not possess. This means that you need to have a good understanding of prerequisites that your students demonstrate. It also means that you need to examine your assessments carefully to know what prerequisites are required. For example, suppose you want to test math reasoning skills. Your questions are based on short paragraphs that provide needed information. In this situation, math reasoning skills can be demonstrated only if students can read and understand the paragraphs. Thus, reading skills are prerequisites. If students do poorly on the assessment, their performance may have more to do with a lack of reading skills than with math reasoning.

Another type of prerequisite skill is concerned with test taking. Some students bring better test-taking skills to an assessment than other students do, such as knowing to read directions carefully, pacing, initially bypassing difficult items, checking answers, and eliminating wrong answers to multiple-choice items rather than looking for the right answer. These skills are not difficult for students to learn, and it is advisable to make sure all students are familiar with these skills prior to assessment.

Avoiding Teacher Stereotypes

Stereotypes interfere with your objectivity. It is your responsibility to judge each student on his or her performance on assessment tasks, not on how others who share characteristics of the student perform. Although you should not exclude personal feelings and intuitions about a student, it is important to separate these feelings from performance. Stereotypes are judgments about how groups of people will behave based on characteristics such as gender, race, socioeconomic status, physical appearance, and other characteristics. It is impossible to avoid stereotypes completely because of our values, beliefs, preferences, and experiences with different kinds of people. However, we *can* control the influence of these prejudices.

Stereotypes can be based on groups of people, such as "jocks have less motivation to do well," "boys do better in math," "students from a particular neighborhood are more likely to be discipline problems," and "children with a single parent need extra help with homework." You can also *label* students with words such as *shy, gifted, smart, poor, learning disabled, leader,* and *at-risk.* These labels can affect your interactions and evaluations by establishing inappropriate expectations.

Avoiding Bias in Assessment Tasks and Procedures

Another source of bias can be found in the nature of the actual assessment task—the contents and process of the test, project, problem, or other task. Bias is present if the assessment distorts performance due to the student's ethnicity, gender, race, religious background, and so on. Popham (1995) has identified two major forms of assessment bias: offensiveness and unfair penalization.

Offensiveness occurs if the content of the assessment offends, upsets, distresses, angers, or otherwise creates negative affect for particular students or a subgroup of students. This negative affect makes it less likely that the students will perform as well as they otherwise might, lowering the validity of the inferences. Offensiveness occurs most often when stereotypes of particular groups are present in the assessment. Suppose a test question portrayed minority groups in low-paying, low-status jobs, and white groups in high-paying, high-status jobs. Students who are members of the minority group may understandably be offended by the question, mitigating their performance. Here is an example of a biased mathematics test question that may result in offensiveness:

> Juan Mendez gathers lettuce for his income. He receives fifteen cents for every head of lettuce he picks. Juan picked 270 heads of lettuce on Tuesday. How much money did he make?

Unfair penalization is bias that disadvantages a student because of content that makes it more difficult for students from some groups to perform as compared to students from other groups. That is, bias is evident when an unfair advantage or disadvantage is given to one group because of gender, socioeconomic status, race, language, or other characteristic. Suppose you take an aptitude test that uses rural, farm-oriented examples. The questions deal with types of cows and pigs, winter wheat, and farm equipment. If you grew up in a suburban community, do you think you will score as well students who grew up on a farm? Similarly, will a student whose primary language is Spanish have an equal opportunity to demonstrate oral reading skills in English as students whose primary language is English? Do test items containing sports content unfairly advantage boys? Here is a reading comprehension test question that is biased with unfair penalization:

> Write a persuasive essay about the advantages of sailing as recreation. Include in your essay comparisons of sailing with other types of recreation such as hiking, swimming, and bowling.

For many years, standardized tests used content that was more familiar to students from middle-class backgrounds than to minorities from poor backgrounds. This meant that the tests contained vocabulary, pictures, names, situations, and other life experiences that were more familiar to middle-class students, resulting in unfair penalization. Although publishing companies now carefully screen test items to remove this sort of bias, teachers, quite inadvertently, may structure tests and other assessments that *are* biased. It's not that teachers deliberately produce biased assessments. It is most often unconscious and quite innocent. For these reasons, bias can be minimized by having others review your assessments, looking specifically for the types of bias presented here and, of course, by your own sensitivity to bias when creating the assessments. It should be noted that assessment tasks are not necessarily biased solely on the basis of differential performance by minority groups or other groups students may be members of. For example, just because Asian Americans score higher on the SAT than Native or African Americans does not mean that the SAT is biased to give an unfair advantage to Asian Americans.

Cultural differences that are reflected in vocabulary, prior experiences, skills, and values may influence the assessment. These differences are especially important in our increasingly diverse society and classrooms. Consider the following examples of how cultural background influences assessment:

- Knowledge from the immediate environment of the student (e.g., large city, ethnic neighborhood, rural, coastal, etc.) provides a vocabulary and an indication of the importance or relevance of assessment tasks.
- Depending on the culture, rules for sharing beliefs, discussion, taking turns, and expressing opinions differ.
- Respect and politeness may be expressed differently by students from different backgrounds (e.g., not looking into another's eyes, silence, squinting as a way to say no, looking up or down when asked a question).
- Learning style differences—which are exhibited in preferences for learning alone or in a group, for learning by listening or reading, for reflective or impulsive responses, and in the ability to think analytically or globally—influence a student's confidence and motivation to complete assessment tasks.

The influence of these differences will be minimized to the extent that you first understand them and then utilize multiple assessments that will allow all students to demonstrate their progress toward the learning target. If an assessment technique or approach advantages one type of student, another technique may be a disadvantage to that type of student. By using different types of assessments, one provides a balance to the other. Students unable to respond well to one type of assessment will respond well to another type. This points out an important principle of high-quality assessment—*never rely solely on one method of assessment*. However this does not mean that you should arbitrarily pick different methods. You need to select your assessments on the basis of what will provide the fairest indication of student achievement for *all* your students.

Another type of assessment task bias that has received a lot of attention recently is the need to accommodate the special abilities of exceptional children. An assessment is biased if performance is affected by a disability or other limiting characteristic when the student actually possesses the knowledge or skill being measured. In other words, when assessing exceptional students, you need to modify the assessment task so that the disabling trait is not a factor in the performance. For example, students with hearing loss may need written directions to complete an assessment that you give orally to other students. Chapter 12 deals with assessing mainstreamed students in the regular class in some detail.

POSITIVE CONSEQUENCES

The nature of classroom assessments has important consequences for teaching and learning. Ask yourself these questions: How will the assessment affect student motivation? Will students be more or less likely to be meaningfully involved? Will their motivation be intrinsic or extrinsic? How will the assessment affect how and what students study? How will the assessment affect my teaching? How much time will the assessment take away from instruction? Will the results allow me to provide students with individualized feedback? What will the parents think about my assessments? High-quality assessments have consequences that will be positive, for both students and yourself.

Positive Consequences on Students

The most direct consequence of assessment is that students learn and study in a way that is consistent with your assessment task. If the assessment is a multiple-choice test to determine the students' knowledge of specific facts, then students will tend to memorize information. On the other hand, if the assessment calls for extended essays, students tend to learn the material in larger, related chunks, and they practice recall rather than recognition when studying. Assessments that require problem solving, such as performance-based assessments, encourage students to think and apply what they learn. A positive consequence, in this sense, is the appropriate match between the learning target and the assessment task.

Assessments also have clear consequences on student motivation. If students know what will be assessed and how it will be scored, and if they believe that the assessment will be fair, they are likely to be more motivated to learn. Is the assessment structured so that students will be able to show their best performance?

Motivation also increases when the assessment tasks are relevant to the students' backgrounds and goals, challenging but possible, and structured to give students individualized feedback about their performance. What good is a high score on an easy test? Authentic assessments provide more active learning, which increases motivation. Giving students multiple assessments, rather than a single assessment, lessens fear and anxiety. With less apprehension, risk taking, exploration, creativity, and questioning are enhanced.

Finally, the student–teacher relationship is influenced by the nature of assessment. When teachers construct assessments carefully and provide feedback to students, the relationship is strengthened. Conversely, if students have the impression that the assessment is sloppy, not matched with course objectives, designed to trick students (like some true/false questions we have all answered!), and provide little feedback, the relationship is weakened. How quickly do you return papers or tests to students? What type of comments do you write on papers or projects? Assessment affects the way students perceive the teacher and gives them an indication of how much the teacher cares about them and what they learn.

Positive Consequences on Teachers

Like students, teachers are affected by the nature of the assessments they give their students. Just as students learn depending on the assessment, teachers tend to teach to the test. Thus, if the assessment calls for memorization of facts, the teacher tends to teach lots of facts; if the assessment requires reasoning, then the teacher structures exercises and experiences that get students to think. The question, then, is how well your assessments promote and encourage the teaching you want and what you want your students to learn.

There is often a trade-off between instructional time and the time needed for assessment. If your assessments require considerable time for preparation, administration, and scoring, then there is less time for instruction.

A goal of high-quality assessments is that they will lead to better information and decision making about students. Will the assessment help you make more valid judgments, or will it tend to make judgments about students more difficult? As a result of assessment, are you likely to label students inappropriately?

Finally, assessments may influence how you are perceived by others. Are you comfortable with school administrators and parents reviewing and critiquing your assessments? What about the views of other teachers? How do your assessments fit with what you want to be as a professional?

PRACTICALITY AND EFFICIENCY

High-quality assessments are practical and efficient. It is important to balance these aspects of assessment with previously mentioned criteria. As I have already pointed out, time is a limited commodity for teachers. It may be best, on the one hand, to use extensive performance-based assessments; but if these assessments take away too much from instruction or energy needed for other professional activities, it may be better to think about less time-consuming assessments. Essentially, ask yourself this question: Is the information obtained worth the resources and time required to obtain it? Other factors to consider include your familiarity with the method of assessment, the time required of students to complete the assessments, the complexity of administering the assessment, the ease of scoring, the ease of interpretation, and cost. We'll consider each briefly.

Teacher Familiarity with the Method

Teachers need to know about the assessment methods they select. This includes knowledge of the strengths and limitations of the method, how to administer the assessment, how to score and properly interpret student responses, and the appropriateness of the method for given learning targets. Teachers who use assessment methods that they are not familiar with risk time and resources for questionable results.

Time Required

Other things being equal, it is desirable to use the shortest assessment possible that provides credible results. In other words, gather only as much information as you need for the decision or other use of the results. The time required should include how long it takes to construct the assessment, how much time is needed for students to provide answers, and how long it takes to score the results. The time needed for each of these aspects of assessment is different for each method of assessment. Multiple-choice tests take a long time to prepare but a relatively short time for students to complete and for teachers to score. Thus, if you plan to use this format over and over for different groups of students, it is efficient to put in considerable time preparing the assessment as long as you can use many of the same test items each semester or year (keep objective tests secure so you don't have to construct an entirely new test each time). Essay tests, on the other hand, take less time to prepare but take a long time to score. Performance-based assessments are probably most time-intensive (in preparation, student response time, and scoring). For all types of assessments, reuse questions and tasks whenever possible.

Another consideration in deciding about time for assessment is reliability. The reliability of a test or other assessment is directly related to its length—the longer the test the greater the reliability. In general, assessments that take thirty or forty minutes provide reliable results for a single score on a short unit. If separate scores are needed for subskills, more time may be needed. A general rule of thumb is that six to ten objective items are needed to provide a reliable assessment of a concept or specific skill.

Complexity of Administration

Practical and efficient assessments are easy to administer. This means that the directions and procedures for administration are clear and that little time and effort is needed. Assessments that require long, complicated directions and setup, like some performance-based assessments, are less efficient and may, due to student misunderstanding, have adverse effects on reliability and validity.

Ease of Scoring

It is obvious that some methods of assessment, such as objective tests, are much easier to score than other methods, such as essays, papers, and oral presentations. Like other traits, scoring needs to match your method and purpose. In general, use the easiest method of scoring appropriate to the method and purpose of the assessment. Objective tests are easiest to score and contribute less scoring error to reliability. Scoring performance-based assessments, essays, papers, and the like are more difficult because more time is needed to ensure reliability. For these assessments it is more practical to use rating scales and checklists rather than writing extended individualized evaluations.

Ease of Interpretation

Objective tests that report a single score are usually easiest to interpret, and individualized written comments are more difficult to interpret. Many subjectively evaluated products are given a score or grade to enhance ease of interpretation. It is necessary to provide sufficient information so that whatever interpretation is made is accurate. Often grades or scores are applied too quickly without enough thought and detailed feedback to students. This can be partially remedied by sharing a key with students and others that provides meaning to different scores or grades. Interpretation is easier if you are able to plan, prior to the assessment, how to use the results.

Cost

Because most classroom assessments are inexpensive, cost is relatively unimportant. It would certainly be unwise to use a more unreliable procedure assessment just because it costs less. Some performance-based assessments are exceptions, because the cost of materials can be an important factor. Like other practical aspects, it is best to use the most economical assessment, other things being equal. But economy should be thought of in the long run, and unreliable, less expensive tests may eventually cost more in further assessment.

SUMMARY

High-quality classroom assessments provide reliable, valid, and useful measures of student performance. Quality is enhanced when the assessments meet several important criteria, summarized as follows:

- One criterion is to match the method of assessment to learning targets. Knowledge targets are matched best with objective tests, reasoning targets with essays, and affective targets with observation and student self-reports. Performance-based assessments are best for measuring skills and products.
- Validity is the degree to which a score-based inference is appropriate, reasonable, and useful. Inferences are valid or invalid—not tests.
- Different types of evidence are used to establish the validity of classroom tests, the most important of which is content-related evidence.
- Whether it is face validity, a test blueprint, or instructional validity, the teacher's professional judgment is needed to ensure that there is adequate content-related evidence.
- Construct-related evidence is provided by theoretical, logical, and statistical analyses.
- Reliability is used to estimate the error in testing. It measures the degree of consistency when several items measure the same thing and stability when the same measures are given across time.
- Different sources of error should be taken into consideration when interpreting test results.
- Assessment is fair if it is unbiased and provides students with a reasonable opportunity to demonstrate what they have learned.
- Fairness is enhanced by student knowledge of learning targets prior to instruction, the opportunity to learn, the attainment of prerequisite knowledge and skills, unbiased assessment tasks and procedures, and by teachers who avoid stereotypes.
- Positive consequences on both teachers and students enhance the overall quality of assessment, particularly the effect of the assessments on student motivation and study habits. Assessments need to take into consideration the teacher's familiarity with the method, the time required, the complexity of administration, the ease of scoring and interpretation, and cost in order to determine the assessment's practicality and efficiency.

SELF-INSTRUCTIONAL REVIEW EXERCISES

1. Should teachers be concerned about relatively technical features of assessments such as validity and reliability? Why or why not?

2. Match the description with the type of assessment.

___ **(1)** Based on verbal instructions	**a.** Objective
___ **(2)** Made up of questionnaires and surveys	**b.** Essay
___ **(3)** Selection or supply type	**c.** Performance-based
___ **(4)** Constructs unique response to demonstrate skill	**d.** Oral question
___ **(5)** Constructed response either restricted or extended	**e.** Observation
___ **(6)** Used constantly by teachers informally	**f.** Self-report

3. For each of the following situations or questions, indicate which assessment method provides the best match (objective, O, essay, E, performance-based, P, oral question, OR, observation, OB, and self-report, SR).

   a. Mrs. Keen needs to check students to see if they are able to draw graphs correctly like the example just demonstrated in class.
   b. Mr. Garcia wants to see if his students are comprehending the story before moving to the next set of instructional activities.
   c. Ms. Powell wants to find out how many spelling words her students know.
   d. Ms. Tanner wants to see how well her students can compare and contrast the Vietnam War with World War II.
   e. Mr. Johnson's objective is to enhance his students' self-efficacy and attitudes toward school.
   f. Mr. Greene wants to know if his sailing clinic students can identify different parts of a sailboat.

4. Indicate if each of the following statements is correct or incorrect. Explain why.

   a. Validity is impossible without strong reliability.
   b. A test can be reliable and without validity.
   c. A valid test is reliable.

5. Mr. Nelson asks the other math teachers in his high school to review his midterm to see if the test items represent his learning targets. Which type of evidence for validity is being used?

   a. Content-related
   b. Criterion-related
   c. Instructional
   d. Construct-related

6. The students in the following lists are rank ordered, based on their performance on two tests of the same content (highest score at the top, next highest score second, etc.) Do the results suggest a reliable assessment? Why or why not?

Test A	*Test B*
Germaine	Ryann
Cynthia	Robert
Ryann	Steve
Steve	Germaine
Robert	Cynthia

7. Which aspect of fairness is illustrated in each of the following assessment situations?

   a. Students complained because they were not told what to study for the test.
   b. Students studied the wrong way for the test (e.g., they memorized content).
   c. The teacher was unable to cover the last unit that was on the test.
   d. The story students read, the one they would be tested on, was about life in the northeast during winter. Students who had been to that part of the country in winter showed better comprehension scores that students who had rarely even seen snow.

8. Is the following test item biased? Why or why not?

> Ramon has decided to develop a family budget. He has $2,000 to work with and decides to put $1,000 into the mortgage, $300 into food, $200 into transportation, $300 into entertainment, $150 into utilities, and $50 into savings. What percent of Ramon's budget is being spent in each of the categories?

9. Why is it important for teachers to consider practicality and efficiency in selecting their assessments, as well as more technical aspects like validity and reliability?

ANSWERS TO SELF-INSTRUCTIONAL REVIEW EXERCISES

1. Yes, but not in the way psychometricians do with published, standardized tests. Validity and reliability are essential to fairness, proper interpretation of assessments, and to teacher decision making. Both validity and reliability are best estimated by teacher judgment and logical analysis, not statistically unless the statistics are easily provided.

2. (1) d, (2) f, (3) a, (4) c, (5) b, (6) e.

3. a. OB, b. OR, c. O, d. E, e. SR, f. O.

4. a. Yes, if the score is not consistent or stable the inference will likewise not be consistent or stable, hence inaccurate and invalid. b. Yes, a measure of the circumference of your big toe is very reliable but not very valid for measuring your ability to read. c. No, tests are not valid or invalid, only inferences are.

5. a.

6. Not very reliable. Germaine scored highest on Test A but near the bottom on Test B; Robert scored at the bottom on Test A but near the top on Test B. A reliable assessment would result in nearly the same rank ordering for both tests.

7. a. Student knowledge of assessment. b. Student knowledge of assessment. c. Opportunity to learn. d. Biased content.

8. Probably not. For bias to exist, it needs to be fairly obvious. In this example, a minority group name is used, but it would be unlikely to elicit negative affect from Hispanic members of the class. There is no content that is clearly biased.

9. Because the time you have is limited, and priorities need to be made so that you balance instruction with assessment.

SUGGESTIONS FOR ACTION RESEARCH

1. Interview a teacher and ask about the types of assessments he or she uses. See if there is a match between the assessment methods and targets consistent with Figure 3.2. Also ask about validity and reliability. How does the teacher define

these concepts, and how are they determined informally, if at all, by the teacher? How does the teacher account for error in testing? Finally, ask about additional criteria for making assessments fair and unbiased. Does the teacher make it clear to students what they will be tested on? Do all students have the same opportunity to do well?

2. Prepare a table of specifications for a test of this chapter. Include all the major target areas. Compare your table with those of other students to see how similar you are with respect to what you believe is most important to assess. Also include examples of test items.

3. Ask a group of high, middle, or elementary students, depending on your interest in teaching, about what they see as fair, high-quality assessment. Ask them to generate some qualities that they believe contribute to good assessments, and then ask them specifically about each of the criteria in the chapter. Also, ask them how different kinds of assessments affect them; for example, do they study differently for essay and multiple-choice tests?

4

ASSESSMENT PRIOR TO INSTRUCTION

A hallmark of an effective teacher is being able to match instructional activities with the knowledge, skills, and affect students bring to the classroom. Consequently, an important assessment process takes place prior to formal instruction. This occurs before the school year begins, continues for the first week or two of school, and occurs again whenever needed throughout the school year as new topics are introduced. You have set your general learning goals. High-quality initial

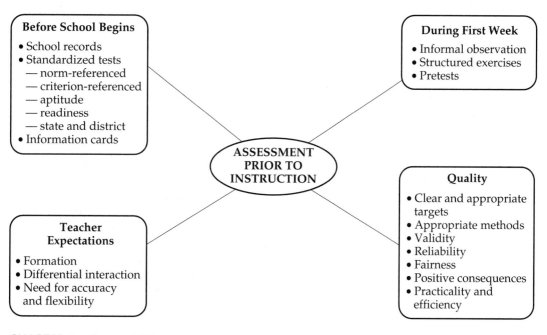

Before School Begins
- School records
- Standardized tests
  — norm-referenced
  — criterion-referenced
  — aptitude
  — readiness
  — state and district
- Information cards

During First Week
- Informal observation
- Structured exercises
- Pretests

ASSESSMENT PRIOR TO INSTRUCTION

Teacher Expectations
- Formation
- Differential interaction
- Need for accuracy and flexibility

Quality
- Clear and appropriate targets
- Appropriate methods
- Validity
- Reliability
- Fairness
- Positive consequences
- Practicality and efficiency

CHAPTER 4   Concept Map

assessments are needed before more specific learning targets, instructional activities, and subsequent assessments are finalized.

Important planning decisions are made prior to formal instruction. These decisions can be made thoughtfully and with reflection because there is less sense of immediacy. During this time, then, you will be able to gather and process assessment information that will help you make decisions concerning questions such as the following:

> Do students have the content knowledge and intellectual skills to handle the material?
> Are students likely to be interested in this content?
> How can I plan for instruction that will motivate these particular students?
> What are the implications of individual differences among the students?
> Are some students likely to be far behind others? If so, how can this be accommodated?

Answers to these questions will allow you to base planning decisions concerning grouping, activities, content, and other instructional elements on current abilities, interests, and potential for learning. It is difficult to be responsive to students' strengths, weaknesses, and needs with appropriate individualization unless you *know* what those strengths, weaknesses, and needs are. Assessments for planning purposes occur prior to the start of school, during the first few days or weeks, and throughout the year when you are beginning new instructional units or beginning a new semester. We consider each of these planning periods in this chapter.

BEFORE SCHOOL BEGINS: WHAT DO YOU KNOW ABOUT YOUR STUDENTS?

Prior to the start of the school, it is likely that you will have some knowledge of the students you will be teaching. There certainly is no lack of available information. School records, test scores, comments from other teachers, sibling performance, and other sources of information are readily available. The teachers' lounge may be the source of much discussion about students. Although there is disagreement about *how much* teachers should know about their students before they have them in class, it is probable that you will know *something*. Not only will the teacher use this information to plan instruction, it may also influence the teacher's initial expectations about what students are capable of achieving, and may, in turn, determine how the teacher interacts with the students. We will consider four major sources of information—school records, standardized test scores, state and district tests, and information cards—and we will examine how expectations may be formed from each source. These sources provide objective data that will often offset the myths that result from gossip and hearsay.

School Records

The major preclass systematic source of information about students is school records. These records, often contained in a student's cumulative file, include report cards, written comments from other teachers, information about or from parents, inventories, results of standardized testing, attendance, health records, special placements, portfolios of student work, and other information. The specific types of information contained in school records will depend on school policies and procedures.

Some teachers choose to examine information in these records before school begins with the thought that it is best to know as much as possible about the backgrounds of their students. Most teachers, on the other hand, do not want to know too much about their students from other sources. These teachers prefer to use their own interactions with the students as the primary pre-instruction source of information. They are wary of forming inappropriate expectations on the basis of other information.

This is how Betty, an elementary teacher, expresses it (Davis, 1995, p. 187):

I usually look at the report cards at the beginning of the year . . . but I guess I like to form my own judgments of kids . . . and not really go by exactly what it says in here. . . . I would rather see for myself.

As indicated in Figure 4.1, there are both advantages and disadvantages to using information in school records before meeting the students. On the positive side, reviewing student records will help you get to know and understand your students

FIGURE 4.1   Advantages and Disadvantages of Using School Records

Advantages	Disadvantages
Provides additional information to help understand students	Information can be outdated
Helps teachers know students more quickly	Student changes may be overlooked
Previous accomplishments are not forgotten	Standardized test results may be misinterpreted
Provides long-range perspectives on the students	May prevent teachers from making an objective assessment
Prevents needless repetition of some assessments	First impressions may be inaccurate
Enhances grade level and school-to-school transitions	May lead to inappropriate teacher expectations
Identifies specific areas in which teachers need to look or gather additional evidence	Teachers are unable to view students with a "clean slate"
Helps prevent inaccurate teacher expectations	Previous information may be biased, invalid, or unreliable
Allows instruction to begin more quickly	

more quickly. You can reinforce previous accomplishments and avoid repeating unnecessary material in class. School records can identify areas that you need to gather further information on to more fully understand the students. Perhaps most importantly, school records can help you establish accurate and realistic expectations.

On the negative side, information in school records can be outdated or inaccurate, and recent changes in students may be overlooked. Such records may lead the teacher to have preconceived ideas that lead to inappropriate expectations.

My view is that the advantages far outweigh the disadvantages as long as certain precautions are taken. Most of the disadvantages arise from inappropriate interpretations of the information. Because teachers need to know as much as possible about their students, information from a variety of sources provides a more complete picture than the teacher is able to form on his or her own. For example, when grades, standardized test scores, and teacher comments point to the same conclusion, the inference you make about the student is more valid. It is also wise to look for patterns of achievement that may occur over several years. Particularly in elementary school, prior knowledge of students will help provide smooth transitions from one grade to the next, especially when students move from one school to another. Here is how one elementary teacher puts it (Davis, 1995, pp. 157–158):

> *I always look at the parent's occupation to see if their parents are working outside the home . . . which gives me an idea of perhaps how hectic their schedules might be. . . . I look to see how much education the parents have . . . so that I might weigh the experiences the child will get outside of school. . . . I look at the report card. . . . I many times look for behavioral problems with that child . . . to check to see how the child did socially. . . . I try to glance at them . . . from the cumulative folder at the beginning of the school year. . . . I glance at the report card and see overall how that child did.*

An effective teacher should regard preclass information tentatively, combining it with his or her own observations and initial assessments of the students. Initial impressions should be treated as hypotheses that may be confirmed or disproved with subsequent assessments. Others' insights and previous student performance can augment your evaluations during the first few days of school so that instruction can begin as soon as possible. This is helpful as long as you are able to resist forming rigid expectations.

Most teachers want to know about special characteristics of students that will require instructional accommodations. It is important to know about physical or serious emotional difficulties. For example, if a student is on medication for hyperactivity, teachers need to know what the side effects are and what to do if the medication is not taken as prescribed. Some physical challenges of students will require certain room arrangements. You will also want to know if a student is receiving special services for a learning disability. Often it is helpful to know of any difficult home situations that could affect student performance. At the very least, elementary teachers need to know whom to contact at home and who may be picking up or dropping off students.

One component of most school records is summaries of the results of various standardized tests. It is especially important to interpret this information properly. We will look at these tests briefly as a separate source of information to be used prior to instruction.

Standardized Tests

Standardized tests have been much criticized over the past few years as having few positive implications for teaching. The argument is made that because of broad coverage and infrequent testing, heavy reliance on objective formats, encouragement to "teach to the test," cultural bias, and inappropriate ranking and comparing students, the information from these tests is not very helpful. Despite these criticisms, however, it is likely that standardized testing will continue, if for no other reason than it has traditionally been used to provide the public with information for accountability. Parents expect to see such test scores and have learned to rely on them as measures of achievement.

Although results from these tests, when used appropriately, can provide helpful information for instructional planning, the main problem is that some teachers who do not know the limitations of these tests tend to overuse the results, drawing invalid conclusions about the ability or prior achievement of their students. This typically occurs when results of standardized assessments are used as the sole criterion for making decisions about instruction. As we will see, results from these tests should always be used with other types of evidence, such as teacher observation and classroom assessments. Also, some teachers do not use standardized test results at all because they are unsure about how to interpret the scores.

In this chapter, we will consider standardized tests in the context of instructional planning. In Chapter 13 I will present a more complete discussion of the nature of these tests. Five different types of standardized tests may be used for classroom planning: norm-referenced achievement test batteries, criterion-referenced achievement test batteries, aptitude tests, readiness tests, and state or district achievement tests.

Norm-Referenced Standardized Achievement Test Batteries

Norm-referenced standardized achievement test batteries are the most common types of standardized tests. They are characterized by some qualities shared by other types of large-scale standardized tests, including high technical quality, precise directions for administration, uniform scoring procedures, equivalent or comparable forms, and test manuals for interpretation of the scores. When standardized tests are *norm-referenced* it means that national samples of students have been used as the *norming* group for interpreting relative standing. Because these tests are designed to be used in different schools throughout the country, they tend to provide broad coverage of each content area to maximize potential usefulness in as many schools as possible. Thus, close inspection of the objectives and types of test items is needed to determine how well the test matches the emphasis in the local curriculum.

A test *battery* means that several individual tests are normed on the same national sample. This allows us to compare the scores of the different tests to determine students' strengths and weaknesses. Such comparisons are only possible when the tests have used the same national sample. It cannot be done with different standardized tests that have different norming groups.

The results of test batteries are reported by objective or skill area. Some tests, such as the *Metropolitan Achievement Tests*, the *Stanford Achievement Tests*, and the *California Achievement Tests* have *diagnostic* batteries. These batteries have more items in each area than the survey forms of the tests, which allows for greater confidence when comparing achievement levels. Each battery is identified with a descriptive title, such as spelling, punctuation, letter recognition, fraction computations, graphs, and so on, but the best way to be sure about the match between what the battery says it is testing and your instructional planning is to examine the objectives and the type of test items that are used (you won't be able to review items from the actual tests because they are secured). With knowledge of the objectives and the nature of the items, particularly difficulty level, your interpretations of the scores are more relevant.

Figure 4.2 shows the areas that are covered by the Iowa Test of Basic Skills. Note in this example that the skills reported are fairly specific.

Two types of scores are reported for each student. One type of score indicates how the student's performance compares to that of the norming group. The scores that indicate this relative standing are typically percentile rank, grade equivalent, or a type of standard score.

The *percentile rank*, or *percentile score*, indicates the percentage of the *norm group* that is at or below the same raw score. In other words, the percentile score tells us the percentage of the norm group that the student outscored. The percentile score is based on the number of items answered correctly, but it does not indicate the *percentage* of items answered correctly. Thus, a student scoring at the 70th percentile did better on the test than 70 percent of the norming group (70 percent of the norming group scored below this student; 30 percent above).

Because the percentile rank is calculated by comparison to the norming group, the nature and characteristics of this group determine the score. Thus, if the norming group is representative of the entire nation, a percentile score using this group will not be the same as scores determined by local norms. If the local community and school are stronger academically than the rest of the nation, the local norm percentile rank scores will be lower, even though the student answered the same number of items correctly. All of this shows how an accurate interpretation of percentiles on standardized tests depends on the norm group, and the norm group for many tests can be national, local, regional, suburban, or urban. If the norm group is local, it is important to remember that, by definition, half of the students will be above the 50th percentile and half will be below the 50th percentile.

FIGURE 4.2   Example of Iowa Test of Basic Skills: Battery Skills Analysis Report

Iowa Tests of Basic Skills

Service 1: Student Criterion-Referenced Skills Analysis

Student:	**Long, Michael**	Building:	Linden	Sex:	M
I.D. No.:		Bldg. Code:	303	Grade:	1
Class/Group:	Ms Olson	System:	Dalen Community	Lvl/Form:	7/K
Norms:	Spring 1992	Birth Date:	05/86	Test Date:	03/93
Order No.:	000-A33-73804-00-001	Age:	06-10	Page:	302

	Reading			Language			Mathematics			Core	Social		SRCS		Word	Math
	Vocab-ulary	Compre-hension	Total	Listening	Language	Total	Concepts	Problems	Total	Total	Studies	Science	of info	Composite	AN	Compu-tation
Standard Score	153	148	150	154	159	156	176	156	166	157	150	159	162	157	135	161
Grade Equivalent	1.9	1.7	1.8	2.0	2.3	2.1	3.3	2.3	2.7	2.3	1.8	2.3	2.5	2.2	1.1	2.5
Nat'l %ile Rank	62	52	58	69	76	72	98	70	91	74	54	75	85	74	22	91
Nat'l Stanine	6	5	5	6	6	6	9	6	8	6	5	6	7	6	3	8

Skills	(Class N)	Number of Items	Number Attempted	Number Correct this Student	Percent Correct this Student	Class Average Percent Correct	National Average Percent Correct
Word Analysis	(21)	30	30	16	53	78	70
Initial Sounds		5	5	2	40	77	69
Rhyming Sounds: Words		5	5	3	60	90	69
Letter Substitutions		6	6	4	67	89	85
Word Building		7	7	5	71	85	75
–Vowel Sounds		7	7	2	29	55	56
Comprehension	(21)	40	40	21	53	65	60
+Cue: Word Identification		7	7	7	100	88	75
Factual Meaning		15	15	7	47	62	60
Inferential Meaning		16	16	5	31	58	54
+Evaluative Meaning		2	2	2	100	69	53
Listening	(21)	31	31	22	71	75	64
–Literal Meaning		3	3	0	0	38	44
Inferential Meaning		6	6	3	50	68	61
Concept Development		5	5	4	80	73	59
Predicting Outcomes		5	5	5	100	87	72
Following Directions		4	4	3	75	90	63
Sequential Relationships		4	4	3	75	76	71
Visual Relationships		4	4	4	100	86	73
Language	(21)	42	42	30	71	83	61
Developmental Language		5	5	4	80	88	59
Shared Linguistic Class		5	5	3	60	82	60
- Spelling in Context		11	11	5	45	82	67
+Capitalization		5	5	5	100	91	56
Punctuation: Context		5	5	3	60	76	59
Usage and Expression		11	11	10	91	82	61
Math Concepts	(21)	29	29	27	93	78	70
Number Systems		9	9	8	89	76	65
Whole Numbers		3	3	3	100	84	82
Geometry		4	4	4	100	82	80

(continued)

FIGURE 4.2 (*Continued*)

Skills	(Class N)	Number of Items	Number Attempted	Number Correct this Student	Percent Correct this Student	Class Average Percent Correct	National Average Percent Correct
Measurement		4	4	4	100	88	82
Fractions and Money		4	4	3	75	79	57
Number Sentences		4	4	4	100	75	67
Estimation: Standard Rounding		1	1	1	100	29	47
Problem Solving	(21)	27	27	18	67	61	57
Problem Solving		16	16	11	69	63	59
Single-Step: +/−		6	6	5	83	62	66
Single-Step: ×/÷		3	3	0	0	57	51
Multiple-Step		2	2	2	100	50	55
Problem-Solving Strategies		5	5	4	80	73	58
Data Interpretation		11	11	7	64	58	54
Read Amounts		3	3	2	67	76	74
Compare Quantities		6	6	3	50	46	46
Interpret Relationships		2	2	2	100	67	50
Social Studies	(21)	31	31	22	71	78	69
History		4	4	3	75	74	61
Geography		6	6	5	83	75	69
−Economics		9	9	4	44	78	68
Political Science		5	5	3	60	81	76
Sociology & Anthropology		7	7	7	100	81	71
Science	(21)	31	31	23	74	77	67
Nature of Science		9	9	6	67	78	70
Life Science		10	10	9	90	83	60
Earth and Space		2	2	1	50	43	37
Physical Sciences		6	6	3	50	66	66
Health and Safety		4	4	4	100	96	89
Sources of Information	(21)	28	28	23	82	77	59
Map Reading		11	11	9	82	78	54
Locate & Describe		5	5	4	80	75	54
Determine Direction		2	2	1	50	76	53
Determine Distance		2	2	2	100	88	60
Living Conditions		2	2	2	100	76	50
Reference Materials		17	17	14	82	77	62
Alphabetizing		5	5	5	100	86	68
Table of Contents		6	6	4	67	60	50
Dictionary		6	6	5	83	87	68
Math Computation	(21)	27	27	25	93	86	71
Add Whole Numbers		14	14	12	86	83	73
Subtract Whole Numbers		13	13	13	100	89	68
Thinking Skills	(21)						
Focus/Information-Gathering		18	18	13	72	73	65
Remembering		34	34	24	71	80	70
Organizing		64	64	49	77	77	65
Analyzing		78	78	58	74	78	62
Generating		49	49	31	63	69	59
Integrate/Evaluate		16	16	11	69	60	58

Source: Reprinted with the permission of The Riverside Publishing Company. From the Iowa Tests of Basic Skills, copyright © 1993 by the University of Iowa. All rights reserved.

Percentile scores are very useful in indicating relative strengths and weaknesses. If a student scores consistently higher in mathematics than in language arts, then it can be concluded that the student is stronger in mathematics than language arts (at least as defined by the tests). However, this relative strength does not indicate, in a more diagnostic way, specific skills that should be addressed or remediated. This interpretation is dependent on the *number* of *relevant* items answered correctly. This is determined by the percentage correct and an inspection of the nature of the objectives measured by the test items.

A grade equivalent score is commonly reported and commonly misinterpreted. There is a practical quality to expressing performance in relation to grade level, but this is easily misleading. *Grade equivalent* (GE) scores are expressed in terms of a year and month in school, assuming a ten-month school year. Thus, a 5.2 GE refers to fifth grade, second month (some tests will delete the decimal and report the score as 52). This means that the student's raw score on the test is the same as the median score that would be obtained by the norming group of students who are in the fifth grade, second month. As with other norm-referenced measures, then, GEs indicate a student's standing in relation to the norming group. Consider Jack, a third grader who has obtained a GE of 5.7 on his mathematics achievement test. Does this mean that Jack is achieving above grade level? Does it suggest that Jack could do as well as most other fifth graders? Should he be promoted to the fifth grade? The answer to each of these questions is no. What we *can* say is that Jack has achieved about the same as students in the norming group who are in the seventh month of the fifth grade, if such students actually took the test. Compared to the other third graders in the norming group, Jack is above average, but this does not tell us much about how he could do with fifth-grade material or whether he should be in a different grade. If Jack had taken a test designed for the fifth grade, he may not have achieved a score as high as 5.7. Grade-equivalent scores are useful for measuring growth or progress, and, like standard scores, they can be averaged for making group comparisons.

Standard scores are transformed or derived from raw scores for convenience, comparability, and ease of interpretation. These scores are typically based on the normal curve, and simply provide different ways of expressing the results. For example, the results of aptitude tests and the SAT are reported as standard scores, not as the number of items answered correctly. An increasingly popular type of standard score for standardized tests is the stanine. A *stanine* indicates about where a score lies in relation to the normal curve of the norming group. Stanines are reported as single-digit scores from 1 to 9. A stanine of 5 indicates that the score is in the middle of the distribution; stanines 1, 2, and 3 are considered below average; 7, 8, and 9 are above average; and stanines of 4, 5, and 6 are about average. Think of each stanine as representing a part of the normal curve, as illustrated in Figure 4.3. Although there is a precise, statistically determined procedure for determining stanines, it is practical to use the range from 1 to 9 as a simple, easily understood way to indicate relative standing. A disadvantage of the stanine is that even though you know the area of the normal curve the score lies in, you don't know what part of this area the score is in. In this sense, stanines are less precise than percentile rank.

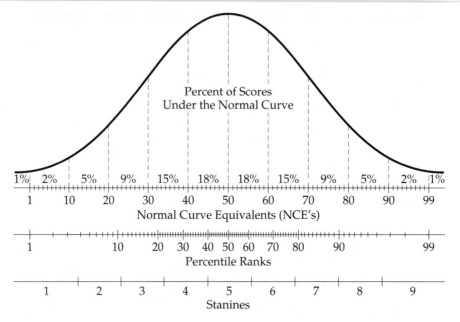

FIGURE 4.3   Normal Curve Percentile Ranks and Stanines

Source: "More Mileage: Interpretation of Student Test Scores." Reprinted with permission of The River-side Publishing Company. From the Iowa Tests of Basic Skills, copyright © 1993 by the University of Iowa. All rights reserved.

For example, percentile scores of 42 and 58 have the same stanine score of 5. How-ever, when stanine scores differ by more than one, it is probable that there is a meaningful difference between achievement in those areas. That is, if the reading stanine score is 5 and the mathematics stanine 7, it is likely that the student is demonstrating stronger achievement in mathematics. Also, remember that the sta-nine is calculated on the basis of the norming group.

A second type of score that is commonly reported on achievement test batter-ies is the raw number or percentage of items answered correctly. This is illustrated in Figure 4.2 on pages 81–82. These raw scores, by themselves, are not very mean-ingful. As previously indicated, it is necessary to review the objectives to judge the level of performance that is demonstrated. Also note that in some cases there are only a few items in each area. Thus, carelessness or a lucky guess is relatively more important in determining the final score for that skill or content area.

The specific type of report of standardized test scores for individual students varies from district to district. The more general format simply lists the scores in the form of a profile. The profile typically contains the names of the subtests and two or three types of norm-referenced scores. The profile illustrated in Figure 4.4 has additional information on skills that are assessed in different subtests. In Fig-ure 4.5 on page 87, the subtest scores are graphed without the skills.

FIGURE 4.4   Example of Iowa Test of Basic Skills: Individual Profile

Iowa Tests of Basic Skills

Service 12a: Individual Performance Profile

Student:	**Maxit, Ryan**
I.D. No.:	
Class/Group:	Lambert
System:	Port Charles
Order No.:	901-A4000052-00-002

Building:	Washington
Bldg Code:	99C001101
Grade:	2
Level:	8

Form:	K
Test Date:	4/94
Norms:	Spring 1992
Page:	561

SS=Standard Score
GE=Grade Equivalent

NCE=Normal Curve Equivalent
NPR=Nat'l %ile Rank (■■)

N Att=Number Attempted
%C=Percent Correct

					National Percentile Ranks											
	Scores				**Low**			**Average**					**High**		
Tests	**SS**	**GE**	**NCE**	**NPR**	**1**	**10**	**25**	**40**	**50**	**60**	**75**	**90**	**99**
Vocabulary	177	3.3	60	68									
Reading Comprehension	168	2.8	50	50									
Reading Total	172	3.0	54	58									
Listening	162	2.5	42	36									
Language	164	2.6	45	41									
Language Total	163	2.5	43	37									
Math Concepts	175	3.3	59	66									
Math Problems	178	3.4	61	69									
Math Total*	174	3.2	58	65									
Core Total*	170	2.9	52	54									
Social Studies	157	2.2	37	27									
Science	196	4.5	75	88									
Sources of Information	166	2.7	48	46									
Composite*	171	2.9	53	56									
Word Analysis	172	3.1	53	56									
Math Computation	169	2.9	52	53									

*Includes Mathematics Computation

Total Items	N Att.	%C Student	%C Nation	Skills		Low	Avg	High
31	31	65	54	*Vocabulary*	Vocabulary			
5	5	60	64	*Word Analysis*	Initial Sounds: Words			
5	5	100	81		Letter Substitutions			
5	5	80	73		Word Building: Vowels			
11	9	64	72		Vowel Sounds			
3	3	67	60		Silent Letters			
3	3	100	58		Affixes			
24	24	75	68	*Comprehension*	Factual Meaning			
16	15	50	61		Inferential Meaning			
3	3	100	61		Evaluative Meaning			
3	3	33	71	*Listening*	Literal Meaning			
6	6	67	55		Inferential Meaning			
6	6	50	59		Concept Development			
4	4	50	72		Predicting Outcomes			

(continued)

FIGURE 4.4 *(Continued)*

Total Items	N Att.	%C Student	%C Nation	Skills		Low	Avg	High
4	4	50	60		Following Directions			
4	4	75	63		Sequential Relationships			
4	4	75	71		Visual Relationships			
5	5	40	65	*Language*	Developmental Lang			
5	5	60	68		Shrd Characters Class			
11	11	91	67		Spelling in Context			
11	11	73	71		Capitalization			
5	5	40	64		Punctuation: Context			
17	17	53	64		Usage and Expression			
4	4	100	71	*Math Concepts*	Number Systems			
3	3	67	75		Whole Numbers			
5	5	80	69		Geometry			
6	6	67	69		Measurement			
4	4	50	61		Fractions and Money			
6	6	67	56		Number Sentences			
3	3	67	40		Estimation: Stndrd Rnd			
22	22	64	55	*Math Problem Solving*	Problem Solving			
5	5	60	72		Single-Step: + & −			
4	4	50	35		Single-Step: × * ÷			
6	6	67	50		Multiple-Step			
7	7	71	57		Prob-Solv Strategy			
8	8	88	71		Data Interpretation			
2	2	100	60		** Read Amounts			
4	4	75	82		Compare Quantities			
2	2	100	59		** Interpret Relationship			
4	4	50	61	*Social Studies*	History			
6	5	50	67		Geography			
8	8	50	73		Economics			
6	6	67	70		Political Science			
7	7	86	71		Sociology & Anthro			
9	8	89	66	*Science*	Nature of Science			
6	6	83	79		Life Science			
5	5	80	74		Earth and Space			
8	8	75	63		Physical Sciences			
3	3	100	81		Health and Safety			
17	17	53	57	*Sources of Info*	Map Reading			
6	6	50	64		Locate & Describe			
2	2	0	49		** Determine Direction			
5	5	60	49		Determine Distance			
4	4	75	63		Living Conditions			
17	17	76	73		Reference Materials			
5	5	60	72		Alphabetizing			
6	6	67	67		Table of Contents			
6	6	100	80		Dictionary			
17	17	82	69	*Math Computation*	Add Whole Numbers			
13	13	54	67		Subtract Whole Nos			
19	19	79	70	*Thinking Skills*	Focus/Info-Gathering			
40	38	73	68		Remembering			
59	59	61	63		Organizing			
86	86	67	66		Analyzing			
63	62	67	66		Generating			
18	18	61	57		Integrate/Evaluate			

**1 and 2 item skills are not graphed

FIGURE 4.5   Example of Iowa Test of Basic Skills: Profile Narrative Report

Iowa Tests of Basic Skills

Service 2a: Profile Narrative Report—Parent Copy

Student:	**Pickering, Amanda**	Building:	Weber	Grade:	4
I.D. No.:		Bldg. Code:	304	Lvl/Form:	10/K
Class/Group:	Ness	System:	Dalen Community	Test Date:	03/93
Norms:	Spring 1992	Birth Date:	01/83	Page:	311
Order No.:	000-A33-76044-00-001	Sex:	F		

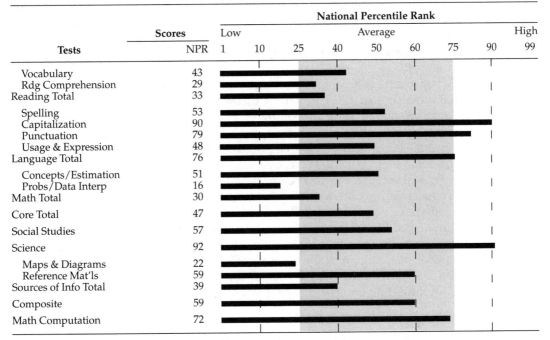

NPR: Nat'l %ile Rank

Amanda was given the Iowa Tests of Basic Skills in March, 1993. She is in fourth grade at Weber in Dalen Community.

Amanda's Composite score is the best indicator of her overall achievement on the tests. Amanda's Composite national percentile rank of 59 means that she scored higher than 59 percent of fourth-grade students nationally. Her overall achievement appears to be about average for fourth grade.

A student's ability to read is related to success in many areas of schoolwork. Amanda's Reading Comprehension score is somewhat below average when compared with other students in fourth grade nationally.

Basic skills can be compared with each other to determine a student's strengths and weaknesses. The following are areas of relative strength for Amanda: Capitalization, Punctuation, and Science. Some of these strengths might be used to help improve other areas.

The following areas are relative weaknesses which appear to need the most work: Reading, Math Problems and Data Interpretation, and Maps and Diagrams.

Source: Reprinted with the permission of The Riverside Publishing Company. From the Iowa Tests of Basic Skills, copyright © 1993 by the University of Iowa. All rights reserved.

Many publishers of standardized tests are able to customize reports for individual states or districts. These reports indicate specific skills and may include standards that are set by the state or district. The skills are reported to match local educational learning goals, which allows you to more easily interpret student strengths and weaknesses for instructional planning. Figure 4.6 illustrates this type of report.

Criterion-Referenced Standardized Achievement Tests

In recent years, testing companies have made criterion-referenced standardized tests available. The procedures for developing these tests are very similar to what teachers do for classroom tests. General goals and more specific learning targets or objectives are identified, and then items are constructed to measure these targets or objectives. The items are reviewed and field-tested to ensure high technical quality. The prerequisite skills for each grade or topic are often identified. This is especially helpful information for determining whether students have the needed skills to move ahead.

Many testing companies offer tailor-made criterion-referenced tests for individual states or districts. The state or district selects the objectives it wants measured from a large bank of objectives provided by the publisher. Once the objectives are identified, appropriate items are pulled from a large bank of items. For example, the *Multiscore System*, published by The Riverside Publishing Company, offers more than 1,500 objectives and 5,500 test items. These tests are especially helpful because they can be matched so well with local learning goals.

The scores from criterion-referenced tests will be reported as the percentage of items answered correctly, or mastery/nonmastery. It is important to know who has set the standard for mastery/nonmastery, particularly for tests that are not customized for the district. Other guidelines for interpreting these test scores for instructional planning are summarized in Figure 4.7 on page 90. The suggestions emphasize that you should use your own professional judgment about the adequacy of the definition of skill or area assessed and the items that measure it.

Aptitude Tests

Standardized aptitude tests measure a student's cognitive ability, potential, or capacity to learn. This ability is determined by both in-school and out-of-school experiences. Thus, aptitude tests are less specifically tied to what is taught in school than are achievement tests. Actually aptitude tests differ in the degree to which school learning is assessed. Some aptitude tests, like the *Stanford-Binet Intelligence Scale* and the *Wechsler Intelligence Scales*, are broad measures of ability, while others are more specific to course content.

Aptitude tests are developed to enable you to predict future achievement. They provide a measure of current developed ability, not innate capacity that cannot change. This level of ability is helpful in planning instruction in two ways: knowing the general capabilities students bring to the class in different areas and knowing the discrepancies between aptitude and achievement.

FIGURE 4.6   Example of State Testing: Customized Skills Report

Riversize 2000 Customized Skills Report

Service 29b: Class Diagnostic Report—Reference Number: 010

Class/Group:		Building:		Grade:	5
System:	River Falls ISD	Bldg. Code:		Level:	11
Norms:	Spring 1992	Test Date:	05/22/92	Page:	10
Order No.:	000-005926-001==	Form:	K		

		Count for Averages	# of Items Correct	Average # of Items Correct	System Defined Cut Score	# At or Above Cut Score	% At or Above Cut Score
LANGUAGE ARTS							
Goal One	A Recognize Recall Summarize	254	17.7/	29	15	186	73%
	B Question Reading Rationale	254	7.2/	11	6	187	74%
	C Read for Various Purposes	254	33.5/	50	25	209	82%
	D Sensitive to Difficulties	254	36.4/	56	28	203	80%
	E Use Appropriate Inferences	254	15.1/	21	11	215	85%
	F Integration of Information	254	29.5/	41	21	217	85%
	G Justify & Explain Answers	254	36.4/	56	28	203	80%
Goal Two	A Clear Logical Organization	254	12.2/	18	9	220	87%
	B Use Stand. Written English	254	25.8/	41	21	184	72%
	C Revise, Edit and Proofread	254	25.8/	41	21	184	72%
Goal Three	A Diff of Poetry Drama Fictn	254	3.5/	5	3	193	76%
	B Diff Types of Factual Lit	254	5.5/	7	4	224	88%
	C Selected Lit History Works	254	5.9/	11	6	140	55%
	D Selected Lit Philos Works	254	6.6/	8	4	239	94%
	E Elements of Fict, Non-Fict	254	5.4	8	4	217	85%
	F Literary Themes	254	4.0	6	3	213	84%
	G Symbol, Allegory and Myth	254	1.7	3	2	154	61%
Goal Four	A Diversity of Language Conv.	254	5.7	7	4	233	92%
	B Language Origin and Change	254	50.8	82	41	189	74%
	C English Grammar	254	28.0	40	20	232	91%
MATHEMATICS							
Goal One	A Read, Write & Name Numbers	257	5.0/	8	4	188	73%
	B Perform Number Operations	257	48.8/	74	37	214	83%
	C Translate Word Problems	257	18.6/	31	16	172	67%
	D Ordering Numbers	257	1.8/	3	2	161	63%
	E Appl of Number Properties	257	4.6/	6	3	234	91%
	F Use Factors and Multiples	257	2.5/	3	2	227	88%
	G Appl of Computatn, Problem	257	18.6/	31	16	172	67%
Goal Two	A Interpretation of Ratios	257	4.0/	6	3	205	80%
	B Appl of Ratio & Proportion	257	1.2/	2	1	205	80%
	C Interpretation of Percents	257	1.4/	3	2	116	45%
	D Application of Percents	257	1.4/	3	2	116	45%
Goal Three	A Estimation of Measurement	257	1.2/	3	1	222	86%
	B Relating Length, Area, Vol.	257	1.0/	3	1	200	78%
	C Appl of Select Measurement	257	1.5/	3	2	116	45%
Goal Four	A Use Expressions, Equations	257	2.0	3	2	186	72%
	B Ability to Solve Equations	257	3.8	5	3	224	87%
	C Translate Verbal Descriptn	257	1.9	3	2	170	66%
	D Ability to Perform Operatn	257	1.7	3	2	135	53%

Source: Reprinted with the permission of The Riverside Company. From the Iowa Tests of Basic Skills, copyright © 1993 by the University of Iowa. All rights reserved.

FIGURE 4.7   Suggestions for Interpreting Criterion-Referenced Standardized Tests

1. Check the specificity and clarity of the definitions of the achievement domains and skills that are assessed. They should be delimited, clearly specified, and match well with your instructional plans.
2. Are there a sufficient number of items that measure each separate skill or objective? If there are fewer than six items, interpret with caution or combine with other items into larger clusters. With a small number of objective items, the influence of guessing increases, which decreases reliability.
3. How difficult are the test items? You will need to inspect sample items to gauge difficulty. Answering fewer items that are more difficult may mean the same thing as answering all easy items correctly.
4. Base your interpretation on what is measured by reviewing sample items, as well as on what the publisher says the items measure.

Source: Linn, R. L. & Gronlund, N. E., *Measurement and Assessment in Teaching,* 7th Edition, copyright © 1995, p. 442. Adapted by permission of Prentice-Hall, Upper Saddle River, New Jersey.

An understanding of the general ability levels of your students will help you design instructional experiences and group students appropriately. Suppose one class has an average aptitude score of 83 and another a score of 120. Would you use the same teaching materials and approaches in each of these classes? Similarly, would you give the same assignments to individual students who differ widely in ability? Research in aptitude-treatment interactions suggests that student achievement is maximized when the method of instruction or learning activity matches the aptitude. For example, low-ability students may need remediation, while high-ability students would benefit most from enrichment activities. For cooperative learning, it is best to form groups that have mixed levels of aptitude.

Aptitude tests are also used for determining *expected* learning by examining any discrepancy between ability and achievement. If there is a large discrepancy, and if other information is consistent, a student may be an underachiever. Many standardized test services provide a report that includes both aptitude and achievement test score results, and presents predicted sores (see Figure 4.8). This makes the determination of discrepancy easier, but what is a "large" discrepancy? A complete answer to this question goes beyond what can be presented in this chapter because it depends on some statistical procedures. One rule of thumb, however, is that when the discrepancy is greater than ten percentile points it may be significant. Another significant discrepancy is when stanines differ by two. On some standardized test score reports you will see percentile "bands." If the bands for achievement do not overlap those for aptitude, then a significant discrepancy is indicated.

Readiness Tests

Readiness tests are actually a specialized type of aptitude test. However, readiness tests, because of the high number of items from specific skill areas, can also be used diagnostically to determine the skills students need to improve if they are to be successful in school. Thus, readiness tests both predict achievement and diagnose strengths and weaknesses.

FIGURE 4.8 Example of Cognitive Abilities Test: Individual Profile Narrative

Iowa Tests of Basic Skills Cognitive Abilities Test

Individual Profile Narrative

Student:	**Olson, Terry**				
I.D. No.:		Building:	Johnson Elem	Grade:	4
Class/Group:	Canfield	Bldg. Code:		Level:	9/B
System:	River Falls	Birth Date:	07/13/82	Form:	K/5
Norms:	Spring 1992	Sex:	M	Test Date:	05/92
Order No.:	000-005926-001==	Age:	10	Page:	9

	Predicted Scores		Obtained Scores		National Percentile Rank					
					Low			Average		High
Iowa Tests of Basic Skills	GE	NPR	GE	NPR	1 10	25		50	75	90 99
Vocabulary		66		85						
Comprehension		64		88						
Reading Total		65		87						
Spelling		72		59						
Capitalization		72		75						
Punctuation		76		58						
Usage & Expression		72		58						
Language Total		73		64						
Math Concepts & Est.		87		71						
Math Problems		81		78						
Math Total		83		74						
Composite	4.8	80	4.6	74						
Math Computation		78		70						

■ Predicted   ▱ Obtained

			Age Scores		Grade Scores	National Percentile Rank					
						Low			Average		High
Cognitive Abilities Test	Number Attempted	Raw Score	SAS	NPR	NPR	1 10	25		50	75	90 99
Verbal	75	56	108	69	71						
Quantitative	60	54	126	95	95						
Nonverbal	65	51	116	84	87						
Composite	200	161	117	83	84						

GE = *Grade Equivalent*, the grade and month in that grade in which a student will usually perform on the test the same as Terry did.
NPR = *National Percentile Rank*, indicating Terry's standing with his peers across the nation. The graph shows how he did on a scale of 1 to 99 for each test.
SAS = *Standard Age Score*. 100 is an average score.

Terry's Composite score is derived from the tests listed above it and gives the general picture. Overall, Terry did very well.

A glance at the graph will tell you Terry's scores as compared to the Composite are relatively low in Spelling, and relatively high in Comprehension.

An examination of Terry's test document gives us insight into his strengths and weaknesses.
Strengths: **Comprehension**—Inferences; **Vocabulary**
Weaknesses: **Spelling**—Consonants and Vowels; **Math Concepts**—Number Systems, Equations, and Fractions

Predicted Scores. Scores from the CogAT generate predictions of how well a student will perform on the achievement test. They are graphed together for comparison. Terry performed better than expected in Vocabulary and Reading Comprehension. Terry performed less than expected in Spelling, Punctuation, Usage & Expression, Math Concepts & Estimation, and Math Computation.

Most readiness tests are used in early elementary grades and for reading. The tests are helpful in identifying particular skills and knowledge to plan instruction and in designing remedial exercises. For example, the *Boehm Test of Basic Concepts—Revised* assesses student comprehension of the basic verbal concepts that are needed for comprehension of verbal communication (e.g., concepts such as many, smallest, nearest). Reading readiness tests are helpful in identifying skills that need to be mastered, such as visual discrimination of letters, auditory discrimination, recognition of letters and numbers, and following instructions. Readiness tests should *never* be used as the sole criterion for determining whether a child has the skills and knowledge to begin kindergarten or first grade. Scores from these tests should always be used with other information to provide a more comprehensive evaluation of readiness.

State and District Achievement Tests

Many states and districts develop and use their own achievement tests. These tests are typically closely aligned with local learning goals and targets, so they can be very useful. However, the technical quality of the tests may not be high. Consequently, it is necessary to look carefully at the procedures used in the development of the tests. How were the items initially generated? Were the items matched to specific learning goals and targets? What evidence for reliability is provided? How were the items reviewed? Were the items screened for racial and sexual bias? What pilot testing was conducted? Usually, large school districts and states do a pretty good job of test development, but you still need to ask the right questions and get satisfactory answers.

Uses of Standardized, State, and District Tests

I have mentioned throughout this discussion how different types of standardized and other large-scale tests could be used for planning instruction prior to the beginning of the year and during the first week. These suggestions, and some others, are included in Figure 4.9. Remember that results from this type of testing should *never be used as the only source of information to make decisions about instruction.* Rather, it is important to use several sources of information to provide an accurate portrait of your students.

Information Cards

At the elementary level, it is common to complete some kind of information card or sheet that provides the students' new teachers with a summary of important information. These cards are especially helpful if they are targeted to placements in groups. For example, the last reading or mathematics unit completed by a student can be indicated to give the teacher a sense of where to begin instruction. It is a convenient way to communicate any special problems or to note special circumstances that may be difficult to clarify in a cumulative folder. Often these cards are for teachers' eyes only and are not part of the cumulative folder. It is not uncommon for teachers to review the cards and destroy them. Figure 4.10 illustrates what an information card might look like.

FIGURE 4.9   Suggestions for Using Standardized, State, and District Tests

1. Use results for identifying the level and range of student ability. In conjunction with other information, these tests can provide objective evidence of the students' learning ability and achievement.
2. Use differences between different subjects or skills to identify the students' relative strengths and weaknesses. Focus instruction on improving weak areas, especially if the weak areas are consistent for a group of students. Use aptitude tests for ability, norm-referenced achievement tests to identify general strengths and weaknesses, criterion-referenced tests to identify specific strengths and weaknesses, and readiness tests to identify learning errors or deficiencies.
3. Use results to provide an initial perspective of overall ability and achievement. In conjunction with other information, use the results to establish realistic expectations. Do not form fatalistic expectations from low test scores, nor unrealistically high expectations from high test scores.
4. Use test results to identify specific weaknesses in students that may be hindering progress.
5. Use results to identify discrepancies between ability and achievement. Interpret with caution; verify with other evidence.
6. Use results for modifying learning targets. Initial learning targets can be modified by test results. If students are weak in an important area, new targets can be established. Targets that students have already attained can be changed to the right level.
7. Use results, with other evidence, for initial student grouping.
8. Use results to identify areas that need further investigation. Standardized tests are like car temperature gauges—the scores can indicate that something is wrong, but further investigation is needed to confirm the nature of the problem. This may be accomplished by checking other records of a student's performance, talking with other teachers who have had the student, closely observing the student's in-class performance, and asking the student to perform specific tasks that can confirm difficulties.

Name _____	**Grouping/Placement**	Placement for Year
Grade _____ Sex _____ DOB_____	**Information Card**	19 _____ /_____
Student # _____ Tel _____		Grade _____

Reading Placement

GRP   Open Court   (Circle One)

Beginning Level: _____ Unit: _____

Grade Avg. for Year: E   S   M   N   (Circle One)
                       A   B   C   D   U

Comments: _____

_____

Math Placement

Basic Math Facts at Grade Level:
    Mastery/Non-mastery   (Circle One)

CSMP: Successful/Unsuccessful   (Circle One)

Grade Avg. for Year: E   S   M   N   (Circle One)
                       A   B   C   D   U

Comments: _____

_____

Pertinent Information:

General Behavior:	☐ Excellent	☐ Good	☐ Average	☐ Poor		
General Work Habits:	☐ Excellent	☐ Good	☐ Average	☐ Poor		
Special Services Rec'd:	☐ Reading	☐ Chapter 1	☐ LD	☐ Gifted	☐ Speech	☐ Other
Confidential Folder:	☐ Yes	☐ No				

Health Problems: _____

Retained in Grade _____ Year _____

Moved to New Classroom: _____ Grade _____ Month/Year

Comments: _____

Current Teacher _____   Form # 1085-1989

FIGURE 4.10   Example of an Information Card

AFTER THE FIRST WEEK: NOW WHAT DO YOU KNOW ABOUT YOUR STUDENTS?

Once school has started, you will make more targeted pre-instructional assessments to learn about your students. The nature of these assessments will vary considerably by grade level and general learning goals. At the elementary level, teachers are usually concerned about both academic and social dimensions, while at the secondary level, teachers tend to focus on academic preparation, ability, and student interest in the subject. Teachers tend to view this information as much more important than information gleaned from previously taken tests. The information comes mainly from two sources—informal observation and structured exercises—and is usually gathered during the first week of the year or semester.

Informal Observation

Most pre-instructional assessment consists of informal observation. During the first few days of school, teachers are constantly looking for any clues about the nature of their students. These observations are made from spontaneous student behavior. There are typically four steps involved: collecting information, interpreting the information, synthesizing the information, and naming the characteristic of the student the observation describes (Gordon, 1987).

During the first step, the teacher observes student appearance and behavior. What type of clothes does the student wear? Is the student clean? Does the student talk with other students? What nonverbal cues are present? What kind of vocabulary does the student use? How well does the student speak? How does the student's face look? Is the student courteous? Does the student volunteer to answer questions? It is not a matter of looking for certain types of appearance or behavior. Rather, the observations come from the initiatives of the students. Like a good physician, with experience, effective teachers know what to attend to.

The second step is interpreting what has been observed. At this point, teachers make judgments about what the appearance or behavior means. For example, a teacher may form the following tentative explanations:

> "Tom is always late to school and unprepared. I wonder if there is a situation at home that I need to know about?"
> "Anne is eager to answer almost every question with a smile. She is listening and motivated to learn and participate."
> "Tim doesn't participate much and rarely looks directly at me when I speak to him. This may mean he has low self-esteem."
> "Jane does not interact much with the other students. Perhaps she is not well liked by them."

In each case, an interpretation is made from the observation. It is this interpretation that provides meaning.

Naturally, different teachers can observe the same behavior and come up with different interpretations. In this sense, informal observations are *subjective*. That is, meaning is derived only by professional judgment of what is observed. Of course, it is possible for an observation to be *biased*, or heavily influenced by what the teacher wants to see or wants to believe. Your own perspectives, preferences, and attitudes will influence how you interpret your observations. Because each of us views the world differently, differences in interpretations can be expected. What is important is to understand how your background may influence your interpretations, and that it is best to obtain corroborating interpretations provided by different sources of information (e.g., another teacher or more structured assessment).

In the third step, interpretations are synthesized into meaningful traits or characterizations of the students. This involves inductive thinking whereby several separate interpretations are pulled together to form a tentative conclusion about the trait or characteristic (e.g., "Tom is motivated," "Erin is from a dysfunctional home," "Jose is way behind on social skills"). At this point it is important to be aware of the need to have a sufficient number of interpretations so that the synthesis provides an accurate description. It is also helpful to use others' interpretations to validate your own.

The fourth step is naming the trait or characteristic. This step is idiosyncratic in that your definitions of terms such as *motivated, behind, uncooperative, easily distracted, talkative, able,* and so on, are not necessarily the same as others' definitions. Thus, how you characterize a student or class has meaning according to your definition of the trait. Furthermore, the more general name of the trait is what is likely to be remembered and to influence subsequent interactions. That is, you are less likely to remember the specific behaviors and more likely to recall that the student was self-confident, lazy, shy, capable, and the like.

As shown in Figure 4.11, it is important to emphasize the cyclical nature of these informal observations. As you begin to make observations and interpretations, you will arrive at tentative syntheses. Then, you will make further observations and interpretations to confirm or change these tentative conclusions.

Structured Exercises

A good approach to evaluating current student knowledge and skills is to design informal, structured exercises that will provide you with an opportunity to observe

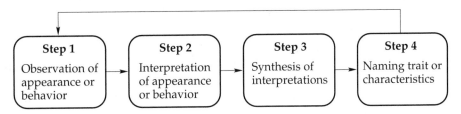

FIGURE 4.11   Steps in Informal Observation

students in the context of specific performance situations. These exercises are not like a formal pretest, but they are more structured than informal observation.

One approach is to design a class activity in which all the students participate. This could be a writing assignment, an oral presentation, or group work. For example, asking students to write about their summer vacation can help to identify language arts skills. Students can interview each other about their summer vacations and make short presentations to the class. Games can be used to observe students' math skills. Students can be asked to read aloud. A common technique is to ask students to write information about themselves on cards, such as names of family members, hobbies, and interests. Any one of these demonstrations of knowledge or skills would not be sufficient for instructional planning, but as you build a portrait of your students from many such observations, and combine this information with previous test scores, student records, and comments from other teachers, by the end of the first week of school you will have a pretty accurate idea of the strengths and weaknesses of your students.

One aspect of successful structured exercises is to keep them *nonthreatening*. This is important because you want to minimize student anxiety, which may be high anyway at the beginning of the year. Obviously, it is best not to grade the exercise. In addition, you will want to arrange the conditions to be as comfortable as possible. Reading orally to a small group or only to you is probably less threatening than reading to the entire class. If students are able to work at their own pace, without strict time constraints, they are more likely to feel less threatened. Comparisons between different students should be avoided.

Pretests

During the first few days of school, some teachers ask students to complete a formal pretest of the content that will be covered. The pretest would supposedly indicate what students know and don't know, or what they can or cannot do. However, for several reasons it is doubtful that the information from a pretest will be very helpful in planning instruction. First, at least in the fall, students have returned from vacation and have probably not thought too much about world history, algebra, or other school subjects. Their actual or true knowledge may not be reflected on a surprise test. With some review, the knowledge would be much better. Second, it is hard to motivate students to do their best on such tests. What do they have to gain by trying hard to answer the questions? This is especially true for older students. Third, to be helpful diagnostically, the pretest would need to be fairly long and detailed, which would be difficult to find time for during the first week. Finally, presenting students with a pretest may not be the best way to start a class. Asking students what they know about something they will learn may be intimidating and create anxiety about the class (on the other hand, a pretest can communicate to students that the teacher is serious about learning). For these reasons, formal pretests are not used very often. The validity of the information is questionable, and the effect on the classroom environment and teacher–student relationships may be negative. If you do use a pretest, do not grade it or average it into final grades.

If a pretest is to be used successfully, it needs to be short and targeted to specific knowledge and skills. Students need to be motivated to do their best work, and the teacher needs to make it clear to students that the purpose is to help them learn more and help the teacher plan more effective instruction. The results may suggest the need for further diagnostic assessment. Cheri Magill, a German teacher, puts it this way:

> *Preassessment was a very important part of my diagnosing the content knowledge of students taking German. When planning my first lessons for them I incorporated short diagnostic tests designed to let me know their degree of skill in manipulating specific sentence patterns, verb tenses, article forms, and declinations of nouns. This information, once analyzed, helped me identify what content to emphasize and what content I could safely ignore. Knowing that students could not, for example, correctly form the past tense of certain verbs was not enough. Further assessment was needed to determine exactly what stood in the way. Was it the meaning of the verb? Was it how to correctly form the participle? Was choosing and/or conjugating the correct helping verb the problem? Was word order an issue? Getting the data from student performance on these short diagnostic tests helped me assess their needs and better plan instruction at the appropriate level of difficulty for them.*

Notice that for Cheri, the pretests helped her assess student needs. The information was used with other assessments to plan instruction.

TEACHER EXPECTATIONS

Some teachers may not want to review student records or test scores because they want to avoid forming inappropriate expectations. This is a valid concern, but the real issue is not whether expectations will be acquired, but forming *realistic, accurate* expectations that are flexible. Teacher expectations are beliefs about what students are capable of knowing or doing, and pre-instructional assessments are important in forming these beliefs. You *will* have expectations. They can not be avoided. What you want to do is make sure they are as unbiased as possible, relevant to the subject matter to be taught.

Expectations are based on a number of different student attributes, including socioeconomic status, test scores, classroom performance, appearance, knowledge of siblings, name, gender, and race. The expectations may affect the nature of the interactions the teacher has with the students, which can, in turn, affect subsequent student performance. This cycle of influences is illustrated in Figure 4.12 on page 98.

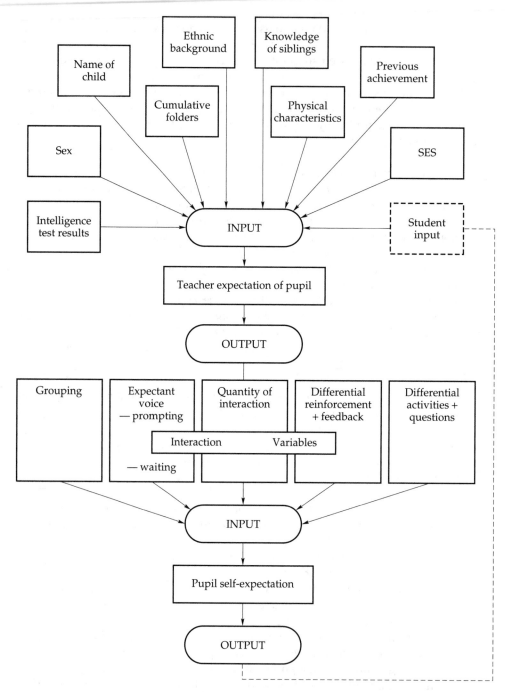

FIGURE 4.12   The Behavioral Cycle between Teacher Input and Learner Output

Source: Braun, C., "Teacher Expectation: Sociopsychological dynamics." *Review of Educational Research, 46,* 206. Copyright © 1976 by the American Educational Research Association. Reprinted by permission of the publisher.

In its worst form, teacher expectations can be self-fulfilling and detrimental. Students become what is expected of them. According to Good and Brophy (1994), the process looks like this:

1. Early in the year, teacher expectations are formed.
2. The teacher interacts differently with the students, consistent with these expectations.
3. This treatment informs students about what they may achieve or what behavior is appropriate for them.
4. If the teacher's treatment is consistent over time, and students do not resist, it will affect the self-concept and classroom conduct of the students.
5. Subsequent student behavior reinforces the teacher's initial expectations.
6. Eventually, student achievement is affected: high-expectation students will achieve at their potential, low-expectation students will achieve below their potential.

As I have previously indicated, I think that it is best for teachers to obtain as much information as possible on their students so that their expectations will be accurate. Classroom observation and classroom performance of the student are what teachers use most to form initial expectations. Standardized tests and other external sources of information are helpful because they are independent of what are sometimes a teacher's unconsciously biased perceptions. If anything, teachers tend to dismiss low test scores in their evaluations of students. This is a safe approach; if you are going to err, err toward more positive expectations. It is better, however, to have realistic expectations of students. This will allow you to target instruction more accurately, and it will help to provide appropriate evaluations of student performance. For example, is it best to give similar feedback to two students who perform the same when one student has high ability and the other low ability? Probably not. Your feedback will depend on how the performance is related to ability. If your perception of the student's ability is not accurate, your feedback will be less helpful than it could be.

HIGH QUALITY PRE-INSTRUCTIONAL ASSESSMENT

Teacher assessments of students prior to instruction form the foundation for many instructional decisions and influence the nature of subsequent interactions between the teacher and students. So it is very important to employ certain procedures and approaches that will enhance the quality of these assessments. Not surprisingly, these procedures, summarized in Figure 4.13 on page 100, can be organized around the more general points made in Chapter 3 regarding high-quality assessments.

Clear and Appropriate Learning Targets

Before you begin to examine information about your students, you need to establish clear learning targets that are not too specific. These targets should include some idea of the criteria that you will use to evaluate student learning. My suggestion is

FIGURE 4.13   Criteria for Ensuring High-Quality Pre-Instructional Assessments

Clear and Appropriate Learning Targets. Base pre-instructional assessments on initial unit
   learning targets.
Appropriateness of Assessment Methods. Match the method of assessment with the
   learning targets.
Validity. Strengthen the validity of your inferences by using multiple methods over time
   and looking for discrepancies.
Reliability. Reduce error in pre-instructional assessment by using multiple methods and
   giving students the benefit of the doubt.
Fairness. Avoid inappropriate expectations by using procedures to reduce bias.
Positive Consequences. Consider the effect of the pre-instructional assessments. Will they
   promote student learning?
Practicality and Efficiency. Use assessments that are familiar and not too time-consuming.

to begin with unit targets. Consider different types of targets as well. Once the targets are identified, you can design pre-instructional assessments to give you information that will have a direct influence on your modification of the targets. You
may find that the emphasis you had originally intended for certain targets needs to
be changed to better meet the needs of your students. For example, suppose you
have mostly reasoning and skill targets before the class begins. If it appears that
your class will contain a high percentage of low-ability students, you may need to
rethink this emphasis. It may be more appropriate to include more knowledge targets to provide students with the prerequisite skills they need.

Appropriateness of Assessment Methods

Your methods of pre-instruction assessment need to match with the type of information you need. Generally, the strengths of pre-instructional assessment methods
are similar to those in Chapter 3. For knowledge targets, it is best to examine test
scores from previous years and ask knowledge questions during the first week.
Reasoning and skill targets are assessed by aptitude test scores, informal observation, and performance on structured exercises. Product targets can be assessed by
looking at student work from the previous year (portfolios are good for this type of
assessment). Affect targets will depend on your informal observations of the students and their interactions with each other.

Validity

Pre-instruction assessments are valid if the inferences you make about your students are accurate. To enhance validity, you need to use multiple assessment methods for each learning target and look for consistency with these results. I cannot
stress enough how important it is to *never rely on a single source of information*. Be
careful not to allow inferences about some targets to influence inferences about
other targets. For example, you may infer that a particular student has weak writ-

ing skills. Before you conclude that the student is also weak in reading and has poor vocabulary, you need to gather information about each of these areas. It would be invalid to conclude that the student had poor reading skills by examining only his or her writing skills.

It will also be helpful to look for consistency across time. Once you have formulated an initial impression, examine further student behavior for evidence that would be inconsistent with this impression. Give the student opportunities to demonstrate behavior that would be inconsistent with your impression. Given such opportunities, consistent behavior would provide evidence for valid inferences.

Reliability

Remember that reliability is concerned with how much error is present in the assessment. Multiple assessments reduce the overall error, as will those that are longer. That is, standardized test scores are more reliable than your informal observations over a day or two. Keep a proper perspective about error. Realize that any single assessment may be determined more by error than anything else, and give students the benefit of pre-instructional assessments that are borderline. When in doubt, ask other teachers for their independent judgments.

Fairness

A fair pre-instructional assessment is one that provides an equal opportunity to all students. This means that your interpretation of the information is not influenced by race, gender, ethnic background, handicapping condition, or other factors unrelated to what is being assessed. It is important to remain unbiased and give every opportunity to each student.

Positive Consequences

You will want to conduct pre-instructional assessment so that the results will have positive consequences for you and your students. If the information is viewed as helpful, this attitude will facilitate positive consequences. You should feel more confident about your teaching as you plan instruction on an assessment foundation. If you use the information to form realistic expectations, your behavior toward the students will communicate positive, realistic messages about what they will achieve.

Practicality and Efficiency

Like all assessments, those done prior to instruction need to be practical and efficient. It will be most productive to use information that you are familiar with and that will not take too much time. For example, you may find that the specific skills listed on standardized test reports for your students are too numerous to consider individually. You may find it helpful to look for specific grades or teacher comments in cumulative files, making note of unusual or conflicting information that will need further investigation. During the first week, your assessments need to be simple and direct, providing sufficient information but not more than you need for planning. Whatever methods and approaches you use, try to be as clear as possible about how you will use the information *before* you collect it. It is easy to test with the thought that the results may be of use, but often, because this has not been specified, the information is collected but never used.

SUMMARY

Assessment occurs prior to instruction to facilitate instructional planning. Some information is available before school begins, though the most relevant information is gathered by the classroom teacher after school begins. Major points in the chapter for effective use of pre-instructional assessment include the following:

- Before school begins information is contained in school records, standardized tests, and information cards. School records contain grades, teacher comments, and other data. It is recommended that teachers carefully review this information to learn as much as possible about their students in order to form accurate yet flexible expectations.
- Information in school records should be combined with teacher observations and other direct assessments.
- Different types of standardized tests and their report formats are introduced as providing important information.
- Proper interpretation of scores from norm-referenced standardized tests depends on the nature of the norm group and understanding relative standing as indicated by percentile rank, grade equivalent, and other standard scores.
- Test batteries can indicate strengths and weaknesses; some reports show achievement in specific skills.
- Criterion-referenced standardized tests measure performance on clearly defined skills or areas.
- Aptitude and readiness tests measure capacity to learn.
- During the first week, teachers use informal observation, structured exercises, and pretests to supplement existing information.
- Informal observation is done by observing student behavior, interpreting it, synthesizing, and naming the trait or characteristic. Nonthreatening, informal exercises are used to assess specific skills.
- Pretests should be short and should not interfere with establishing a positive classroom climate.
- Teacher expectations are teacher beliefs about what students are capable of achieving.
- Expectations are formed from many sources of information prior to instruction. These expectations should be realistic, avoiding negative self-fulfilling prophecies.
- Criteria for high-quality pre-instructional assessment are presented.

SELF-INSTRUCTIONAL REVIEW EXERCISES

1. Summarize the advantages and disadvantages of using information in school records to learn about students before school starts. Do you agree that it is best to know as much as possible about your students? Why or why not?

2. What kind of information would lead one to conclude that a student has clear weaknesses in a particular skill?

3. How is it possible for all school districts in a state to be above the 50th percentile on a standardized norm-referenced test?

4. Refer to Figure 4.2 on page 81. What are the national percentile scores for Michael in reading and mathematics problems? In general, how does Ms. Olson's class compare to the national norm group?

5. Now look at Figure 4.4 on page 85. What are Ryan's strengths and weaknesses?

6. Indicate whether each of the following characteristics refers to a norm-referenced test (NR), criterion-referenced (CR), aptitude (A), or state (S) standardized test. More than one may apply to each characteristic.

   a. Reports scores as percentage of items correct.
   b. Shows capacity to learn.
   c. Reports grade equivalents.
   d. Reports percentile scores.
   e. Readiness test.

7. Using Figure 4.12 on page 98 as a general guide, draw a diagram that illustrates a teacher expectation that has applied to you or one that you have observed. Label each part of the diagram so you can identify each step the expectation process.

ANSWERS TO SELF-INSTRUCTIONAL REVIEW EXERCISES

1. Refer to Figure 4.1 on page 77 for the advantages and disadvantages of using school records. The major issue related to knowing as much as possible about the students before you meet them is your confidence about forming appropriate expectations. As long as you keep in mind the need to be flexible in your expectations, more information is better than less.

2. When the information from several different sources suggests the same conclusion, when there is a pattern of performance for several years, and when your own informal assessment coincides with what is in school records.

3. Because norms are established in one year (e.g., 1990) and then used for several more years, and current scores (1995) are compared to the 1990 norms. Before new norms are established, all the school districts may target skills assessed on the test.

4. Reading percentile is 58, mathematics problems is 70. With some exceptions, Ms. Olson's class scored quite a bit higher than the national norm group.

5. Overall Ryan shows average achievement in comparison to the national norm. He appears to be relatively weak on developmental language and punctuation, but he

appears to be strong on spelling. Ryan is about average in math concepts and math problem solving. He is strong in number systems.

6. a. clearly CR, some NR and S, not A; b. A; c. NR; d. NR, A, maybe S; e. A.

7. This answer will vary depending on the individual student, but it should correspond to the figure. Remember that expectations will not influence students unless there is differential teacher behavior. In other words, fully operational expectations include both the teacher's belief about students and the teacher's behavior toward the students.

SUGGESTIONS FOR ACTION RESEARCH

1. Ask for access to school records to review the contents. For several students, determine if the information is consistent. For example, are standardized test scores and grades consistent? Compare the composite picture of some students as determined from a review of their records with observations of them in the classroom and teacher's comments.

2. Interview several teachers about how they use information about their students prior to instruction. Ask them what data they use and why, and how they gain access to it. If they do not use specific sources of information, like pretests, ask them why they do not. Ask them if there is special information that they like to have about all their students, and on what they base their expectations of their students.

3. Observe some students informally in a classroom and make some judgments about their academic strengths and weaknesses. Then compare your judgments with those of the teacher or school records. Ask the teacher what you could do to make more accurate judgments.

4. Examine the standardized test score reports that are commonly used in schools in your area. Identify some examples of student scores that would indicate a discrepancy between ability and achievement, and between achievement in different areas.

5. Locate a standardized test manual to determine the definition of some of the knowledge and skills that are assessed. Through a review of the objectives and sample items, compare what the test is assessing to what is taught in a local school curriculum.

5

ASSESSING STUDENT PROGRESS

Based on assessments done before school and during the first week, you have set your learning targets and planned your lessons. Now is the time for instruction. As we have seen, teaching is fast paced and hectic. Many different tasks and events occur simultaneously, and decisions must be made quickly. Research has shown that in this complex environment, effective teachers employ a process of beginning instruction, assessing student progress, making decisions about what to do next,

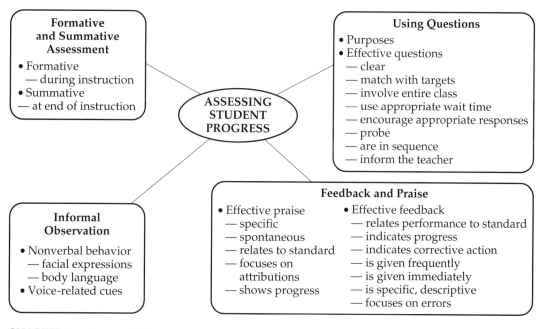

Formative and Summative Assessment

- Formative
  — during instruction
- Summative
  — at end of instruction

Using Questions

- Purposes
- Effective questions
  — clear
  — match with targets
  — involve entire class
  — use appropriate wait time
  — encourage appropriate responses
  — probe
  — are in sequence
  — inform the teacher

ASSESSING STUDENT PROGRESS

Informal Observation

- Nonverbal behavior
  — facial expressions
  — body language
- Voice-related cues

Feedback and Praise

- Effective praise
  — specific
  — spontaneous
  — relates to standard
  — focuses on attributions
  — shows progress
- Effective feedback
  — relates performance to standard
  — indicates progress
  — indicates corrective action
  — is given frequently
  — is given immediately
  — is specific, descriptive
  — focuses on errors

CHAPTER 5   Concept Map

responding to students, and revising planned instruction as appropriate. All of this happens very quickly. Jeremy Lloyd is a high school mathematics teacher. This is how he characterizes the importance of decision making and assessment:

> *Teachers need to create a warm and trusting classroom. Students need to trust their teachers not to make unrealistic demands, move too quickly through new material, or lead them too far, too soon, from the comfort zone of knowledge they have already mastered. Teachers moving too quickly will "lose" their students. Teachers will gain their students' trust when they move forward cautiously, stopping often to review progress with students, and providing them with opportunities to ask questions. This is especially important when students are being challenged to be creative and engage in different kinds of problem solving. The teacher must be able to gauge when "enough is enough" for a while, and then bring the class together again for some reassurance and confidence-building through some "lower level" learning. Then the class can go back to working on riskier learning targets. When the class is engaged in this kind of work, the teacher, more than ever, needs honest and straightforward feedback from students. They must feel comfortable about letting their teacher know exactly what they are thinking and feeling; at the same time the teacher is constantly conducting checks for understanding.*

A key element in this process is continuous monitoring on the part of teachers to ascertain their students' reactions to instruction and students' progress toward understanding the content or accomplishing the skill. How is the flow of activities? How are students responding to the activities? Are they interested and attentive? Should I speed up or slow down? Should I give more examples? Here is where good assessment is essential to effective teaching. You need to know what to look for in your students while you deliver instruction, how to interpret what you see and hear, how to respond to the students, and then how to adjust your teaching. In this chapter, we will look at the two primary methods you use to assess students while teaching—observation and asking questions—as well as how you provide helpful feedback.

FORMATIVE AND SUMMATIVE ASSESSMENT

Two terms will help clarify assessment during instruction: formative and summative assessment. *Formative assessment* occurs during a lesson or unit to provide ongoing feedback to the teacher and student. The purpose of formative assessment is to provide corrective actions as instruction occurs to enhance student learning. It consists of informal observation, questioning, student responses to questions, homework, worksheets, and teacher feedback to the student. Formative assessment is integrated with instruction on a daily basis. It is flexible and idiosyncratic.

In contrast, *summative assessment*, or *formal* assessment, takes place at the end of a unit of study. Its primary purpose is to document student performance after

FIGURE 5.1   Characteristics of Formative and Summative Assessments

	Formative	Summative
Purpose	To monitor and improve instruction and student learning	To document student performance on a learning unit
Time of Assessment	During instruction	After instruction is completed
Assessment Techniques	Informal observation, listening to student questions and responses to teacher questions	Chapter tests, final exams, reports, term papers, projects
Use of Information	To improve a process while it is still going on	To judge success of student learning and instruction, and to identify systematic student errors
Structure	Flexible, informal	Fixed, formal, standardized for all students

Source: Adapted from Airasian, P. W. (1994). *Classroom Assessment* (2nd ed.). New York: McGraw-Hill, Inc., p. 136.

instruction is completed. We are all quite familiar with this type of assessment in the form of term papers, chapter achievement tests, final exams, and research projects. Summative assessments are also used to identify patterns in the errors that students make. This is accomplished by examining wrong answers to discern systematic mistakes. Often such an analysis is helpful in making decisions about the type of instruction a student needs.

We will be examining several types of summative assessment methods in the next few chapters. This chapter focuses on formative assessments. Figure 5.1 summarizes the characteristics of both types of assessment.

INFORMAL OBSERVATION

For most teachers no assessment activity is more pervasive than the informal observation of student behavior. Teachers constantly look at students and listen to what is occurring in the class. These observations are made to determine such things as:

- the nature of student participation in class discussion
- the kinds of questions asked
- the interpersonal skills used in cooperative groups
- the correctness of student responses to questions

- the nature of student responses to examples
- how students react to an assignment
- how students react to grades on a test
- the verbal skills demonstrated in expressing thoughts
- the pacing of a lesson
- whether more examples are needed
- which students to call on
- the interest level of the students
- the degree of understanding demonstrated in student answers

This list could go on and on. Informal observation is unstructured in the sense that there is no set format or procedure, but it is not random. For example, effective teachers learn to observe key students in each class who show their reactions more clearly than others. Some of these students are vocal and stand out, while others are quiet leaders.

We will first consider the observation of nonverbal behavior, then we will look at vocal cues such as pauses and tone of voice.

Assessing Nonverbal Behavior

Teachers greatly rely on students' body language, facial expressions, and eye contact to accurately observe and interpret student behavior. These actions are called *non*verbal because the message is communicated by something about the student other than the content of what the student says. These nonverbal cues are often more important than what is said. According to Mehrabian (1971), as much as 93 percent of a message is communicated by nonverbal factors. Some of this is through general appearance and behavior such as body language, gestures, and facial expressions, and some is communicated by vocal cues that accompany what is said, such as tone of voice, inflection, pauses, and emphasis.

Nonverbal behaviors help you assess both meaning and emotion. For instance, we rely on facial and bodily expressions to determine the actual intent of the message. The nonverbal cues punctuate verbal messages in much the same way exclamation points, question marks, boldfacing, and italics focus the meaning of written language. Knapp (1978) suggests that this punctuation occurs in the following ways:

- *Confirming or Repeating.* When nonverbal behavior is consistent with what is said verbally, the message is confirmed or repeated. For instance, when Sally gave the correct answer to a question, her eyes lit up (facial expression), she sat up straight in her chair and her hand was stretched up toward the ceiling (body motion), and her answer was animated and loud (voice quality). She indicated nonverbally as well as verbally that she knew the answer.
- *Denying or Confusing.* Nonverbal and verbal messages are often contradictory, suggesting denial or confusion. For example, Ms. Thomas has just asked her

class if they are prepared to begin their small group work. The students say yes, but at the same time look down with confused expressions on their faces. The real message is that they are not really ready, despite what they have said.

- *Strengthening or Emphasizing.* Nonverbal behavior can punctuate what is said by adding emotional color, feelings, and intensity. These emotions strengthen or emphasize the verbal message. Suppose Mr. Terrell suggested to Teresa that she take the lead in the next school play. Teresa responds by saying, "No, I wouldn't want to do that," while she shakes her head, avoids eye contact, and becomes rigid. Teresa doesn't just mean no, she means NO! If she really wanted to take the lead her nonverbal behavior would contradict her verbal response.
- *Controlling or Regulating.* Nonverbal behavior can be used to control others and regulate the nature of the interaction. In a cooperative learning group, you may observe that when Tom goes to ask David for some help, David controls the conversation by looking away.

You will find that emotions and feelings are communicated more clearly and accurately by nonverbal than verbal cues. Not only is nonverbal behavior the richest source of information on affect, it is the most stable and consistent. Because most nonverbal behavior is not consciously controlled, the messages are relatively free of distortion and deception. It is really not difficult, when you consciously attend to appropriate nonverbal behavior, to determine mood, mental states, attitudes, self-assurance, responsiveness, confidence, interest, anger, fear, and other affective and emotional dispositions. This is especially helpful when the nonverbal message conflicts with the verbal one. That is, *how* students say something, through their nonverbal behavior, is as important, if not more so, than *what* they say. Think about a student who answers a question but does so with a slow, low voice, looking away. Even if the answer is correct, these nonverbal cues are telling you something important about the student's level of confidence and affect. Your interpretation would be different for a student who looked directly at you, spoke with authority, and whose face displayed excitement. In this section we will look at how specific nonverbal behaviors communicate different meanings and emotions, and how teachers respond to these cues.

Facial Expressions

The face is the most important source of nonverbal information because it is the primary outlet for emotions and it rarely distorts meaning. The face projects a great variety of messages, in part because of the complex and flexible set of muscles. To know what to look for it is best to focus on three areas: the brows and forehead; the eyes, lids, and nose; and the lower face. The upper portion of the face is more likely to indicate feelings of concern and anger (e.g., the brows are lowered and drawn together in anger). The lower area, particularly the mouth, will communicate happiness and amusement. Smiles, frowns, twisted lips, a raised chin, a clenched mouth, and other expressions are also fairly clear in what they communicate.

Let's see how you do with a short test of facial meaning (The Facial Meaning Sensitivity Test, Leathers, 1986). In Figure 5.2 you will find ten photographs of different facial expressions. Match the following emotions with the pictures below:

Facial Meaning	*Photograph #*	*Facial Meaning*	*Photograph #*
Disgust	_____	Contempt	_____
Happiness	_____	Surprise	_____
Interest	_____	Anger	_____
Sadness	_____	Determination	_____
Bewilderment	_____	Fear	_____

FIGURE 5.2   The Facial Meaning Sensitivity Test

Source: Leathers, D. G., *Successful nonverbal communication: Principles and applications*, 3rd ed., copyright © 1997, p. 36. All rights reserved. Reprinted by permission of Allyn & Bacon.

The correct choices are disgust = 1, happiness = 3, interest = 8, sadness = 10, bewilderment = 2, contempt = 9, surprise = 7, anger = 6, determination = 4, and fear = 5.

For the purposes of teaching, you will need to be especially careful to attend to facial expressions of bewilderment and interest. Teachers use these emotions extensively to gage student understanding and motivation. Emotions similar to bewilderment are confusion, doubt, frustration, and puzzlement. Obviously these cues suggest that the student is not understanding or is not progressing. Interest conveys anticipation, excitement, and attention. These emotions are important as an indication of attention.

The most informative aspect of the face is the eye and the nature of eye contact. Eye contact indicates a readiness to communicate, and continued direct eye contact signifies confidence and competence. Students who use positive eye contact, who look directly at you and watch your movements, are probably attentive and interested.

Averted eyes often suggest an unwillingness to respond, a lack of confidence, or a general sense of apathy. For example, if a student looks down before responding, looks away from teachers when interacting with them, keeps eyes downcast, or looks at the ceiling, a reasonable interpretation is that the student may lack confidence, knowledge, or skills, and may have other negative emotions. When most of the students in a class start looking around the room, at each other and out the window, it indicates that they have lost interest and are not involved. This may mean that students do not understand well enough, or it may mean they are bored (in some cultures the lack of eye contact may indicate respect for an authority figure or older person, and not a lack of self-confidence or other negative feeling).

The pupils of the eyes convey the intensity of emotion shown more generally in the face. They tend to enlarge as we become more interested in something, more emotionally aroused, and more happy with positive anticipation. Pupils contract as we become less interested and have more negative emotions such as sadness, sorrow, and indifference.

Body Language

Like facial expressions and voice, body language, movement, and posture communicate messages. The meaning associated with different bodily cues is best understood by considering five categories of nonverbal behavior, each of which is based on a different function or purpose: emblems, illustrators, affect displays, regulators, and adapters (Ekman & Friesen, 1969).

An *emblem* is a body cue that has a direct one- or two-word verbal translation. Emblems are used to consciously communicate a particular message. There are many emblems, such as holding up your hand with your palm facing the other person (which means "wait"), putting your finger to your puckered lips ("quiet"), and waving toward yourself ("come over"). Most of these emblems are substitutes for words.

Although there has not been much research on emblems in schools, you should be aware of possible cross-cultural differences. For example, nodding your head in the United States means that you agree, while in Japan it acknowledges only that you have received the other person's message.

An *illustrator* is used to increase clarity and awareness and to augment what is being said. It reinforces the strength of the emotional message. For example, holding your fingers close together augments "small," and pointing to an object clarifies what you intend to communicate about. If a student's fist is clenched, it may indicate anger in association with what the student has verbalized.

The third type of bodily communication is the *affect display*. These cues show emotion through the position and posture of the body and certain gestures. If the student has a rigid, tense, slumped body with arms and legs crossed, the affect is negative and defensive. Students with open, relaxed bodies who lean toward the teacher and do not fidget or tap something communicate positive affect, attention, and confidence. Suppose you notice that a student has one hand to her mouth and the other arm clenched to her body. How would you interpret this body language? It is likely that the student is not very confident about the lesson or assignment and generally has negative emotions that will probably interfere with learning.

Regulators are used to indicate the initiation, length, and termination of verbal messages. Students use these cues to inform the teacher about whether they want to initiate a response, are finished with a comment or thought, or want to continue speaking. An obvious initiation regulator is to raise the hand or index finger. Other initiation regulators include eye contact, head nodding, smiles, and raised eyebrows. When students do not want to make a comment, they may use such "turn-denying" behaviors as staring at something (especially looking down at the desk) and slumping in the chair. Students who want to continue speaking may lean toward you, use gestures to punctuate their thoughts, and display an enthusiastic, expectant face.

The final category to describe different functions is the *adapter*. Adapters are a rich source of information about attitudes, levels of confidence, and anxiety. They include behaviors such as picking at oneself, chewing nails, and fidgeting (these indicate nervousness, anxiety, and concern). Covering the face with one's hands indicates that a message is undesirable, painful, or unpleasant.

Assessing Voice-Related Cues

Voice-related cues include tone of voice, loudness, intensity, pauses, silences, voice level, inflection, word spacing, emphases, and other aspects of voice that add color to the content of what is said. The potential of vocal cues to provide information about a student's level of understanding, confidence, and emotional state is exceeded only by facial expressions.

A summary of recent research on the relationship between vocal cues and messages is presented in Figure 5.3 (Leathers, 1986). Although this research has not been conducted with teacher/student dyads or groups, the findings do have important implications. For example, on the basis of vocal cues you would expect students who are confident in their knowledge or skill to be relatively loud rather than quiet, to have a rather rapid speaking rate, to speak in a high pitch, and to speak fluently with few pauses, "ahs," sentence changes, throat clearings, word repetitions, and incomplete sentences. Students who are unsure of their knowledge or ability to perform a skill are likely to speak quietly, in a low pitch with little variety, and to speak slowly with many pauses and frequent throat clearings. The student who lacks confidence will speak nonfluently, the voice will be flat, more like a monotone rather than showing variety in pitch and rate. Research has also determined that persons who demonstrate little variation in pitch and rate tend to be viewed as introverts, lacking assertiveness and dynamism. Voices that are clear, articulate, and confident are viewed as positive.

You will need to be careful not to infer lack of knowledge, confidence, anxiety, or motivation *solely* on the basis of vocal cues. Like nonverbal behavior, voice is one of many pieces of evidence that you need to consider to make an accurate assessment.

The challenge of being a teacher is being able to observe these nonverbal and verbal cues, make appropriate interpretations, and then take corrective action when needed. To help you with this I have prepared a table that combines different types of nonverbal behaviors and vocal cues in relation to particular messages students send (Figure 5.4 on page 114).

FIGURE 5.3   Vocal Cues and Messages

Vocal Cue	Message
Loudness	*Loud*—competent, enthusiastic, competent, forceful, self-assured, excited *Quiet*—anxious, unsure, shy, indifferent
Pitch (musical note voice produces)	*High*—excited, explosively angry, emotional *Low*—calm, sad, stunned, quietly angry, indifferent *Variety*—dynamic, extroverted
Rate	*Fast*—interested, self-assured, angry, happy, proud, confident, excited, impulsive, emotional *Slow*—uninterested, unsure, unexcited, unemotional
Quality (combination of attributes)	*Flat*—sluggish, cold, withdrawn *Nasal*—unattractive, lethargic, foolish

FIGURE 5.4   Messages Students Convey through Nonverbal Behavior and Vocal Cues

Message	Facial Expressions	Body Language	Vocal Cues
Confident	Relaxed, direct eye contact; pupils enlarged	Erect posture; arms and legs open; chin up; hands waving; forward position in seat	Fluent; few pauses; variety in tone; loud
Nervous	Tense; brows lowered; pupils contracted	Rigid; tense; tapping; picking	Pauses; "ah" sounds; repetition; shaky; soft; fast; quiet
Angry	Brows lowered, drawn together; teeth clenched	Fidgety; hands clenched; head down	Loud or quiet; animated
Defensive	Downcast eyes; pupils contracted; eyes squinted	Arms and legs crossed; leaning away; leaning head on hands	Loud; animated
Bored	Looking around; relaxed; pupils contracted	Slumped posture; hands to face	Soft; monotone; flat
Frustrated	Brows together; eyes downcast; squinting	Tense; tapping; picking; placing fingers or hands on each side of head	Pauses; low pitch
Happy	Smiling, smirking; relaxed; brows natural; pupils enlarged	Relaxed; head nodding; leaning forward	Animated; loud; fast
Interested	Direct eye contact; brows uplifted	Leaning forward; relaxed; opening arms and legs; nodding; raising hand or finger	Higher pitch; fast
Not Understanding	Frowning; biting lower lip; squinting eyes; looking away	Leaning back; arms crossed; head tilted back; hand on forehead; fidgeting; scratching chin; leaning head on hands	Slow; pauses; "ah," "um," "well" expressions; low pitch; monotone; quiet; soft

I also asked some teachers to summarize the nonverbal behavior and vocal cues they attend to, how they interpret what they see and hear, and the action they take following their observation and interpretation. Examples of the teachers' responses include the following:

Nonverbal Behavior	Interpretation	Action
Students start to look around the room and at each other.	Some students are not understanding; some may be bored.	Refocus students; review previous lesson; reteach lesson; regroup students.
Room quiets; students are writing in their notebooks.	Students are motivated and on-task.	Keep going—it may not last long!
Students pull materials from desk quickly.	Students understand the assignment.	Begin monitoring individuals.
Many students wave hands eagerly.	Students are confident of answer.	Ask students to write answers so most will participate or call on lower-ability students.
Students slump in chairs, look down, and avoid eye contact when questions are asked.	Students seem to be losing contact or no longer understand.	Use a "mind capture" to refocus student attention. Cautiously, encourage students to ask questions.
Some students are sleeping in class.	May be boredom or fatigue.	Check to see which students have jobs and how much they work.
Students squint and adjust the focus of their eyes.	Indicates a lack of understanding, frustration, or boredom.	Rephrase the question or ask the students what it is that they do not understand.

Sources of Error in Informal Observation

In a busy classroom, it's difficult to make continuous informal observations that are accurate, whether of individual students or groups. Some of the more common errors that teachers make in their informal observations and interpretations are presented in Figure 5.5 on page 116. To make accurate, reliable observations, it is best to first learn what to look for and listen to. Next, you need to be aware of the types of errors that are possible and consciously monitor yourself so that these errors are not made. Finally, it is helpful if you are able to use a few simple procedures:

- Ask yourself, is the verbal message consistent with the nonverbal behavior? Is this behavior normal or unusual?
- Plan time to do informal observation while not actively teaching a lesson to the entire class (e.g., during seat work, small group work, and individual interactions).

FIGURE 5.5   Sources of Error in Informal Observation

1. Leniency or generosity	Teachers as observers tend to be lenient or generous.
2. Primacy effects	Teacher's initial impressions have a distorting effect on later observations.
3. Recency effect	Teacher's interpretations are unduly influenced by their most recent observation.
4. Logical generalization errors	Teacher makes assumptions that some nonverbal behavior generalizes to other areas (e.g., lack of confidence in math means lack of confidence in English).
5. Failure to acknowledge self	Teacher fails to take into account his or her influence on the students.
6. Unrepresentative sampling	Teacher erroneously interprets behaviors that do not accurately reflect the student or do not occur frequently enough to provide a reliable measure.
7. Observer bias	Teacher's preconceived biases and stereotypes distort the meaning of what is observed.
8. Failure to consider student perspective	Teacher fails to obtain student interpretations that would clarify the teacher's impressions.
9. Student reactions to being observed	Some students may get nervous or uneasy when observed by teachers (e.g., students would behave differently if the teacher were not present).
10. Lack of consideration for the rapid speed of relevant action	Teacher may miss critical behaviors because of the speed of what occurs in the classroom.
11. Lack of consideration for the simultaneity of relevant action	Teacher may fail to account for more than one message being sent at the same time.
12. Student faking	Teacher may fail to realize that students are faking (e.g., eye contact and nodding does not always indicate engagement); as students become more sophisticated they develop strategies to make themselves appear to be on task.

Source: Adapted from Evertson, G., & Green, J. (1986). Observation as inquiry and method, p. 183. In M. C. Wittrock (Ed.), *Handbook of research on teaching* (3rd ed., pp. 162–213). New York: Macmillan.

- Keep a list of possible errors from Figure 5.5 in a place where you can refer to it quickly, such as in your desk. Make a habit of referring to the list frequently.
- When possible during the school day, write down informal observations, your interpretations, and the action you took. Be sure to keep the interpretations separate from the observations.
- At the end of the day, set aside a few minutes to record, briefly, important informal observations. Refer to your notes each week to look for patterns and trouble spots that need attention.
- If you are unsure about what a nonverbal behavior may mean, and the implications are serious, check them out with the student during an individual conference. For example, if you are picking up from nonverbal behavior that a student does not understand a procedure, even though the student's answers are correct on worksheets, ask the student directly about how he or she felt about the procedure and inquire about the student's confidence. You may dis-

cover that the student was concerned with other things at the time, and this affect was being displayed.

- Consciously think about informal observations of behavior in relation to student understanding and performance of learning targets. Those that directly relate to the targets are most important.
- Don't be fooled by students who appear to be on task and interested but aren't.

Remember, do not base an interpretation solely on the basis of a single nonverbal behavior or vocal cue.

USING QUESTIONS TO ASSESS STUDENT PROGRESS

Good instruction involves much more than simply presenting information and giving students assignments to work on. Effective teaching requires constantly monitoring your students' understanding during instruction. You will be unable to stop teaching and give a quiz or other type of formal assessment every time you want to see if students are learning. Along with observing nonverbal behavior, teachers rely heavily on how students answer questions during instruction to know if the students understand what is presented or can perform skills. Thus, the questions teachers ask in the classroom and subsequent teacher–student interaction are essential components of effective instruction. Oral questioning, therefore, is the predominant method of assessing student progress during instruction. Most teachers ask hundreds of questions each day (Morgan & Saxton, 1991). Except for lecturing, some type of questioning in student–teacher interactions is the most frequently used instructional strategy.

Questioning typically occurs in three formats: teacher-led reviews of content, discussions, and recitations. The review may be a fast-paced drill that is designed to cover specific knowledge. Discussions are used to promote student questioning and exchange ideas and opinions to clarify issues, promote thinking, generate ideas, or solve a problem. Recitations, the most common format for questioning, are in between reviews and discussions. In a recitation, the teacher asks questions as part of the presentation of material to engage students in what they are learning. Questions are blended with teacher talk to promote student understanding of the content and to monitor comprehension. In each of these formats, teachers use oral questioning during instruction to serve a number of important purposes (Kissock & Iyortsuun, 1982; Morgan & Saxton, 1991), only one of which is assessing student progress.

Purposes of Questioning

Teachers use questions for five major purposes: to involve students in the lesson, to promote students' thinking and comprehension, to review important content, to control students, and to assess student progress. We will review the first four purposes briefly, then discuss in greater depth the use of questioning for formative assessment.

Questions can conveniently and efficiently grab students' attention and engage them in the lesson. Questions can challenge beliefs, provoke students, and get them to think about the topic under discussion by creating a sense of cognitive dissonance, imbalance, or disequilibrium. Second, questions can promote student reasoning and comprehension by helping them think through and verbalize their ideas. By actively thinking through answers to questions, student understanding is enhanced. Learning is also enhanced by listening to the answers of other students, because these answers may represent a way of expressing ideas that makes more sense to the student than the way the teacher explains things.

Third, questions signal to students important content to be learned and provide an opportunity for students to assess their own level of understanding in these areas. The types of questions asked also indicate how the students should prepare to demonstrate their understanding. For instance, if you ask questions that compare and contrast (e.g., How were presidents Carter and Clinton similar?), this will cue students that they need to learn about how these presidents were similar and different, not just characteristics of each one. If you ask simple recall questions (e.g., What three major legislative initiatives occurred during the Clinton presidency?), you will tell your students that they need to memorize the names of these initiatives.

Fourth, questions are used to control student behavior and manage the class. Questions asked at random to different students—and which require brief, correct answers—maintain student attention. Teachers often ask a specific question to a student who is not paying attention to stop inappropriate behavior. Conversely, questions can be used to reinforce good behavior. Questions are also used to refocus students and to remind them of the classroom rules and procedures. Through the use of good questions students will keep actively involved in learning, preventing opportunities for student misbehavior.

The final purpose of questioning is to obtain information about student understanding and progress. This is accomplished if the questions are effective and elicit information that will help you. We will review characteristics of good questions and questioning skills in relation to this purpose.

Characteristics of Effective Questioning to Assess Student Progress

Your goal is to ask questions during instruction that will provide you with accurate information about what students know and can do. With this goal in mind, the following suggestions and strategies will help you:

1. State Questions Clearly and Succinctly So That the Intent of the Question Is Understood.   Students understand the question if they know how they are to respond. Questions are vague to students if there are too many different possible responses or if the question is too general. With such a question, students wonder, "What does he mean?" Because they are unsure of what is intended, they are less likely to be willing to answer the question, and you are less likely to find out what they know. This occurs for a single vague question and for run-on questions (ones in which two or more questions are asked together). For example, if a fourth-grade teacher wants to determine current student understanding of noun–verb agreement in sentences, an inappropriately vague question might be:

What is wrong with the sentences on the board?

It would be better to ask:

> Read each of the three sentences on the board. In which sentence or sentences is there agreement between the noun and the verb? In which one or ones is there disagreement? How would you correct the sentence(s) in which the verb and noun do not agree?

Other questions that are too vague:

> What did you think about this demonstration?
> What about the early explorers of America?
> Can you tell me something about what you learned?
> What do you know about the solar system?

2. Match Questions with Learning Targets. The questions you ask should reflect your learning targets, the degree of emphasis of different topics that will be assessed more formally in a unit test, and the difficulty of learning targets. Ask more questions and spend more time questioning with difficult learning targets. This will give you sufficient information to make sure students understand. Try to ask questions in rough proportion to how you will eventually test for student learning. We have all been in classes where much class time was spent discussing something that was covered only lightly on the test. Try to avoid this.

Matching questions to learning targets means that the questions should be phrased to elicit student responses that are required in the learning target. For this purpose, most oral questions will correspond to either knowledge or reasoning targets. Knowledge targets focus on remembering and understanding. Questions that assess knowledge targets often begin with *what*, *who*, *where*, and *when*. For example, "What is the definition of exacerbate?" "What is the sum of 234 and 849?" "When did Columbus discover America?" "Who is Martin Luther King?" These are examples of knowledge questions that generally require factual recall or rote memorization of dates, names, places, and definitions. The questions are *convergent* in that there is only one correct answer. Other knowledge questions go beyond simple factual recall and assess student understanding and comprehension. Students are required to show that they grasp the meaning of something by answering questions that require more than rote memory, for example, "What is the major theme of this article?" "What is an example of a metaphor?" and "Explain what is meant by the phrase 'opposites attract'?" "How do you find the area of a parallelogram?" These questions are convergent in the sense that there is a single correct answer, but the answers are unique for each student. More thinking is required than simple rote memory. These types of questions are effective when you want to assess more than one student in whole group instruction since each student is using his or her own words for the answer. If there is only one way to state the correct answer, only one student can answer it correctly.

Reasoning questions require more time to respond to. These questions are generally *divergent* in that more than one answer can be correct or satisfactory. In a reasoning question, the teacher is asking students to mentally manipulate what they know to analyze, synthesize, problem-solve, create, and evaluate. Reasoning questions will include words or intents like *distinguish, contrast, generalize, judge, solve, compare, interpret, relate,* and *predict,* such as "Relate the causes of the Civil War to the causes of World War I. How are they the same and how are they different?" "What was the implication of the story for how we live our lives today?" "What would happen if these two liquids were mixed?" As you might imagine, reasoning questions are excellent for promoting student thinking and discussion, but they are not as effective as knowledge questions for assessing student progress.

It is generally recommended that teachers balance knowledge with reasoning questions to keep student attention and enhance a broad range of student abilities.

3. Involve the Entire Class.   You will want to ask questions to many different students in your class, rather than allowing a few students to answer most questions. Balance is needed between students who volunteer and those who don't, high- and low-ability students, males and females, and students near and far from you. It is easy to call on the same students most of the time, so it's best to be aware of who has and who has not participated. If you are judging the progress of the class as a whole, it is especially important to obtain information from different students, although normally if your better students are confused or having difficulty, chances are good that this is true for the rest of the class as well. If slower students respond correctly, then most students are ready to move on.

Involvement will be enhanced if everyone's responses are supported. One technique for engaging most students is to address the question to the class as a whole, allow students time to think about a response, and then call on specific students. This encourages all the students to be responsible for an answer, not just a single student if you call the name first. Teachers who restrict their questioning to a small group of students are likely to communicate inappropriate expectations. Also, it is most fair if all students have the opportunity to benefit from the practice of answering questions.

4. Allow Sufficient Wait Time for Student Responses.   A more accurate assessment of what students know will occur if students have sufficient time to think before responding to each question. Students need this time to process their thoughts and formulate their answers. Research shows that some teachers have difficulty waiting more than a single second before cuing a response, calling on another student, or rephrasing a question. It has been shown that when teachers can wait three to five seconds, the quality and quantity of student responses are enhanced. There is an increase in the length of responses, unsolicited but appropriate responses, speculative responses, responses to reasoning questions, and a decrease in failures to respond (Good & Brophy, 1994). It follows from these findings that longer wait time will result in better assessment. Answers are better and more representative for the class as a whole.

It may be difficult for you to wait more than a couple of seconds because the silence may seem like it has been much longer. It's helpful to tell students directly that such wait time is not only expected, but required, so that immediate responses do not take opportunities away from students who need a little more time. This will help alleviate your own insecurity about having so much silence during a lesson. Reasoning questions will naturally require more wait time than knowledge questions.

5. Give Appropriate Responses to Student Answers.   Your responses to student answers will be very important for gathering valid information about student progress, because your style and approach—the climate and pattern of interaction that is established—will affect if and how students are likely to answer your questions. Each student's response should be acknowledged with some kind of meaningful, honest feedback. Feedback is part of ongoing assessment because it lets students know, and confirms for you, how much progress has been made. In the course of a class recitation or discussion, this feedback is usually a short, simple phrase indicating correctness, such as answering, "right," "correct," "yes," or maybe by doing something as simple as nodding your head. We will consider more about feedback later in this chapter.

6. Avoid Questions Answered by a Yes or No.   There are two reasons to avoid yes/no questions or other questions that involve a choice between stated alternatives. First, if there are two alternatives, such as those available when answering a yes/no or true/false question, students can guess the correct answer 50 percent of the time. After a while, students tend to key into teacher behaviors or the way such a question is phrased to guess correctly. In any event, you will need to ask many yes/no questions to assess student progress accurately.

Second, these types of questions do not reveal much about a student's understanding of the content. They are not very diagnostic in nature. If you want to use such questions, do so sparingly and as a warm-up to questions that are better able to assess student learning. Adding a simple *why* after an answer to a yes/no question will increase its diagnostic power considerably. It is better to use these types of questions with students individually rather than in groups.

7. Probe Initial Responses When Appropriate.   Probes are specific follow-up questions. Use them to better understand how students arrived at an answer, their reasoning, and the logic of their response. Examples of probes include words and phrases such as "Why?" "How?" "Explain how you arrived at that solution," and "Please give me another example."

8. Avoid Tugging, Guessing, and Leading Questions.   Asking these types of questions makes it difficult to obtain an accurate picture of student knowledge and reasoning. Tugging questions ask students to elaborate or expand their answers without indicating what the student should focus on. They are usually vague questions or statements that follow what the teacher judges to be an incomplete answer. For example, "Well . . . ?" "And . . . ?" or "So . . . ?" are tugging questions. It is better to use a specific probe. For example, if the question is "Why were cities built near water?" and a student answered "So the people could come and go more easily," a tugging question would be "And what else?" A better probe would be "How did coming and going affect the travel of products and food?"

Guessing questions obviously elicit guessed answers from students, for example, "How many small computer businesses are there in this country?" This type of question is useful in getting students' attention and getting students to think about a problem or area, but it is not helpful in assessing progress.

Leading questions, like rhetorical questions, are more for the teacher to pace a lesson than for obtaining information about student knowledge. Therefore, these types of questions ("That's right, isn't it?" or "Let's go on to the next chapter, ok?") should be avoided.

9. Avoid Asking Students What They Know.   It will not usually be too helpful to ask students directly if they know or understand something. The question might be something like "Do you know how to divide fractions?" or "What do you know about the War of 1812?" or "Is everyone with me?" Students may be reluctant to answer such questions in class because of possible embarrassment, and if they do answer, the tendency is to say they know and understand when the reality is that they don't. However, if your relationship with your students is good, asking them if they understand or know something may work well.

Another approach, with older students, is to distribute a sheet at the beginning of class that lists all of the subject areas you plan to teach. Then, ask the students to check off the subjects they know about or to indicate the degree to which they are confident of knowing a specific content area. Assure them that their answers will remain anonymous. Like oral questions, however, this strategy is generally not as good as asking direct questions that require the student to demonstrate understanding, knowledge, or skills.

10. Ask Questions in an Appropriate Sequence.   Asking questions in a planned sequence will enhance the information you receive to assess student understanding. Good sequences generally begin with knowledge questions to determine if students know enough about the content to consider reasoning questions. For example, consider the following situation. After having her students read an article about the United States military involvement in Haiti in 1994, Mrs. Headly asks the question, "Should the United States stay in Haiti and enforce the local laws until a new government is formed?" Students give some brief opinions, but it's clear that this reasoning question is premature. She then asks some knowledge questions to determine whether students understand enough from the article to ask other reasoning questions, such as "What was the condition of Haiti prior to the United States involvement?" "Historically, what has happened in Haiti the last two times a new government has taken control?" "How did the people of Haiti receive the American soldiers?" Such questions also serve as a review for students to remind them about important aspects of the article. Once students show that they understand the conditions and history, then divergent questions that require reasoning would be appropriate.

Figure 5.6 summarizes the do's and don'ts of using effective questioning to assess student progress toward understanding learning targets.

FIGURE 5.6   Do's and Don'ts of Effective Questioning

Do	Don't
State questions clearly and succinctly.	Ask yes/no questions.
Match questions with learning targets.	Ask tugging questions.
Involve the entire class.	Ask guessing questions.
Allow sufficient wait time for students to respond.	Ask leading questions.
Give appropriate responses to student answers.	Ask students what they know.
Probe when appropriate.	Direct questions at just those students you know will answer correctly.
Sequence questions appropriately.	

PROVIDING FEEDBACK AND PRAISE

As I have already pointed out, an essential component of assessment is use of the information gathered. One way teachers use assessment information is to know how to respond to students after they demonstrate their knowledge, reasoning, skill, or performance. The teacher's response is termed *feedback*—the transfer of information from the teacher to the student following an assessment. Thus, one purpose of assessment while teaching is instructional; another purpose is to provide teachers with information that will help them make decisions about the frequency and nature of feedback to students. Of course in one sense feedback is also provided in the form of grades on unit tests and report cards, though normally grades offer very limited feedback. Our discussion will focus on the characteristics of effective feedback that are provided both during and after instruction. In Chapter 12 feedback in the form of grades is discussed in greater detail.

Research literature, as well as common sense experiences, has confirmed that the right kind of feedback is essential for effective teaching and learning. Corrective feedback is needed for learning, and assessment is needed to provide the feedback. The key is that the feedback must be *useful* and *helpful*. A simple definition of feedback is confirming the correctness of an answer; that is, whether it is right or wrong. This is what we do with most tests—tell students what they got right and what they missed; it is also the extent of the feedback many teachers give to a student's answers to oral questions—"Good," "That's right," "Close," and so on. Feedback of this nature is only part of what students need to improve their learning. Students also need to know *why* their performance was graded as it was and what *corrective procedures*, if any, are needed to improve their performance.

To further illustrate the importance of effective feedback, consider these two examples. First, good coaching requires effective feedback. For Ryann, a gymnast, her goal is to earn a score of 10. After Ryann has completed a routine the judges give her a score of, say, 8.5 or 9.2. This is analogous to a teacher giving a student a score or grade. But simply knowing the score doesn't help Ryann know what she needs to change to improve her score. When the judge immediately indicates, specifically, why certain points were deducted, then Ryann knows what to work on. Furthermore, if the judge or coach tells Ryann how she can correct the skill, she has the corrective procedures needed. Similarly, if a student receives a 70 percent on a test, the student knows that he or she has not done well, but unless otherwise indicated, this information alone does not tell the student what to do next. Or suppose you just started to learn golf. You miss the ball. Your skill level is obviously low. But knowing that is not enough. You need to get feedback about *why* you missed it. Is it because of your stance, your hand grip, the position of your head, your backswing, or some other aspect of your swing? When the teacher tells you precisely what you did wrong, what you need to correct, and how you can correct it, effective feedback has been provided.

Characteristics of Effective Feedback

Feedback is helpful when it has the following six characteristics (Elawar & Corno, 1985; Kindsvatter, Wilen, & Ishler, 1992; Wiggins, 1993):

1. Relates performance to standards
2. Indicates progress
3. Indicates corrective procedures
4. Is given frequently and immediately
5. Is specific and descriptive
6. Focuses on key errors

1. *Relate Performance to Standard.* The first of these essential components is that the feedback shows how the performance compares to a standard, exemplar, or goal. As emphasized previously, it is important for students to know the standards they will be judged against prior to learning and assessment. This makes it much easier for you to show students how their performance compares to this standard and for students to self-assess their work. You can write standards on the board, show exemplars of student work, and reinforce the meaning of scores and grades to make this process more efficient. Word your feedback to refer to these standards; for example, "John, your paper did not include an introductory paragraph, as shown here on our exemplar," or "Your answer is partially correct but, as I said in my question, I am looking for an example of a sentence with both adjectives and adverbs." Student self-assessment can be promoted by asking students to critique their work according to the examples that you provide.

2. *Indicate the Progress Students Have Made.* Progress is indicated by placing the feedback in the context of previous and expected performance. This encourages the student and helps to define what needs to be done next, for example, "Maria, your division has improved by showing each step you have used in your work. Now you need to be more careful about subtraction."

3. *Indicate Corrective Action That Students Can Take.* Corrective action is something pragmatic and possible. It gives students specific actions that they can engage in to improve. As an example, "You have made seven errors in the use of commas in your paper. Please refer to chapter three in your text and review the rules for using commas" or "Your understanding of how to use adverbs can be enhanced if you work through a computer program that is available." Such feedback explains how to correct the performance.

4. *Give Feedback Frequently and Immediately If Possible.*   The best kind of feedback is given continually as we perform. This goal is not usually possible in classrooms, except with the help of recent computer programs, but feedback in a frequent and timely fashion is much better than only getting it after the performance is completed. When Ryann does gymnastics, her coach gives her feedback on how well she is performing as she does her routine, not just after she has finished ("straighten your legs, point your toes, lift your chin, smile"). It is more difficult for students to change what was learned than it is for them to adjust their current behavior or when learning something for the first time. Consequently, you will not want to have long periods of teaching and learning time without feedback. This is one reason why frequent testing is recommended, even though testing by itself does not assure adequate feedback. Of course, this assumes that tests are returned promptly, which they certainly should be, if you want to use the results as feedback to improve learning.

You will provide more frequent, immediate feedback if you (1) develop or select activities with built-in opportunities for feedback; (2) circulate to monitor individual work, making comments to students; (3) provide exemplars and directions to students so they can self-assess; (4) use examples of ongoing student work to show all students mistakes and corrections; and (5) use techniques during recitation to monitor the progress of all students. The last suggestion can be achieved by having students complete practice exercises individually, then giving the answer, and ask for a show of hands of those answering correctly. At the elementary level you can ask students to close their eyes and raise their hands if they got the answer correct or if a particular choice was correct; for example, "Close your eyes. If you think A was correct, raise your hand."

5. *Give Specific and Descriptive Feedback.*   It is important to be as specific and descriptive as possible when giving feedback. If the feedback is vague or general it will not be helpful to the student; it will only communicate a sense of whether the performance was good or bad. If feedback is comparative rather than descriptive, there is little to gain by it. For example, saying to a student "You did better than most students in the class" is comparative, and as feedback it indicates nothing about what was correct or incorrect, or how the student can improve. A descriptive statement specifies in exact terms the nature of the performance; for example, "Your speech was delivered too quickly. It will help you to pronounce each word more slowly and to pause between each sentence" or "I really liked the way you read your story this morning. You pronounced the words very clearly and spoke enthusiastically." How often have you received feedback like "good work," "nice job" "excellent," "awkward," and "ok"? What did these vague messages mean? Feedback like this provides very little that is helpful.

Research shows that middle and high school students find written teacher comments on assignments and papers most helpful when the comments provide constructive criticism. This suggests that you should make specific, descriptive comments on errors or incorrect strategies, and that you should balance this criticism with comments about progress and positive aspects of the student's work.

6. *Focus Feedback on Key Errors.*   It is not very practical to provide detailed and specific feedback to every student on homework and other assignments. You will need to make some choices about what to focus on, and it is best to determine what the most significant error is or what changes will be most helpful to the student. For example, it is relatively easy to comment on misspellings and grammatical errors on student papers, but is this the most important aspect of the paper the student needs feedback about? A study of sixth-grade teachers demonstrated that feedback can be improved dramatically when teachers use four questions as a guide (Elawar & Corno, 1985, p. 166). The first question helps the teacher focus on significant errors; the remaining questions summarize, in a different way, the other characteristics of effective feedback:

a. What is the key error?
b. What is the probable reason the student made this error?
c. How can I guide the student to avoid this error in the future?
d. What did the student do well that I could note?

Characteristics of Effective Praise

Most teachers use praise ubiquitously in the classroom. It can be thought of as a type of feedback to the student, but it is also used frequently to control student behavior and for classroom management. In general, research shows that teachers use too much praise and use it inappropriately as positive reinforcement (Good & Brophy, 1994).

Like effective feedback, praise can be helpful to students if it draws attention to student progress and performance in relation to standards. It is also a good type of message to accompany other types of feedback. This is especially true when the praise focuses on student effort and other internal attributions so that students know that their efforts are recognized, appreciated, and connected to their performance.

Praise is most effective when it is delivered as a spontaneous but accurate message, giving the teacher's genuine reaction to student performance, and when it includes a specific description of the skill or behavior that is commended. You should praise students simply and directly, in natural language, without gushy or dramatic words. A straightforward, declarative sentence is best. For example, say: "Good; you did a wonderful job of drawing the vase; your lines are clear and the perspective is correct," not "Incredible!" or "Wow!" Try to be specific about what you are praising, and include your recognition of the student's effort. For example, say "This is an excellent job of paraphrasing the story. It is well organized and you have captured each of the major elements of the story. I like the way you kept at this assignment and worked hard to provide the detail you did." Call attention to progress and evidence of new skills. For instance, say "I notice that you have learned to move sentences around with the blocking feature on your computer. Keep learning new ways to improve your computer and writing skills."

Try to use as many different phrases as you can when praising. If you say the same thing over and over it may be perceived as insincere with little serious attention to the performance. This is especially true if the phrase is a vague generality like "good" or "nice job." It is also best to keep your verbal praise consistent with your nonverbal behavior. Students pick up very quickly and accurately teachers' nonverbal messages. So if the performance really is good, and progress is demonstrated, say your praise with a smile, using a voice tone and inflection that communicates warmth and sincerity.

Additional useful guidelines for effective praise are given in Figure 5.7.

FIGURE 5.7   Guidelines for Effective Praise

Effective Praise	Ineffective Praise
1. Is delivered contingently	1. Is delivered randomly or unsystematically
2. Specifies the particulars of the accomplishment	2. Is confined to global reactions
3. Shows spontaneity, variety, and other signs of credibility; suggests clear attention to the student's accomplishment	3. Shows a bland uniformity that suggests a conditioned response made with minimal attention
4. Rewards attainment of specified performance criteria (which can include effort criteria, however)	4. Rewards mere participation, without consideration of performance processes or outcomes
5. Provides information to students about their competence or the value of the accomplishments	5. Provides no information at all or gives students little information about their status
6. Orients students toward better appreciation of their own task-related behavior and thinking about problem solving	6. Orients students toward comparing themselves with others and thinking about competing
7. Uses student's own prior accomplishments	7. Uses the accomplishments of peers as the context for describing student's present accomplishment
8. Is given in recognition of noteworthy effort or success at difficult (for this student) tasks	8. Is given without regard to the effort expended or the meaning of the accomplishment
9. Attributes success to effort and ability, implying that similar success can be expected in the future	9. Attributes success to ability alone or to external factors such as luck or task difficulty (easy)
10. Fosters endogenous attributions (students believe that they expend effort on the task because they enjoy the task or want to develop task-relevant skills)	10. Fosters exogenous attributions (students believe that they expend effort on the task for external reasons, e.g., to please the teacher, win a competition or reward, etc.)
11. Focuses students' attention on their own task-relevant behavior	11. Focuses students' attention on the teacher as an external authority figure who is manipulating them
12. Fosters appreciation of, and desirable attributions about task relevant behavior after the process is completed	12. Intrudes into the ongoing process, distracting attention from task-relevant behavior

Source: Brophy, J. (1981). Teacher praise: A functional analysis. *Review of Educational Research, 51,* p. 26. Copyright © 1981 by the American Educational Research Association. Reprinted by permission of the publisher.

SUMMARY

This chapter focused on what you can do to improve instruction by obtaining appropriate information from students as they learn. Key points in the chapter include the following:

- Assessing student progress consists of a teacher monitoring students and their academic performances to inform instructional decision making and the nature of feedback given to students.
- Formative assessment provides ongoing feedback from students to teachers and from teachers to students; summative assessment measures student learning at the end of a unit of instruction.
- Informal observation includes the teacher "reading" nonverbal behavior such as facial expressions, eye contact, body language, and vocal cues. These behaviors indicate student emotions, dispositions, and attitudes.
- Emotion is communicated best through facial expression. Eye contact is key to assessing attentiveness, confidence, and interest.
- Body language includes emblems, illustrators, affect displays, regulators, adapters, body movement, and posture.
- Voice-related cues such as pitch, loudness, rate, and pauses indicate confidence and emotions.
- Errors in informal observation are often associated with when the observations are made, sampling of student behavior, and teacher bias.
- Teachers use questions to involve students, promote thinking, review, control students, and assess student progress. Effective questions are clear, matched with learning targets, and involve the entire class. Allow sufficient wait time for student responses. Avoid yes/no, tugging, guessing, and leading questions, and keep questions in the proper sequence.
- Effective feedback relates performance to standards, progress, and corrective procedures. It is given frequently and immediately, and it focuses specifically and descriptively on key errors.
- Effective praise is sincere, spontaneous, natural, accurate, varied, and straightforward. It focuses on progress, internal attributions, specific behaviors, and corrective actions.

SELF-INSTRUCTIONAL REVIEW EXERCISES

1. To sharpen your interpretation of facial expressions, match the following pictures to the ten emotions listed in the chapter from Figure 5.2 on page 110.

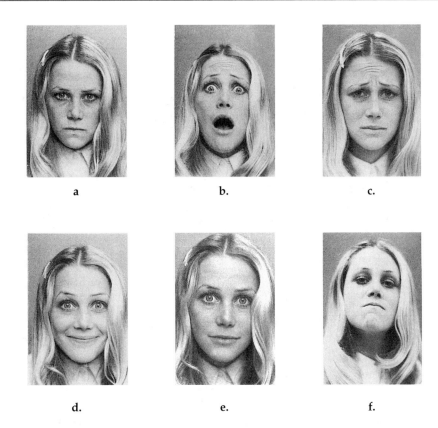

a   b.   c.

d.   e.   f.

2. Identify each of the following examples of body language as an emblem (E), illustrator (I), affect display (AD), regulator (R), or adapter (A).

   a. Student leans toward you and raises both hands immediately after you ask a question.
   b. Student points to the pencil sharpener as if to ask, "May I sharpen my pencil?"
   c. It seems that Johnny is always chewing on the end of his pencil.
   d. You notice that Ken is picking at his cuticles.
   e. Mary is sitting upright in her chair, arms on desk, chin up, with an expectant expression on her face.
   f. Sam uses his hands to show how large the fish was.

3. Match the messages most likely to be conveyed with the descriptions provided. Each message may be used once, not at all, or more than once.

_____ **(1)** Pauses when speaking; eyes downcast   **A.** Confident

_____ **(2)** Eyebrows uplifted; speaks fast; raises hand   **B.** Nervous

_____ **(3)** Looks around room; slumped in chair with   **C.** Angry
head resting in one hand

_____ **(4)** Direct eye contact; speaks clearly with few   **D.** Defensive
pauses; uses variety in tone

_____ **(5)** Enlarged pupils; chin up; arms open   **E.** Bored

_____ **(6)** Taps pencil; rigid body; pupils contracted   **F.** Frustrated

_____ **(7)** Loud; eyebrows lowered; hands make fists   **G.** Happy

_____ **(8)** Arms and legs crossed; leans away   **H.** Interested

4. Mr. Bush had observed Trent over the past few days carefully because he was concerned that Trent would revert to his old pattern of cheating by looking at others' papers. What observation error is Mr. Bush most susceptible to, and why?

5. Mrs. Greene saw Renee staring out the window, obviously not concentrating on her work. Since Renee is a good student and this is not very typical of her, Mrs. Greene ignores the behavior. What type of observation error was Mrs. Greene careful *not* to make in this situation? What error is possible in her interpretation?

6. Why is it important to match the type of question you ask students in class with your learning targets?

7. How would a teacher preface a question to make sure students took sufficient time to think about the answer before responding?

8. What type of question—convergent or divergent—would be best to determine if students knew how to find the area of a rectangle?

9. Evaluate each of the following forms of feedback on the basis of the six characteristics in the chapter and in Figure 5.7 on page 127.

   a. "Lanette, that was a great job you did yesterday!"
   b. "Jeff, your writing is improving. Your *b*s are much better because you are making a straighter line and not a loop."
   c. "Robert, you have a good report. Your grammar is excellent, although you have some problems with sentence structure. The conclusion is incomplete. Work harder on providing more detail."

10. Indicate whether each of the following is characteristic of effective praise (EP) or ineffective praise (IP). If ineffective, indicate why.

   a. "Sally, you did the best in the class!"
   b. "Jon, I can see by your work that you are really good in math."
   c. "This shows that you did the report well because you worked hard and because you are a good writer."

    d. "Good work, this time you doubled the length and width before adding them to find the perimeter of the rectangle."

    e. "You typed thirty-five words a minute with seven mistakes. This was among the best in the class."

ANSWERS TO SELF-INSTRUCTIONAL REVIEW EXERCISES

1. a. anger, b. fear, c. sadness, d. happiness, e. interest, f. determination.

2. a. R, b. E, c. A, d. A, e. AD, f. I.

3. (1) F, (2) H, (3) E, (4) A, (5) A, (6) B, (7) C, (8) D.

4. Mr. Bush is using previous behavior to motivate his informal observations, so his initial impressions may distort what he finds (primacy effect). He may also have a preconceived idea about what Trent would do (observer bias).

5. At least Mrs. Greene did not commit the error of unrepresentative sampling, since this was not a common occurrence. However, her interpretation that Renee was not thinking about her lesson may not be accurate. If this type of behavior became frequent and extensive, Mrs. Greene would want to ask Renee to get her perspective.

6. Matching questions with targets (1) helps to clarify to students what is important, (2) allows you to check student understanding of targets, (3) reinforces learning, and (4) balances emphasis given to each target.

7. The easiest way is the most direct—simply tell the students to wait a certain number of seconds before answering (e.g., fifteen or thirty seconds). You can also ask them to write their answer, then think about it, before responding orally.

8. Convergent; only one or two possible ways are correct.

9. a. Poor in almost all respects. Feedback is not specific or descriptive, it is not related to standards, nor does it focus on key errors. It is not given immediately, and no corrective actions are suggested.
b. This is pretty good feedback as praise. It is specific, descriptive, and focuses on improvement. However, it might be better to include areas to improve as well.
c. This feedback seems okay at first; you may well have received something like this many times. But when you look closely at what is said, the feedback is weak. The teacher does not indicate how Robert can improve nor does the teacher identify Robert's specific mistakes or problems in either sentence structure, conclusion, or providing detail. The teacher has indicated there is "improvement," but this is not a clear indication of progress. The teacher also does not say how Robert can improve his difficulties, only that he has them.

10. a. IP; too general, compares performance only to others.
b. IP; too general, and attributes success only to ability.
c. EP; although general, still attributes success to both effort and ability (internal factors).
d. EP; specific, shows progress.
e. Both EP and IP; on the one hand the praise is specific, but on the other hand success is indicated by comparison to others.

SUGGESTIONS FOR ACTION RESEARCH

1. While in a classroom, informally observe students' nonverbal behavior. It would be best if another observer could also sit in on the class so that you could compare notes. Take a sheet of paper and draw a line down the middle. On the left-hand side, record a description of the nonverbal behavior—such as a facial expression, body language, or vocal cue—and on the right side, summarize your interpretation of each one. It would be interesting to check these out with the teacher for accuracy.

2. Ask a teacher about the kinds of questions he or she asks, and what kinds of student responses are typical. Compare the teacher's comments to the suggestions for effective questioning presented in Figure 5.6 on page 123. If possible, observe the teacher and record examples of effective and ineffective questioning.

3. Ask a group of students about the kind of feedback they get from teachers. Ask questions about how the feedback affects them.

4. Observe how teachers in two or three different classrooms use praise. What kind of praise is given by each teacher? What is the effect of the praise on the students? How could the praise you observe be improved?

6

ASSESSING KNOWLEDGE: OBJECTIVE ITEMS

You have taught your students, using assessment to inform your instructional decision making. Now you need to see how much your students have really learned and if there are patterns of errors that require additional instruction. It's time for the weekly, unit, chapter, or semester test or quiz. These are summative assessments, *formal*, or *official* ones, that all of us have had to take to demonstrate how much we

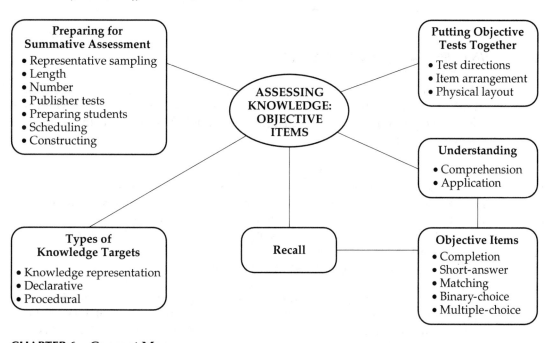

CHAPTER 6   Concept Map

knew about specified subject matter or other information, or to exhibit what skills we have acquired. You will use these assessments to decide how much students have learned. Thus, results of these assessments have important consequences for students because they affect grades, placement in special classes or groups, and conferring of honors.

In this chapter and the next three, we will see how different learning targets can be conceptualized and how appropriate assessment methods can be used to measure each type of learning. The logic here is that *the nature of the learning target is what should determine which assessment method is used.* That is why chapter titles refer to type of target as well as type of assessment. As was pointed out in Chapter 3 (Figure 3.2 on page 50), some assessment methods measure certain targets better than others. Your job is to first refine your learning targets, select the most appropriate type of assessment, prepare the assessment so that it will meet the criteria of high quality, administer it, then score and interpret the results.

Knowledge learning targets are the ones most commonly assessed in tests and quizzes given after instruction. As you can probably attest to from your own experience, most tests require students to remember facts, definitions, concepts, places, and so on, usually by either recall or recognition. Some tests go beyond simple memorization and assess understanding. In this chapter, we will examine different types of knowledge targets and the objective assessment methods that do the best job of measuring them. In subsequent chapters, we will examine reasoning, skills and products, and affect targets, which for the most part are best measured with different assessment methods. We will begin, though, with some important considerations for preparing for any type of summative assessment.

PREPARING FOR ASSESSMENT AFTER INSTRUCTION

As you think about how to construct the summative assessment, a number of preliminary steps will be helpful. The first step is to review what you think you want to do in light of the criteria for ensuring high-quality assessments that were presented in Chapter 3:

1. Do I have clear and appropriate learning targets?
2. What method of assessment will match best with the targets?
3. Will I have good evidence that the inferences from the assessments will be valid?
4. How can I construct an assessment that will minimize error?
5. Will my assessment be fair and unbiased? Have students had the opportunity to learn what is being assessed?
6. Will the assessment be practical and efficient?

There are additional considerations when setting out to construct summative assessments, including how you will obtain a representative sample of what has been learned, the length and number of assessments, whether you should use tests provided by publishers, how students should be prepared for the assessment, when the assessment should be scheduled, and when you should construct the assessment.

Representative Sampling

Most assessments *sample* what students have learned. It is rare, except for quizzes over short lessons, that you will assess everything that is included in your learning targets. There simply is not enough time to assess each fact or skill. Rather, you will select a sample of what students should know and then assume that the way they respond to assessments of this sample is typical of how they would respond to additional assessments of the entire unit. If you do a good job with this, your inference about what students know about the unit will be valid.

As pointed out in Chapter 3, an important step in representative sampling is preparing a test blueprint or outline. This set of specifications is helpful because it indicates what students are responsible for learning. When assessment items are based on this outline, there is a greater likelihood that the sampling will be reasonable. You will literally be able to look at the blueprint to see how the sampling came out. Without a test blueprint or some type of outline of content there is a tendency to oversample areas that you particularly like, those that were covered most recently, and to overload the assessment with a disproportionately large number of questions about simple facts (mainly because these questions are much easier to write).

Another consideration when preparing a representative sampling is to construct or select the appropriate number of items for the assessment. Suppose you are preparing a test for a six-week social studies unit on early civilizations, and you want to assess how much knowledge the students retained. How many items will be needed? Thirty? Sixty? Eighty? In the absence of any hard and fast rules, a couple rules of thumb will help determine how many items are sufficient. First, a minimum of ten items is needed to assess each knowledge learning target that encompasses the unit. Thus, if one learning target is that "students will identify the location of twenty-five ancient cities on a map," preparing a test that asks them to identify ten of the twenty-five would be reasonable. Which ten, you may be thinking? You can select randomly if all the cities are equally difficult to locate. Normally, however, your sampling will be purposeful so that a good cross section of difficulty would be selected (in this case, different types of cities).

With more specific learning targets, as few as five items can provide a good assessment. For example, you can get a pretty good idea if a student knows how to multiply three-digit numbers from five questions that require students to supply answers. When reasoning, performance, and other skills are being assessed, we are usually confined to one or just a few items because they take so much time. You need to be careful in these instances that the item is appropriate and that other criteria for high-quality assessment are met.

Length and Number of Assessments

Knowing how many items or questions are needed, you must then decide how many separate assessments will be given and then the length of each one. This decision will depend on several factors, including the age of the students, the length of classes, and the types of questions. One rule of thumb, though, is that the time allocated for assessment is sufficient for all students to answer all the questions. We generally do not want to use *speeded* tests in school when it is important to obtain a fair assessment of what students know and can do. This is because speeded tests, which require students to answer as quickly as possible to obtain a high score, increase the probability of other factors, such as anxiety and test-taking skills, to influence the result.

There is an obvious relationship between the number and length of assessments. Many short assessments can provide the same, if not better, information than a single long assessment. It will help you to focus on length first without regard to the number of assessments. This will indicate what is needed for a high-quality assessment. Then you can decide whether what is needed is best given in one large block of time, three smaller tests, weekly assessments, or whatever other considerations suggest is best. If you wait until the end of a unit to begin constructing your assessment, you may find that there is insufficient time to administer an assessment that meets other high-quality criteria. What typically happens in this situation is that content-related evidence for validity is weakened because the sampling is not adequate.

The age of students and the related length of classes are other important considerations. Kindergarten and first-grade students have very short attention spans, so summative assessments will usually last only five to ten minutes. Attention spans and stamina increase with age, but it is still best to use many short assessments rather than one or two long ones for elementary students. Thus, in later elementary grades, summative assessments typically should last between fifteen and thirty minutes.

Ironically, when students are old enough to have longer attention spans they are in middle or high schools where the length of the class usually determines the maximum length of the assessment. Consequently, most teachers plan unit and other summative assessments to last one class period, approximately forty-five minutes. In this situation, you need to provide time for directions and student questions so you have to be careful not to end up with a speeded test. With block scheduling and other innovations more time is now available for assessment, but you will need to decide how much time is too much during a single day.

Another important influence on the length of time it takes students to complete an assessment is the type of item used. Obviously, essay items require much more time to complete than objective items. It also takes students longer to complete short-answer items than multiple-choice or true/false questions. The nature of the subject is also important. For example, in a test of simple knowledge in a content area, students can generally answer as many as two to four items per minute. For more difficult objective items, one per minute is a general rule of thumb. In math, students may need as long as three or four minutes for each item. Experience will be your best guide. Initially, try some assessments that are short so you can get an idea of how long it takes students to complete each item. Using practice questions will also give you an idea about the number of items that would be reasonable in a unit test. The best practice is to give your students too much time rather than too little time to complete the assessment.

Use of Assessments Provided by Publishers

You will receive ready-made tests from textbook and instructional packages that can be used for summative assessments. These tests are prepared by the publisher for chapters and units. Some of these tests are adequate and may be useful if you remember a few key points. First, you can't assume that just because a test is provided that it is reliable or that the results will be valid. You will need to review the test carefully to make sure that fundamental principles of good assessment are followed. Second, a decision to use *any* type of assessment—whether provided in instructor's materials, by other teachers, or by yourself—is always made *after* you have identified the learning targets that you will assess. The prepared test may be technically sound, but if there is not a good match between what it tests and what you need tested, it should not be used in its entirety. For example, many publisher's tests asses a range of skills rather than those covered by the unit. Also, because these tests are often prepared by someone other than the textbook author(s), it is relatively easy to stress some sections too much and hardly cover others. Third, check the test carefully to make sure the language and terminology are appropriate for your students. The author of the test may use language that is not consistent with the text or the way you have taught the material. The vocabulary and sentence complexity may not be at the right level for your students. Fourth, the number of items for each target needs to be sufficient to provide a reliable measure.

The obvious advantage of using these tests is that they can save you a great deal of time, especially when the test is provided in a format that can be easily copied. Feel free, however, to use only part of the prepared test or to modify individual questions as appropriate. Often the best use of the textbook test is to get ideas that provide a good starting point for you to prepare your own test. It is rare that publisher's tests would be appropriate without some modification.

Preparing Students for Summative Assessments

Your objective in summative assessment is to obtain a fair and accurate indication of student learning. This means that you need to take some simple, yet often neglected, steps to prepare your students so that they will be able to demonstrate what they know and can do (see Figure 6.1).

The first step is to make sure that all your students have adequate test-taking skills, such as paying attention to directions, reading each item in its entirety before answering it, planning and outlining responses to essay questions, and pacing themselves while answering the questions (as one teacher told me, "When I first

FIGURE 6.1   Preparing Students for Summative Assessments

- Teach test-taking skills.
- Familiarize students with test length, format, and types of questions.
- Teach to the test (do not teach *the* test).
- Review prior to the test.
- Tell students when the test is scheduled.

gave math tests students would include the item number with the problem; for example, if item 2 was 3 + 4, they would answer 9—incorrect answer but they knew how to add!"). Students should be directed to answer all questions (guessing is rarely penalized in classroom tests, though you don't want to encourage mindless guessing). If there is a separate sheet for recording responses, teach students to check the accuracy of their answers.

A second step is make sure students are familiar with the format and type of question and response that will be needed on the test. This is accomplished by giving students practice test items. If time is available, it is very instructive to have students practice writing test items themselves. This is good for review sessions. Familiarity with the type of question will lessen test anxiety. Of course, you don't want to teach the test—that is, use examples in class that are identical to the test items—or give students practice on the test items before they take the test. It's fine to teach *to* the test, in the sense that you want to instruct students on what they will eventually be tested. It's also helpful to students if they know the length of the test and how much the test will count in their grade.

A review of the unit or chapter learning targets is both fair and helpful. There are several purposes for the review: to reacquaint students with material taught early in the unit, to allow students an opportunity to ask questions for clarification, to reemphasize the important knowledge and skills that students should focus on, and to provide an opportunity for students to check their understanding of what will be tested.

Finally, you will want to tell students, as soon as possible after beginning the unit, when the test is scheduled. This gives students an adequate period of time to prepare for the test. Can you remember when a teacher announced for the first time that "we will have a test tomorrow"? The lack of time to prepare and review for the test contribute to student anxiety and lessens the validity of the results.

Scheduling the Assessment

To give students the best opportunity to show what they have learned you need to be careful when scheduling the test. Try to avoid giving a test on days that make it difficult for students to perform to their capability (e.g., homecoming, right after spring vacation, or after a pep rally). Also, try to schedule the test when you know you will be present, not when the class has a substitute.

When Summative Assessments Should Be Constructed

Summative assessments need to be planned and put together well in advance of the scheduled testing date. A good procedure is to construct a general outline of the test based on your learning targets and a table of specifications. This would not include the development or selection of specific items, but it provides enough information to guide you in instruction. As the unit proceeds, you can make decisions about the format of the test and begin to construct individual items. The final form of the test should be prepared no later than the review session. How else will you be able to provide a good review and inform students about what to expect on the test? But don't try to finalize the test too soon. You will find that as you teach, your learning targets will most likely change somewhat, or the emphasis you place on certain topics is not as you planned. These expected instructional variations should be reflected in the test. Consequently, you want to allow the test and instruction to influence each other while teaching the content or skills.

With this summary of considerations for preparing any type of summative assessment, we now turn to knowledge targets and objective items.

TYPES OF KNOWLEDGE TARGETS

The simple phrase "what students should know" is used frequently as a concept for inclusion of important learning outcomes and standards. But this phrase is also pretty vague. We need to be much more specific about what is meant by "know" and "knowledge." Once this is accomplished, appropriate assessment methods can be selected that will foster as well as measure the type of learning that is desired.

Knowledge Representation

Until recently, Bloom's taxonomy provided a definition of *knowledge* for many educators. In this scheme, knowledge is the first, and "lowest," level of categories in the cognitive domain, in which knowledge is defined as remembering something. All that is required is that the student recall or recognize facts, definitions, terms, concepts, procedures, principles, or other information.

The contemporary view of knowledge is that remembering is only part of what occurs when students learn. You also need to think about how the knowledge is represented in the mind of the student. *Knowledge representation* is how information is constructed and stored in long-term and working memory (Gagne, Yekovich, & Yekovich, 1993). There are different types of knowledge representations. We will examine two that have direct application to assessment: declarative and procedural.

Declarative Knowledge

Declarative knowledge is information that is retained about something, knowing that it exists. The nature of the information learned can be ordered hierarchically, depending on the level of generality and understanding that is demonstrated (Marzano, Pickering, & McTighe, 1993) and the way the knowledge is represented. At the "lowest" level, declarative knowledge is similar to Bloom's first level— remembering or recognizing specific facts about persons, places, events, or content in a subject area. The knowledge is represented by simple association or discrimination, such as rote memory. At the highest level, declarative knowledge consists of concepts, ideas, and generalizations that are more fully understood and applied. This type of knowledge involves understanding in the form of comprehension or application, the next two levels in Bloom's taxonomy. Thus, for our purposes here, declarative knowledge can exist as recall or understanding, depending on the intent of the instruction and how the information is learned. Assessments of declarative knowledge will likewise measure recall or understanding.

The nature of the representation moves from rote memorization and association of facts to generalized understanding and usage. This is a critical distinction for both learning and assessment. As pointed out in Chapter 1, constructivist views contend that students learn most effectively when they connect new information meaningfully to an existing network of knowledge.

Constructivists believe that new knowledge is acquired through a process of seeing how something relates, makes sense, and can be used in reasoning. This notion is quite different from memorized learning that can be demonstrated for a test. Although I don't want to suggest that some rote memorization is not appropriate for students, I do want to point out that your learning targets can focus on recall or understanding types of declarative knowledge, and that your choice of assessment method and test items will be different for each of these.

Let's look at some examples of declarative knowledge. One of the most important types of information students learn about is geometric shapes. Each shape is a concept (mental structures that use physical characteristics or definitions to classify objects, events, or other things into categories). If students learn the concept of "rectangle" at the level of *recall*, then they simply memorize a definition or identify rectangles from a set of different shapes that look like the ones they studied in class. If students *understand* the concept of rectangle, however, they will be able to give original examples and identify rectangles of different sizes, shapes, and colors they have never seen before. Each of these levels of learning is "knowing something," but the latter is much closer to true student mastery and what constructivists advocate. Also, because these levels are hierarchical, understanding requires recall. Thus, it may be better to state learning targets that require understanding but teach and test for recall as well because one is a prerequisite to the other.

Procedural Knowledge

Procedural knowledge is knowing how to do something. It is knowledge that is needed for carrying out an action or solving a problem. What is demonstrated is knowledge of the strategies, procedures and skills students must engage in; for example, how to tie shoes, how to divide fractions, how to check out library books. Like declarative knowledge, procedural knowledge can be demonstrated at different levels. At the level of recall, students simply identify or repeat the needed steps. Understanding is indicated as students explain in their own words (comprehension) and actually use the steps in executing a solution (application).

Definitions of the two major types of knowledge are presented in Figure 6.2; examples are provided in Figure 6.3. These learning target categories will be used to present examples of test items throughout the remainder of the chapter. The most effective methods of assessing knowledge are conveniently grouped into measuring recall or understanding.We will now consider how different types of objective items can be used to assess the various knowledge targets, beginning with recall knowledge.

FIGURE 6.2 **Definitions of the Levels of Declarative and Procedural Knowledge**

Level	Declarative Knowledge	Procedural Knowledge
Recall	Restates, defines, identifies, names, reproduces, or selects *specific facts, concepts, principles, rules, or theories.*	Restates, defines, identifies, names, reproduces, or selects *correct procedure, steps, skills, or strategies.*
Understanding: *Comprehension*	Converts, translates, distinguishes, explains, provides examples, summarizes, interprets, infers, or predicts, in own words, *essential meanings of concepts and principles.*	Converts, translates, distinguishes, explains, provides examples, summarizes, interprets, infers, or predicts, in own words, *correct procedure, steps, skills, or strategies.*
Understanding: *Application*	Uses existing knowledge of concepts, principles, and theories, in new situations, to solve problems, interpret information, and construct responses.	Uses existing knowledge of correct procedures, steps, skills, or strategies, in new situations, to solve problems, interpret information, and construct responses.

FIGURE 6.3 **Examples of Declarative and Procedural Knowledge**

Declarative Knowledge

Recall	Is able to define the word "democracy."
Understanding (comprehension)	Is able to give three examples of countries with democracies.
Understanding (application)	Is able to determine whether a new country has a democracy by its description.

Procedural Knowledge

Recall	Is able to identify, in correct order, steps in the scientific method.
Understanding (comprehension)	Is able to explain if a set of procedures follows the scientific method.
Understanding (application)	Is able to demonstrate in writing the correct use of the scientific method to solve a novel problem.

ASSESSING RECALL KNOWLEDGE

Both declarative and procedural recall knowledge are best assessed with objective tests. This section presents suggestions for using these types of items and tests, along with examples. You will determine which of these objective methods to use based on their strengths and weaknesses in relation to your teaching situation and personal likes and dislikes. You need to be comfortable with whatever method you use, and this consideration is probably more important than other factors such as ease of construction and scoring. The suggestions for writing each type of item are applicable to assessing understanding and reasoning as well.

Completion and Short-Answer Items

The most common and effective way to assess recall knowledge is simply to ask a question and require the students to answer it from memory. These types of questions are called *constructed-response* (or *supply*) items, because students provide their answers. Supply items in which the student responds to an incomplete statement are *completion items*; a brief response to a question is a *short-answer item*.

Completion Items

The completion item offers the least freedom of student response, calling for one answer for each blank in a sentence. Responses may be in the form of words, numbers, or symbols. If properly constructed, completion items are excellent for measuring how well students can recall facts due to the following strengths: (1) they are easy to construct, (2) their short response time allows a good sampling of different facts, (3) guessing contributes little to error, (4) scorer reliability is high, (5) they can be scored more quickly than short-answer or essay items, and (6) they provide more valid results than a test with an equal number of selected-response items (e.g., multiple-choice). There are only two limitations of using completion items to measure recall. The first is in the scoring. It takes more time to score completion items than selected-response items, and if the sentence is not well written more than one answer may be possible. A second limitation is that younger students may be confused by completion items.

The following suggestions for constructing completion items use examples that measure either declarative or procedural recall knowledge. The suggestions are summarized in the form of a checklist in Figure 6.4.

1. Paraphrase Sentences from Textbooks and Other Instructional Materials. It is tempting to lift a sentence verbatim from materials the students have studied, and replace a word or two with blanks. However, statements in textbooks, when taken out of context, are often too vague or general to be good completion items. Also, you don't want to encourage students to memorize phraseology in the text.

FIGURE 6.4   Checklist for Writing Completion Items

1. Is verbatim language from instructional materials avoided?
2. Is recall knowledge being assessed?
3. Is a single, brief answer required?
4. Is the blank at the end of the sentence?
5. Is the length of each blank the same?
6. Is the precision of a numerical answer specified?
7. Is it worded to avoid verbal clues to the right answer?

Consistent with constructivistic principles, you want students to connect what they learn with what they already know, even when it is recall. Thus, you want to paraphrase or restate facts in words that are different from those students have read.

Examples

The textbook statement is "James Buchanan, elected president in 1856, personally opposed slavery."

> *Poor:* James Buchanan, elected president in 1856, personally opposed _____ .
>
> *Improved:* The name of the president who was elected in 1856, and who thought slavery was unacceptable, was _____ .

2. Word the Sentence So That Only One Brief Answer Is Correct.   The single greatest error in writing completion items is to use sentences that can be legitimately completed by more than one response. This occurs if the sentence is too vague or open-ended.

Examples

> *Poor:* Columbus first landed on America _____ .
> *Improved:* Columbus first landed on America in _____ .
> *Better:* Columbus first landed on America in the year _____ .

In the first example students could logically provide correct answers having nothing to do with the year. In the improved version an answer like "a boat" would be correct.

3. Place One or Two Blanks at the End of the Sentence.   If blanks are placed at the beginning or in the middle of the sentence, it may be more difficult for students to understand what response is called for. It is easier and more direct to first read the sentence and then determine what will complete it correctly. (That's why it's called a *completion* item!)

Examples

> *Poor:* In 1945, _____ decided to have the atomic bomb dropped on Japan.
> *Improved:* The name of the president who decided to have the atomic bomb dropped on Japan in 1945 was _____ .

You also will not want to use several blanks in a single sentence. This will confuse students and measure reasoning skills as much, if not more, than recall.

Example

> *Poor:* The name of the _____ who decided to have the _____ _____ dropped on _____ in 1945 was _____ .

4. If Answered in Numerical Units, Specify the Unit Required.   For completion items that require numerical answers, the specific units or the degree of precision should be indicated.

Examples

> *Poor:* The distance between the moon and the earth is _____ .
> *Improved:* The distance between the moon and the earth is _____ miles.

5. Do Not Include Clues to the Correct Answer.   Test-wise students will look for clues in the way sentences are worded and the length of blanks that may indicate a correct answer. The most common wording errors are using single or plural verbs and wording the sentence so that the blank is preceded by "a" or "an." These clues can be eliminated by avoiding verb agreement with the answer, by using "a(an)," and by making all blanks the same length.

Examples

> *Poor:* The two legislative branches of the United States federal government are
>   the _____ and the _____ _____ _____ .
> *Improved:* The two legislative branches of the United States federal government are the _____ and the _____ .

Short-Answer Items

Short-answer items, in which the student supplies an answer consisting of one word, a few words, or a sentence or two, are generally preferred to completion items for assessing recall targets. First, this type of item is similar to how teachers phrase questions and direct student behavior during instruction. This means that the item is more natural for students. Students are familiar with answering questions and providing responses to commands that require recall (e.g., "Write the definition of each of the words on the board"). Second, it is easier to write these items to more accurately measure knowledge. Typically, teachers make fewer errors when writing short-answer items than they do when writing completion items.

Short-answer items are usually stated in the form of a question (e.g., "Which state is surrounded by three large bodies of fresh water?"). They can also be stated in general directions (e.g., "Define each of following terms"), and they can require responses to visual stimulus materials (e.g, "Name each of the countries identified with arrows A–D").

Like completion items, short-answer items are good for measuring recall knowledge because it is possible to focus on a specific fact, students can respond to many items quickly, a good sample of knowledge is obtained, guessing is avoided, scoring is objective, and results are generally more valid than what is obtained from selected-response formats. Also, like completion items, the disadvantages are primarily in the scoring. Figure 6.5 summarizes the following suggestions in a checklist format.

FIGURE 6.5   Checklist for Writing Short-Answer Items

1. Is only one answer correct?
2. Is it clear to students that the required answer is brief?
3. Are questions from textbooks avoided?
4. Is the precision of a numerical answer specified?
5. Is the item written as succinctly as possible?
6. Is the space designated for answers consistent with the length required?
7. Are words used in the item too difficult for any students?

1. State the Item So That Only One Answer Is Correct.   Be sure that the question or directions are stated so that what is required in the answer is clear to students. If more than one answer is correct, the item is vague and the result is invalid. If you are expecting a one word answer, use a single, short blank.

Examples

> *Poor:* Where is the Eiffel Tower located?
> *Improved:* In what country is the Eiffel Tower located? *or* Name the country in which the Eiffel Tower is located.

Obviously in the first item students could give several responses—Europe, Paris, France—each of which would be technically correct.

2. State the Item So That the Required Answer Is Brief.   Remember that short-answer items have answers that are short! Keep student responses to a word or two, or a short sentence or two if necessary, by properly wording the item, offering clear directions, and providing space or blanks that indicate the length of the response. In the directions, state clearly that students should not repeat the question in their answer.

Examples

> *Poor:* What does the term *reptile* mean? _____
> _____
>
> *Improved:* Name three characteristics of reptiles.
>
> 1. _____
> 2. _____
> 3. _____

3. Do Not Use Questions Verbatim from Textbooks or Other Instructional Materials.   Most textbooks include review questions and questions for study. You don't want to use these same questions on tests because it encourages rote memorization of answers.

4. Designate Units Required for the Answer.   Students need to know the specific units and the degree of precision that should be used in their answer. This will avoid the time students may take to try to figure out what is wanted—such as asking a question for clarification during the test—and it will mitigate scoring difficulties.

Examples

> *Poor:* When was president John F. Kennedy killed?
> *Improved:* In what year was president John F. Kennedy killed?

5. State the Item Succinctly with Words Students Understand.   It is best to state questions or sentences as concisely as possible, and to avoid using words or phrases that may be difficult for some students to understand.

Examples

> *Poor:* What was the name of the extraordinary president of the United States who earlier had used his extensive military skills in a protracted war with exemplary soldiers from another country?
> *Improved:* What United States general defeated the British and later became president?

Matching Items

Matching is one of three types of selected-response items that are used to assess knowledge. Matching items measure effectively and efficiently the extent to which students know related facts, associations, and relationships. Some examples of such associations include terms with definitions, persons with descriptions, dates with events, and symbols with names.

The major advantage of matching is that it makes it possible to obtain a very good sampling of recall knowledge. As such, it is beneficial to use matching when there is a great amount of factual information within a single topic. Matching is easily and objectively scored. Constructing good matching items is more difficult than creating completion or short-answer items, but it is not as difficult as preparing multiple-choice items. However, it is relatively easy to construct matching items that are weak measures. This usually occurs when there is insufficient material to include in the item and you add irrelevant information that is unrelated to the major topic that has been targeted for assessment.

In a matching item, the items on the left are called the *premises*. In the right-hand column are the *responses*. The student's task is to match the correct response with each of the premises. As long as the following suggestions are followed, matching items are excellent for measuring recall knowledge that includes associations.

1. Make Sure Directions Are Clear to Students.   Even though matching items are familiar to students, it is helpful to indicate in writing (or orally for young students) the basis for the matching and where and how student responses should be recorded. Generally, letters are used for each response in the right-hand column, and students are asked to write the selected letter next to each premise. Younger students can be asked to draw lines to connect the premises to the responses. It is important in the directions to indicate that *each response may be used once, more than once, or not at all*. This lessens the probability that, through a process of elimination, guessing will be a factor in the results.

2. Include Homogeneous Premises and Responses.   Avoid putting information from different lessons in the same matching item. You wouldn't want to include recent scientists, early U.S. presidents, and sports figures in the same item. Even though what is homogeneous will vary from one person to another, this principle is the one most violated. For example, it would make good sense to use matching to test student knowledge of important dates during the Civil War. It would not be a good idea to contain both dates and men's names as responses. Testing homogeneous material with matching is effective for fairly fine discriminations among facts. For example, matching dates with events in one of the Civil War battles provides greater discrimination than matching dates with major battles.

3. Use Four to Eight Premises.   You do not want to have too long a list of premises. A relatively short list will probably be more homogeneous and will be perceived by students as more fair.

4. Keep Responses Short and Logically Ordered.   Usually the responses include a list of one- or two-word names, dates, or other terms. Definitions, events, and descriptions are in the premise column. Students will be more accurate in their answers if the responses are in logical order. Thus, if responses are dates they should be rank ordered by year; words or names should be alphabetized. Like premises, keep the number of responses to eight; ten at the most. Longer lists waste students' time and contribute to error by including reasoning abilities as part of what is needed to answer the item correctly.

5. Avoid Grammatical Clues to Correct Answers.   Like completion items, you will need to be careful not to make matches obvious by using grammatical clues, such as verb tense agreement.

Example

The following is an example of a good matching item. Notice the complete directions, responses on the right in logical order, and homogeneous content (achievements of early presidents).

> *Directions:* Match the achievements in Column A with the names of presidents in Column B. Write the letter of the president who had the achievement on the

line next to each number. Each name in Column B may be used once, more than once, or not at all.

Column A	Column B
_____ 1 Second president	A. John Adams
_____ 2 President when there were no severe external threats to the country	B. John Quincy Adams
	C. Andrew Jackson
_____ 3 Declined to run for a third term	D. Thomas Jefferson
_____ 4 Wrote the Declaration of Independence	E. James Madison
	F. James Monroe
_____ 5 Last of the presidents from Virginia	G. George Washington

Suggestions for writing matching items are summarized in Figure 6.6.

True/False and Other Binary-Choice Items

When students select an answer from only two response categories, they are completing a *binary-choice* item. This type of item may also be called *alternative-response, alternate-response,* or *alternate-choice.* The most popular binary-choice item is the true/false question; other types of options can be right/wrong, correct/incorrect, yes/no, fact/opinion, agree/disagree, and so on. In each case, the student selects one of two options.

Binary-choice items are constructed from propositional statements about the knowledge. A *proposition* is a declarative sentence that makes a claim about content or relationships among content. Simple recall propositions include the following:

Lansing is the capital of Michigan.
Peru is in the southern hemisphere.
The area of a square is found by squaring the length of one side.
Petosky is the name of a type of rock.

These propositions provide the basis for good test items because they capture an important thought or idea. Once the proposition is constructed, it is relatively easy to keep it as is, rephrase and keep the same meaning, or change one aspect of

---

FIGURE 6.6   Checklist for Writing Matching Items

1. Is it clear how and where students place their answers?
2. Is it clear that each response may be used once, more than once, or not at all?
3. Is the information included homogeneous?
4. Are there more responses than premises?
5. Are the responses logically ordered?
6. Are grammatical clues avoided?
7. Is there only one feasible answer for each premise?
8. Is the set of premises or responses too long?

the statement and then use it for a binary-choice test item. As such, the items provide a simple and direct measure of one's knowledge of facts, definitions, and the like, as long as there is no exception or qualification to the statement. That is, one of the two choices must be *absolutely* true or false, correct or incorrect, and so on. Some subjects, like science and history, lend themselves to this type of absolute proposition better than others.

There are several advantages to using binary-choice items. First, the format of such questions is similar to what is asked in class, so students are familiar with the thinking process involved in making binary choices. Second, short binary items provide for an extensive sampling of knowledge because students are able to answer many items in a short time (two to five items per minute). Third, these items can be written in short, easy-to-understand sentences. Compared to multiple-choice items, binary-choice questions are relatively easy to construct. Finally, scoring is objective and quick.

The major disadvantage of binary items is that they are susceptible to guessing, particularly if the item is poorly constructed. Students can guess the correct answer 50 percent of the time, and often test-wise students can find clues to the correct answer. Thus, a combination of some knowledge, guessing, and poorly constructed items that give clues to the correct answer will allow some students to score well even though their level of knowledge is weak. Binary items are also weak in providing diagnostic information about what students know and don't know.

Writing good binary-choice items begins with propositions about major knowledge targets. In converting the propositions to test items, you will need to keep the items short, simple, direct, and easy to understand. This is best accomplished by avoiding ambiguity and clues. The following suggestions, summarized in Figure 6.7, will help accomplish this.

1. Write the Item So That the Answer Options Are Consistent with the Logic in the Sentence.   The way the item is written will suggest a certain logic for what type of response is most appropriate. For example, if you wanted to test spelling knowledge, it wouldn't make much sense to use true/false questions; it would be better to use correct/incorrect as options.

FIGURE 6.7   Checklist for Writing Binary-Choice Items

1. Does the item contain a single proposition or idea?
2. Is the type of answer logically consistent with the statement?
3. Are the statements succinct?
4. Is the item stated positively?
5. Is the length of both statements in an item about the same?
6. Do the correct responses have a pattern?
7. Are unequivocal terms used?
8. Does the item try to trick students?
9. Is trivial knowledge being tested?
10. Are about half the items answered correctly with same response?

2. Include a Single Fact or Idea in the Item.   For assessing recall knowledge, avoid two or more facts, ideas, or propositions in a single item. This is because one idea or fact may be true and the other false, which introduces ambiguity and error.

Example

> *Poor:*   T   F   California is susceptible to earthquakes because of the collision between oceanic and continental plates.
>
> *Improved:*   T   F   Earthquakes in California are caused by the collision between oceanic and continental plates.

3. Avoid Long Sentences.   Try to keep the sentences as concise as possible. This allows you to include more test items and will reduce ambiguity. Longer sentences tend to favor students who have stronger reading comprehension skills.

Example

> *Poor:*   T   F   A cup with hot water that has a spoon in it will cool more quickly than a similar cup with the same amount of hot water that does not have a spoon in it.
>
> *Improved:*   T   F   Hot water in a cup will cool more quickly if a spoon is placed in the cup.

4. Avoid Insignificant or Trivial Facts and Words.   It is relatively easy to write "tough" binary-choice items that measure trivial knowledge. Avoid this by beginning with what you believe to be significant learning targets.

Examples

> *Poor:* Charles Darwin was twenty-two years old when he began his voyage of the world.
>
> *Improved:* An elephant spends about fifteen hours a day eating and foraging.

5. Avoid Negative Statements.   Statements that include the words *not* or *no* are confusing to students and make items and answers more difficult to understand. Careful reading and sound logic become prerequisites for answering correctly. If the knowledge can only be tested with a negatively worded statement, be sure to highlight the negative word with boldface type, underlining, or all caps.

Example

> *Poor:* United States senators are not elected to six-year terms.
>
> *Improved:* United States senators are elected to six-year terms.

6. Avoid Clues to the Answer.   Test-wise students will look for specific words that suggest that the item is false. When adjectives and adverbs such as *never, all, every, always,* and *absolutely* are used, the answer is usually false. Also, avoid any kind of pattern in the items that provides clues to the answer, such as all true items being longer, alternating true and false answers, tending to use one type of answer more than the other, or all the items being either true or false.

7. Do Not Try to Trick Students.   Items that are written to "trick" students by including a word that changes the meaning of an idea or by inserting some trivial fact should be avoided. Trick items undermine your credibility, frustrate students, and provide less valid measures of knowledge.

8. Avoid Using Vague Adjectives and Adverbs.   Adjectives and adverbs such as *frequent, sometimes, occasionally, typically,* and *usually* are interpreted differently by each student. It is best to avoid these types of words because the meaning of the statement is not equivocal.

9. Write Questions So That about 50 Percent of the Answers Are True.   Don't worry about having exactly half of the correct answers true and half false. But do be careful not to create a pattern where on most tests most of the items are true or false. Students catch on quickly to such patterns, which increases their chance of guessing the correct answer. It follows, then, that you also do not want to construct a test in which all of the items are either true or false.

Multiple-Choice Items

As you are well aware, multiple-choice items are used widely in schools, even though they may *not* provide the best method for assessing recall knowledge (see Figure 3.2 on page 50). Multiple-choice items have a *stem,* in the form of a question or incomplete statement, and three or more *alternatives.* The alternatives contain one correct or best answer and two or more *distractors.* For measuring recall knowledge, it is usually best to use a question as the stem and to provide one correct answer. A direct question is preferred for several reasons: it is easier to write, it forces you to state the complete problem more clearly in the stem, its format is familiar to students, it avoids the problem of grammatically tailoring each alternative to the stem, and questions place less demand on reading skills to understand the problem. Questions are clearly better for younger students. Items that assess the "best" answer allow for greater discrimination and are very effective for measuring understanding. In this type of item, each alternative is technically correct, but one answer is better than the others.

Multiple-choice questions offer several advantages. Like other select-response items, they can provide a broad sampling of the knowledge. The scoring is easy and objective, and it's good to give students practice on the type of items they are likely to encounter on standardized tests.

However, there are also disadvantages. Multiple-choice questions take longer to answer than other types of objective items, and consequently they do not sample as well. Also, it is relatively difficult to write multiple-choice items, especially good distractors. Many teachers find that it isn't too hard to come up with one or two good distractors, but the third or fourth ones are often giveaways to students. This increases the probability that students will guess the right answer. Students learn that the way to study for multiple-choice items is to read and reread the material to focus on recognition. Much less energy is spent to recall information. Thus, like other selected-response items, the type of mental preparation prompted by multiple-choice items is not consistent with more contemporary theories of learning and information processing. As we will see, this is less problematic when the learning target is focused on understanding.

Suggestions for writing multiple-choice items are summarized in the following points and in Figure 6.8, on page 154, in the form of questions. When you need to write the items, begin with the stem, then the correct response, and finally the distractors.

1. Write the Stem as a Clearly Described Question or Task. You want the stem to be meaningful by itself. It should clearly and succinctly communicate what is expected. If the stem makes sense only by reading the responses, it is poorly constructed. It is best, then, to put as much information as possible in the stem and not the responses, as long as the stem does not become overly wordy. The general rule is this: use complete stems and short responses. This reduces the time students need to read the items and reduces redundant words. Of course, you will not want to include words in the stem that are not needed; the stem is longer but is still as succinct as possible. In the end, a good indicator of an effective stem is if students have a tentative answer in mind quickly, before reading the options.

Examples

Poor: Validity refers to

    a. the consistency of test scores.
    b. the inference made on the basis of test scores.
    c. measurement error as determined by standard deviation.
    d. the stability of test scores.

Improved: The inference made on the basis of test scores refers to

    a. reliability.
    b. stability.
    c. validity.
    d. measurement error.

Poor: What is the length of the table?

    a. 1 foot
    b. 3 feet
    c. 15 inches
    d. 24 inches

Improved: What is the length of the table in feet?

    a. 1
    b. 2
    c. 3
    d. 4

2. Avoid the Use of Negatives in the Stem.   Using words like *not* and *except* will confuse students and create anxiety and frustration. Often students simply overlook the negative, which leads to invalid results. It also takes longer to respond to such items. So try to word the stem positively. In cases where knowing what not to do is important, as in knowing rules of the road for driving, the negative stem is fine as long as the negative word is emphasized.

Examples

> *Poor:* Which of the following is not a mammal?
>
>   **a.** Bird
>   **b.** Dog
>   **c.** Horse
>   **d.** Whale
>   **e.** Cat
>
> *Improved:* Which of the following is a mammal?
>
>   **a.** Bird
>   **b.** Frog
>   **c.** Whale
>   **d.** Fish
>   **e.** Lizard

3. Write the Correct Response with No Irrelevant Clues.   There should not be any difference between the correct answer and distractors that would clue the student to respond on some basis other than the knowledge being tested. Common mistakes include making the correct response longer, more elaborate or detailed, more general, or more technical. Qualifiers such as *usually, some,* and *generally* are clues to the correct answer.

4. Write the Distractors to Be Plausible yet Clearly Wrong.   The distractors are useless if they are so obviously wrong that students do not even consider them as possible answers. The intent of a multiple-choice item is to have students *discriminate* among *plausible* answers. Distractors should appear to be possibly correct to poorly prepared students. Poor distractors contain content that is plainly wrong, grammatical inconsistencies, qualifiers such as *always* or *never*, or they state the opposite of the correct answer.

Examples

> *Poor:* Which of the following is the largest city in the United States?
>
>   **a.** Michigan
>   **b.** London
>   **c.** New York
>   **d.** Berlin

Improved: Which of the following is the largest city in the United States?

    a. Los Angeles
    b. Chicago
    c. New York
    d. Miami

Poor: The first step in writing is to

    a. always rewrite.
    b. outline.
    c. grammatically correct.

5. Avoid Using "All of the Above," "None of the Above," or Other Special Distractors. These phrases are undesirable for a number of reasons. "All of the above" is the right answer if only two of the options are correct, and some students may select the first item that is correct without reading the others. Only when students need to know what *not* to do would "none of the above" be appropriate. Be sure to avoid options like "A and C but not D" or other combinations. Items with this type of response tend to measure reasoning ability as much as knowledge, and, especially for measuring recall knowledge, the items take far too long to answer.

6. Use Each Alternative as the Correct Answer about the Same Number of Times. If you have four possible alternatives, about 25 percent of the items should have the same letter as the correct response (20 percent if there are five alternatives). This avoids a pattern that can increase the chance that students will guess the correct answer. Perhaps you have heard the old admonition from test-wise students, "when in doubt, pick C." There is some truth to this for test writers who are not careful to use all the alternatives equally as the correct one.

FIGURE 6.8   Checklist for Writing Multiple-Choice Items

1. Is the stem stated as clearly, directly, and simply as possible?
2. Is the problem self-contained in the stem?
3. Is the stem stated positively?
4. Is there only one correct answer?
5. Are all the alternatives parallel with respect to grammatical structure, length, and complexity?
6. Are irrelevant clues avoided?
7. Are the alternatives short?
8. Are complex alternatives avoided?
9. Are options placed in logical order?
10. Are the distractors plausible to students who do not know the correct answer?
11. Are correct answers spread equally among all the choices?

ASSESSING STUDENT UNDERSTANDING: COMPREHENSION AND APPLICATION

As pointed out earlier in this chapter, comprehension and application are two types of knowing through which students demonstrate their understanding of something. We will consider each with some examples, using the aforementioned objective test methods. Other methods of assessment, such as essays and interpretive items, are also good for measuring student understanding. We will consider these methods in the next chapter.

Assessing Comprehension with Objective Items

Comprehension is demonstrated when students understand, in their own words, the essential meaning of the concept, principle, or procedure. They show this by providing explanations and examples, by converting and translating, and by interpreting and predicting. These mental operations have been hierarchically categorized into three levels: translation, interpretation, and extrapolation. Objective test items can be written for each level.

In *translation*, students demonstrate that they comprehend by retaining essential meaning when the known concept or message is put in different words or symbols. Examples of translation include restating a definition, using words that convey the same meaning, showing or producing new examples of something, translating a foreign language, and explaining a trend from a graph. *Interpretation* means that students can explain why or how, can identify which aspects of a problem are important to the answer, and can draw inferences. Examples of interpretation would be understanding charts, maps, and graphs. *Extrapolation* is being able to make inferences about the consequences of something. This could involve predicting trends, formulating hypotheses and conclusions, and recognizing probable results.

Objective test items that assess recall knowledge can be changed easily to assess comprehension. To tap into translation, simply change the words used to describe or define something so that it is not verbatim from the instructional materials. Higher levels of comprehension require more work. Suppose that as a student you have learned that "photosynthesis is the process by which plants use light to make glucose." The following examples show how to measure this knowledge as either recall or comprehension.

Examples

Recall Knowledge (short-answer): Define photosynthesis: _____

_____

Comprehension (translation, completion): Sunlight is used by plants to make energy
in a process called _____ .

Comprehension (interpretation, short-answer): Explain how plants get energy
from the sun. _____

_____

Comprehension (extrapolation, short-answer): What would happen to plants if they did not receive any sunlight for a long time?

Comprehension (extrapolation, binary-choice): T F   Plants that receive 50 hours of light will produce more glucose than plants that receive 10 hours of light.

Recall Knowledge (multiple-choice): The process by which plants use light to make glucose is called

   a. respiration.
   b. photosynthesis.
   c. energizing.
   d. growing.

Comprehension (translation, multiple-choice): In plants, sugar is made by energy from the sun in what is called

   a. respiration.
   b. photosynthesis.
   c. energizing.
   d. growing.

Comprehension (extrapolation, multiple-choice): Which of the following is most consistent with the process of photosynthesis?

   a. Plants that have light do not need to make glucose.
   b. Plants that have less light make less glucose.
   c. Glucose is produced from plants prior to photosynthesis.
   d. Energy is stored in plants as glucose.

Other examples of objective items that assess comprehension are illustrated in Figure 6.9.

FIGURE 6.9   Examples of Objective Items Assessing Comprehension

Learning Target: **Students understand the nature of food chains.**

Items

Completion:	Toxic chemicals can get in our bodies from what farmers spray on plants because of the _____ _____.
Short-Answer:	Explain how a plant, a mouse, a snake, and a human can be part of a food chain.
Binary-Choice:	T F Farmers rotate their crops to make sure each crop gets the same amount of sun.
Multiple-Choice:	Which of the following would make fish travel through the ocean as if they were in a stream ?

   a. Current
   b. Waves
   c. Tide
   d. Wind

Assessing Application with Objective Items

Understanding is demonstrated through application when the students are able to *use* what they know to solve problems in a *new* situation. This is a more sophisticated type of understanding than comprehension, and it includes the ability to interpret new information with what is known and to apply rules, principles, and strategies to new problems and situations. Obviously this is a very important type of learning target, since we want students to apply what they learn in school to new situations outside of school. Knowing something well enough to apply it successfully to new situations is called learning for *transfer*. The goal is to have sufficient understanding to transfer what is known to different situations.

Perhaps the best example of learning for application is mathematics. At one level, students can memorize the steps for solving certain kinds of math problems—that is, what to do first, second, and so forth. They may even show some comprehension by being able to explain the steps in their own words. But if they cannot apply the steps to new problems and get the right answer, we conclude that they really don't *understand* the process. That's why we give math tests with new problems. Students learn procedural knowledge in math, hopefully at the application level. In many ways, understanding mathematics is demonstrated by successful application. Likewise, much of what we do in language arts instruction is focused on understanding at the application level. Students learn rules for grammar, sentence structure, to write drafts prior to final copy, and reading skills. We conclude that they actually understand how to read and write by demonstrating their skill with new material.

Application is effectively measured with objective test items at one level. As we will see in the next two chapters, interpretive and essay items, and performance-based assessments, take application to a higher level.

Your goal with objective application items is to construct an item that contains new data or information that the student must work with to obtain the answer. The extent of newness determines; to some extent; item difficulty. Items that contain completely new or unfamiliar material are generally more difficult than items in which there are only small differences between what was learned and the content of the question. This is why students may be able to solve new mathematics computational problems well but have trouble applying the same procedures to word problems that put the question in a new context.

The key feature of application items, then, is presenting situations that the students have not previously encountered. There are several strategies for constructing such items. One approach is to present a fictional problem that can be solved by applying appropriate procedural knowledge. For example, if students have learned about electricity and resistance, the following objective questions would test at the application level.

Examples

Application

1. Shaunda has decided to make two magnets by wrapping wire around a nail and attaching the wires to a battery so that the electric current can create a

magnetic force. One magnet (A) uses thin wire and one magnet (B) uses thick wire. Which magnet will be the strongest?

a. A
b. B
c. A and B will be the same
d. Cannot be determined from the information provided

2. T   F   Other things being equal, an electric stove with greater resistance will be hotter than a stove with less resistance.
3. To increase the heat produced from his electric iron, Mr. Jones would _____ the resistance.

Other examples of objective application items include the following:

Examples

1. What happens to water pollution when farmers use *less* fertilizer?
    _____

2. A researcher investigated whether a new type of fertilizer would result in greater growth of corn plants. What is the independent variable?

    a. Growth of corn plants
    b. The researcher
    c. Type of fertilizer
    d. Amount of sunlight

3. William is given a $2.00 allowance each week. He wants to save enough money to go to the movie, which costs $4.00, and buy some candy and a soft drink at the movie. The candy will cost $1.50 and the drink will cost $2.50. How many weeks will William have to wait before he can go to the movie and buy the candy and soft drink?

    a. 2
    b. 3
    c. 4
    d. 5

PUTTING OBJECTIVE TESTS TOGETHER

You will need to consider a few guidelines for putting the objective test together. These guidelines are also important for other types of items and for tests that combine objective with essay or performance-based questions. The guidelines include suggestions for directions, arranging items, and the physical layout of the test.

Preparing Test Directions

According to Gronlund (1993) test directions should include the following:

1. Purpose
2. Time allowed for completing the test
3. Basis for responding
4. Procedures for recording answers
5. What to do about guessing
6. How constructed-response items will be scored

The purpose of the test should be made clear to students well in advance of the testing date. This is usually done when the test is announced. Students need to know why they are taking the test and how the results will be used. A written statement of purpose will clarify the purpose for both students and parents, though usually the purpose is given to students orally.

Students need to know *exactly* how much time they will have to complete the test. It is helpful to indicate to students how they should distribute their time among various parts of the test. It is best to allow plenty of time for students so that they do not feel rushed. As indicated earlier, students can be expected to complete at least one multiple-choice and two binary-choice items per minute, but the actual time will depend on the difficulty of the items and student preparation. Obviously elementary students will take more time than high school students. Your judgments about how many items to include will improve with experience. In the beginning, err on the side of allowing too much time.

The basis for responding simply refers to what students are to do in order to answer the question, that is, how to respond. This should be a simple and direct statement (e.g., "Select the correct answer," or "Select the best answer"). The procedure for responding indicates how students show their answers, whether they circle the answer, write the answer next to the item, write the word in the blank, and so on. If computations are to be shown, tell the students where they should write them. It is best to have young children answer directly on the test, next to the answer. For older students, scoring is much easier if the answers are placed on a separate piece of paper.

In a test where all the items are of the selection type, students may ask about whether there is a penalty for guessing. In classroom tests it is very rare that you find a correction for guessing. The best practice is to be very clear to students that they should try to answer each item (e.g., "Your score is the total number of correct answers, so answer every item").

The final suggestion for directions concerns the scoring criteria for constructed-response items. For these items it is important to clearly indicate the basis on which you will grade the students' answers. We will explore this in greater detail in the next chapter.

Arranging Items

Arranging items by level of difficulty (e.g., easy items first, then difficult ones) has little effect on the results. If you think your students gain confidence by answering the easiest items first, it's fine to order the items by increasing difficulty. The most important consideration in arranging items is item type. Keep all the items that use the same format together. Thus, keep all the multiple-choice items in one section, all the matching items in another, and so on. This reduces the number of times students need to shift their response mode. It also minimizes directions and makes scoring easier. Generally it is best to order items, in sections determined by type, based on how quickly students can answer. Items answered more quickly, such as completion and binary-choice, would generally come first, followed by multiple-choice and short-answer items. If possible, it is best if the items are grouped according to learning targets, keeping assessments of the same target or content together.

Physical Layout of the Test

Objective test items need to be formatted so that they are easy to read and answer. A few commonsense suggestions help to achieve this goal. First, all the information needed to answer an item should be on the same page. This means that items should be on only one page. Avoid having part of an item on one page and the rest of the item on another page. Second, do not crowd too many items onto a page. Although we all need to be careful about wasting paper, a test that is crowded is likely to contain more errors than one that has reasonable spacing and white space. This means that multiple-choice alternatives should not be listed horizontally on the same line. Rather, it is best if the alternatives are listed vertically below the item.

Examples

> *Poor Format:* The movement of animals from one environment to another between summer and winter is called (a) conditioning (b) hibernation (c) territorial reflex (d) migration.
>
> *Improved Format:* The movement of animals from one environment to another between summer and winter is called
>
> **a.** conditioning.
> **b.** hibernation.
> **c.** territorial reflex.
> **d.** migration.

Finally, the format of the test should enhance scoring accuracy and efficiency. For older students, it is best to use a separate answer sheet that can be designed for scoring ease. This can be accomplished by simply repeating the directions and listing the items by number. Students circle or write in their answers. If you have students answer on the same piece of paper that contains the questions, leave blanks to the left of each binary-choice, multiple-choice, or matching item, and blanks on the right-hand of the page for completion items. For younger students, it is best to minimize transfer of answers by having them circle or underline the correct answer or write the answer in the space provided in the item.

SUMMARY

This chapter has examined the nature of knowledge learning targets and objective test items that can be used to assess students on these targets. Suggestions for preparing summative assessments and assembling an objective test were also presented. Major points include the following:

- Preparation for summative assessment includes appropriately sampling what students are responsible for knowing, having the appropriate length and number of assessments, carefully using the tests provided by publishers, preparing students, properly scheduling the assessment, and allowing instruction to influence the final makeup of the test.
- Knowledge can be classified as declarative or procedural and recall or understanding.
- Declarative recall knowledge emphasizes memorization of facts, concepts, and principles.
- Declarative knowledge as understanding involves greater generalization and connection with existing knowledge.
- Procedural recall knowledge emphasizes memorization of skills, steps, and procedures.
- Procedural knowledge as understanding emphasizes the application of process skills to new problems and situations.
- Understanding is defined by comprehension and application.
- Comprehension is demonstrated through translation, interpretation, and extrapolation.
- Completion and short-answer items are effective if memorization is avoided, a single brief answer is correct, wording is understood by all students, and the specific nature and length of the answer is clearly implied.
- Matching items are effective for assessing student understanding of related facts or concepts as long as responses are short, premises and responses are homogeneous, lists are logically ordered, no grammatical clues are given, and no more than ten premises are in one matching item.
- Binary-choice items, like true/false items, are effective if they are clearly, succinctly, and positively stated as single propositions or statements.
- Multiple-choice items are effective if they are clearly and directly stated with one correct answer, include plausible distractors, and do not provide clues to the correct answer.
- Student understanding for application is assessed with objective items when previously learned facts or skills are used to solve problems in novel situations.
- Objective tests are put together by considering the directions, proper arrangement of the items, and correct formatting of the contents of the test.

SELF-INSTRUCTIONAL REVIEW EXERCISES

1. Match the descriptions in column A with the criteria for constructing summative assessments in column B. Each criterion may be used once, more than once, or not at all.

Column A

_____ (1) Revision of a test provided in instructional materials
_____ (2) Use of test blueprint
_____ (3) Teaching test-taking skills
_____ (4) Using an adequate number of items for each area
_____ (5) Providing time for student questions
_____ (6) Chapter review

Column B

a. Representative sampling
b. Length of assessment
c. Number of assessments
d. Use of publisher's test
e. Preparing students
f. Scheduling assessments

2. Identify each of the following descriptions as declarative (D) or procedural (P), and as recall (R) or understanding (U).

   a. Define procedural knowledge.
   b. What is the sequence of steps in preparing an objective test?
   c. Give an example of a multiple-choice item that measures application.
   d. List three suggestions for constructing matching items.
   e. Predict whether students will have questions about how to answer the items in the test.
   f. Review the strategy a teacher has used to construct binary-choice test items to determine if they can be improved.

3. Match the suggestions or descriptions from column A with the type(s) of objective items in column B. Each type of item may be used once, more than once, or not at all; each suggestion or description may have more than one correct match.

Column A

_____ (1) Generally more time-consuming to construct
_____ (2) Scoring may be a problem
_____ (3) Effectively measures relations
_____ (4) Conveniently constructed from knowledge propositions
_____ (5) Responses ordered logically
_____ (6) Correct answers spread equally among all possible choices
_____ (7) Verbatim language from textbooks is avoided
_____ (8) Uses clear, concise statements
_____ (9) Uses blanks of equal length

Column B

a. Completion
b. Short-answer
c. Matching
d. Binary-choice
e. Multiple-choice

4. Using the checklists for writing objective items, evaluate each of the following items and revise it so that it will be improved.

   (1) The _____ _____ are sloping ledges that are formed underwater next to most continents such as Australia and North America.
   (2) How does energy from the sun affect the earth?

(3) Match the states with the characteristics.

_____ Florida	**a.** St. Augustine
_____ New York	**b.** Bordered by Missouri and Minnesota
_____ Michigan	**c.** Alamo
_____ Colorado	**d.** Jamestown
_____ Iowa	**e.** Outer Banks
_____ Texas	**f.** Lincoln
_____ Utah	**g.** Largest city
_____ Illinois	**h.** Great Lake state
_____ Virginia	**i.** Great Salt Lake
_____ North Carolina	**j.** Denver

(4) Estimate each product by rounding.

a. $65 \times 15 =$ _____
b. $3.7 \times 4.3 =$ _____
c. $556 \times 121 =$ _____

(5) T   F   Students do not construct their own answers to every type of item except multiple choice.

(6) Circle the best answer.

Michigan is a (a) great lake state, (b) state in which the rocky mountains are located, (c) example of a state that is west of the Mississippi, (d) none of the above.

(7) Circle the correct answer.

Biodegradable substances are

a. nonrenewable resources.
b. materials that can be broken down into substances that are simpler and do not result in environmental pollution.
c. becoming less popular.
d. like fossil fuels.

ANSWERS TO SELF-INSTRUCTIONAL REVIEW EXERCISES

1. 1. d, 2. a, 3. e, 4. a, 5. b, 6. e.

2. a. DR, b. PR, c. DU, d. DR, e. DU, f. PU.

3. 1. e; 2. a, b; 3. c; 4. a, d; 5. c, e; 6. d, e; 7. a, b, c, d, e; 8. a, b, c, d, e; 9. a.

4. (1) This may be lifted verbatim from the instructional material requiring memorization of a definition. The blanks are not at the end of the sentence. The length of the blanks gives a clue to the correct answer. It is not a concise statement, including only what is needed to answer the item.

Revision: The sloping ledge formed underwater next to most continents is the

_____ _____.

(2) This is poorly worded because many answers could be correct. There is no indication of how long the answer should be, and it is possible that a "correct" answer could be several sentences long—hardly short-answer!

Revision: Name two sources of energy from the sun that affect the earth. _____

_____.

(3) There are probably too many items in one list. Additional responses should be included as distractors. Better to have states listed on the right. Directions are inadequate. Format is difficult to score. Premises are not homogeneous and are on the wrong side. Do not mix cities with historical figures, geographic descriptions, and state mottos.

Revision: On the line next to each number in column A, write the letter of the state from column B that matches the geographic descriptions. Each state may be used once, more than once, or not at all.

Column A   *Column B*

_____ **(1)** Is bordered by three Great Lakes   **a.** New York

_____ **(2)** Contains part of the Rocky Mountains   **b.** Virginia

_____ **(3)** Has an upper and lower peninsula   **c.** Ohio

_____ **(4)** Is bordered by the Ohio and   **d.** Michigan

           Mississippi rivers   **e.** Texas

_____ **(5)** Contains the Blue Ridge Mountains   **f.** Colorado

                                                         g. Illinois

                                                         h. Maryland

                                                         i. North Carolina

(4) The weakness of this item is in the formatting. It would be better to give space next to each problem and have students list their answers on the right hand side of the page.

Revision: Estimate each product by rounding. Show your work next to each problem and write your answer in the column on the right side of the page.

a. $65 \times 15 =$ a. _____

b. $3.7 \times 4.3 =$ b. _____

c. $556 \times 121 =$ c. _____

(5) The negatives in this item make it very hard to understand. State more directly the proposition to be tested. Directions need to be included.

Revision: If the statement is true, circle T; if it is false, circle F.
T   F   Students construct answers to multiple-choice items.

(6) The directions should indicate "correct" answer, not "best" answer. The alternatives should be listed vertically under the stem. The stem should be long, the alternatives short. Alternative (c) does not fit grammatically and is not concise. "None of the above" should be avoided.

Revision: Circle the correct answer.

Which of the following is a characteristic of Michigan?

a. It is surrounded by the Great Lakes.
b. It contains the Rocky Mountains.
c. It is a single peninsula.
d. It borders the Atlantic Ocean.

(7) The correct answer, **b,** is obvious due to the complexity of the sentence in relation to the others. Fossil fuels are also biodegradable, so more than one correct answer is possible. The stem is short and the correct alternative long. It is more clearly stated as a question.

Revision: Circle the correct answer.

What type of material is broken down by decomposers into simpler substances that do not pollute the environment?

a. Nonrenewable
b. Biodegradable
c. Fossil fuel
d. Decomposition

SUGGESTIONS FOR ACTION RESEARCH

1. Collect some examples of objective item tests. Analyze the items and the format of the test in relation to the suggestions provided in the chapter. Show how you would improve the items and format of the test.
2. Find ten examples of objective items that measure different types of knowledge targets (e.g., recall, declarative, procedural, understanding). Change items that measure recall knowledge to ones that measure understanding or application knowledge.
3. Conduct an interview with two teachers and ask them about how they construct objective items. Ask them if they use each of the test preparation guidelines (i.e., sampling, using publisher's tests, and so on). Ask them to give you some advice about putting together an objective test, and see if their advice is consistent with the suggestions in the chapter.
4. With another student, make up a knowledge test of the content of this chapter that could be taken in one hour. Begin with a table of specifications or outline, and indicate the learning targets. Include recall, understanding, and application items. Give the test to four other students for their critique, and then revise the test as needed. Show the original test and the revised one to your supervisor or teacher for his or her critique and further suggestions. Keep a journal of your progress in making up the test. What was difficult? How much time did it take? What would have made the process more efficient?

7

ASSESSING KNOWLEDGE AND REASONING: OBJECTIVE AND ESSAY ITEMS

In Chapter 6, we reviewed knowledge targets and how objective items can efficiently assess these targets. In this chapter, we examine the assessment of reasoning—how students use their knowledge for more complex thinking. As we will

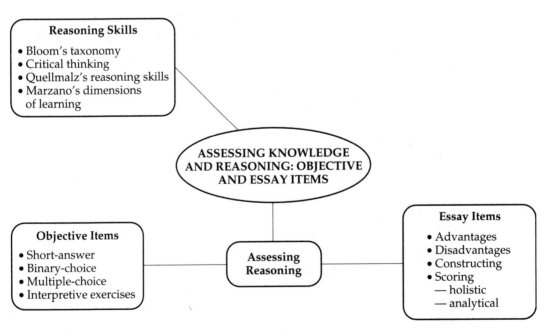

Reasoning Skills

- Bloom's taxonomy
- Critical thinking
- Quellmalz's reasoning skills
- Marzano's dimensions of learning

ASSESSING KNOWLEDGE AND REASONING: OBJECTIVE AND ESSAY ITEMS

Objective Items

- Short-answer
- Binary-choice
- Multiple-choice
- Interpretive exercises

Assessing Reasoning

Essay Items

- Advantages
- Disadvantages
- Constructing
- Scoring
  — holistic
  — analytical

CHAPTER 7   Concept Map

see, there are different ways to conceptualize cognitive skills such as thinking and reasoning. Two methods, the interpretive exercise and the essay question, are emphasized as the preferred approaches if using a paper-and-pencil test to assess these skills. In Chapter 8, we will see how performance-based assessments also provide an excellent way to assess reasoning.

WHAT ARE REASONING SKILLS?

In Chapter 2, reasoning targets were defined as the use of knowledge for reasoning and problem solving. This suggests that reasoning is something students do with their knowledge, a kind of cognitive or mental operation that employs their understanding to some end. Reasoning is more than recall, comprehension, or simple application. Of course, knowledge targets, like reasoning, involve some type of thinking skill. Thinking occurs in the most fundamental process of remembering something, just as it does in demonstrating understanding and reasoning. It is in the nature of the thinking, however, that knowledge is distinguished from reasoning.

Reasoning, as I have conceptualized it here, involves some kind of mental manipulation of knowledge. The task is to employ knowledge to interpret and draw inferences, solve a problem, make a judgment or decision, or engage in creative or critical thinking. Thinking is not normally content-free. Thus, I find it helpful to identify three components to reasoning. One is the mental skill needed to perform the task; a second is the declarative or procedural knowledge needed; and the third is the task itself. These ingredients differentiate cognitive skills such as analysis, comparison, and discrimination from the problem-solving or interpretation task. The mental skills are used in conjunction with knowledge to perform the task (see Figure 7.1). Even though we are sometimes interested in

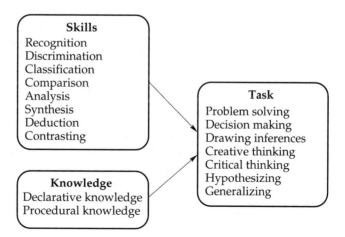

FIGURE 7.1   Major Components of Reasoning

teaching and assessing students on their ability to perform certain types of mental operations, such as analysis or deductive logic, we don't normally test these skills directly. Rather, we are usually interested in the *use* of these skills to demonstrate understanding (knowledge) or to perform a problem-solving tasks in subject matter domains.

Assessing reasoning skills is challenging because the target is difficult to define. It is one thing to note the importance of teaching and testing "higher-order thinking" skills or "reasoning" skills, but operationalizing these general ideas into specific assessment targets is far from straightforward. The literature on thinking and reasoning identifies three distinct conceptualizations, each based in a different academic discipline. Educators have emphasized mental skills, as illustrated by Bloom's taxonomy. Psychologists have focused on the application of problem-solving strategies and processes. Philosophers have contributed to our understanding of deductive and inductive logic and to what is called "critical thinking." Each of these disciplines has had a different focus, but all could be labeled as thinking skills or reasoning in a broad sense. I will briefly present four thinking skill/reasoning frameworks that have been developed on the basis of these perspectives. Each represents a different way to organize, label, and define thinking skills.

I want to emphasize that selecting a way to operationalize thinking skills is up to you—there is no single right or best way. But assessing reasoning or thinking skills, no matter how one defines them in general, requires close attention to the nature of the specific mental operation involved. The following four frameworks are presented to give you suggestions and examples for developing reasoning targets.

Bloom's Taxonomy of the Cognitive Domain

Bloom's taxonomy has been described and, as previously noted, it is both the most used and the most dated conceptualization of thinking. This taxonomy has popularized the term *higher order thinking skills* because the six levels are interpreted by most to be hierarchical (hence some are considered higher than others). The difficulty I have with using this taxonomy for assessing reasoning is that it does not address very well the tasks that are commonly completed by students, such as problem solving and making inferences. Two of the levels, analysis and synthesis, are important cognitive skills, but only application and evaluation address tasks that students complete. Also, conceptualizing the taxonomy as hierarchical does not make much practical sense. The third level, application, is considered lower than analysis, whereas comprehension, as measured by making an inference, is at the second level. Is the ability to make an inference a prerequisite for analysis? My experience is that trying to teach and test as if the taxonomy is a hierarchy is unrealistic. For me, it makes more sense to first identify the task, then examine the cognitive skills needed to complete the task, rather than to delay evaluation until skills in other levels are demonstrated. Furthermore, Bloom's taxonomy has now been incorporated into more contemporary conceptualizations.

Ennis's Taxonomy of Critical Thinking Dispositions and Abilities

Critical thinking is defined by Ennis (1987) as "reasonable reflective thinking that is focused on deciding what to believe or do" (p. 10). Ennis notes that critical thinking *involves* higher order thinking skills, but the act of thinking critically must include a decision or judgment about a belief, action, or answer, as well as appropriate dispositions. Critical thinking is being able to carefully analyze a knowledge claim or information to judge its merit and worth in relation to the action or belief that results. It is not so much a matter of deriving a correct answer or solution to a problem as being able to evaluate and weigh information and evidence to make an informed judgment. In the end, some judgments are better than others. Thus, there is a goal or purpose to critical thinking. Separating the thinking skills from the action or belief is similar to what I have pointed out in Figure 7.1 on page 167.

Dispositions refer to a frame of mind that is important for critical thinking, such as being willing to remain open-minded, a desire to consider all viewpoints, seeking clear statement of the problem or question, and striving for unbiased information. These dispositions are part of what makes someone a good critical thinker. Not only must students know when to ask questions to clarify information or seek new data, they also must have an inclination to do so.

To promote "reasonable" thinking in making judgments, Ennis lists a number of abilities that should be employed. The "best" judgment results from being able to apply these abilities successfully. From a practical standpoint, the abilities are organized in a series of steps that are employed in the process of critical thinking. Being able to both follow the steps and use the abilities enables students to reason effectively. The steps constitute procedural knowledge. Being able to list the critical thinking abilities is declarative knowledge. Using the steps and abilities in reasoning is critical thinking. From an assessment standpoint, then, the task students are required to complete needs to be structured to determine if students are able to use particular abilities in making judgments. For example, you can design a paragraph that includes unreliable or biased sources of information. If students make their judgments without taking into consideration limitations due to the unreliability or bias, then it can be concluded that this aspect of their critical thinking is weak.

Figure 7.2 on p. 170 presents the steps involved in critical thinking, along with the critical thinking abilities required and practical examples. Assessment of critical thinking as reasoning begins with identifying the task—the judgment that the student needs to make. Information is presented to the student, which is formulated to assess specific critical thinking abilities. Thus, you may purposefully in-

FIGURE 7.2   Critical Thinking Steps and Abilities

Steps	Abilities	Examples
Clarify problem.	Identify or formulate a question; put the problem in context; ask questions or seek information to clarify the problem.	Which medication should Troy choose? What background factors would affect Troy's choice? Does Troy have any other options?
Gather information.	Distinguish verifiable facts from value claims; determine the credibility of a source; distinguish relevant from irrelevant information, claims, or reasons; detect bias.	What information is based on opinion about the medications and what is based on objective evidence? Should the information from drug companies be used? Is it important to know that a medication tastes good? Would a company representative be biased about the company's medication?
Make inferences.	Recognize logical inconsistencies in deductive reasoning; recognize unwarranted claims or generalizations from inductive reasoning.	The medication worked well with adults, but will it work as well with children? If the medication should not be used with adults, does this mean it shouldn't be used with children?
Conduct advanced clarification.	Identify unstated assumptions; identify ambiguous or illogical arguments; determine the strength of an argument; detect fallacy labels such as straw person, name calling, and non sequitur; detect inconsistencies; detect stereotypes; consider alternative judgments; distinguish cause and effect from relationships.	How good is the evidence that a particular medication will be effective? Is a particular argument for a medication reasonable? Is calling one of the medications silly and insignificant important? What are the advantages and disadvantages of each medication?
Make a judgment.	Decide on an answer, solution, or course of action.	Selecting a medication and providing reasons for the decision.

Source: Adapted from: Ennis, R. H. (1987). A taxonomy of critical thinking dispositions and abilities. From *Teaching thinking skills* by Baron and Sternberg. Copyright © 1987 by W. H. Freeman and Company. Used with permission; Norris, S. P., & Ennis, R. H. (1989). *Evaluating critical thinking.* Pacific Grove, CA: Midwest Publications; and Beyer, B. K. (1985). Critical thinking: What is it? *Social Education, 22,* 270–276.

clude some illogical arguments or unreliable sources of information to see if students are able to recognize these and use them appropriately in defending their judgments. As we will see, essay-type test questions are best for this type of assessment because students can be asked to defend their judgments or answers. However, objective items are also useful in detecting whether students realize that, for instance, a specific fact presented is irrelevant.

Quellmalz's Framework for Reasoning Skills

Quellmalz (1987) conducted an analysis of the different ways of conceptualizing thinking and reasoning skills that had been presented in the literature. She concluded that the various frameworks contained five common elements that make sense for teaching and assessment: recall, analysis, comparison, inference, and evaluation.

Recall is quite similar to Bloom's knowledge and comprehension categories and to the ways recall and comprehension are defined in Chapter 6. It refers to verbatim repetition, translation, or identification. This mastery of subject matter content and procedures was included as a type of thinking because subsequent forms of reasoning arise from applying a knowledge base. I maintain, however, that it is important to separate simple recall from understanding.

Analysis is used in essentially the same way as it is in Bloom's taxonomy. In this operation, students divide a whole into component parts. This includes identification of the parts, the relationships among different parts, and the relation of parts to the whole. With this skill, students are able to break down, differentiate, categorize, sort, or subdivide.

The third element, comparison, is concerned with reasoning about similarities and differences. This skill is one in which the student compares, contrasts, and relates. Simple comparisons are done by pointing out one or a few similarities and differences, for example, by asking "How are two sentences the same or how are they different?" More complex comparisons require reasoning with many attributes or components.

Comparison is contained within Bloom's analysis category, but it is separated out by Quellmalz because often students are asked to first analyze and then compare. What is actually being measured in compare-and-contrast questions is the student's understanding of the dimensions that are being compared. For this reason, I think of such questions more as a way to assess understanding than reasoning. Perhaps a specific thinking skill is being utilized, but it falls short of reasoning.

Inference requires deductive or inductive thinking. In a deductive task, students are asked whether one thing follows from another. Often, students are given a generalization or principles and are asked to identify or construct a correct conclusion. For example, giving students a fact like "Jane is taller than Shuanda, and Shuanda is taller than Frank," then asking "Is Jane taller or shorter than Frank?" is a task that requires deductive thinking. Inductive reasoning involves reaching a reasonable conclusion or generalization from information provided. Other thinking skills that require inference include hypothesizing, predicting, and synthesizing.

In the final kind of reasoning, evaluation, students express or defend an opinion, judgment, or point of view. This is essentially the same as critical thinking. Students justify, explain, argue, and criticize.

The appeal of Quellmalz's work is that the types of reasoning are easily applied to different subjects. Figure 7.3 presents examples of what are labeled "higher order" reasoning skills. The limitation of this framework, however, is that the emphasis is on the cognitive skills rather than tasks such as problem solving or critical thinking.

Marzano's Dimensions of Learning

Marzano and his colleagues (Marzano, 1992; Marzano, Pickering, & McTighe, 1993) offer an instructional framework for organizing learning outcomes into five major categories (see Figure 7.4). Each of the categories represents a type of thinking that is important for successful learning. The dimensions of learning framework was ini-

FIGURE 7.3 Applications of Quellmalz's Framework of Higher Order Reasoning Skills

	Science	Social Science	Literature
Analyze	Identify the components of a process or the features of animate and inanimate objects.	Identify the components of an argument or the elements of an event.	Identify the components of literary, expository, and persuasive discourse.
Compare	Compare the properties of objects or events.	Compare the causes and effects of separate events and of social, political, economic, cultural, and geographic features.	Compare meanings, themes, plots, characters, settings, and reasons.
Infer	Draw conclusions, make predictions, pose hypotheses, tests, and explanations.	Predict, hypothesize, conclude.	Explain characters' motivations in terms of cause and effect.
Evaluate	Evaluate the soundness and significance of findings.	Evaluate the credibility and significance of arguments, decisions, and reports.	Evaluate form, believability, significance, completeness, and clarity.

Source: Quellmalz, E. S. (1987). Developing reasoning skills. From *Teaching thinking skills* by Baron and Sternberg, p. 91, Table 5-3. Copyright © 1987 by W. H. Freeman and Company. Used with permission.

FIGURE 7.4   Dimensions of Learning

Dimension 1:   Positive Attitudes and Perceptions about Learning

Dimension 2:   Acquiring and Integrating Knowledge
- Declarative knowledge
- Procedural knowledge

Dimension 3:   Extending and Refining Knowledge
- Comparing
- Classifying
- Making inductions
- Making deductions
- Analyzing errors
- Creating and analyzing support
- Analyzing perspectives
- Abstracting

Dimension 4:   Using Knowledge Meaningfully
- Decision making
- Investigation
- Experimental inquiry
- Problem solving
- Invention

Dimension 5:   Productive Habits of Mind
- Being clear and seeking clarity
- Being open-minded
- Restraining impulsivity
- Being aware of your own thinking
- Evaluating the effectiveness of your actions
- Pushing the limits of your knowledge and abilities
- Engaging intensely in tasks even when answers or solutions are not immediately apparent

Source: Adapted from Marzano, R. J. (1992). *A different kind of classroom: Teaching with dimensional learning.* Alexandria, VA: Association for Supervision and Curriculum Development; and Marzano, R. J., Pickering, D., & McTighe, J. (1993). *Assessing student outcomes: Performance assessment using the dimensions of learning model.* Alexandria, VA: Association for Supervision and Curriculum Development.

tially developed to show teachers how to use recent research and theory on learning, particularly constructivist ideas, to organize, plan, and execute instruction.

The instructional emphasis of the framework makes it ideal for identifying learning targets that are practical. The first dimension, positive attitudes and perceptions about learning, and the fifth one, productive habits of mind, are concerned with what I have called affect, and will be reviewed in Chapter 10. The second learning dimension, acquiring and integrating knowledge, is conceptually the same as what has been covered in Chapter 6, including the distinction between declarative and procedural knowledge. Dimensions 3 and 4 (referred to as "complex" thinking or "reasoning strategies") are concerned with reasoning as I have defined it in this chapter. Dimension 3, extending and refining knowledge, emphasizes how students use thinking skills to extend and refine their knowledge to demonstrate understanding. This includes inductive and deductive thinking, analysis, and making comparisons. Dimension 4, using knowledge meaningfully, includes most of the reasoning tasks in Figure 7.1 on page 167. Here students use their knowledge to make decisions, conduct an investigation or experiment, solve a problem, and develop something unique. Two of the reasoning tasks identified in this dimension, decision making and problem solving, are used frequently by teachers.

Problem solving involves finding a solution that overcomes some kind of obstacle. This involves identifying the problem and obstacle, developing possible solutions, testing solutions, and finally evaluating the solutions. The steps in this process, then, include the following:

1. Identify the general problem.
2. Clarify the problem.
3. Identify and describe relevant constraints or obstacles.
4. Identify the most important obstacles.
5. Identify possible solutions.
6. Choose the best solutions.
7. Apply or test the best solutions.
8. Monitor effect of each solution.
9. Select the best solution.

To assess problem solving, you will need to construct a task that lends itself to these steps and then ask questions that address the ability of the student to apply the steps successfully in order to arrive at a best solution. The reasoning learning target should also include each of the steps.

Decision making is similar to problem solving, but it may or may not involve obstacles or constraints. The critical characteristic is that there are alternative, competing choices. In decision making, students need to understand the desired goal or result, evaluate the alternatives in terms of the criteria related to the situation, and select a plan, task, course of action, or make a choice on the basis of their evaluations. Solutions or choices are not correct or incorrect; it is in the evaluations of the relative merits of the alternatives and during the following process of decision making that students demonstrate their competencies. Like problem solving, then, to assess decision making you need to specify clearly the steps and criteria for your evaluations.

The kind of thinking that is needed for each dimension is translated easily into questions that are applicable for all disciplines. In Figure 7.5, each of the complex reasoning skills in dimensions 3 and 4 is defined, along with examples.

The four reasoning frameworks I have presented are summarized in matrix format in Figure 7.6 on page 176. This figure allows you to compare the different definitions of reasoning and major components to determine more easily which might be most closely related to the reasoning learning targets in your discipline or classroom. However, don't feel that you must adopt any single framework in its entirety. It's fine to pick and choose, mix and match, and adapt as appropriate.

FIGURE 7.5 Definitions and Examples of Thinking Processes in Dimensions 3 and 4

Thinking Process	Definition	Example
Comparison	Describes similarities and differences between two or more items.	Your task is to identify similarities and differences among different sizes of government.
Classification	Organizes items based on specific characteristics.	Classify various waste materials on the basis of smell, toxicity, bulk, and any other attributes.
Induction	Creates a generalization from information.	Observe the behavior of six different people and synthesize your observations into three or four general ways people tend to behave.
Deduction	Describes logical consequences of generalizations or principles.	Observe the following news clip and indicate whether the clip is an example of biased reporting.
Error analysis	Identifies and describes specific errors in information or processes.	Review recent news reports and give examples of inaccurate information.
Constructing support	Develops well-articulated argument for or against a specific claim or assertion.	Residents of a rural community are objecting to a proposal to build a landfill on their farmland because it will pollute their water. Do you agree with their argument? Why or why not?
Abstracting	Identifies underlying theme or pattern from situations or information.	Describe the major events people experience when going to the doctor. Is the process the same for going to the dentist?
Analyzing perspectives	Considers opposing positions and the reasoning that supports each position.	Write two letters to the editor, one in support of and one against allowing prayer in the schools.
Decision making	Makes a selection among apparently equal alternatives.	If you were Harry Truman, would you have decided to drop an atomic bomb on Hiroshima? What factors would be important in your decision?
Investigation	Examines and systematically inquires about something.	What were the important determining events that led to the U.S. military involvement in Vietnam?
Problem solving	Develops and tests a method or product for overcoming obstacles or constraints to reach a desired outcome.	How can the United States reduce the high number of violent crimes?
Experimental inquiry	Tests hypotheses that have been generated to explain a phenomenon.	Observe what happens when the population of mice is increased in this area. How can you explain what happened? What would happen if the population of mice were decreased?
Invention	Develops something unique or makes unique improvements to a product or process.	How would you change the way bills are passed in Congress to improve our system of government?

Source: Adapted from Marzano, R. J., Pickering, D., & McTighe, J. (1993). *Assessing student outcomes: Performance assessment using the dimensions of learning model.* Alexandria, VA: Association for Supervision and Curriculum Development.

FIGURE 7.6   Comparison of Reasoning Frameworks

	Definition	Major Components
Bloom's Taxonomy	Higher-order thinking skills	Application (apply in novel situations, predict effects) Analysis (distinguishing, checking consistency) Synthesis (combining, reducing) Evaluation (logical inconsistencies, fallacies, adequacy of evidence, judgment of quality or worth of something)
Ennis's Critical Thinking	Decision making or judgment about the merits and worth of a belief or action	Dispositions (clarify problems, gather information, make inferences, conduct advanced clarification, make judgment) Skills (detecting bias, irrelevancies, source credibility, logical inconsistencies, fallacies, unwarrranted claims, illogical arguments, stereotypes)
Quellmalz	Higher-order reasoning skills	Analysis (identity components) Comparison (contrasts, relates, similarities, differences) Inference (deductive, inductive thinking) Evaluation (judgment)
Marzano	Complex thinking or reasoning strategies	Extending and refining knowledge (comparing, classifying, inducting, deducting, analyzing errors, constructing support, abstracting, analyzing perspectives) Using knowledge meaningfully (decision making, investigation, problem solving, experimental inquiry, invention)

ASSESSING REASONING

Before we consider several methods that do a good job of assessing reasoning, I want to emphasize two points. First, remember that each of the assessment methods we discuss in this book can be used to measure any learning target. Reasoning can be measured by objective items and recall knowledge can be evaluated in student essays or performance-based products. However, some methods are better than others for assessing particular types of targets. This is why I have emphasized particular methods in the chapter on assessing knowledge and different methods for assessing reasoning. Second, normally when we assess reasoning we are also measuring how much students know. This is clearly illustrated in the scoring criteria for many essay items, in which students are graded for demonstrating an understanding of certain concepts or principles. But there is an important trade-off. Items that do well in assessing reasoning cannot begin to sample the *amount* of knowledge that can be tested with simple objective items.

We will look at how the objective items discussed in Chapter 6 work for assessing reasoning, and then we will review two paper-and-pencil test methods that are better suited for assessing reasoning but that aren't as good for assessing knowledge—interpretive exercises and essays. In the next chapter, we will examine performance-based products and their potential for assessing knowledge, reasoning, and skills.

Objective Items

Objective items can be used to measure the isolated thinking skills required for reasoning tasks. We will consider some examples, but there are far too many thinking skills to cover all of them with each type of item. The suggestions for writing items in Chapter 6 are also applicable here.

Short-Answer

Short-answer items can assess thinking skills when students are required to supply a brief response to a question or situation that can be understood only by the use of the targeted thinking skills. Reasoning tasks, like decision making and critical thinking, are not assessed very well with short-answer items.

Examples

(Comparing) List three ways the recession of the 1980s was like the depression of the 1920s.

(Comparing) How does a pine tree differ from an oak tree?

(Comparing) Name one difference between vertebrate and invertebrate animals.

(Deductive reasoning) Coach Greene substitutes his basketball players by height, so that the first substitute is the tallest player on the bench, the next substitute is the next tallest, and so forth. Reginald is taller than Sam, and Juan is taller than Reginald. Which of these three players should Coach Greene play first?

(Credibility of a source) The principal needs to decide if the new block schedule allows teachers to go into topics in greater detail. He can ask a parent, teacher, or a principal from another school. Who should he ask to get the most objective answer?

(Analysis/prediction) People want health insurance but they don't want to be forced to buy it from a company in their community. The law says that a person must buy health insurance from a company in his or her community. What action by the people is most likely?

(Investigating) Several paper towel companies claim that their product absorbs more liquid than the other brands. Design an experiment to test the absorbency of each brand of paper towel.

(Analysis) List the anatomical structures of the kidney, explain the function of each part, and describe how they all work together.

Binary Choice

Binary-choice items can be used to assess reasoning in several different ways. Students can be asked to indicate whether a statement is a fact or opinion:

Examples

If the statement is a fact, circle F; if it is an opinion, circle O.

> F   O   Literature is ancient Rome's most important legacy.
> F   O   The word *Mississippi* has eleven letters.
> F   O   The best way to wash a car is with a sponge.

Additional reasoning skills can be assessed using the same approach by developing some statements that are examples of the skill and some statements that are not examples. This can be done with many of the critical thinking skills (e.g., identifying stereotypes, biased statements, emotional language, relevant data, and verifiable data).

Examples

If the statement is an example of a stereotype, circle S; if it is not a stereotype, circle N.

> S   N   Mexican Americans are good musicians.
> S   N   Women live longer than men.

If emotional language is used in the statement, circle E; if no emotional language is used, circle N.

> E   N   Health insurance reform is needed so that poor people with serious injuries will be able to lead productive lives.
> E   N   Health insurance is going to cost a lot of money.

Logic can be assessed by asking if one statement follows logically from another:

Examples

If the second part of the sentence explains why the first part is true, circle T for true; if it does not explain why the first part is true, circle F or false.

> T   F   Food is essential *because* it tastes good.
> T   F   Plants are essential *because* they provide oxygen.
> T   F   Reggie is tall *because* he has blue eyes.

Multiple Choice

Simple multiple-choice items can be used to assess reasoning in two ways. One way is to focus on a particular skill, like the binary-choice items, to determine if students are able to recognize and use that skill. A second use is to assess the extent to which students can use their knowledge and skills in performing a problem-solving, decision-making, or other reasoning task. The first use is illustrated with the following examples:

Examples

(Distinguishing fact from opinion) Which of the following statements about our solar system is a fact rather than an opinion?

a. The moon is made of attractive white soil.
b. Stars can be grouped into important clusters.
c. A star is formed from a white dwarf.
d. Optical telescopes provide the best way to study the stars.

(Identifying assumptions) When Patrick Henry said "give me liberty or give me death," his assumption was that

a. everyone would agree with him.
b. Thomas Jefferson would be impressed by the speech.
c. if he couldn't have freedom he might as well die.
d. his words would be taught to students for years.

(Recognizing bias) Peter told the group that "the ill-prepared, ridiculous senator has no business being involved in this important debate." Which words make Peter's statement biased?

a. important, senator
b. important, business
c. ill-prepared, ridiculous
d. debate, involved

(Comparison) One way that insects are different from centipedes is that

a. they are different colors.
b. one is an arthropod.
c. centipedes have more legs.
d. insects have two body parts.

(Analysis) Reginald decided to go sailing with a friend. He took supplies with him so he could eat, repair anything that might be broken, and show him where on the lake he could sail. Which of the following supplies would best meet his needs?

a. bread, hammer, map
b. milk, bread, screwdriver
c. map, hammer, pliers, screwdriver
d. screwdriver, hammer, pliers

(Synthesis) What is the main idea in the following paragraph?

Julie picked a pretty blue boat for her first sail. It took her about an hour to understand all the parts of the boat, and another hour to get the sail on. Her first sail was on a beautiful summer day. She tried to go fast but couldn't. After several lessons she was able to make her boat go fast.

   a. sailing is fun
   b. Julie's first sail
   c. sailing is difficult
   d. going fast on a sailboat

The next few examples show how multiple-choice items can be used to assess the students' ability to perform a reasoning task.

Examples

(Hypothesizing) If there were a significant increase in the number of hawks in a given area,

   a. the number of plants would increase.
   b. the number of mice would increase.
   c. there would be fewer hawk nests.
   d. the number of mice would decrease.

(Problem solving) Farmers want to be able to make more money for the crops they grow. But there are too many farmers growing too many crops. What can the farmers do to make more money?

   a. try to convince the public to pay higher prices
   b. agree to produce fewer crops
   c. reduce the number of farmers
   d. work on legislation to turn farmland into parks

(Critical thinking) Peter is deciding which car to buy. He is impressed with the sales representative for the Ford, and he likes the color of the Buick. The Ford is smaller and gets more miles to the gallon. The Buick takes larger tires and has a smaller trunk. More people can ride in the Ford. Which car should Peter purchase if he wants to do everything he can to ensure that his favorite lake does not become polluted?

   a. Ford
   b. Buick
   c. either car
   d. can't decide from the information provided

(Predicting) Suppose that the midwest United States, which grows most of the country's corn, suffered a drought for several years and produced much less corn than usual. What would happen to the price of corn?

   a. The price would rise.
   b. The price would fall.
   c. The price would stay the same.
   d. People would eat less corn.

Interpretive Exercises

The best type of objective item for assessing reasoning is usually the interpretive exercise. This type of item consists of some information or data, followed by several objective questions. The questions are based on the information or data, which can take the form of maps, paragraphs, charts, figures, a story, a table of data, or pictures. The form of the question makes it possible to ask questions that require interpretation, analysis, application, and other reasoning skills.

    Interpretive exercises have four major advantages over other types of items. First, because there are several questions about the same information, it is possible to measure more reasoning skills in greater depth. Second, because information is provided, it is possible to separate the assessment of the reasoning skills from content knowledge of the subject. If content is not provided in the question, as is the case with most multiple-choice items, then a failure to provide a good answer could be attributed to either the student's lack of knowledge or lack of reasoning skill. In the interpretive exercise, students have all or most of the information needed as part of the question, so successful performance provides a more direct measure of reasoning skill. Clearly, the intent of the exercise is to assess how students use the information provided to answer questions. If students know ahead of time that the information will be provided, then they can concentrate their study on application and other uses of the information. Thus, you need to make choices. That is, is it more important for students to memorize physics formulas or practice applying the formulas to new problems?

    A third advantage of the interpretive exercise is that it is possible to use material that students will encounter in everyday living, such as maps, newspaper articles, and graphs. Consistent with constructivist learning theory, this connects the material better with the student, increasing meaningfulness and relevance. Finally, because interpretive exercises provide a standard structure for all students and are scored objectively, the results tend to be more reliable. Students are unable to select a reasoning skill they are most proficient with, as they can do with essay questions. They must use the one called for in each question. Like all objective items, the scoring is efficient, especially if the answers are not of the short-answer type. This is an important consideration in comparing interpretive exercises with essays and performance-based products, which are also used extensively for assessing reasoning skills.

Interpretive exercises have three significant limitations. The first is that they are rather time-consuming and difficult to write. Not only do you need to locate or develop the information or data that will be new for the students and at the right difficulty level, which could take considerable time, but you also need to construct the objective questions (the multiple-choice ones will take longest). The information you first identify may need to be modified, and most teachers are not accustomed to writing several objective items for a single passage or example. For these reasons, teachers tend to use items that have already been prepared by curriculum and textbook publishers.

A second limitation is that you are unable to assess how students organize their thoughts and ideas, or know whether students can produce their own answers without being cued. Third, many interpretive exercises rely heavily on reading comprehension. This puts poor readers at a distinct disadvantage. It takes them longer to read the material for understanding, let alone reason with it. This disadvantage holds for other types of items that require extensive reading as well, but it is especially troublesome for interpretive exercises.

Whether you develop your own interpretive exercises or use ones that have already been prepared, the following suggestions will help ensure high quality (see Figure 7.7 for a checklist summary).

1. Identify the Reasoning Skills to Be Assessed Prior to Selection or Development of the Interpretive Exercise. The sequence you use is important because you want the exercise to fit your learning targets, not have learning targets determined by the interpretive exercise. This is especially important given the number of different conceptualizations of thinking and reasoning skills. What may be called "critical thinking" or "analysis" in a teachers' manual may not coincide with what you think the target is. You need to have a clear idea of the skill to be assessed and then select or develop the material that best fits your definition.

2. Keep Introductory Material as Brief as Possible. By keeping the introductory material brief you will minimize the influence of general reading ability. There should be just enough material for students to complete the reasoning task.

3. Select Similar but New Introductory Material. Reasoning skills are best measured with material that is new to the students. If the material is the same as

---

FIGURE 7.7 Checklist for Writing Interpretive Exercises

1. Are reasoning targets clearly defined before writing the exercise?
2. Is introductory material brief?
3. Is introductory material new to the students?
4. Are there several questions for each exercise?
5. Does the exercise test reasoning?

what was covered in class, you will measure rote memory rather than reasoning. The goal is to find or develop examples that are similar to what students have already studied. The material should vary slightly in form or content, but it should not be completely new. A good strategy to use to accomplish this is to take passages, examples, and data students have been exposed to and alter them sufficiently so that correct answers cannot be given by memory.

4. Construct Several Test Items for Each Exercise.   The test items can be short answer, multiple choice, binary choice, or other objective formats. By asking more than one question for each exercise, you will obtain a better sample of the proficiency of students' reasoning skills. It would be particularly inefficient to have a very long introductory passage and a single question. One common approach for asking questions is to give the students a key of possible answers and have them apply the key to selected aspects of the introductory material (key-type item). For example, if after reading a passage students are asked to judge the relevance of different parts of the passage, the key could simply be:

Key:	A	if the statement is relevant
	B	if the statement is irrelevant

Or if you are testing for student ability to distinguish facts from opinions:

Key:	F	if the statement is a fact
	O	if the statement is an opinion

If you use a key, do not mix different types of reasoning tasks in the same key (e.g., you wouldn't want to put relevant, irrelevant, fact, and opinion in the same key). Like a matching item, the choices should be homogeneous.

5. Construct Items So That the Answers Are Not Found in the Introductory Material.   Remember, you are testing reasoning skills, not knowledge, understanding, or the student's ability to find the correct answer in the material. You also do not want to use questions that can be answered without even reading the introductory material. This happens when students' general knowledge is such that they can determine the correct answer from the question alone.

Interpretive exercises are illustrated in the following four examples. Note that many different formats can be utilized. The reasoning skills and tasks that are assessed are indicated in parentheses next to name of each example.

Example 1. Interpretive exercise[1] (drawing inferences, analyzing perspectives)

Two citizens spoke at the city council meeting. Here are their statements. Use the information to help you answer questions 10 through 13.

Citizen A

The Bower House should be restored and used as a museum. A museum would help the people of the community learn about their heritage and would attract tourists to Grenville. We should not sell the property to the Opti Company. Grenville has grown too quickly, and a factory would bring even more people into the area. In addition, a factory's industrial waste would threaten the quality of our water.

Citizen B

Grenville needs the Opti factory. The factory would provide needed jobs. The tax money it would bring into the community would help improve our streets, schools, and other city services. A museum, on the other hand, would hurt our local economy. Taxes would have to be raised to pay for the restoration of the Bower House. A museum would not create enough jobs to solve our unemployment problem.

Key: Write the letter A next to each statement that Citizen A would most likely agree with. Write the letter B next to each statement that Citizen B would most likely agree with.

            (10) Jobs are the foundation of a community.
            (11) Pollution problems will multiply.
            (12) We are in danger of losing the history of our community.
            (13) Hanging on to the past hurts the future.

Example 2. Interpretive exercise (recognizing the relevance of information)

Sally lost her pencil on her way to school. It was red and given to her by her grandmother. She wanted the teacher to ask the class if anyone found the pencil.

Key: Circle *yes* if the information in the sentence will help the class find the pencil.
    Circle *no* if the information in the sentence will not help the class find the pencil.

    yes no   **1.** The pencil was new.
    yes no   **2.** Sally rides the bus to school.
    yes no   **3.** The pencil is red.
    yes no   **4.** The pencil was a present from Sally's grandmother.
    yes no   **5.** The pencil had a new eraser.
    yes no   **6.** The teacher knows Sally's grandmother.

Example 3. Interpretive exercise (analysis, inference, error analysis)

Based on Figure 7.8, circle T if the statement is true and F if the statement is false.

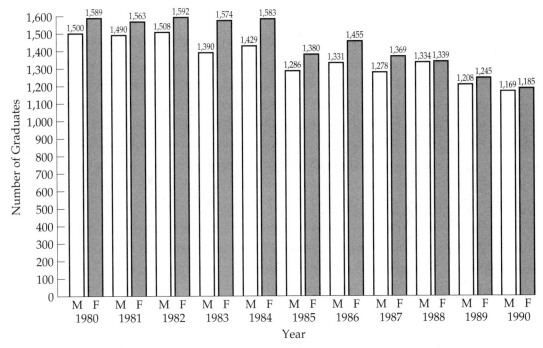

Note: numbers in thousands

FIGURE 7.8 **Number of Male and Female Students Graduating from High School in the United States**

Source: U.S. Department of Education, Office of Educational Research and Improvement. (1994). *Digest of education statistics,* p. 188.

T F   In 1990, more female than male students graduated from high school.

T F   From 1980 to 1990, the percentage of female students graduating from high school increased gradually.

T F   Overall, the best year for graduating students was 1987.

T F   From 1980 to 1990, more female than male students graduated from high school.

Answer each of the following questions:

In what years did more male students than female students graduate? _____

In what year was there the greatest difference between the percentage of male and female graduates? _____

Example 4. Interpretive exercise (inference, prediction)

Review and complete Figure 7.9, below.

FIGURE 7.9   Earth Science

Wind and Weather in Transgaea

The map below shows the three most common kinds of winds that blow across the imaginary continent of Transgaea. Each wind is generated by a different air mass.

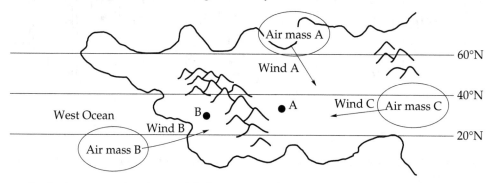

Study the map and make careful observations about the air masses and the winds they generate. Then make inferences about the relative temperature and moisture content of each wind. Record your inferences in the table below.

Wind	Temperature	Moisture content
A		
B		
C		

What inferences can you make about the average annual precipitation at Points A and B on the map?

It is June, Wind B is blowing, and there is relatively cold air over much of Transgaea. Predict the weather for Point B.

Source: Earth Science, Critical Thinking Worksheets. Copyright © 1989 by Addison-Wesley Publishing Company. Reprinted by permission.

Essay Items

Essay items can effectively assess both knowledge and reasoning skills. It is generally understood that essays can tap complex thinking by requiring students to organize and integrate information, interpret information, give arguments, give explanations, evaluate the merit of ideas, and conduct other types of reasoning. Although objective formats are clearly superior for measuring recall knowledge, the essay, as an extension of the short-answer format, is an excellent way to measure understanding and mastery of complex information, such as how students explain procedures or put together many discrete facts into a meaningful whole. Research on student learning habits shows that when students know they will face an essay test they tend to study by looking for themes, patterns, relationships, and how information can be organized and sequenced. In contrast, when studying for objective tests, the students tend to fragment information and memorize each piece.

Examples

Explain how the fertilizers farmers use to grow crops may pollute our lakes and streams.
What happens to food after it is eaten to produce energy for the body?
Describe the major events that led up to the beginning of the Civil War.
Give an example, new to me and not one from class, of how the law of supply and demand would make prices of some products increase.

Usually, essay items that assess knowledge require relatively brief answers. These may be called *short-essay* or *restricted-response essay* to distinguish them from short-answer items, even though the length of the answer does not necessarily indicate the type of target being measured. We will focus here on both *extended-response* and *restricted-response* essay items, although the extended-response format is the best one for assessing reasoning targets.

Advantages and Disadvantages

The major advantage of using essay questions is that complex thinking and reasoning skills can be assessed. Essays motivate better study habits and provide students with flexibility in how they wish to respond. Written responses allow you to evaluate the ability of students to communicate their reasoning. Compared to developing objective items that measure reasoning, essay items are less time-consuming to construct. However, it still takes considerable time to construct a *good* essay question.

The major disadvantages to essay items are related to scoring student responses. Reading and scoring answers is very time-consuming, especially if done conscientiously so that meaningful feedback is given to students. From a practical standpoint, most teachers find that they can give only a few essay items. Scoring essays is also notoriously unreliable. Suppose two teachers score the same essays; if the scoring is reliable, the results for each student would be the same for both teachers. Experience and research suggests that this rarely happens. There is almost certain to be some difference in the way the teachers would evaluate the student responses. This is the result of variations in the weight each teacher gives to different aspects of the answers, the professional standards of each teacher, and the individual moods of each teacher.

In most classrooms, only a single individual, the teacher, judges the answers, and variations in mood, halo effects, expectations, the order in which students are evaluated, and other factors, will affect the professional judgments that are made. This is not meant to imply that it is inappropriate to use subjective judgments in scoring. You *want* to be able to make judgments; that's one reason for using the essay format. When done appropriately, these judgments are professional, not intuitive. We will review guidelines for ensuring high-quality scoring shortly.

A final shortcoming of essay items is that they do not provide for very good sampling. The essay cannot sample content knowledge well because, since students must have time to think about and then write responses, relatively few questions are asked. This is why it is generally better to use objective items to assess content knowledge. Sampling is also limited to the reasoning skills that are assessed. For example, a single extended-response essay item that asks students to make a decision based on information provided may give you a good indication of one or two reasoning skills, while several shorter items could sample different types of skills.

Constructing Essay Items

Essay items will be strengthened by adhering to the following suggestions, summarized in Figure 7.10. In the next section we will review important principles for scoring student answers.

1. Construct the Item to Elicit Skills Identified in the Learning Target. Once the reasoning skill is identified, the wording in the question needs to be such that the specific skill(s) will need to be used to answer the question. This is easier with restricted-response items that focus on a single reasoning skill. With extended-response items, the scoring criteria can be matched to the skills assessed. A good way to begin writing the item to match the target is to start with a standard stem, then modify it as needed for the subject and level of student ability. Some examples of such items are illustrated in Figure 7.11.

2. Write the Item So That Students Clearly Understand the Specific Task. After reading an essay item, students ask, "What does the teacher want in my answer?" If the assessment task is described ambiguously, so that students interpret what is called for in the answer differently, many responses will be off target. Such responses lead to flawed interpretations by teachers. For students who misinterpret the task, you don't know if they have the targeted skill or not, leading to invalid conclusions.

To clearly set forth the nature of the task, try to make the essay question as specific as possible. Don't be hesitant about stating the desired response explicitly.

FIGURE 7.10   Checklist for Writing Essay Items

1. Is the targeted reasoning skill measured?
2. Is the task clearly specified?
3. Is there enough time to answer the questions?
4. Are choices among several questions avoided?

FIGURE 7.11   Sample Item Stems for Assessing Reasoning

Skill	Stem
Comparing	Describe the similarities and differences between . . . . . Compare the following two methods for . . . . .
Relating cause and effect	What are major causes of . . . ? What would be the most likely effects of . . . ?
Justifying	Which of the following alternatives would you favor and why? Explain why you agree or disagree with the following statement.
Summarizing	State the main points included in . . . . Briefly summarize the contents of . . . .
Generalizing	Formulate several valid generalizations from the following data. State a set of principles that can explain the following events.
Inferring	In light of the facts presented, what is most likely to happen when . . . ? How would Senator X be likely to react to the following issue?
Classifying	Group the following items according to . . . . What do the following items have in common?
Creating	List as many ways as you can think of for . . . . Make up a story describing what would happen if . . . .
Applying	Using the principle of . . . as a guide, describe how you would solve the following problem. Describe a situation that illustrates the principle of . . . .
Analyzing	Describe the reasoning errors in the following paragraph. List and describe the main characteristics of . . . .
Synthesizing	Describe a plan for proving that . . . . Write a well-organized report that shows . . . .
Evaluating	Describe the strengths and weaknesses of . . . . Using the given criteria, write an evaluation of . . . .

Source: Linn, R. L., & Gronlund, N. E., *Measurement and assessment in teaching*, 7th Edition, copyright © 1995, pp. 226–227. Adapted by permission of Prentice-Hall, Upper Saddle River, New Jersey.

Examples

> *Poor:* Why do Haitian farmers have trouble making a living?
> *Improved:* Describe how the weather, soil, and poverty in Haiti contribute to the plight of farmers. Indicate which of these three factors contributes most to the difficulties farmers experience, and give reasons for your selection.
> *Poor:* How was World War I different from World War II?
> *Improved:* How were the social and political factors leading up to World War I in Germany different from those leading up to World War II? Focus your answer on the ten-year period that preceded the beginning of each war.

You can see that in each of these "poorly" worded items students have too much freedom to write about any of a number of aspects of either Haiti or differences between the wars.

Another way to clarify to students the nature of the task is to indicate the criteria for scoring their answer in the question. This can be labeled a scoring plan, scoring criteria, or attributes to be scored. It essentially tells the student what you will be looking for when grading their answers. This is particularly important if the organization of the response or writing skills are included as criteria.

Examples

For Scoring Writing Skills

- Organization
- Clarity
- Appropriateness to audience
- Mechanics

For Scoring an Argument

- Distinguishing between facts and opinions
- Judging credibility of a source
- Identifying relevant material
- Recognizing inconsistencies
- Using logic

For Scoring Decision Making

- Identifying goals or purpose
- Identifying obstacles
- Identifying and evaluating alternatives
- Justifying a choice of one alternative

3. Indicate Approximately How Much Time Students Should Spend on Each Essay Item.   You should have some idea of how much time students will need to answer each item. For restricted-response questions, the amount of time needed is relatively short and easy to estimate. For extended-response items, the estimate is more difficult. You can get some idea by writing draft answers, and as you gain more experience the responses of previous students to similar questions will be helpful. Take into consideration the writing abilities of your students, and be sure that even your slowest writers can complete their answers satisfactorily in the time available. (You want to assess reasoning, not writing speed!) If you are unsure about the time needed, err by providing more time than is needed rather than less time.

4. Avoid Giving Students Options as to Which Essay Questions They Will Respond To.   Many teachers provide students with a choice of questions to answer. For example, there may be seven questions, and the teacher will tell students to answer their choice of three of the seven. Students love such questions because they can answer the items they are best prepared for. They will especially like this approach if they know before taking the test that they will have a choice. Then they can restrict their study to part of the material, rather than to all of it (you can avoid this by telling students *you* will select the items they will write on).

But giving students a choice of questions means that each student may be taking a different test. Differences in the difficulty of each question are probably unknown. This makes scoring more problematic, and your inferences of student ability less valid. It is true that you can't measure every important target, and giving students a choice does provide them with an opportunity to do their best work. However, this advantage is outweighed by difficulties in scoring and making sound inferences.

Scoring Essays

Scoring essay question responses is difficult because each student writes a unique answer and because there are many distractions that affect scoring reliability. Obviously scoring is subjective, so it is important to practice a few procedures to ensure that the professional judgments are accurate.

The following guidelines will help (see Figure 7.12).

1. Outline What Constitutes a Good or Acceptable Answer as a Scoring Key. This should be completed prior to administering or scoring student responses. If done before the test is finalized, an outline provides you with an opportunity to

FIGURE 7.12   Checklist for Scoring Essays

1. Is the answer outlined prior to testing students?
2. Is the scoring method—holistic or analytic—appropriate?
3. Is the role of writing mechanics clarified?
4. Are items scored one at a time?
5. Is the order in which the papers are graded changed?
6. Is the identity of the student anonymous?

revise the stem or question on the basis of what you learn by delineating the response. It's important to have the points specified before reading student answers so that you are not unduly influenced by the initial papers you read. These papers can set the standard for what follows. The scoring key provides a common basis for evaluating each answer. An outline lessens the influence of other extraneous factors, such as vocabulary or neatness.

2. Select an Appropriate Scoring Method.   There are two ways to score an essay: holistically or analytically. In *holistic* scoring, the teacher makes an overall judgment about the answer, giving it a single score or grade. The score can be based on a general impression or on attending to several specific scoring criteria to come up with a single score for each essay. This is often accomplished by placing essays in designated piles that represent different degrees of quality. The holistic method is most appropriate for extended-response essays (in which the responses are not limited and are generally long).

Analytic scoring is achieved by giving each of the identified criteria separate points. Thus, there would be several scores for each essay, and probably a total score that results from adding all the component scores. Analytic scoring is preferred for restricted-response questions (for which there is a limit to the amount of response the student provides). The advantage of analytic scoring is that it provides students with more specific feedback (though this should not replace individualized teacher comments). However, analytic scoring can be very time-consuming, and sometimes adding scored parts does not do justice to the overall student response. To avoid excessive attention to specific factors, keep the number of features to be scored analytically to three or four.

3. Clarify the Role of Writing Mechanics.   Suppose you are a biology teacher and you use essay questions. Does it matter if students spell poorly or use bad sentence structure? Such writing mechanics can certainly influence your overall impression of an answer, so it is important to decide early about whether, and to what extent, these factors are included as scoring criteria. Regardless of how you decide to incorporate writing mechanics, it is generally best to give students a separate score for these skills (as long as it was one of your targets) and not add this score into the total.

4. Use a Systematic Process When Scoring Many Essays at the Same Time.
When faced with a pile of papers to grade, it's tempting to simply start with the first paper, grade all the questions for that student, and then go on to the next. To lessen the influence of order and your own fatigue, however, it is best to score one item at a time for all students, and to change the order of the papers for each question. Reliability will increase if you read all responses to question 1 in one order, all responses to question 2 in a different order, and so on. This avoids the tendency to

allow the answer a student gives to the first question to influence subsequent evaluations of the remaining questions. It is also best to score all answers to each item in one sitting, if possible. This helps you to be consistent in applying criteria to the answers.

5. If Possible, Keep the Identity of the Student Anonymous.   It is best not to know whose answer you are grading. This avoids the tendency to be influenced by impressions of the student from class discussion or other tests. This source of error, which is probably the most serious one that influences results, is difficult to control because most teachers get to know the writing of their students. You can have students put their names on the back of the papers, but the best guard is to be consciously aware of the potential bias to keep it minimized.

SUMMARY

This chapter has focused on the assessment of reasoning skills. Teachers need to first clearly identify the skills they want to assess and then use appropriate methods of assessment wisely. The following points summarize the chapter:

- Reasoning is mental manipulation of knowledge for some purpose. Many different thinking skills are involved.
- Three perspectives on thinking and reasoning, from education, psychology, and philosophy, have contributed different ideas about how to operationalize and categorize the skills.
- Bloom's taxonomy represents a popular, though dated framework for identifying reasoning skills.
- Critical thinking involves the application of evaluative thinking skills, such as identifying irrelevant information, analyzing an argument, detecting bias, and using deductive logic, to decide what to do or believe.
- Quellmalz's framework combines other conceptualizations to result in five major types of reasoning: recall, analysis, comparison, inference, and evaluation.
- Marzano's dimensions of learning has five levels: positive attitudes about learning, acquiring and integrating knowledge, extending and refining knowledge, using knowledge meaningfully, and productive habits of mind. Using knowledge includes decision making, problem solving, investigation, experimental inquiry, and invention. Each of these processes has steps that can be identified and assessed.
- Reasoning targets are best assessed by interpretive exercises and essay items, though objective questions can be used effectively to measure specific thinking skills.

- Binary-choice items are good for assessing a student's ability to discriminate among differences such as fact or opinion, relevant or irrelevant, and biased or unbiased.
- Multiple-choice items can be used to assess thinking and reasoning skills, but they are difficult to write.
- Interpretive exercises include information or data followed by objective questions that require students to reason about what was presented. Because most of the knowledge needed for the answer is usually present in the item, it provides a good measure of reasoning.
- Good interpretive items are difficult to write and may penalize students who are not good readers.
- Each interpretive item should have relatively short, familiar, but new introductory material and several questions that do not measure recognition of the introductory material used in class.
- Essay items allow students to show their reasoning skills by constructing an answer.
- Extended-response essays are best for assessing complex reasoning tasks such as decision making and problem solving, while restricted-response items are better for assessing specific thinking skills or knowledge and comprehension.
- The major disadvantage of essays is in the scoring, which is time-consuming and fraught with many potential sources of error.
- Good essay items clearly define the task for students, specifically in terms of the skills that will be assessed. Students should know about how much time to spend on each essay item, and the option to choose items should be avoided.
- The scoring of essays is enhanced if an outline of an acceptable answer is made before testing students; if the correct method of scoring is used (holistic or analytical); if the scoring is done by question, not by student; if the order of papers is changed; and if student papers are anonymous.

SELF-INSTRUCTIONAL REVIEW EXERCISES

1. Identify the thinking or reasoning skill or task illustrated by each of the following examples, using this key:

    A analysis
    S synthesis
    C critical thinking
    D decision making
    P problem solving
    I inference
    E evaluation

    a. Suppose you were President Johnson and had to decide whether to send more troops to Vietnam. What would you do? Why would you do it?

    b. State your reasons for agreeing or disagreeing with the following statement: Religious people are more likely to help others.

    c. Given what you know about sailing, what would most likely occur if a novice sailor tried to sail directly into the wind?

    d. Examine three different human cultures. What is common for all three of the cultures, and what principle about being human does this suggest?

    e. Examine four recent presidential speeches. Is any part of the speeches the same?

    f. How can the United States reduce the rate of teenage pregnancies?

    g. Suppose you had to choose between increasing taxes to reduce the U.S. budget deficit or decreasing federal spending to reduce the deficit. Which would you choose? Why? How would your choice affect retired persons?

    h. Examine the data on birth rates. What is likely to happen to the birth rate by the year 2010? Why?

2. Indicate whether each of the following would be best measured by an objective item (O), an interpretive exercise (I), or an essay question (E).

    a. Discerning the meaning of a series of pictures.

    b. Asking students about the validity of an argument used in a debate tournament.

    c. Analyzing a passage to identify irrelevant information and opinions.

    d. Being able to construct a logical argument.

    e. Knowing the sequence of steps involved in problem solving.

    f. Giving examples of the principle of tropism.

    g. Being able to distinguish critical thinking from decision making.

    h. Determining if Michelangelo would be regarded as a great artist if he lived today and, if so, why.

    i. Identifying several valid generalizations from the data presented.

3. Evaluate the following interpretive exercise based on the weather map in Figure 7.13 on page 187. What are its strengths and how could it be improved? What reasoning skills does it assess?

    Directions. Pretend you are a weather forecaster. Read the weather information and then answer the questions.

    a. What four cities can expect rain?

    b. What will the weather be like in Chicago and Los Angeles?

    c. Which cities will have the highest temperatures?

    d. Which city will have a partly cloudy day?

    e. In what part of the United States will there be a high pressure area?

    f. In what direction will the warm front be moving?

    g. Would you go to the beach in Miami on August 31 to get a suntan? Why or why not?

4. Evaluate the following essay question. What learning targets does it appear to assess? How could it be improved?

    Do you think freedom of the press should extend to the irresponsible sensationalism of Hearst during the era of the Spanish-American War? Justify your answer.

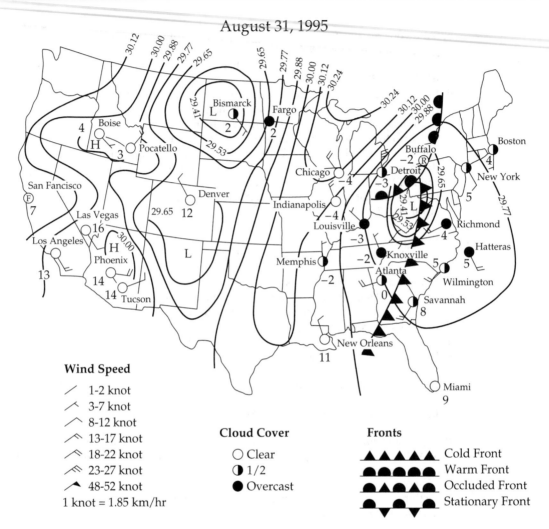

FIGURE 7.13   Forecasts and Temperatures

Source: Perkins, Otho E. (1987). *Earth Science: A Cambridge Work-A-Text*. New York: Globe Book Company, Inc., p. 187.

ANSWERS TO SELF-INSTRUCTIONAL REVIEW ITEMS

1. a. D, b. C, c. I, d. S, e. A, f. P, g. C, h. I.

2. a. I, b. I or E, c. I, d. E, e. O, f. E, g. O, h. E, i. I.

3. The general format of the question is appropriate, and it is good to have several questions on the material presented. Introductory information is kept to a minimum. Presumably students have been studying weather maps; this one should be new. Clearly the questions cannot be answered correctly unless the student can understand the map.

The format of the questions could be improved so that students check or circle correct answers rather than taking time to write their answers (e.g., What will the weather be like in Chicago and Los Angeles? a. fair b. cloudy c. rainy d. windy). This would reduce the time students need to answer the questions and the time needed for scoring. The reasoning target assessed by the question is primarily inference. Question 7 assesses deductive reasoning. Application and understanding targets are also assessed. The assessment could be improved by asking additional questions about wind speed and direction and barometric pressure.

4. This essay question assesses evaluation and critical thinking skills. A decision must be made with reasonable justification. It also assesses constructing support and deductive reasoning. The item could be improved by indicating how much time students should take in answering it, by indicating scoring criteria, and by providing more specific information about what is expected. Including the word *irresponsible* gives students a clear tip to what the teacher is looking for. Phrases like *justify your answer* give students some direction but are vague. What level of detail is expected? How many reasons are adequate? What is meant by *justify*? There should also be an indication of the total points for the item.

SUGGESTIONS FOR ACTION RESEARCH

1. Devise some reasoning learning targets for this chapter or one of the previous chapters. Then construct four objective and two essay items that would assess these targets.
2. Provide examples of five of Marzano's or Quellmalz's reasoning skills from the discipline you teach. Share your examples with two other students for their critique.
3. Write an essay question with criteria for scoring and examples of responses that would be graded A, B, and C. Give the question, scoring criteria, and examples of responses with grades deleted to four other students for them to grade. Compare their judgments with the grades you assigned.
4. Examine two or three textbooks written for the area in which you wish to teach, either teacher's editions or the ones students use, and identify examples of the reasoning or thinking skills that are assessed. Then match the skills in the textbooks with the frameworks presented in the chapter.
5. Ask a teacher how he or she conceptualizes reasoning skills and how these skills are measured in the classroom. Compare the teacher's responses to the checklists presented in the chapter.
6. Observe some students as they take a test that assesses reasoning skills. How much time does it take them to formulate an answer? How much time does it take to write an answer? If possible examine their responses. How would you evaluate their work?

ENDNOTE

1. Adapted from California Achievement Test 5 Performance Assessment Component, CTB/Macmillan/McGraw-Hill, 1993, p. 39.

8

ASSESSING KNOWLEDGE, REASONING, SKILLS AND PRODUCTS: PERFORMANCE-BASED ASSESSMENTS

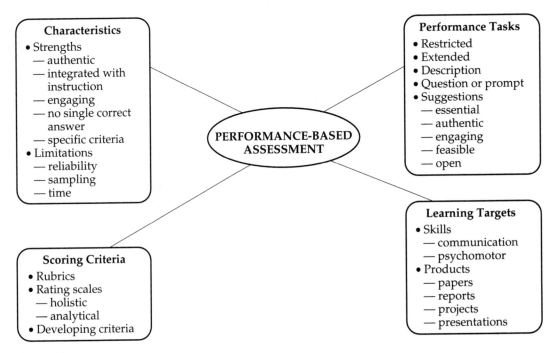

Characteristics
- Strengths
  — authentic
  — integrated with instruction
  — engaging
  — no single correct answer
  — specific criteria
- Limitations
  — reliability
  — sampling
  — time

Performance Tasks
- Restricted
- Extended
- Description
- Question or prompt
- Suggestions
  — essential
  — authentic
  — engaging
  — feasible
  — open

PERFORMANCE-BASED ASSESSMENT

Scoring Criteria
- Rubrics
- Rating scales
  — holistic
  — analytical
- Developing criteria

Learning Targets
- Skills
  — communication
  — psychomotor
- Products
  — papers
  — reports
  — projects
  — presentations

CHAPTER 8   Concept Map

In the last two chapters, we examined what are often called conventional *paper-and-pencil* methods of assessment. These techniques have been used effectively for many years to assess knowledge targets and, to a lesser extent, to assess reasoning targets. With greater emphasis on reasoning and being able to apply learning to situations and problems that are more like real life, there has recently been an explosion of interest in assessments that require students to *do* something, not simply know it or know how to do it. That is, it is one thing to demonstrate written knowledge about how to give a speech, but actually giving the speech represents a different kind of learning target. Students are required to show what they can do, not simply tell what they know or would do. This chapter focuses on these new assessments.

WHAT IS PERFORMANCE-BASED ASSESSMENT?

Simply put, a *performance-based* assessment is one in which the teacher observes and makes a judgment about the student's demonstration of a skill or competency in creating a product. Performance-based is shorthand for *performance-and-product* based. The emphasis is on the students' ability to use their knowledge and skills to produce their own work. In some cases this is an actual performance, like singing, playing the piano, or doing gymnastics. In other cases, this ability is expressed through a product, such as a completed paper, project, or solution. Over the past decade, educators have taken what is best about performance-and-product assessment and used these principles to assess targets that previously were measured mostly by conventional objective tests. In doing this, however, the field has been deluged by confusing terms and definitions.

The term *performance-based assessment* is synonymous with *performance assessment*. Other terms, such as *authentic assessment* and *alternative assessment* are sometimes used interchangeably with performance assessment, but they actually mean something different. An *alternative* assessment is any method that differs from conventional paper-and-pencil tests, most particularly objective tests. Examples of alternative assessments include observations, exhibitions, oral presentations, experiments, portfolios, interviews, and projects. Some think of essays as a type of alternative assessment because they require students to construct responses.

Authentic assessment involves the direct examination of a student's ability to use knowledge to perform a task that is like what is encountered in real life or in the real world. Authenticity is judged in the nature of the task completed and in the context of the task (e.g., in the options available, constraints, and access to resources). Like any performance assessment, students plan, construct, and deliver an original response, and explain or justify their answers. The students are aware of the criteria and standards by which the work will be judged prior to beginning their work.

Performance-based assessment may or may not be authentic. In fact, we find that authenticity in terms of the real-world use of knowledge is one of several characteristics of performance-based assessment that is a matter of degree. Some performance-based assessments are more authentic than others. Figure 8.1 on page 200 summarizes the characteristics of performance-based assessments.

FIGURE 8.1   Characteristics of Performance-Based Assessments

- Students perform, create, construct, produce, or do something.
- Reasoning skills are needed and assessed.
- Involves sustained work, often days and weeks.
- Calls upon students to explain, justify, and defend.
- Performance is directly observable.
- Involves engaging ideas of importance and substance.
- Relies on trained assessor's judgments for scoring.
- Multiple criteria and standards are prespecified and public.
- There is no single "correct" answer.
- If authentic, grounded in real-world contexts and constraints.

Most of these characteristics are typically present to some extent in a performance-based assessment. But be careful. Because the term *performance assessment* is so popular, test publishers and some educators have come to use it as a label for constructed response interpretive exercises and essay items. All of this may seem confusing, but it reflects reality. It's as if there is an ideal for what a performance-based assessment should look like, and many variations are in practice. Popham (1995) points out that some performance-based assessment proponents contend that there are three essential components to a performance-based assessment: multiple criteria, prespecified quality standards, and judgmental appraisal.

STRENGTHS AND LIMITATIONS OF PERFORMANCE-BASED ASSESSMENTS

The major benefits of performance-based assessments are tied closely to instruction. This explains much of the appeal of the approach. The intent is to integrate instruction and assessment, so that what is taught in the classroom is reflected in measures of student performance, and what is tested drives appropriate instruction. Learning occurs while students complete the assessment. Teachers interact with students as they do the task, providing feedback and prompts that help students learn. Good performance-based assessment models need instruction; the performance assessment tasks are sometimes the same as instructional activities. Opportunities are provided for teachers to assess the reasoning processes students use in their work. Because the assessments are usually tied to real-world challenges and situations, students are better prepared for such thinking and performance once out of school. Also like real life, students justify their thinking and learn that there often is no single correct answer. In this way, the assessments influence the instruction to be more meaningful and practical. Students value the task more because they view it as rich rather than superficial, engaging rather than uninteresting, and active rather than passive.

As pointed out in Chapter 1, much instruction is now based on constructivistic principles of learning, with an emphasis on applied reasoning skills and integrated subject matter. Performance-based assessments are better suited to measure these kinds of targets than are objective tests. Students are more engaged in active learning as a part of the assessment because that is what they need to perform successfully (as contrasted with memorizing information). Because the emphasis is on what students *do*, skills are more directly assessed and there are more opportunities to observe the process students use to arrive at their answer or response. Students who traditionally do not perform well on paper-and-pencil tests have an opportunity to demonstrate their learning in a different way.

Another advantage of performance assessments is that they force teachers to identify multiple, specific criteria for judging success. Teachers share these criteria with students prior to the assessment so that the students may use them as they learn. In this way, students learn how to evaluate their own performance through self-assessment. They learn how to ask questions and, in many assessments, how to work effectively with others.

Wiggins (1993) makes the point that performance-based assessment is simply applying the teaching/learning methods used successfully for years in the adult world. Musicians, artists, athletes, architects, and doctors all learn by getting feedback on what they do, and the important goal is not what they know but how what they know is demonstrated in practice. Thus, an important advantage of performance-based assessment is that this same approach can be applied to learning all content areas. It helps instruction target more important outcomes.

Finally, performance-based assessment motivates educators to explore the purposes and processes of schooling (Jamentz, 1994). Because of the nature of the assessments, teachers revisit their learning goals, instructional practices, and standards. They explore how students will use their classroom time differently and whether there are adequate resources for all students.

Bill Hadley, a high school mathematics teacher, illustrates how performance-based assessment can transform the classroom (Stenmark, 1991, p. 12):

> *In my general math classes this past year I decided not to give separate stand-alone tests but to assess my students' growth and understanding of mathematics through the use of performance assessments. . . . I assigned groups or pairs of students certain tasks to perform. Then by coaching, observing, and interviewing the students as they worked on these tasks, I was able to assess their knowledge and growth. The information I received was much more comprehensive and complete, and I found that I was able to give the students grades that I thought very accurately reflected their progress. . . . This positive experience with alternative assessment forms and with integrating assessment and instruction will enable me to employ similar methods more often in my other classes. I have discovered that tests do not have to be a primary or necessary type of assessment . . . traditionally structured tests seem to be an impediment to effective instruction.*

The limitations of using performance assessment lie in three areas: reliability, sampling, and time. Unfortunately, performance-based assessments are subject to considerable measurement error, which lowers reliability. Like essay items, the major source of measurement error with performance-based assessments lies in the scoring. Because scoring requires professional judgment, there will be variations and error due to bias and other factors, similar to what affects evaluating essay answers. Although procedures exist that can minimize scoring error—such as carefully constructed criteria, tasks, and scoring rubrics; systematic scoring procedures; and using more than one rater—rating reliability is likely to be lower than what is achieved with other types of assessment. Inconsistent student performance also contributes to error. That is, student performance at one time may differ noticeably from what the student would demonstrate at another time (this might occur, for example, if on the day of the performance the student is ill). Both of these factors then, scoring error and inconsistency, contribute to unreliability.

Because it takes a lot of time for students to do performance-based assessments, you will have relatively few samples of student achievement and ability. Furthermore, we know that performance on one task may not provide a very good estimate of student proficiency on other tasks. This means that if you intend to use the results of performance-based assessment to form conclusions about capability in a larger domain of learning targets, you need to accumulate information from multiple tasks. This usually takes several months. Although the lack of generalization to a larger domain of targets is offset by greater depth and richness of information, you need to be careful in making properly constrained inferences (validity). In situations where a great amount of knowledge and understanding is to be demonstrated, such as in content areas, performance-based assessments will not provide a very good measure of the targets because of the lack of generalization.

The third major limitation of performance-based assessment concerns time. First, it is very time-consuming to construct good tasks, develop scoring criteria, administer the task, observe students, and then apply these criteria to student performance. For performances that cannot be scored later, adequate time needs to be taken with each student as he or she performs the task. Second, it is difficult to interact with all students in a timely fashion, and give them meaningful feedback as they learn and make decisions. Finally, it is difficult to estimate the amount of time students will need to complete performance-based assessments, especially if the task is a new one and if students are unaccustomed to the format and expectations.

LEARNING TARGETS FOR PERFORMANCE-BASED ASSESSMENTS

Teachers in some fields have been using performance-based assessment for years because their learning targets require students to demonstrate skills or to generate a product (this applies to subjects such as art, music, typing, athletics, writing, reading). Skills include the student's accomplishment of reasoning, communication, and psychomotor proficiencies. Products are completed works, such as term papers, reports, projects, and other assignments in which students use their skills and knowledge. What is new about performance-based assessment is that it is now being advocated for assessing understanding and for formal statewide testing. Because the method of assessment for both of these uses has mainly been objective paper-and-pencil tests, the popularity of performance assessment has represented a major change in what and how we assess students. Our experience to date indicates that substantial difficulties arise when using performance-based assessments for statewide accountability testing. However, for the right targets in the classroom, performance-based assessments can be very effective and will enhance student learning. We'll turn now to these types of appropriate learning targets.

Skills

The reasoning skill targets delineated in Chapter 7 are often cited in describing performance assessment outcomes. Typically, students are given a problem to solve or are asked to make a decision based on information provided. The types of targets are essentially the same as those identified in Chapter 7. What is different is the nature of the task and the scoring criteria used to judge student answers. If the characteristics in Figure 8.1 (page 200) are evident, the assessment can be called "performance-based," although sometimes it's neither easy nor necessary to know for sure if this label is accurate. If a student is asked to explain how he or she arrived at a particular answer to a problem to the class, is this a performance-based assessment because the student is performing a reasoning skill? From the standpoint of the learning target, a performance-based assessment is appropriate, but it may be that the nature of the task and the *scoring* of the result do not contain enough characteristics from Figure 8.1 to be an example of a performance-based assessment. In other words, we can call just about anything students do "performances," but that's not the same as implementing a systematic performance-based assessment as discussed here.

Communication Skills

Learning targets focused on communication skills involve student performance of reading, writing, speaking, and listening. For reading, targets can be divided into process—what students do before, during, and after reading—and outcome—what students get from the reading. Reading targets for elementary students progress from process skills such as being able to handle a book appropriately (e.g., right side up, turning pages), to word analysis skills (e.g., decoding, phonological awareness, and blending), to skills needed for comprehension and understanding (such as discrimination, contextual cues, inference, blending, sequencing, and identifying main ideas). For effective performance-based assessment, each of these areas would need to be delineated as specific targets. For instance, a word identification target may include naming and matching uppercase and lowercase letters, recognizing words by sight, recognizing sounds and symbols for consonants at the beginnings and ends of words, and sounding out three-letter words. For older students, reading targets focus on comprehension and reading efficiency. These include stating main ideas; identifying the setting, characters, and events in stories; drawing inferences from context; and reading speed. More advanced reading skills include sensitivity to word meanings related to origins, nuances, or figurative meanings; identifying contradictions; and identifying possible multiple inferences. All reading targets should include the ability to perform a specific skill for novel reading materials. A variety of formats should also be represented.

Writing skill targets are also determined by a student's grade level. For young students, the emphasis is on their ability to construct letters and copy words and simple sentences legibly. For writing complete essays or papers, elaborate delineations of skills have been developed. Typically, important dimensions of writing are used as categories. In Vermont, for example, student writing targets for public school grades 4 through 8 are as follows:

Purpose:	Clarity of purpose; awareness of audience and task; clarity of ideas
Organization:	Unity and coherence
Details:	Appropriateness of details to purpose and support for main point(s) of writers response
Voice/tone:	Personal investment and expression
Usage, Mechanics and Grammar:	Correct usage (tense formation, agreement, word choice), mechanics (spelling, capitalization, punctuation), grammar, and sentence construction

Other dimensions can be used when the writing skill being measured is more specific, such as writing a persuasive letter, a research paper, or an editorial. Writing targets, like those in reading, should include the ability to perform the skill in a variety of situations or contexts. That is, if students have been taught persuasive writing by developing letters to editors, the student may write a persuasive advertisement or speech to demonstrate that he or she has obtained the skill. Because writing is so easily collected and stored, it is also easy to provide students with examples of writing that illustrate the target prior to their demonstrating their competence. Writing is also used extensively for portfolios, which will be discussed in greater detail in the next chapter.

Oral communication skill targets can be generalized to most or all situations, or it can be focused on a specific type of oral communication such as giving a speech, singing a song, speaking a foreign language, or competing in a debate. When the emphasis is on general oral communication skills, the targets typically center around the following three general categories (Airasian, 1994):

Physical expression:	Eye contact, posture, facial expressions, gestures, and body movement
Vocal expression:	Articulation, clarity, vocal variation, loudness, pace, and rate
Verbal expression:	Repetition, organization, summarizations, reasoning, completeness of ideas and thoughts, selection of appropriate words to convey precise meanings

A more specific set of oral communication skill targets is illustrated in the following guidelines for high school students.[1]

A. Speaking clearly, expressively, and audibly

   1. Using voice expressively
   2. Speaking articulately and pronouncing words correctly
   3. Using appropriate vocal volume

B. Presenting ideas with appropriate introduction, development, and conclusion

   1. Presenting ideas in an effective order
   2. Providing a clear focus on the central idea
   3. Providing signal words, internal summaries, and transitions

C. Developing ideas using appropriate support materials

   1. Being clear and using reasoning processes
   2. Clarifying, illustrating, exemplifying, and documenting ideas

D. Using nonverbal cues

   1. Using eye contact
   2. Using appropriate facial expressions, gestures, and body movement

E. Selecting language to a specific purpose

   1. Using language and conventions appropriate for the audience

For specific purposes the skills are more targeted. For example, if a student were giving a persuasive speech, the target could include such factors as the establishment of initial interest, whether interest is sustained, persuasiveness, dependency on notes, and logic, as well as more general features such as posture, enunciation, and eye contact.

Psychomotor Skills

There are two steps in identifying learning targets for psychomotor skills. The first step is to describe clearly the physical actions that are required. These may be developmentally appropriate skills or skills that are needed for specific tasks. I have divided the psychomotor area into five categories in Figure 8.2 on page 206 to help you describe the behavior: fine motor skills (such as holding a pencil, focusing a microscope, and using scissors), gross motor actions (such as jumping and lifting), more complex athletic skills (such as shooting a basketball or playing golf), some visual skills, and verbal/auditory skills for young children.

The second step is to identify the level at which the skill is to be performed. One effective way to do this is to use an existing classification of the psychomotor domain (Simpson, 1972). This system is hierarchical. At the most basic level is *perception*, the ability to use sight, smell, hearing, and touch to be aware of a stimulus. The second level is *set*, which is a state of readiness to take action. The next level is *guided response*, which involves imitating a behavior or following directions.

FIGURE 8.2   Examples of Psychomotor Skills

Fine Motor	Gross Motor	Complex	Visual	Verbal and Auditory
Cutting paper with scissors	Walking	Perform a golf swing	Copying	Identify and discriminate sounds
Drawing a line	Jumping	Operate a computer	Finding letters	Imitate sounds
Tracing	Balancing	Drive a car	Finding embedded figures	Pronounce carefully
Eye-hand coordination	Throwing	Dissect a frog	Identifying shapes	Articulate
Penmanship	Skipping	Perform back walkover on balance beam	Discriminating on the basis of attributes such as size, shape, and color	Blend vowels
Coloring	Pull-ups	Operate a microscope		Use proper lip and tongue placement to produce sounds
Drawing shapes	Hopping	Sail a boat		
Connecting dots	Kicking	Operate a press drill		
Pointing				
Buttoning				
Zipping				

The fourth level is reached when an action becomes habitual and is done correctly with confidence. This is called *mechanism*. *Complex overt response* is the fifth level, which involves correct actions comprising complex skills. The sixth level is *adaptation*, through which students can make adjustments to suit their needs. The final and highest level is *origination*, which refers to creating new actions to solve a problem. This classification scheme is summarized in Figure 8.3, along with some examples. You can use the levels to determine the nature of the target for the skills identified from step 1. For instance, suppose you are interested in assessing your students' abilities to write capital letters correctly. At one level students need to be able to identify the letter, perhaps by locating an example of it on the wall (the perception level). Then they need to be physically prepared to write correctly (the set level—pencil sharpened, paper in the correct position), followed by being able to copy letters from the board (guided response). Then they can demonstrate their skill when drafting paragraphs (mechanism), and alter the shapes to accommodate different widths between lines (adaptation).

Products

Products for performance-based assessment are completed works that include to some degree most of the characteristics in Figure 8.1 on page 200. For years, students have done papers, reports, and projects. What makes these products different when used for performance-based assessment is that they are more engaging, more authentic, and are scored more systematically with public criteria and standards. For example, rather than having sixth graders report on a foreign country by summarizing the history, politics, and economics of the country, students write

FIGURE 8.3   **Major Levels in the Psychomotor Domain**

Description	Examples
1. *Perception*. Uses the sense organs to obtain cues that guide motor activity; ranges from sensory stimulation (awareness), through cue selection, to translation.	Chooses appropriate letters based on sounds made by the teacher. Detects different sounds from a machine. Relates music to a particular dance step.
2. *Set*. Readiness to take a particular action; includes mental, physical, and emotional set. Perception is an important prerequisite.	Explains sequence of steps in building a bookcase. Shows proper batting stance. Shows desire to learn keyboarding.
3. *Guided response*. Concerned with the early stages of learning a complex skill. Includes imitation, trial and error.	Performs shooting a basketball free-throw shot as demonstrated. Applies first-aid bandage as shown. Repeats a dance step.
4. *Mechanism*. Concerned with habitual responses that can be performed with some confidence and proficiency. Less complex than the next level.	Writes smoothly and legibly. Operates a slide projector efficiently. Performs a dance step gracefully.
5. *Complex overt response*. Skillfully performs acts that require complex movement patterns, such as highly coordinated motor activities. Proficiency indicated by quick, smooth, and accurate performance, requiring a minimum of effort.	Operates a power saw skillfully. Demonstrates skill in driving a car. Plays the violin skillfully.
6. *Adaptation*. Concerned with skills so well learned that they are modified to fit special requirements or to meet a problem situation.	Modifies swimming stroke based on roughness of the water. Changes basketball jump shot due to defense played.
7. *Origination*. Creates new movement patterns to fit a particular situation or problem.	Creates a new dance step. Composes a song. Originates a new procedure for operating a machine.

Source: Linn, R. L., & Gronlund, N. E., *Measurement and assessment in teaching*, 7th Edition, copyright © 1995, pp. 538–539. Adapted by permission of Prentice-Hall, Upper Saddle River, New Jersey.

promotional materials for the country that would help others decide if it would be an interesting place to visit. In chemistry, students are asked to identify an unknown substance. Why not have them identify the substances from a local landfill, river, or body of water? In music, students can demonstrate their proficiency and knowledge by creating and playing a new song. Figure 8.4 on page 208 presents some other examples, with varying degrees of authenticity.

FIGURE 8.4   Performance-Based Products Varying in Authenticity

Relatively Unauthentic	Somewhat Authentic	Authentic
Indicate which parts of a garden design are accurate.	Design a garden.	Build a garden.
Write a paper on zoning.	Write a proposal to change fictitious zoning laws.	Write a proposal to present to city council to change zoning laws.
Answer a series of questions about what materials are needed for a trip.	Defend the selection of supplies needed for a hypothetical trip.	Plan a trip with your family, indicating needed supplies.
Explain what you would teach to students learning to play basketball.	Show how to perform basketball skills in practice.	Play a basketball game.
Listen to a tape and interpret a foreign language.	Hold a conversation with a teacher in a foreign language.	Hold a conversation with a person from a foreign country in his or her native language.

As a learning target, each product needs to be clearly described in some detail so that there is no misunderstanding about what students are required to do. It is not sufficient to simply say, for example, "Write a report on one of the planets and present it to the class." Students need to know about the specific elements of the product (e.g., length, types of information needed, nature of the audience, context, materials that can be used, and what can be shown to the audience) and how they will be evaluated. One effective way to do this is to show examples of completed projects to students. These are not meant to be copied, but they can be used to communicate standards and expectations. In other words, show examples of the target to the students. If the examples can demonstrate different levels of proficiency, so much the better. A good way to generate products is to think about what people in different occupations do. What is it that a city planner does? What would an expert witness produce for a trial? How would a map maker create a map that is easy to understand? What kinds of stories does a newspaper columnist write? How would an advertising agent represent state parks to attract tourists? In the next section, we will examine criteria for good performance-based tasks.

CONSTRUCTING PERFORMANCE-BASED TASKS

Once learning targets have been identified and you have decided that a performance-based assessment is the method you want to use, three steps remain. The first is to construct the performance task students will be engaged in; the second is to develop the task description; the third is to write the specific question, prompt, or problem the students will receive (Figure 8.5).

FIGURE 8.5 Steps in Constructing Performance-Based Tasks

The performance-based task is what students are required to do in the performance assessment, either individually or in groups. The tasks can vary by subject and by level of complexity. Some performance tasks are specific to a content area, while others integrate several subjects and skills. With regard to level of complexity, it is useful to distinguish two types: restricted and extended.

Restricted- and Extended-Type Performance-Based Tasks

Restricted-type tasks target a narrowly defined skill and require relatively brief responses. The task is structured and specific. These tasks may look very similar to short essay questions and interpretive exercises that have open-ended items. The difference is in the relative emphasis on characteristics listed in Figure 8.1 on page 200. Often the performance-based task is structured to elicit student explanations of their answer. Students may be asked to defend an answer, indicate why a different answer is not correct, tell how they did something, or show some other aspect of their reasoning. In contrast, short essay questions and interpretive exercises are designed to infer reasoning from correct answers. While restricted-type tasks require relatively little time for administration and scoring in comparison with extended-type tasks (providing greater reliability and sampling), it is likely that fewer of the important characteristics of authentic performance-based assessments are included.

Some restricted-type performance-based tasks are as follows:

Construct a bar graph from data provided.
Demonstrate a short conversation in French about what is on a menu.
Read an article from the newspaper and answer questions.
Review a zoning map of a city and indicate changes that would encourage more commercial development.
Flip a coin ten times, make a prediction about what the next ten flips of the coin will be, and explain why.
Listen to the evening news on television and explain if you believe the stories are biased.
From the information given on three bar graphs showing the amount of carbohydrates, fats, and protein in two new food bars, select the one that would be most healthy. Justify your answer.
Using your own words and illustrations, construct a poster that explains the parts of flowers.
Sing a song.
Type at least thirty-five words per minute with fewer than six mistakes.
Show how to adjust the display of a computer screen.

Construct a circle, square, and triangle from the materials provided that have the same circumference.

Write a term paper on the importance of protecting forests from being converted to farmland.

Using scissors, cut the outlined figures from the page.

Recite a poem.

Many publishers now provide performance-based assessments in a standardized format, and most of these will contain restricted-type tasks.

Extended-type tasks are more complex, elaborate, and time-consuming. Often, extended-type tasks include collaborative work with small groups of students. The assignment usually requires students to use a variety of sources of information (e.g., observations, library, interviews). Judgments will need to be made about which information is most relevant. Products are typically developed over several days or even weeks, with opportunities for revision. This allows students to apply a variety of skills and makes it easier to integrate different content areas and reasoning skills.

It is not too difficult to come up with ideas for what would be an engaging extended-type task. As previously indicated, one effective approach is to think about what people do in different occupations. Another way to generate ideas is to check curriculum guides and teacher's editions of textbooks because most will have activities and assignments that tap student application and reasoning skills. Perhaps the best way is to generate ideas by brainstorming with others, especially members of the community. They can be particularly helpful in thinking about authentic tasks that involve reasoning and communication skills. Here are a few ideas that could be transformed into extended-type tasks:

Design a playhouse and estimate cost of materials and labor.

Plan a trip to another country, include the budget and itinerary, and justify why you plan to visit certain places.

Conduct a historical reenactment (e.g., the Boston Tea Party, the Lincoln–Douglas debates, a Civil War battle).

Diagnose the problem and repair a car.

Design an advertisement campaign for a new or existing product.

Publish a newspaper.

Design a park.

Create a commercial.

Write and perform a song.

Prepare a plan for dealing with waste materials.

Design and carry out a study to determine which grocery store has the lowest prices.

Once you have a general idea for the task, you need to develop it into a more detailed set of specifications.

Descriptions of Performance-Based Tasks

The performance-based task needs to be specified so that it meets the criteria for good performance-based assessment and is clear to students. This is accomplished by preparing a *task description*. The purpose of the task description is to provide a blueprint or listing of specifications to ensure that essential criteria are met, that the task is reasonable, and that it will elicit desired student performance. The task description is not the same as the actual format and wording of the question or prompt that is given to students; it is more like a lesson plan. The task description should include the following:

> content and skill targets to be assessed
> description of student activities
> group or individual help allowed
> resources needed
> teacher role
> administrative process
> scoring procedures

It is essential that the specific content or skill targets to be assessed are clearly described. This is needed to make certain that the activities and scoring will be well matched to ensure valid assessment as well as practical assessment. Think about what students will actually do to respond to the question or solve the problem. Will they consult other experts, use library resources, and/or do experiments? Are they allowed to work together or is it an individual assignment? What types of help from others are allowed? Is there sufficient time to complete the activities? Once the activities are described, the resources needed to accomplish them can be identified. Are needed materials and resources available for all students? What needs to be obtained prior to the assessment? It will be helpful to describe your role in the exercise. Will you consult your students or give them ideas? Are you comfortable with what you will do and adequately prepared for it? What administrative procedures are required? Finally, what scoring procedures will you use? Will scoring match the learning targets? Is adequate time available for scoring? Do you have the expertise needed to do the scoring? Is it practical?

Once the task description is completed and you are satisfied that the assessment will be valid and practical, you are ready to prepare the specific performance-based task question or prompt.

Question or Prompt for Performance-Based Task

The actual question, problem, or prompt that you give to students will be based on the task description. It needs to be stated so that it clearly identifies what the final outcome or product is, outlines what students are allowed and encouraged to do, and explains the criteria that will be used to judge the product. A good question or prompt also provides a context that helps students understand the meaningfulness and relevance of the task. A performance-based prompt is illustrated in Figure 8.6, in which the important components previously described are pointed out.

Because it takes considerable time to construct good performance tasks, you will want to use ones that have already been developed. The Association for Curriculum and Instruction (ASCD) has sponsored an *Authentic Assessment Network*. The network publishes a newsletter and facilitates opportunities for interested educators to plan and implement performance-based assessments by customizing information to meet the needs of individual members. The National Center for

---

FIGURE 8.6   Performance-Based Task Prompt

Comparison Task

Grade level range: Upper Elementary–Middle

Working in pairs, list as many insects as possible. Come up with a classification system that focuses on key characteristics of the insects and place the insects from your list in the appropriate categories. Do the same classification procedure two more times, but from the following perspectives:

- An exterminator (sample categories: insects found in homes, flying insects, crawling insects, insects commonly found in kitchens, insects that prefer dark basements).
- A frog (sample categories: insects that fly above water, insects that can swim, insects that would make a big meal, insects that would make a little meal).

⎫ Nature of Final Product

You will have to consult various resources (materials in the classroom, peers, adults, and so on) to obtain the information necessary to classify the insects accurately. When you turn in your three classification systems, include a list of the resources you used and explain in a short paragraph which were most and least useful. Be ready to share with the class some interesting things you discovered as a result of doing these classifications.

⎫ What Students Are Required to Do

You will be assessed on and provided rubrics for the following:

1. Your understanding of the characteristics of insects.
2. Your ability to specify important defining characteristics of the categories.
3. Your ability to accurately sort the identified elements into the categories.
4. Your ability to effectively use a variety of information-gathering techniques and information resources.

⎫ Criteria Used to Judge the Product

Source: Adapted by permission from Marzano, R. J., Pickering, D., & McTighe, J. (1993). *Assessing student outcomes: Performance assessment using the dimensions of learning model.* Alexandria, VA: Association for Supervision and Curriculum Development, p. 51.

Research on Evaluation, Standards, and Student Testing (CRESST) has a number of helpful resources, including a newsletter, technical reports, and an Internet gopher server that includes an Alternative Assessments in Practice Database with listings of assessments from more than 250 sources. CRESST is also making available samples of performance-based assessments in different subject areas and grade levels through ERIC (Educational Resources Information Center). The Council of Chief State School Officers (CCSSO) sponsors the Student Assessment Consortium, which includes information about the development of prototype assessment exercises. The New Standards Project, sponsored by the National Center on Education and the Economy (NCEE) is preparing performance-based assessments in several subject areas. Other good sources for tasks are national professional organizations, such as the National Council of Teachers of Mathematics, state departments of education, the Mid-Continent Regional Educational Laboratory, and the Northwest Regional Education Laboratory.

Whether you develop your own tasks or use intact or modified existing ones, you will want to evaluate the task on the basis of the following suggestions (summarized in Figure 8.8, page 216) and criteria summarized in Figure 8.7, page 214) .

1. The Task Should Integrate the Most Essential Aspects of the Content Being Assessed with the Most Essential Skills.   Performance-based assessment is ideal for focusing student attention and learning on the big ideas of a subject, the major concepts, principles, and processes that are important to a discipline. If the task encourages learning of peripheral or tangential topics, or specific details, it is not well suited to the goal of performance-based assessment. Tasks should be broad in scope. Similarly, reasoning and other skills essential to the task should represent essential processes. The task should be written to integrate content with skills. For example, it would be better to debate important content or contemporary issues rather than something relatively unimportant. A good test for whether the task meets these criteria is whether what is assessed could be done as well with more objective, less time-consuming measures.

Example

> *Poor:* Estimate the answers to the following three addition problems. Explain in your own words the strategy used to give your answer.
>
> *Improved:* Sam and Tyron were planning a trip to a nearby state. They wanted to visit as many different major cities as possible. Using the map, estimate the number of major cities they will be able to visit on a single tank of gas (fourteen gallons) if their car can get twenty-five miles to the gallon.

2. The Task Should Be Grounded in Real-World Contexts.   This suggestion lies at the heart of authentic performance-based assessment. Your goal is to use an authentic task, one that is similar to what students might encounter outside of school. Tasks that apply only to what students do in school are rarely authentic, though it may not be possible to have a task that is completely real.

FIGURE 8.7   Criteria for Performance Tasks

Essential	• The task fits into the core of the curriculum. • It represents a "big idea."	vs. Tangential
Authentic	• The task uses processes appropriate to the discipline. • Students value the outcome of the task.	vs. Contrived
Rich	• The task leads to other problems. • It raises other questions. • It has many possibilities.	vs. Superficial
Engaging	• The task is thought-provoking. • It fosters persistence.	vs. Uninteresting
Active	• The student is the worker and decision maker. • Students interact with other students. • Students are constructing meaning and deepening understanding.	vs. Passive
Feasible	• The task can be done within school and homework time. • It is developmentally appropriate for students. • It is safe.	vs. Infeasible
Equitable	• The task develops thinking in a variety of styles. • It contributes to positive attitudes.	vs. Inequitable
Open	• The task has more than one right answer. • It has multiple avenues of approach, making it accessible to all students.	vs. Closed

---

Source: Reprinted with permission from *Mathematics Assessment: Myths, models, good Questions, and practical Suggestions,* by Jean Kerr Stenmark, copyright © 1991 by the National Council of Teachers of Mathematics. All rights reserved.

Example

> *Poor:* Compare and contrast different kinds of literature.
>
> *Improved:*[2] You have volunteered to help your local library with its literacy program. Once a week after school, you help people learn how to read. To encourage your students to learn, you tell them about the different kinds of literature you have read, including poems, biographies, mysteries, tall tales, fables, and historical novels. Select three types of literature and compare them, using general characteristics of literature and the specific characteristics of each genre that you think will help your students see the similarities and differences among the types of literature. Create a table or chart to visually depict the comparison.

Notice also how the improved version integrates content, language arts, with two skills, comparison and communication.

3. Structure the Task to Assess Multiple Learning Targets.   As pointed out in the first suggestion, it is best if the task assesses both content and skill targets. Within each of these areas there may be different types of targets. For instance, assessing content may include both knowledge and understanding and, as in the example above, both reasoning and communication skills. It is also common to include different types of communication and reasoning skills in the same task (e.g., students provide both a written and oral report or need to think critically and synthesize to arrive at an answer). Often, because several targets are assessed, different modes of evaluation are used, such as observation and reading reports.

4. Structure the Task So That You Can Help Students Succeed.   Good performance-based assessment involves the interaction of instruction with assessment. The task needs to be something that students learn from, which is most likely when there are opportunities for you to increase student proficiency by asking questions, providing resources, and giving feedback. In this kind of active teaching, you are intervening as students learn, rather than simply providing information. Part of teachability is being certain that students have the needed prerequisite knowledge and skills to succeed.

5. Think Through What Students Will Do to Be Sure That the Task Is Feasible. Imagine what you would do if given the task. What resources would you need? How much time would you need? What steps would you take? It should be realistic for students to implement the task. This depends both on your own expertise and willingness, and on the costs and availability of equipment, materials, and other resources so that every student has the same opportunity to be successful.

6. The Task Should Allow for Multiple Solutions.   If a performance-based task is properly structured, more than one correct response is not only possible, but encouraged. The task should not encourage drill or practice for which there is a single solution. The possibility of multiple solutions encourages students to personalize the process, and makes it easier for you to demand that students justify and explain their assumptions, planning, predictions, and other responses. Different students may take different paths in responding to the task.

7. The Task Should Be Clear.   An unambiguous set of directions that explicitly indicates the nature of the task is essential. If the directions are too vague, students may not focus on the learning targets or may waste time trying to figure out what they should be doing. A task such as "Give an oral report on a foreign country" is too general. Students need to know the reason for the task, and the directions should provide sufficient detail so that students know how to proceed. Do they work alone or with others? What resources are available? How much time do they have? What is the role of the teacher? Here is an example of a clearly defined task (Marzano, Pickering, & McTighe, 1993, p. 61):

> *We will be reading George Orwell's* 1984, *which could be described as a work of projective investigation. We will also be studying what was happening in the world around the time this book was written, the decade of the 1940s.*

**FIGURE 8.8   Checklist for Writing
Performance-Based Tasks**

1. Are essential content and skills targets integrated?
2. Are multiple targets included?
3. Is the task authentic?
4. Is the task teachable?
5. Is the task feasible?
6. Are multiple solutions and paths possible?
7. Is the nature of the task clear?
8. Is the task challenging and stimulating?
9. Are criteria for scoring included?

> *First, working in small groups, your task is to select specific events, ideas, or trends from the 1940s and show how Orwell projected them into the future. You'll be given a chart on which you can graphically depict these connections.*
>
> *Second, each person is to select a field of study that interests you (economics, science and technology, health care, fashion, sports, literature, the arts, politics, sociology) and select current events, ideas, and trends in that field, with an emphasis on areas where there is some controversy or disagreement.*
>
> *Finally, using your knowledge of the field, construct a scenario for the future that makes sense and is a plausible extension of the present. Present your scenario in any way you wish (written prose or poetry, art form, oral or video presentation, etc.). In your presentation, clearly communicate your predictions and how they plausibly extend the present.*

8. The Task Should Be Challenging and Stimulating to Students. One of the things you hope for in a performance-based assessment is that students will be motivated to use their skills and knowledge to be involved and engaged, sometimes for days or weeks. You also want students to monitor themselves and think about their progress. This is more likely to occur when the task is something students can get excited about or can see some relevance for, and when the task is not too easy or difficult. Persistence is fostered if the task is interesting and thought provoking. This is easier if you know the strengths and limitations of your students and are familiar with what kinds of topics would motivate them. One approach is to blend what is familiar with novelty. Tasks that are authentic are not necessarily stimulating and challenging.

9. Include Explicitly Stated Scoring Criteria as Part of the Task. By now you are familiar with this admonition. Specifying criteria helps students understand what they need to do and communicates learning priorities and your expectations. Students need to know about the criteria *prior* to beginning work on the task. Sometimes criteria are individually tailored to each task; others are more generic for several different kinds of tasks. What is shared with students as part of the task, however, may not be the same instrument or scale you use when evaluating their work. For example, for the task in suggestion 7, the following contains part of what you might share with students (Marzano, Pickering, & McTighe, p. 61):

> You will be assessed on and provided rubrics for the following:
>
> 1. Your understanding of the extent to which the present can inform the future.
> 2. Your depth of understanding of major events, ideas, and trends from a field of study.
> 3. Your ability to accurately identify what is already known or agreed upon about the future event.
> 4. Your ability to construct a scenario for some future event or hypothetical past event for which a scenario is not readily available or accepted.
> 5. Your ability to express ideas clearly.
> 6. Your ability to communicate effectively in a variety of ways.

The identification of scoring criteria, and how you translate those criteria to a scale for evaluation, is discussed in the next section. From a practical perspective, the development of the task and scoring criteria is iterative, one influencing the other as both are developed.

Another list of desirable criteria of performance tasks is illustrated in Figure 8.7 on page 214. This figure shows how the characteristics are defined and contrasted with what often occurs with more traditional forms of assessment.

SCORING CRITERIA, RUBRICS, AND PROCEDURES

Once students have completed the task, you must evaluate their performance. Because responses are constructed by students, this is always a matter of reviewing their work and making a professional judgment about the performance. Rather than relying on unstated rules for making these judgments, performance-based assessments include *performance criteria*, what you call on or use to evaluate student proficiency. Performance criteria have been called many things, including *rubrics, scoring rubrics, scoring guidelines,* and *scoring criteria.* Regardless of the term or terms used, what we are concerned about is the nature of the factors that are used to judge the performance.

Criteria

The term *criteria* can be thought of as the narrative descriptions of the performances. This could be something very simple, like "interprets information accurately" or even single words like *exemplary* and *adequate* to something more complex, like "Makes a verifiable prediction that reflects insight into the character of the phenomenon. The prediction is entirely appropriate to the facts, concepts, or principles used to explain the phenomenon." (Marzano, Pickering, & McTighe, 1993, p. 81). Once all the criteria have been identified, a numerical scale is often used to reflect qualitatively different levels of performance. A rubric is the completed package—descriptions with either numbers or verbal labels to summarize levels of proficiency. Coming up with defensible criteria begins with identification of the most important dimensions or traits of the performance. This is a summary of the essential qualities of student proficiency. These dimensions should reflect your instructional goals as well as teachable and observable aspects of the performance. Ask yourself this question: "What is it that distinguishes an adequate from an inadequate demonstration of the target?" Herman, Aschbacher, and Winters make these suggestions for identifying important dimensions:[3]

- What are the attributes of good writing, of good scientific thinking, of good collaborative group process, of effective oral presentation? More generally, by what qualities or features will I know whether students have produced an excellent response to my assessment task?
- What do I expect to see if this task is done excellently, acceptably, poorly?
- Do I have samples or models of student work, from my class or other sources, that exemplify some of the criteria I might use in judging this task?
- What criteria for this or similar tasks exist in my state curriculum frameworks, my state assessment program, my district curriculum guides, my school assessment program?
- What dimensions might I adapt from work done by national curriculum councils, by other teachers?

One of the best approaches is to work backward from examples of student work. These exemplars can be analyzed to determine what descriptors distinguish them. The examples can also be used as *anchor* papers for making judgments, and they can be given to students to illustrate the dimensions. The dimension is the trait you are looking for. For a speech, that dimension might be content, organization, and delivery. Delivery may be divided further into posture, gestures, facial expressions, and eye contact. For a singing performance, you could include pitch, rhythm, diction, and tone quality, and each of these can be further delineated. As you might imagine, you can go into great detail describing dimensions. But to be practical, you need to balance specificity with what is manageable (the next section includes some examples of what is reasonable). How that gets translated to an overall judgment involves the use of some kind of rating scale.

Rating Scales

A rating scale is used to indicate the degree to which a particular dimension is present. It provides a way to record and communicate qualitatively different levels of performance. Several types of rating scales are available; we will consider three: numerical, qualitative, and numerical/quantitative combined.

The numerical scale uses numbers on a continuum to indicate different levels of performance. The number of points on the scale can vary, from as few as three to ten, twenty, or more. The number of points is determined on the basis of the decision that will be made. If you are going to use the scale to indicate low, medium, and high, then three points are sufficient. More points on the scale permit greater discrimination and may provide more diagnostic information. Occasionally a numerical scale will be used without any verbal descriptors or with only minimal descriptors such as *high* and *low* or *excellent* and *poor*. It is much more common to use numbers with qualitative descriptions.

A qualitative scale uses verbal descriptions to indicate student performance. There are two types of qualitative descriptors. One type indicates the different gradations of the dimension. The simplest form is the checklist. This lists different dimensions and provides a way to check whether each dimension was evidenced (Figure 8.9). More complex scales summarize different levels of the dimensions. Some examples of more complete descriptive scales are illustrated in Figure 8.10 on page 220. Notice that there is no indication of or reference to a standard in any of these scales. The idea is to describe the performance accurately, without indicating whether any particular point on any of the scales is considered passing or failing, or without indicating some other type of judgment about what the description means or how it is used. However you should note that there is language that provides the basis for the scale, words such as:

> *consistently, usually, rarely*
> *minimal, partial, complete*
> *never, seldom, occasionally, frequently, always,*
> *consistently, sporadically, rarely*
> *none, some, complete*

FIGURE 8.9   Checklist for Evaluating a Presentation

Japan Presentation Criteria

Content

Yes	No	
_____	_____	**1.** Two or more aspects of Japanese society mentioned.
_____	_____	**2.** The similarity between the United States and Japan presented.
_____	_____	**3.** Explained the difference between the U.S. and Japan.

Presentation

Yes	No	
_____	_____	**4.** Proper grammar used.
_____	_____	**5.** Appropriate eye contact made.
_____	_____	**6.** Varies tone and loudness.
_____	_____	**7.** Enunciates words.
_____	_____	**8.** Speaks clearly.
_____	_____	**9.** Changes facial expressions.
_____	_____	**10.** Faces audience.

Source: Adapted from Bacon, M. (1993). *Restructuring curriculum, instruction, and assessment in the Littleton Public Schools.* Littleton, CO: Littleton Public Schools.

FIGURE 8.10 Examples of Holistic Qualitative Rating Scales

Mathematical Knowledge[1]

Score Level

4   Shows understanding of the problem's mathematical concepts and principles; uses appropriate terminology and notations; executes algorithms completely and correctly.

3   Shows nearly complete understanding of the problem's mathematical concepts and principles; uses nearly correct terminology and notations; executes algorithms completely. Computations are generally correct but may contain minor errors.

2   Shows understanding of some of the problem's mathematical concepts and principles; may contain serious computational errors.

1   Shows very limited understanding of the problem's mathematical concepts and principles; may misuse or fail to use mathematical terms; may contain major computational errors.

Effectively Uses a Variety of Complex Reasoning Strategies[2]

Score Level

4   Demonstrates mastery of a variety of complex thinking processes and consistently applies the processes effectively.

3   Demonstrates competency in a number of complex thinking processes and usually applies the processes effectively.

2   Demonstrates ability in a number of complex thinking processes, but does not have a full complement of skills for managing complex issues.

1   Has a severely limited range of complex thinking skills for managing complex tasks.

Critical Thinking[3]

Level

VI   Demonstrates thorough understanding of many issues; uses extensive knowledge that is factually relevant, accurate, and consistent; conclusion shows analysis evidence, reasonable alternatives, and a number of consequences.

V   Demonstrates clear understanding of scope of task and several main issues; goes beyond documents and adds several relevant ideas; builds conclusion on examination of major evidence; considers several alternatives and possible consequences.

IV   Demonstrates good understanding of task and more than one view; uses main points of information provided and attempts to add to it; conclusion includes information and consideration of general consequences.

III   Shows general understanding of task; main focus is on one issue but discusses at least one other idea; uses information provided and attempts to add to it; conclusion refers to some evidence and consequences.

FIGURE 8.10   *(Continued)*

Level	
II	Shows partial understanding of task; focuses on a single issue; uses basic information provided; may include opinion as well as fact; forms conclusion after limited examination of evidence and little concern for consequences.
I	Shows little understanding or comprehension of task; uses only some of basic information provided; relies on own opinions; forms minimal conclusion based on only one or two pieces of information; no mention of consequences.

Sources: [1]Adapted from Lane, S., Parke, C., & Moskal, B. (1992). Principles for developing performance assessments. Paper presented at the 1992 Annual Meeting of the American Educational Research Association.

[2]Adapted with permission from Marzano, R. J., Pickering, D., & McTighe, J. (1993). *Assessing student outcomes: Performance assessment using the dimensions of learning model.* Alexandria, VA: Association for Supervision and Curriculum Development.

[3]1992 California Assessment Program, California Department of Education, Sacramento, CA. History–Social Science, Grade 11, Scoring Guide: Group Performance Assessment Task. The critical thinking rubric is one of four used for high school history–social science assessment in group performance tasks. Other components include the knowledge and use of history, the communication of ideas, and group and collaborative learning. The rubric should be used with care. The knowledge and critical thinking components outweigh the other two, and using all four components at once is difficult. The authors recommend that users of the rubric use all elements of the entire rubric simultaneously, then focus on the components one at a time, or apply one component at a time over several weeks, then review all rubric dimensions.

These types of scales will also vary according to the number of dimensions in each category. A *holistic* scale is one in which several dimensions are contained in each category of the scale. This is illustrated in the examples in Figure 8.10. If each of the dimensions was rated separately, the scoring would be *analytical*. In holistic scoring, there is a single evaluation based on the overall performance of the student. Analytic scoring results in separate results for each dimension. Holistic scoring is simpler and faster; analytic scoring provides better diagnostic information.

A second type of qualitative scale is one that includes gradations of the criteria and some indication of the worth of the performance. That is, the evaluative component is incorporated in the rating. This is the most frequently used type of rating scale for performance-based assessments. Descriptors like the following are associated with different points on the scale:

novice, intermediate, advanced, superior
inadequate, needs improvement, good, excellent
excellent, proficient, needs improvement
absent, developing, adequate, fully developed
limited, partial, thorough
emerging, developing, achieving
not there yet, shows growth, proficient
excellent, good, fair, poor

Examples of complete rubrics are illustrated in Figure 8.11. Numbers will often accompany different points on the scale. Each of the examples has a holistic scale. Also note that in some categories the dimensions include both what students do and what they don't do. Often, the presence or absence of certain traits is used to provide a summary judgment about a level of performance (e.g., it identifies assumptions but does not synthesize).

FIGURE 8.11   Examples of Complete Scoring Rubrics

Language[1]

1 Inadequate	Grammar and vocabulary are so poor that you cannot understand most of the message.
2 Minimal	Many grammatical mistakes made; uses very simplistic, bland language; uses a "restricted code," a style of communication characterized by simple grammatical structure and concrete vocabulary.
3 Adequate	Few grammatical mistakes made; uses language that is appropriate for the task (e.g., descriptive language when describing, clear and concise language when giving information and explaining, and persuasive language when persuading); uses an "elaborated code," a style of communication characterized by complex grammatical structure and abstract vocabulary.
4 Superior	Few grammatical mistakes made; uses language in highly effective ways to emphasize or enhance the meaning of the message; as appropriate to the task, the speaker uses a variety of language techniques such as vivid language, emotional language, humor, imagery, metaphor, and simile.

Measurement (length, mass, capacity)[2]

Not Understanding	Makes direct comparisons between objects; can order objects according to measure; can distinguish differences in measurements.
Developing	Can compare and order using nonstandard units; can estimate and measure using nonstandard units; can estimate and measure using standard units; can solve related problems.
Understanding/ Applying	Can estimate and measure using standard units; can select appropriate measurement units for task; can use fractional increments to measure; can solve related problems.

Sources: [1]Adapted with permission from The Massachusetts Department of Education.

[2]From *Alternative Assessment*, by Ann Arbor Schools. Copyright © 1993 by Dale Seymour Publications, P.O. Box 10888, Palo Alto, CA 94303. Used with permission.

Developing Scoring Criteria

The process for developing scoring criteria involves several steps. It is helpful to begin by clarifying how the discipline defines different levels of performance. This will give you an idea of the nature and number of gradations that should be used. It is also helpful to obtain samples of how others have described and scored performance in the area to be assessed. This can be done through the same sources that have developed performance tasks, such as national associations, state departments of education, and research organizations such as CRESST.

The second step is to gather performance samples and determine the characteristics of the works that distinguish effective from ineffective ones. The samples could be from students as well as so-called experts in the area. You could start by putting a group of student samples into three qualitatively different piles to indicate three levels of performance. Then examine the samples to see what distinguishes them. The identified characteristics provide the basis for the dimensions of the rating scale. At this point you can review your initial thinking about the scale with others to see if they agree with you. With feedback from others you can write the first draft of the descriptors at each point of the rating scale.

Use the first draft of the rubric with additional samples of student work to verify that it works as intended. Revise as needed, and try it again with more samples of student work until you are satisfied that it provides a valid, reliable, and fair way to judge student performance. Don't forget to use student feedback as part of the process. As you might realize, this entire process is repeated over and over to improve the rubric.

The following suggestions, summarized in Figure 8.12, will provide further help as you develop scoring criteria.

1. Be Sure the Descriptions Focus on Important Aspects of the Performance. There are many ways to distinguish between different examples of student work. You want to use those criteria that are essential in relation to the learning targets you are assessing. Because it is not feasible to include every possible way performances might differ, you need to identify those that are most important. For example, if you are making judgments about writing and use mechanics as one of the criteria, it

FIGURE 8.12   Checklist for Writing and Implementing Scoring Criteria

1. Do descriptions focus on important aspects of the performance?
2. Is the type of rating matched with purpose?
3. Are the traits directly observable?
4. Are the criteria understandable?
5. Are the traits clearly defined?
6. Is scoring error minimized?
7. Is the scoring system feasible?

would not be practical to include every grammatical rule in characterizing the descriptions. Rather, you need to select a few, most important aspects, like tense formation, agreement, and punctuation.

2. Match the Type of Rating with the Purpose of the Assessment. If your purpose is more global and you need an overall judgment, a holistic scale should be used. If the major reason for the assessment is to provide feedback on different aspects of the performance, an analytical approach would be best. Analytical scoring will give you more diagnostic information.

3. The Descriptions of the Criteria Should Be Directly Observable. Try to keep the descriptions focused on behaviors or aspects of products that you can observe directly. You want to use clearly visible, overt behaviors for which relatively little inference is required. Behaviors such as loudness, eye contact, and enunciation are easily and reliably observed. It is best to avoid high-inference criteria that are judged on the basis of behavior, such as attitudes, interests, and effort, because the behaviors are easily faked and are more susceptible to rater error and bias. This means that when the target is affective, the focus needs to be on behaviors that can be directly observed. Avoid the use of adverbs that communicate standards, such as *adequately*, *correctly*, and *poorly*. These evaluative words should be kept separate from what is observed.

Example

> *Poor:* Demonstrates a positive attitude toward learning keyboarding skills.
> *Improved:* Voluntarily gives to the teacher or other students two reasons why it is important to learn keyboarding skills.

4. The Criteria Should Be Written So That Students, Parents, and Others Understand Them. Recall that the criteria should be shared with students prior to instruction. The purpose of this procedure is to encourage students to incorporate the descriptions as standards in doing their work. Obviously, if the descriptions are unclear, students will not be able to apply them to their work, and the meaningfulness of your feedback is lessened. Consequently, pay attention to wording and phrases; write so that students easily comprehend the criteria. A helpful approach to ensure understanding is simple but often overlooked—ask the students! It is also helpful to provide examples of student work that illustrate different descriptions.

5. The Characteristics and Traits Used in the Scale Should Be Clearly and Specifically Defined. You need to have sufficient detail in your descriptions so that the criteria are not vague. If a few general terms are used, observed behaviors are open to different interpretations. The wording needs to be clear and unambiguous.

Example (wood shop assignment to build a letter holder)

Poor: Construction is sound.

Improved: Pieces fit firmly together; sanded to a smooth surface; glue does not show; varnish is even.

6. Take Appropriate Steps to Minimize Scoring Error.   The goal of any scoring system is to be objective and consistent. Because performance assessment involves professional judgment, some types of errors in particular should be avoided to achieve this objectivity and consistency. The most common errors are associated with the personal bias and halo effects of the person who is making the judgment. Personal bias results when there is an inaccurate tendency to rate all students the same. *Generosity error* occurs when the teacher tends to give higher scores; *severity error* results from teachers who use the low end of the scale and underrate students' performances. A third type of personal bias is *central tendency error*, in which students are rated in the middle.

The *halo effect* occurs when the teacher's general impression of the student affects scores given on individual traits or performances. If the teacher has an overall favorable impression, he or she may tend to give ratings that are higher than what is warranted; a negative impression has the opposite effect. The halo effect is mitigated by concealing the identity of the student (though this is not possible with most performance assessments), by using clearly and sufficiently described criteria, and by periodically asking others to review your judgments. Halo effects can also occur if the nature of a response to one dimension, or the general appearance of the student, effects your subsequent judgments of other dimensions. That is, if the student does extremely well on the first dimension, there may be a tendency to rate the next dimensions higher, and students who look and act nice may be rated higher. Perhaps the best way to avoid the halo effect is to be aware of its potential for affecting your judgment and monitoring yourself so that it doesn't occur. Other sources of scoring error, such as order effects and rater exhaustion, should also be avoided.

To be consistent in the way you apply the criteria, rescore some of the first products scored after finishing all of the students, and score one dimension for all students at the same time. This helps avoid order and halo effects that occur due to performance on previous dimensions. Scoring each product several times, each time on a different dimension, allows you to keep the scoring criteria in mind. It is also more efficient than trying to judge all the dimensions of each product together.

7. The Scoring System Needs to Be Feasible.   There are several reasons to limit the number and complexity of dimensions that are judged. First, you need to be practical with respect to the amount of time it takes to develop the scoring criteria and do the scoring. Generally, five to eight different dimensions for a single product are sufficient and manageable. Second, students will only be able to focus on a limited number of aspects of the performance. Third, if holistic descriptions are too complex, it is difficult and time consuming to keep all the facets in mind. Finally, it may be difficult to summarize and synthesize too many separate dimensions into a brief report or evaluation.

SUMMARY

This chapter introduced performance-based assessment as a method to measure skill and product learning targets, as well as knowledge and reasoning targets. Important points made in the chapter include the following:

- In contrast to paper-and-pencil tests, performance-based assessment requires students to construct an original response to a task that is scored with teacher judgment. Students provide explanations, and no single answer is correct.
- Authentic assessment involves a performance-based task that approximates what students are likely to have to do in real-world settings.
- Performance-based assessment integrates instruction with evaluation of student achievement and is based on constructivist learning theory. Multiple criteria for judging successful performance are developed, and students learn to self-assess.
- Major limitations of performance-based assessments include the resources and time needed to conduct them, bias and unreliability in scoring, and a lack of generalization.
- Performance-based assessment is used most frequently with reasoning, skill, and product learning targets.
- Communication skill targets include reading, writing, speaking, and listening.
- Psychomotor skill targets consist of physical actions (fine motor, gross motor, complex athletic, visual, and verbal/auditory) and the level to which the action is demonstrated (perception, set, guided response, mechanism, complex overt response, adaptation, and origination).
- Product targets are completed student works, such as papers, reports, and projects.
- The performance-based task defines what students are required to do.
- Restricted-type tasks target a narrowly defined skill and have a brief response.
- Extended-type tasks target complex tasks and have extensive responses. These may take several days or even weeks to complete.
- The task description needs to clearly indicate the target, student activities, resources needed, teacher role, administrative procedures, and scoring procedures.
- Effective tasks have multiple targets that integrate essential content and skills, are grounded in real-world contexts, rely on teacher help, are feasible, allow for multiple solutions, are clear, are challenging and stimulating, and include scoring criteria.
- Scoring criteria are the bases for evaluating student performances.
- Criteria are narrative descriptions of the dimensions used to evaluate the students.
- Rating scales are used to indicate different levels of performance. Holistic scales contain several dimensions together; analytic scales provide a separate score for each dimension.
- Qualitative rating scales verbally describe different gradations of the dimension. Complete scoring rubrics include both descriptions and evaluative labels for different levels of the dimension.

- Scoring criteria are based on clear definitions of different levels of proficiency and samples of student work.
- High-quality scoring criteria focus on important aspects of the performance, match the type of rating (holistic or analytical) with the purpose of the assessment, are directly observable, are understandable, are clearly and specifically defined, minimize error, and are feasible.

SELF-INSTRUCTIONAL REVIEW EXERCISES

1. How does authentic assessment differ from performance-based assessment?

2. Explain how each of the following words is important in describing the nature of performance-based assessment: *explain, reasoning, observable, criteria, standards, engaging,* and *prespecified.*

3. Identify each of the following as an advantage (A) or disadvantage (D) of performance-based assessment.

   a. resource intensive
   b. integrates instruction with assessment
   c. student self-assessment
   d. scoring
   e. reasoning skills
   f. active learning
   g. use of criteria
   h. length

4. Identify each of the following skills as fine motor (FM), gross motor (GM), or complex (C), and use the hierarchy in Figure 8.3 on page 207 to identify the level of the skill.

   a. making up new dives
   b. tracing a picture of a lion just like the teacher
   c. making cursive capital letters easily
   d. changing running stride to accommodate an uneven surface

5. Classify each of the following as a restricted (R) or extended (E) performance task.

   a. tie shoes
   b. prepare a plan for new city park
   c. construct a building from toothpicks
   d. interpret a weather map
   e. enact the Boston Tea Party
   f. read a tide table

6. Evaluate the following description of a performance-based task. What is missing?

   You have been asked to organize a camping trip in North Dakota. There are seven campers. Indicate what you believe you will need for a three-day trip, and provide reasons for your answer. Also include a detailed itinerary of where you will go while camping. You may use any library resources that you believe are helpful, and you may interview others who have had camping experience. As your teacher, I will answer questions about how you gather information, but I will not evaluate your answer until you have something to turn in.

7. Create a scoring rubric for the task presented in question 6. Show how each of the elements of writing and implementing scoring criteria presented in Figure 8.12 on page 223 is followed in your answer. Include reasoning skills in your rubric.

ANSWERS TO SELF-INSTRUCTIONAL REVIEW EXERCISES

1. Authentic assessment refers to the nature of the task that approximates what is done in the real world. Performance-based assessment involves the construction of responses by students—it may or may not be authentic.

2. Students are required to *explain* their responses as well as to produce them; *reasoning* targets are usually assessed, students use *reasoning* skills to demonstrate their proficiency; student performance is judged by what is directly *observable*; *criteria* are used to judge the adequacy of the performance on the basis of *prespecified standards* that relate a description of the performance to a statement of worth; good performance-based tasks are ones that are *engaging* for students.

3. a. D, b. A, c. A, d. D, e. A, f. A, g. A, h. D.

4. a. C, origination; b. FM, guided response; c. FM, mechanism; d. GM, adaptation.

5. a. R, b. E, c. E, d. R, e. E, f. R.

6. As a performance-based prompt, this isn't too bad; but as a performance task description, it could be improved considerably. There is no indication of the targets, whether this is an individual or group project, the administrative process, and, most important, no indication of the scoring criteria. It is a fairly authentic task and integrates different subjects. It does say something about the role of the teacher and resources, but more detail on both of these aspects could be provided.

7. There will be individual answers to this question, so you'll need to review each other's work by applying the questions in Figure 8.12 on page 223. I would begin with an analysis of the essential understandings and skills needed to plan the trip. This would comprise the dimensions that are evaluated (e.g., the ability to use maps, the ability to understand the impact of terrain and time of year on what will be needed, the extent to which plans follow from assumptions, the logic and soundness of reasons stated). I would then employ a scale to indicate the extent to which each of these dimensions is present (e.g., inadequate, adequate, more than adequate, or absent; developing, proficient, advanced). For example, for the extent to which plans follow from assumptions, you might note the following:

Absent	There is no indication of assumptions or how plans are based on assumptions.
Developing	Assumptions are not clearly stated but implied; plans are not explicitly related to assumptions but are implied.

Proficient	Some assumptions are clearly stated and plans are explicitly related to the assumptions.
Advanced	A comprehensive and well-thought-out list of assumptions is used; assumptions are explicitly related to plans.

SUGGESTIONS FOR ACTION RESEARCH

1. Identify a teacher who is using performance-based assessments and observe students during the assessment. Are they actively involved and on task? Do they seem motivated, even eager to get feedback on their performance? How "authentic" is the task? Can there be more than one correct answer? Is instruction integrated with the assessment? If possible, interview some students and ask them how they react to performance-based assessments. What do they like and dislike about it? How does it compare to more traditional types of assessment? How could it be more effective?

2. Devise a performance-based assessment for some aspect of this chapter. Include the performance-based task and scoring rubric, using the criteria in Figure 8.8 on page 214. Critique the assessments through class discussion.

3. Try out some scoring rubrics with teachers. You will need to formulate learning targets and the performance task. Construct exemplars of student work that illustrate different scores. Ask the teachers to give you some feedback about the scoring rubric. Is it reasonable? Does it allow for meaningful differentiation on important dimensions of the task? Is it practical? Would students understand the rubric? How could the scoring rubric be improved?

4. In a small group with other students, do some research on three examples of performance-based tasks in your field. Do they appear to meet the criteria in Figure 8.8 on page 214? How could they be improved? Be prepared to present your findings to the class for discussion.

ENDNOTES

1. From "District 214's Speech Assessment Rating Guide." (n.d.) Township High School District 214, Arlington Heights, IL.

2. A comparison task from Marzano, Pickering, & McTighe, 1993, p. 50. *Assessing student outcomes: Performance assessment using the dimensions of learning model*. Alexandria, VA: ACSD.

3. Herman, J. L., Aschbacher, P. R., & Winters, L. The National Center for Research in Evaluation, Standards and Student Testing (CRESST). *A Practical Guide to Alternative Assessment*. Alexandria, VA: ASCD, p. 58. Copyright © 1992 by The Regents of the University of California.

9

USING PORTFOLIOS TO ASSESS REASONING, SKILLS, AND PRODUCTS

Portfolios are emerging as a prominent type of alternative assessment. Although the term *portfolio assessment* is an evolving concept, some agreed-upon professional standards have been established. It is becoming increasingly clear that this method of collecting and evaluating student work over time has significant advantages over

Characteristics
- Clear purpose
- Systematic and organized
- Preestablished guidelines
- Student selection of some of the content
- Student self-reflection
- Documented progress
- Clear scoring criteria
- Conferences
- Advantages/ Disadvantages

Implementing
- Review nature of portfolios with students
- Supply content
- Include right number of entries
- Include table of contents
- Include student self-evaluation guidelines

PORTFOLIO ASSESSMENT

Teacher Evaluation
- Checklist of contents
- Portfolio structure
- Individual entries
- Entire contents
- Written comments
- Student-teacher conference

Planning
- Identify learning targets
- Identify use
- Identify physical structure
- Determine sources of content
- Determine self-reflection guidelines
- Determine scoring criteria

CHAPTER 9   Concept Map

more conventional approaches to assessment. But portfolios are much more than student folders, and using them requires some changes in how students are involved in assessment. In this chapter, we will review essential characteristics of effective portfolios, show how they can be integrated with instruction, and illustrate, with examples, how portfolios are designed and implemented.

WHAT ARE PORTFOLIOS?

In many professions, *portfolio* is a very familiar term. Portfolios have constituted the primary method of evaluation in fields such as art, architecture, modeling, photography, and journalism. These professions have realized the value of documenting proficiency, skill, style, and talent with examples of actual work. In education, a *portfolio* can be defined as a purposeful, systematic process of collecting and evaluating student products to document progress toward the attainment of learning targets. Arter and Spandel (1992) point out that portfolios involve student participation in the selection of what is included in the portfolio, specific and predetermined guidelines for the selection of materials and criteria for scoring, and evidence of student self-reflection on what has been accomplished. By including student participation in selection and student self-reflection, there is a clear emphasis on how portfolios are integrated with instruction. This is illustrated nicely by how two secondary teachers define portfolio (Porter and Cleland, 1995, p. 154):

> *A collection of artifacts accompanied by a reflective narrative that not only helps the learner to understand and extend learning, but invites the reader of the portfolio to gain insight about learning and the learner.*

Defined in this way, then, a portfolio has several essential characteristics (Figure 9.1 on page 232). First, a portfolio is *purposeful*. There is a clear reason why certain works would be included and how the portfolio is to be used. Second, rather than reflecting a haphazard collection of examples, the portfolio represents a *systematic* and *well-organized* collection of materials. Third, *preestablished guidelines* are set up so that it is clear what materials should be included. Fourth, students are engaged in the process by *selecting some of the materials* and by continually evaluating and *reflecting* on their work. Fifth, based on clear and well-specified *scoring criteria*, *progress* is documented with the evaluations. Finally, *conferences* are held between teacher and student to review progress, identify areas that need further improvement, and facilitate student reflection.

The idea of documenting progress is an important characteristic which differentiates student portfolios from what professionals prepare. The intent is to integrate portfolios as a component of instruction (Wolf, 1993). Thus, they are used in a formative way, to inform and determine ongoing instruction. Although in the professions portfolios may document progress, their primary purpose is to show one's best or recent work.

FIGURE 9.1   Characteristics of Portfolio Assessment

- Clearly defined purpose and learning targets
- Systematic and organized collection of student products
- Preestablished guidelines for what will be included
- Student selection of some of what is included
- Student self-reflection and self-evaluation
- Progress documented with specific products and/or evaluations
- Clear and appropriate criteria for evaluating student products
- Portfolio conferences between students and teachers

Source: Adapted from Arter, J., & Spandel, V. (1992). Using portfolios of student work in instruction and assessment. *Educational Measurement: Issues and Practice, II*, 36–44.

Because the use of portfolios is relatively recent in schools (with the exception of writing classes) three models appear to be developing in practice (Valencia & Calfee, 1991). However, like other forms of alternative assessment, the precise nature of what is called *portfolio assessment* will be unique to a particular setting. That is, different teachers and school systems use different types of portfolios, depending on their needs and how portfolios fit with other assessments and instruction. The *showcase* portfolio includes student selection of his or her best work. Because the student chooses the work, each profile of accomplishment is unique and individual profiles emerge. This encourages self-reflection and self-evaluation, but makes scoring more difficult and time-consuming because of the unique structure and contents of each portfolio. The *documentation* portfolio is like a scrapbook of information and examples. It may include observations, tests, checklists, and rating scales, in addition to selections by both teachers and students. There is student self-reflection and also external evaluation. The *evaluation* portfolio is more standardized. The purpose is more to assess student learning than to assess instruction, although student self-reflection may be included. Most of the examples are selected by teachers or are predetermined.

Regardless of the specific type or label, however, portfolios have advantages and disadvantages that determine whether you will find them useful in your own teaching. Portfolios combine the strengths of performance-based assessments with the ability to provide a continuous record of progress and improvement. The advantages that result serve as compelling reasons to use portfolios if needed resources are provided (Figure 9.2). Basically, you will want to use portfolios if your instructional goals include improving student self-evaluation and showing concrete evidence of student products that demonstrate improvement. Like any method of assessment, there are limitations and trade-offs, so the choice depends on your overall goals and philosophy of instruction and learning.

Advantages

Perhaps the most important advantage of using portfolios, if you want to focus on improving learning rather than simply documenting performance, is that students are actively involved in self-evaluation and self-reflection (Wolf, 1989). Students become part of the assessment process. They reflect on their performance and accomplishments, critique themselves, and evaluate their progress. This leads to setting goals for further learning. Students learn that self-evaluation is an important part of self-improvement; portfolios encourage and support critical thinking through student self-reflection. Students also apply decision-making skills in selecting certain works to be included and providing justifications for inclusion. In this sense, portfolios are open and always accessible to the student. This is quite different from teachers maintaining a private record of student accomplishments.

Closely related to self-assessment is the notion that portfolios involve collaborative assessment. Students learn that assessment is most effective when it is done with others. In addition to self-reflections, students learn from peer reviews and teacher feedback. They may evaluate the work of others and interact with teachers to come to a better understanding of the quality of their performance.

Another important advantage of portfolios is that they promote an ongoing process wherein students demonstrate performance, evaluate, and revise in order to learn and produce quality work. Assessment is continuous and integrally related to learning. Rather than being only summative, with scores or grades given at the end of an instructional unit, formal and systematic formative evaluation is conducted. This is different from the type of informal feedback teachers give to students, as summarized in Chapter 5. With portfolios, well-developed criteria are used to continually evaluate student progress.

Because portfolios contain samples of student work over time, they focus on self-improvement rather than comparison with others. The samples clearly docu-

FIGURE 9.2   Advantages and Disadvantages of Portfolio Assessment

Advantages	Disadvantages
• Promotes student self-assessment	• Scoring difficulties may lead to low reliability
• Promotes collaborative assessment	• Teacher training needed
• Systematic assessment is ongoing	• Time-consuming to develop criteria, score, and meet with students
• Focus is on improvement, not comparison	• Students may not make good selections of which materials to include
• Focus is on students' strengths—what they can do	• Sampling of student products may lead to weak generalization
• Assessment process is individualized	• Parents may find portfolios difficult to understand
• Allows demonstration of unique accomplishments	
• Promotes performance-based instruction	
• Provides concrete examples for parent conferences	
• Products can be used for individualized teacher diagnosis	
• Flexibility and adaptability	

ment how students have progressed. This helps reinforce the idea that what is most important is how each student, as an individual, improves. This helps to focus the assessment on what is done correctly and on strengths, rather than on weaknesses or what is wrong. Because each student has a unique set of materials in his or her portfolio, assessment and learning are individualized. Thus, portfolios easily accommodate individual differences among students, even though the overall learning targets are the same, and can show unique capabilities and accomplishments. Motivation is enhanced as students see the link between their efforts and accomplishments. From the standpoint of constructivist learning theory, it is desirable to allow this kind of individualization. As we will see, however, this is also a disadvantage when it comes to scoring.

A hallmark of portfolios is that they contain examples of student products. This emphasis on products is helpful in several ways. First, products reinforce the importance of performance-based assessment to students and parents. Products provide excellent evidence to help teachers diagnose learning difficulties, meet with students, and provide individualized feedback. The concrete examples provided by the products are very helpful in explaining student progress to parents. When you have a set of examples in a parent conference, it is much easier to clarify reasons for your evaluations. The emphasis on products also reminds teachers that there is a need to focus on performance activities.

Finally, portfolios are flexible. They can be adapted to different ages, types of products, abilities, interests, and learning styles. There is no single set of procedures, products, or grading criteria that must be used. You have the opportunity to customize your portfolio requirements to your needs and capabilities, to different learning targets, to available resources, and, most importantly, to differences among the students.

Here is how one mathematics teacher describes student reactions to what was obviously a positive experience (Stenmark, 1991, p. 35):

> The students liked the portfolio. They felt it allowed them to "mess up" and not be penalized. They liked being able to choose the quality of the work. A test is only one grade and is not always your best effort. They felt a combination of the two, test and portfolio, was a good measure of what they had learned. The portfolio really was a cumulation of everything I had been trying. It reflected a wide variety of assignments and assessments. It forced me to use and acknowledge the principles of learning that are being uncovered by researchers. The students liked it, and I did too!

Disadvantages

There are some limitations of using portfolios. Like other performance-based assessments, scoring is the major drawback. Not only is scoring time-consuming, research on the reliability of scoring portfolios has shown that it is difficult to obtain high inter-rater reliability. In a recent study of the Vermont Portfolio Assessment Program, low reliability was reported for both mathematics and writing portfolios (average reliability coefficients ranged from .33 to .43) (Koretz, McCaffrey, Klein, Bell, & Stecher, 1993). This investigation of a statewide program provided sobering data on how difficult it is to have consistent scoring when different raters score student portfolios. Such inconsistent scoring results from criteria that are either too general and can be interpreted differently or from such detailed criteria that raters are overwhelmed, and from the inadequate training of raters. Usually, criteria are too general, and raters have not received much training.

In the classroom, there is typically even less training and attention to criteria than what is devoted to statewide programs like the one in Vermont, so one would expect low inter-rater reliability as well. However, there is very little good evidence about the extent to which teachers make errors in judging student portfolios. Because the teacher has extensive knowledge of the student (unlike statewide programs when raters have no knowledge of students), the reliability may be improved by being able to base scoring on a thorough understanding of the student. In the absence of more complete research on teacher scoring of portfolios, it is best to be cautious and augment portfolios with other methods of assessment. Many teachers have found that it is best not to score the portfolios at all, but to use the information to make notes and provide feedback to students.

A second disadvantage of portfolio assessment is that it takes considerable time and other resources to do correctly. From the standpoint of time, you will find that many hours are needed to design the portfolios and scoring criteria, and that many more hours will be spent reviewing, scoring, and conferencing with students and parents. Additional time may be needed to obtain the training to feel confident and implement the portfolios properly. Basically, you need to decide if this amount of time is worth the effort. Let me emphasize that time and resources are needed to do portfolio assessment *correctly*. It's not the same as producing a folder of student work. Unfortunately, surveys of classroom portfolio assessment have found that many such collections are haphazard with poorly constructed criteria (Valencia & Calfee, 1991). Portfolio assessment, when done correctly, is very demanding; it requires time, expertise, and commitment. Because of this, portfolios should not be thought of as an add-on to other forms of assessment.

A final limitation that needs to be considered is the potential for limited generalizability. With portfolios you generalize from the examples and demonstrated performance according to the criteria to broader learning targets. In doing this, we need to be careful that the generalization is justified and that what is in the portfolio provides each student with a fair opportunity to demonstrate his or her level of competency on the general learning target. For example, if you are making judgments about the ability of a student to communicate by writing, and the only types of writing in the portfolio are creative and expository, then the validity of the conclusion about writing more generally is weak.

PLANNING FOR PORTFOLIO ASSESSMENT

The process of planning and implementing portfolio assessment is illustrated in Figure 9.3. In this section of the chapter, we will examine the planning phase of the process, which is represented in the first four steps. These steps are completed prior to implementation. Suggestions for planning are presented in the form of a checklist in Figure 9.4.

Purpose

Designing a portfolio begins with a clear idea about the purpose of the assessment. This involves both the specific learning targets and the use of the portfolio.

Learning Targets

As suggested by the title of this chapter, portfolios are ideal for assessing product, skill, and reasoning targets. This is especially true for multidimensional skills such as writing, reading, and problem solving that are continually improved and demonstrated through products. With extensive self-reflection, critical thinking is an important target. Students also develop metacognitive and decision-making skills. As with other performance-based assessments, portfolios generally are not very efficient for assessing knowledge targets. Sometimes teachers establish a folder of student work to demonstrate knowledge, but this type of evidence is not what is intended in a portfolio.

It will be important to distinguish between learning targets for individual work samples and for the contents of the portfolio as a whole. The targets that reflect all contents tend to be broader and more general, such as "development as a

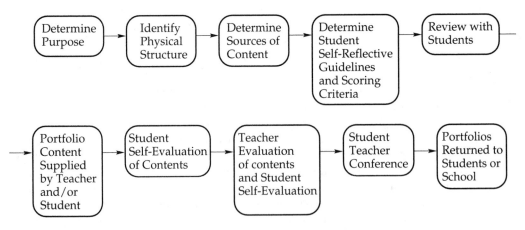

FIGURE 9.3   Steps for Planning and Implementing Portfolio Assessment

FIGURE 9.4   Checklist for Planning Portfolio Assessment

1. Are learning targets clear?
2. Are uses of the portfolio clear?
3. Is the physical structure for holding materials adequate and easily accessed?
4. Are procedures for selecting the content clear?
5. Does the nature of the content match the purpose?
6. Are student self-reflective guidelines and questions clear?
7. Are scoring criteria established?

reader," "adapts writing to audience," "speaks clearly," and "adapts writing style to different purposes." Further examples of learning targets for the portfolio as a whole are illustrated in Figures 9.12, 9.13, and 9.14 on pages 251–253. Notice that the scoring is holistic, which matches the more general nature of the targets.

Uses

I have already mentioned three primary uses for portfolios: documentation, showcasing, and evaluation. You need to indicate the degree to which each one is important because this will influence the contents of the portfolio and the criteria used for evaluation. For example, if the primary purpose is to document typical student work and progress, the portfolio will be highly individualized. It will tend to be a relatively loosely organized collection of samples selected by both the teacher and student, accompanied by both student and teacher evaluations. There are many entries, representing different levels of performance, because the goal is to show what is typical, not necessarily the student's best work. More energy is placed on selecting what would be typical than on systematic evaluation.

If the primary purpose is to illustrate what students are capable of doing, then the orientation is more toward a showcase type of portfolio. Here only the student's best work is included. The emphasis is on student selection, self-reflection, and self-assessment, rather than on standardization for evaluation. This approach uses the portfolio to celebrate and showcase what each individual has achieved. Often teachers display the results in a book or folder. There may or may not be much indication of progress, but the emphasis is clearly on what has been accomplished rather than on improvement.

If the portfolios are used primarily for evaluation, there will be greater standardization about what to include and how the portfolios are reviewed. Most samples are selected by the teacher, and there is an emphasis on scoring.

Some portfolios are used to show parents and others what students have achieved. If this is the primary purpose, more attention needs to be given to what will make sense to parents, with somewhat less attention to student self-reflection. In contrast, if portfolios are used primarily diagnostically and with students to help them progress, then more time is spent with student–teacher conferences during the school day. If the purpose is to help students self-reflect or peer review, then structure and support for these activities needs to be provided.

It may be evident that most teachers implement portfolios with multiple purposes. Because your time and energy is limited, try to identify a *primary* purpose and design the portfolio based on that purpose.

Identify Physical Structure

Once your purpose has been clarified, you need to think about some practical aspects of the portfolio. What will it look like? Most portfolios are contained in envelopes or folders. How large do the folders need to be? Where are they stored so that students can have easy access to them? Do you have boxes to put them in? Some teachers find that putting folders in boxes or files conveys an undesirable message that portfolios are only used at certain times and that they are not an integral, regular aspect of instruction. Putting folders on shelves where they are visible and accessible tells students they are important and should be used continuously. Your choices for these physical demands will influence to some extent what will be put in the portfolios. In addition, you will need to think about the actual arrangement of the documents in the portfolio. Is it done chronologically, by subject area, or by type of document? What materials will be needed to separate the documents?

Determine Sources of Content

The content of a portfolio consists of work samples and student and teacher evaluations. Work samples are usually derived directly from instructional activities, so products that result from instruction are included. The range of work samples is extensive, determined to some extent by the subject. For example, in language arts you could use entries from student journals, book reports, audiotapes of oral presentations, workbook assignments, and poetry. In science, you might include lab reports, questions posed by students for further investigation, drawings, solutions to problems, and pictures of projects.

Select categories of samples that will allow you to meet the purpose of the portfolio. If you need to show progress, select tasks and samples that are able to show improvement. If you need to provide feedback to students on the procedures they use in putting together a report, be sure to include a summary of that process as part of the portfolio. Use work samples that capitalize on the advantages of portfolios, such as flexibility, individuality, and authenticity. The categories should allow for sufficient variation so that students can show individual work. This often means giving students choices about what they can include.

In some school systems, certain *core* items are required to be collected for all students. This is sometimes referred to as an *indicator* system. For example, in language arts the district may require each student to include at least three writing samples, two oral reading passages, reading logs, and four independent reading reports.

To give you a better idea of the types of work samples to include, refer to the examples in Figure 9.5. It is also helpful to consult other sources that include dif-

FIGURE 9.5   Examples of Portfolio Work Samples

Language Arts[1]	Mathematics[2]
• Projects, surveys, reports, and units from reading and writing	• A solution to an open-ended question done as homework
• Favorite poems, songs, letters, and comments	• A mathematical autobiography
• Interesting thoughts to remember	• Papers that show the student's correction or errors or misconceptions
• Finished samples that illustrate wide writing: persuasive, letters, poetry, information, stories	• A photo or sketch made by the student of a student's work with manipulatives or with mathematical models of multidimensional figures
• Examples of writing across the curriculum: reports, journals, literature logs	
• Literature extensions: scripts for drama, visual arts, written forms, webs, charts, time lines, murals	• A letter from the student to the reader of the portfolio, explaining each item
• Student record of books read and attempted	• A report of a group project, with comments about the individual's contribution
• Audiotape of reading	• Work from another subject area that relates to mathematics, such as an analysis of data collected and presented in a graph for social studies
• Writing responses to literacy components: plot, setting, point of view, character development, links to life, theme, literary links and criticism	
• Writing that illustrates critical thinking about reading	• A problem made up by the student
• Notes from individual reading and writing conference	• Art work done by the student, such as string designs, coordinate pictures, and scale drawings or maps
• Items that are evidence of development of style: organization, voice, sense of audience, choice of words, clarity	• Draft, revised, and final versions of student work on a complex mathematical problem, including writing, diagrams, graphs, charts
• Writing that shows growth in usage of traits: growing ability in self-correction, punctuation, spelling, grammar, appropriate form, and legibility	• A description by the teacher of a student activity that displayed understanding of a mathematical concept or relation
• Samples in which ideas are modified from first draft to final product	
• Unedited first drafts	
• Revised first drafts	
• Evidence of effort: improvement noted on pieces, completed assignments	

ferent kinds of portfolios. There are a number of books on portfolio assessment that contain examples,[1] and examples are included in the performance assessment database referenced in the previous chapter. You might also want to subscribe to *Portfolio News* (c/o San Dieguito Union High School District, 710 Encinitas Boulevard, Encinitas, CA 92024) or the *Portfolio Assessment Newsletter* (5 Centerpointe Drive, Suite 100, Lake Oswego, OR 97035) for further ideas and information.

Determine Student Self-Reflective Guidelines and Scoring Criteria

Prior to implementing a portfolio assessment, you need to establish guidelines for student self-reflection and the scoring criteria you will use when evaluating student performance. This needs to be done so that both the guidelines and criteria can be explained to students before they begin instruction. In many cases, students can be involved in the development of self-reflective guidelines and scoring criteria. By working on these together, students will develop greater ownership of the process and will have experience in working collaboratively with you. Because many students are concerned with grades, you will need to be prepared to tell them how their portfolios will be evaluated.

IMPLEMENTING PORTFOLIO ASSESSMENT

Planning is complete. Now you begin the process of actually using the portfolios with your students. This begins with explaining to students what portfolios are and how they will be used. The checklist in Figure 9.6 summarizes the suggestions for effective implementation and use.

Review with Students

Because many students will not be at all familiar with portfolios, you will need to explain carefully what is involved and what they will be doing. Begin with your learning targets, show examples, and give students opportunities to ask questions. Try to provide just enough structure so students can get started without telling them exactly what to do. Put yourself in the student's place—if you had to do this new thing, what would be your response and what would you like to know?

FIGURE 9.6   Checklist for Implementing and Using Portfolios

1. Are students knowledgeable about what a portfolio is and how it will be used?
2. Do students know why portfolios are important?
3. Are students responsible for or involved in selecting the content?
4. Is there a sufficient number of work samples but not too many?
5. Is a table of contents included?
6. Are specific self-evaluation questions provided?
7. Is the checklist of contents complete?
8. Are scoring criteria for individual items and entire contents clear?
9. Are individualized teacher-written comments provided?
10. Are student–teacher conferences included?

Consider some examples of ninth-grade student responses to learning that they will be doing portfolios in their English class (Gold, 1992, p. 22). The teacher reports the following:

> *To introduce the portfolios, I explained that, in addition to completing the reading and essays assigned in the standard syllabus, students would be composing a portfolio of outside writing. Each week they were to find something that sparked their imagination, sympathy, or indignation and then write about it . . . they would continue to file their pieces until June, when they would choose several for grading.*

Some students responded:

> *I hate the idea of doing a portfolio.*
> *I don't want to do all these writings because (1) I never was a good writer, (2) I have always felt writing is a waste of time, (3) I'm afraid I'll be behind the other students.*
> *[It is] just something else to worry about.*
> *Why am I doing this? It will be so boring.*

Obviously these students are skeptical, and this type of reaction may be typical for students who have had little experience with portfolios. You will need to be prepared to help students understand why the process is important. If ungraded, portfolios may be viewed as busywork and not taken very seriously.

Supplying Portfolio Content

Who selects the content of the portfolio—the student, teacher, or both? If both the student and teacher supply samples, what should the proportions be? Are the entries prescribed? Answers to these questions depend on the age and previous experience of students and the purpose of the portfolio. It is not advisable to have preschool and primary students assume sole responsibility for selecting all the samples for their portfolios, though they certainly can be consulted and play an active role in selection. Older students should assume more or even sole responsibility for selection, though even older students who are inexperienced with portfolios will initially need considerable structure. Even if students are responsible for selecting the contents, it will be helpful to provide guidelines about the nature of the works to be included. When the portfolios are used primarily for evaluation, teachers usually make the selections or specifically prescribe what to include.

When deciding who will select the content, you need to consider somewhat conflicting goals. On the one hand, you want to foster student ownership and involvement, which is enhanced when students can decide what to include. On the other hand, you will probably need some degree of standardization with your input so that equitable evidence of student performance and improvement is provided. This is best accomplished with greater teacher control. One effective compromise is for students and teachers to decide together what to include with nonrestrictive guidelines. For example, students can select, in consultation with the teacher, three pieces they believe demonstrate their writing ability and progress for a semester. Another approach is to give students some restrictions and include student explanations of the choices. The teacher might prescribe the categories of writing samples, such as poem, persuasive essay, and technical report, and students would select within each of these categories (Arter & Spandel, 1992). Regardless of who makes the selections, however, there needs to be clear guidelines for what is included, when it should be submitted, and how it should be labeled.

Questions about the number of samples also need to be answered. You will find that too many, indiscriminate samples become overwhelming and difficult to organize, but too few items will not provide enough information to be useful. A portfolio with more complex products that take a longer time to create will have fewer samples than one that illustrates the growth of a number of relatively simple skills. A general rule of thumb for a demonstration portfolio would be to add one sample every week or two, for a total of ten to fifteen different items. For showcase portfolios, as few as three samples may be sufficient. Some teachers differentiate between a *working* portfolio, in which students keep most of their work, and a *display* or *final* portfolio, in which selections are made from the working portfolio. Haertel (1990) suggests a value-added approach, in which students include only those samples that contribute to understanding how the student has improved or progressed. That is, the student or teacher might ask, "What value is added by each piece of evidence?" If a piece doesn't contribute something new, it's not included.

To organize the portfolio, it is best to include a table of contents that can be expanded with each new entry. The table, which should be located at the beginning (some are pasted to the back of the front page of the folder), should include a brief description, date produced, date submitted, and date evaluated. A sample table can be provided, but ownership is enhanced if students have some flexibility to develop their own table or overview. Directions to students could be something like "Suppose someone who doesn't know you is looking at your portfolio and you are not there to tell them important things. What would you need to tell them so that they could follow and understand your portfolio?" (Collins & Dana, 1993, p. 17.)

Here is what Vicki Walker, a middle school mathematics teacher, says about the importance of using a table of contents (Lambdin & Walker, 1994, p. 321):

> *Since I've required a table of contents, I get far fewer portfolios that are just piles of papers with fragmented thoughts attached. Students seem to be more thorough regarding the layout of their work and the overall appearance of their portfolios, perhaps because they have more of a sense of a completed project. Each portfolio now has a definite beginning and end and a clearer vision-at-a-glance of what it contains and what message it is meant to convey. Furthermore, the table of contents allows for easier perusal on my part and has saved me a great deal of time during my evaluation process.*

Student Self-Evaluations

One of the most challenging aspects of using portfolios is getting students to the point where they are comfortable, confident, and accurate in analyzing and criticizing their own work. These *reflective* or *self-evaluation* activities need to be taught. Most students have had little experience with reflection, so one of the first steps in using a portfolio is getting students comfortable with simple and nonthreatening forms of self-evaluation. One useful strategy to accomplish this is to begin with teacher modeling and critiques. Once students understand what is involved by seeing examples (e.g., using an overhead of work from previous, unnamed students), they can begin to engage in their own reflections orally with each other. After they have engaged in these elementary forms of reflection, are they prepared to proceed to more complex self-evaluations (Camp, 1992). This can take several weeks. Simple questions are posed to students, such as:

> Can you tell me what you did?
> What did you like best about this sample of your writing?
> What will you do next?

Eventually students engage in more elaborate self-reflection, as illustrated by the following questions:

> What did you learn from writing this piece?
> What would you have done differently if you had more time?
> What are your greatest strengths and weaknesses in this sample?
> What would you do differently if you did this over?
> What problems or obstacles did you experience when doing this? How would you overcome these problems or obstacles next time?
> Is this your best work? Why or why not?
> What will you do for your next work?
> What was important to you when you did this work?
> If you could work more on this piece of writing, what would you do?
> Which sample would you say is most satisfying? Why?
> Which sample would you say is most unsatisfying? Give specific reasons for your evaluation. How would you revise it so it was more satisfying?
> How did your selection change from rough draft to final copy?
> How did you go about completing this assignment?
> How did you respond to suggestions for improving work samples?

Such reflection is completed for each individual work sample, for groups of pieces, then for the portfolio as a whole. Student responses are insights into how involved students have been in reaching the learning target, what the students perceive to be their strengths, and how instruction can be tailored to meet needs (sometimes a student's perceived strengths are inaccurate and need to be corrected).

Figure 9.7 presents examples of student responses to self-reflective prompts. In this case, students were asked to select a piece of writing "that is important to them," and explain why they made the selection. In this example, the responses from the same three students are indicated, appearing in the same order. The answers, while varied, illustrate what students think about themselves and what they believe they need to work on in the future.

FIGURE 9.7   Student Responses to Self-Reflection Questions

Why did you select this particular piece of writing?

"I believe it's my best piece all year. I think it's a very strong piece."
"It's the most thoughtful piece I have written all year."
"I had to use more references to do this writing, and you can see this by how much more details [sic] are in it."

What do you see as the special strengths of this paper?

"It shows that I can write a unique piece, different from the rest of the crowd."
"The wording and the form."
"I sense a strong ability to spot details from the text."

What was especially important when you were writing this piece?

"I wanted to write something that would stand out, that people would notice. And it was."
"What I thought friendship was all about."
"My main goal was to defend a thesis with as much information as possible."

What have you learned about writing from your work on this piece?

"I can begin to write something, and end up with something totally different."
"Writing a poem wasn't as hard as it seems."
"I have learned that when you are writing you must always stick to the topic."

If you could go on working on this piece, what would you do?

"I would make it longer, taking off the end, making many more levels of anticipation."
"Be more descriptive."
"I would go into the different ways each of the boys handled their tribes."

What kind of writing would you like to do in the future?

"Short stories, POEMS!"
"Narrative."
"I have always wanted to write a murder mystery."

Source: Camp, R. (1992). Portfolio reflections in middle and secondary school classrooms. In K. B. Yancy (Ed.), *Portfolios in the writing classroom.* Urbana, IL: National Council of Teachers of English. Copyright 1992 by the National Council of Teachers of English. Reprinted with permission.

Often students are asked to engage in peer evaluations. These can be very helpful, especially when students are beginning to get used to the idea of self-reflection and the teacher is trying to establish a trusting environment. The focus of peer evaluations is on analysis and the constructive, supportive criticism of strategies, styles, and other concrete aspects of the product. Here are three examples of the type of feedback that you can provide to students. In this situation, students were asked to give advice to one another and to comment on "standout" selections (Lambdin & Walker, 1994, p. 322).

> *When I looked at the portfolio selections with Shawn, I noticed a lot of things I could have done better on. For instance, on my problem-solving section I did not do so good because it was the beginning of the year and I had not really gotten into school yet.*
>
> *I worked with Jeff today. He helped me see many things about my papers but most of all he helped me pick my best work. This is "How many books are in the library?" This work shows reasoning, estimation, observations, and many other things. This is why this work stands out so well. It shows what my work was. This was also challenging and exciting to me. Even though my estimation was 5600 and the actual was 19,000 I still think my reasoning and attitude towards this project was very good [sic].*
>
> *Today I worked with Andrew. Helped me see the things I was doing wrong. I had a codecracker which didn't show a lot but he helped me see how to make it work. He told me to add an explanation about it for it to fit. I think a standout piece is my million's project. It shows everything I need. It has the original problem plus it shows all my work. It has an explanation about the problem and what we did.*

More comprehensive reflection is done on all the contents of the portfolio, at the end of the semester or year. This evaluation focuses much more on the overall learning target. Notice how the following questions are different from what is asked about a single piece or sample in the portfolio (Camp, 1992, p. 76):

What do you notice about your earlier work?

Do you think your writing has changed?

What do you know now that you did not know before?

At what points did you discover something new about writing?

How do the changes you see in your writing affect the way you see yourself as a writer?

Are there pieces you have changed your mind about—that you liked before, but don't like now, or didn't like before but do like now? If so, which ones? What made you change your mind?

In what ways do you think your reading has influenced your writing?

Here is how one twelfth-grade student answered these questions (Camp, 1992, pp. 77–78):

When I look back at my writing from the beginning of the year I realize that I have changed tremendously as a writer. My earlier work is not as explicit and does not seem like anything I would write now. . . . I know now that revising your work adds a great deal to the quality of the piece. If I may quote [my teacher], "Nothing is ever perfect the first time." Each piece of writing we did made me realize more and more things that could make my writing better. After these changes have been made I find that I look upon myself as a better and more sophisticated writer. At the beginning of this year I thought my "Lady and the Tiger" piece was the best I could ever do. When I look at it now I see a lot of places in which I could change it to make it 100% better.

A more structured kind of self-reflection is illustrated in Figure 9.8 for a middle school social studies class.

Student self-reflection can also include comments or a review by parents. One of the advantages of using portfolios is that they are well-suited to parent involvement. At the beginning of the year you will need to inform parents about what portfolios are and how they as parents can actively participate to be helpful. Students can consult their parents when selecting work samples, and parents can help students reflect on their work. Informally, parents can continuously provide advice and encouragement. More formally, parents can complete a form or answer a specific set of questions. A good example of this type of review is illustrated in Figure 9.9 on page 248. Students can then incorporate parent comments and suggestions into their own reflection.

Teacher Evaluation

There are several different ways teachers evaluate the contents of a portfolio. These include checklists of contents, evaluations of the overall quality of how well the portfolio has been put together, evaluations of individual entries, and evaluations of learning targets as demonstrated by all the contents. We'll consider each of these types.

Checklists of Contents

A summary to assure that the contents of the portfolio are complete is often provided in the form of a simple checklist. The checklist can vary according to the level of specificity desired. Examples of checklists for language arts classes are illustrated in Figures 9.10 and 9.11. Figure 9.10 on page 249 shows how a teacher would complete a checklist for an end-of-year portfolio that would become part of what is available for the third-grade teacher. These are not part of the students' cumulative folders, but they are accessible by students and parents as well as by teachers. The checklist in Figure 9.11 on page 250 is intended for students.

FIGURE 9.8   Structured Student Assessment of Portfolio

Personal Assessment of Portfolio

Dear Student: Your portfolio consists of all the writing assignments you have completed in social studies thus far. This form will assist you in monitoring your portfolio and determining the strengths and weaknesses of your writing.

Part I: Read the statements below. Write the number that most honestly reflects your self assessment. (Scale 1–5: 5=strong, 4=moderately strong, 3=average, 2=moderately weak, 1=weak)

_____ **1.** My portfolio contains all of the items required by my teacher.

_____ **2.** My portfolio provides strong evidence of my improvement over the course of the unit.

_____ **3.** My portfolio provides strong evidence of my ability to report factual information.

_____ **4.** My portfolio provides strong evidence of my ability to write effectively.

_____ **5.** My portfolio provides strong evidence of my ability to think and write creatively.

Part II: On the lines below, write the topic of each assignment. Rate your *effort* for each piece. (5=strong effort, 1=weak effort) In the space below write one suggestion for improving that piece.

_____ **1.** _____
_____

_____ **2.** _____
_____

_____ **3.** _____
_____

_____ **4.** _____
_____

_____ **5.** _____
_____

Part III: In assessing my overall portfolio, I find it to be (check one)

Very satisfactory _____   Satisfactory _____
Somewhat satisfactory _____   Unsatisfactory _____

Part IV: In the space below list your goal for the next marking period and three strategies you plan to use to achieve it.

Goal:
Strategies: 1.
                  2.
                  3.

Source: Goerss, D. V. (1993). Portfolio assessment: A work in process. *Middle School Journal, 25*(2), 20–24.

FIGURE 9.9   Example of Parent Review and Evaluation Form

Parent Folder Review and Reflection

Student _____

Reader   _____

Date   _____

   Please read everything in your child's writing folder, including drafts and commentary. Each piece is set up in back-to-front order, from rough draft to final copy. Further, each piece is accompanied by both student and teacher comments on the piece and writing process. Finally, the folders also include written questionnaires where students write about their strengths and weaknesses as writers.

   We believe that the best assessment of student writing begins with the students themselves, but must be broadened to include the widest possible audience. We encourage you to become part of the audience.

   When you have read the folders, please talk to your children about their writing. In addition, please take a few minutes to respond to these questions.

- Which piece of writing in the folder tells you most about your child's writing?
- What does it tell you?
- What do you see as the strengths in your child's writing?
- What do you see as needs to be addressed in your child's growth and development as a writer?
- What suggestions do you have which might aid the class's growth as writers?
- Other comments, suggestions?

Thank you so much for investing this time in your child's writing.

Source: Writing portfolio: Current working model (1992). Used with permission of the Pittsburgh Public Schools, Pittsburgh, PA.

Portfolio Structure Evaluation

Portfolios can be evaluated according to how well students have demonstrated skill in completing the structural requirements, factors such as the selection of samples, self-reflection, and organization. These aspects can be evaluated either by assigning points to each aspect according to a scale (e.g., 5=excellent, 1=poor), by making written comments, or both. When evaluating selections, consider the diversity of the samples, the time periods represented, and overall appropriateness. The quality of student reflection can be judged by the clarity and depth of thought, the level of analysis, and the clarity of communication. Organization can be evaluated by using a checklist to indicate whether required components are included, properly sequenced, and clearly labeled.

Evaluations of Individual Entries

The evaluation of each individual entry in the portfolio can be accomplished with the scoring criteria and rubrics that were discussed in Chapter 8, although often much less standardization is used with portfolios. Many teachers find that more

FIGURE 9.10 Examples of Teacher Portfolio Checklists

(Teacher checks (✓) each item when completed)

Kindergarten Requirements

First Quarter
___ Parent Questionnaire
___ School Adjustment/ Language Checklist
___ Reading Awareness
___ Print Awareness Inventory
___ Dated Writing Sample

Second Quarter
___ Dated Writing Sample
___ Print Awareness Inventory (for those students who became frustrated and/or did not complete inventory)

Third Quarter
___ Dated Writing Sample
___ Print Awareness Inventory (for those students who became frustrated and/or did not complete inventory)

Fourth Quarter
___ Dated Writing Sample
___ Running Record for readers only (all teachers must complete Running Record training by fourth quarter— classroom teachers will be responsible for taking the Running Record)
___ Print Awareness Inventory (for those students who became frustrated and/or did not complete inventory)

*Fourth quarter writing sample and running record, if applicable, are given to the first grade team.

Grade One Requirements

First Quarter
___ Print Awareness Inventory (use with new CCPS students who are at the pre-emergent or emergent levels)
___ Running Record (beginning, developing, and fluent readers)
___ Dated Writing Sample

Second Quarter
___ Dated Writing Sample
___ Story Retelling (all students)

Third Quarter
___ Dated Writing Sample
___ Story Retelling (nonfluent readers only)
___ Reading Comprehension (fluent readers only)
___ Running Record (beginning, developing, and fluent readers)

Fourth Quarter
___ Dated Writing Sample
___ Story Retelling (nonfluent readers only)
___ Reading Comprehension (all beginning, developing, and fluent readers)
___ Running Record (beginning, developing, and fluent readers)

*Fourth quarter writing sample and running record, if applicable, are given to the second grade team.

Grade Two Requirements

First Quarter
___ Running Record (developing and fluent)
___ Dated Writing Sample
___ Comprehension Sample

Second Quarter
___ Running Record (developing and fluent)
___ Dated Writing Sample
___ Comprehension Sample

Third Quarter
___ Running Record (developing and fluent)
___ Dated Writing Sample
___ Comprehension Sample

Fourth Quarter
___ Running Record (developing and fluent)
___ Dated Writing Sample
___ Comprehension Sample

*Fourth quarter writing sample and running record are given to the third grade team.

Source: Chesterfield County Public Schools, Richmond, VA, Elementary Language Arts Department.

FIGURE 9.11   Example of Student Portfolio Checklist

Portfolio Checklist
(For Language Arts Class Only)

Name _____ Date _____

By the end of the year, your portfolio must contain the original copies of the following items:

_____ Student Assessment Letter(s)
_____ Reading Log and Book Reviews
_____ Reading Attitude Survey
_____ Writing Samples

Source: From *Portfolio assessment: Getting started,* by Alan A. De Fina. Copyright © 1992 by Alan A. De Fina. Published by Scholastic Professional Books, New York, p. 79. Reprinted by Permission of Scholastic, Inc.

individualized, informal feedback on work samples is effective and efficient, particularly when many items are included in the portfolio. Furthermore, it is likely that not every entry will be evaluated in the same way. However, it is important to provide sufficient feedback so that students know what has been done well and what needs to be improved.

Evaluation of Entire Contents

The learning targets for the portfolio as a whole are not the same as those for individual entries. Likewise, the criteria for judging progress toward meeting learning targets of all the contents together is different from what is used for each item. The language of the evaluation reflects the more general nature of the target. For example, a portfolio is used to evaluate a student as a reader or writer, while assessments of individual work samples tend to focus on individual attributes, such as letter–sound relationships or use of capital letters. The words used also emphasize the developmental nature of learning because portfolios look at student improvement and progress, thus phrases such as "students demonstrate the ability to understand increasingly complex software programs," "a greater number of self-evaluative criteria applied," "increased understanding of," or "increased ability to." The scoring tends to be holistic because a number of different pieces of evidence are used to arrive at an overall judgment. Here is how one teacher describes holistic scoring for a mathematics portfolio (Stenmark, 1991. p. 37):

> *When it came to grading, I used a holistic method. I sorted portfolios into three main piles and then subdivided within those piles. I found myself basing my decisions on the kinds of assignments selected, tending to value those with writing more than those that showed straight computation, and on the quality of assignments, tending to value those that showed more mathematical understanding.*

Three examples of scoring criteria for overall judgments are illustrated in Figures 9.12, 9.13, and 9.14 on pages 251–253. Two of these forms provide quantitative

KENTUCKY MATHEMATICS PORTFOLIO
HOLISTIC SCORING GUIDE

Scoring Year: Spring _____

An individual portfolio is likely to be characterized by some, but not all, of the descriptors for a particular level. Therefore, the overall score should be the level at which the appropriate descriptors for the portfolio are clustered.

	NOVICE	APPRENTICE	PROFICIENT	DISTINGUISHED
PROBLEM SOLVING — Understanding/Strategies, Execution/Extensions	• Indicates a basic understanding of problems and uses strategies • Implements strategies with minor mathematical errors in the solution without observations or extensions	• Indicates an understanding of problems and selects appropriate strategies • Accurately implements strategies with solutions, with limited observations or extensions	• Indicates a broad understanding of problems with alternate strategies • Accurately and efficiently implements and analyzes strategies with correct solutions, with extensions	• Indicates a comprehensive understanding of problems with efficient, sophisticated strategies • Accurately and efficiently implements and evaluates sophisticated strategies with correct solutions and includes analysis, justifications, and extensions
REASONING	• Uses mathematical reasoning	• Uses appropriate mathematical reasoning	• Uses perceptive mathematical reasoning	• Uses perceptive, creative, and complex mathematical reasoning
MATHEMATICAL COMMUNICATION — Language, Representations	• Uses appropriate mathematical language some of the time • Uses few mathematical representations	• Uses appropriate mathematical language • Uses a variety of mathematical representations accurately and appropriately	• Uses precise and appropriate mathematical language most of the time • Uses a wide variety of mathematical representations accurately and appropriately; uses multiple representations with some entries	• Uses sophisticated, precise and appropriate mathematical language throughout • Uses a wide variety of mathematical representations accurately and appropriately; uses multiple representations within entries and states their connections
UNDERSTANDING/CONNECTING CORE CONCEPTS	• Indicates a basic understanding of core concepts	• Indicates an understanding of core concepts with limited connections	• Indicates a broad understanding of some core concepts with connections	• Indicates a comprehensive understanding of core concepts with connections throughout
TYPES AND TOOLS	• Includes few types; uses few tools	• Includes a variety of types; uses tools appropriately	• Includes a wide variety of types; uses a wide variety of tools appropriately	• Includes all types; uses a wide variety of tools appropriately and insightfully

revised 8/95

PORTFOLIO CONTENTS
- Table of Contents
- Student Signature Sheet
- Letter to Reviewer
- 5–7 Best Entries

BREADTH OF ENTRIES

TYPES
○ INVESTIGATIONS/DISCOVERY
○ APPLICATIONS
○ NON-ROUTINE PROBLEMS
○ PROJECTS
○ INTERDISCIPLINARY
○ WRITING

TOOLS
○ CALCULATORS
○ COMPUTER AND OTHER TECHNOLOGY
○ MODELS/MANIPULATIVES
○ MEASUREMENT INSTRUMENTS
○ OTHERS

○ GROUP ENTRY

WORKSPACE/ANNOTATIONS

PERFORMANCE DESCRIPTORS

PROBLEM SOLVING
- Understands the features of a problem (understands the question, restates the problem in own words)
- Explores (draws a diagram, constructs a model and/or chart, records data, looks for patterns)
- Selects an appropriate strategy (guesses and checks, makes an exhaustive list, solves a simpler but similar problem, works backward, estimates a solution)
- Solves (implements a strategy with an accurate solution)
- Reviews, revises, and extends (verifies, explores, analyzes, evaluates strategies/solutions; formulates a rule)

REASONING
- Observes data, records and recognizes patterns, makes mathematical conjectures (inductive reasoning)
- Validates mathematical conjectures through logical arguments or counter-examples; constructs valid arguments (deductive reasoning)

MATHEMATICAL COMMUNICATION
- Provides quality explanations and expresses concepts, ideas, and reflections clearly
- Uses appropriate mathematical notation and terminology
- Provides various mathematical representations (models, graphs, charts, diagrams, words, pictures, numerals, symbols, equations)

UNDERSTANDING/CONNECTING CORE CONCEPTS
- Demonstrates an understanding of core concepts
- Recognizes, makes, or applies the connections among the mathematical core concepts to other disciplines, and to the real world

Place an X on each continuum to indicate the degree of understanding demonstrated for each core concept.

	DEGREE OF UNDERSTANDING OF CORE CONCEPTS				
	NONE	BASIC	UNDERSTANDING	BROAD	COMPREHENSIVE WITH CONNECTIONS
NUMBER					
MATHEMATICAL PROCEDURES					
SPACE & DIMENSIONALITY					
MEASUREMENT					
CHANGE					
MATHEMATICAL STRUCTURE					
DATA					

FIGURE 9.12   Mathematics Holistic Scoring Guide

Source: Kentucky Department of Education (Office of Curriculum, Assessment, and Accountability), 1995. Used with permission.

FIGURE 9.13   Scoring Criteria for Writing Portfolio (a)

Portfolio Exit Assessment

Student writer _____   Grade _____

Teacher _____   School _____

The contents of this student's portfolio demonstrate (Please circle where appropriate):

	Unsatisfactory Performance			Outstanding Performance	No Evidence to Support Judgment
Accomplishment in Writing	1	2	3	4	NE
• Setting and meeting worthwhile challenges					
• Establishing and maintaining purpose					
• Use of the techniques and choices of the genre					
• Organization, development, use of detail					
• Control of conventions, vocabulary, sentence structure					
• Awareness of the needs of the audience					
• Use of language, sound, images, tone, voice					
• Humor, metaphor, playfulness					
Use of Processes and Resources for Writing	1	2	3	4	NE
• Awareness of strategies and processes for writing					
• Use of processes: prewriting, drafting, revision					
• Awareness of features important to writing					
• Ability to see strengths and opportunities in one's own writing					
• Ability to describe what one sees and knows about writing					
• Use of the classroom social context for writing					
• Use of available experience and resources (one's own, the school's, the community's)					
Development as a Writer	1	2	3	4	NE
• Progress from early to late pieces; growth, development					
• Increased understanding of features and options important to writing					
• Engagement with writing, investment, pursuit					
• Use of writing for different purposes, genres, and audiences					
• Sense of self as a writer, achievements and purposes as a writer					
• Personal criteria and standards for writing					

Source: Used with permission of the Pittsburgh Public Schools, Pittsburgh, PA.

FIGURE 9.14 Scoring Criteria for Writing Portfolio (b)

Portfolio Exit Assessment

Student writer # _____   Grade: _____

School _____   Rater _____

Please circle the appropriate numerical ratings for the contents of this portfolio.

Accomplishment in Writing

- meeting worthwhile challenges
- establishing and maintaining purpose
- use of the techniques and choices of the genre
- control of conventions, vocabulary, sentence structure
- awareness of the needs of the audience (organization, development, use of detail)
- use of language, sound, images, tone, voice
- humor, metaphor, playfulness

Performance Rating

No Evidence Present NE	Inadequate Performance 1	2	3	4	5	Outstanding Performance 6

Use of Processes and Strategies for Writing

- effective use of prewriting strategies
- use of drafts to discover and shape ideas
- use of conferencing opportunities to refine writing (peers, adult readers)
- effective use of revision (reshaping, refocusing, refining)

Performance Rating

No Evidence Present NE	Inadequate Performance 1	2	3	4	5	Outstanding Performance 6

Development as a Writer

- evidence of investment in writing tasks
- increased engagement with writing
- development of sense of self as a writer
- evolution of personal criteria and standards for writing
- ability to see the strengths and needs in one's writing
- demonstration of risk-taking and innovation in interpreting writing tasks
- use of writing for various purposes, genres, and audiences
- progress from early to late pieces; growth, development

Performance Rating

No Evidence Present NE	Inadequate Performance 1	2	3	4	5	Outstanding Performance 6

Source: Used with permisison of the Pittsburgh Public Schools, Pittsburgh, PA.

summaries, while the mathematics portfolio is more comprehensive. You will also want to be sure to include written comments that are individualized for each student. This descriptive summary of performance and progress should highlight changes that have occurred, strengths, and areas that need improvement. It's usually best to point out the strengths and improvements first, then use language to address weaknesses that tells clearly what needs improvement but will not discourage students nor lead them to a sense of futility. Words such as *improving, developing, partial,* or even *novice* are better than *unacceptable* or *inadequate.*

Student–Teacher Conferences

The final step in implementing portfolios, prior to returning them to the student or school file, is conducting a conference with each student to review the contents, student reflections, and your evaluations of individual items and all of the work together as related to learning targets. Actually, conferences with students should be scheduled throughout the year; some suggest having one conference each month at the elementary level. Especially early in the year the conferences can be used to clarify purposes and procedures, answer questions, and establish trust. Although scheduling and conducting these conferences takes time, the sessions provide an important link between students and teachers.

It is best if students are given some guidelines to prepare for each conference. During the conference, do what you can to allow the student to do most of the talking. Have students compare their reflections with your evaluations and make plans for subsequent work. Although weaknesses and areas for improvement need to be covered, show students what is possible and their progress, rather than dwell on what is wrong. Make sure that at the end of the conference there is a plan of action for the future. Limit the conference to no more than ten or fifteen minutes. You may want to have students take notes about what was discussed in the conference, and you may also want to make your own brief notes. Focus on one or two major topics or areas at each conference. This helps ensure a full and thoughtful discussion, rather than a superficial treatment of several areas.

SUMMARY

Portfolios are quickly becoming an important technique for both assessment and instruction. The essence of portfolios is to gather and evaluate, on a continual basis, student products that demonstrate progress toward specified learning targets. By combining principles of performance assessment with student self-reflection, portfolios can be powerful tools to improve student learning. With the flexibility inherent in portfolios, it is possible to individualize assessment so that you can maximize meaningful feedback to each student. Other major points in the chapter include the following:

- Portfolio assessment is systematic and purposeful.
- Portfolio assessment includes student selection of contents and student self-reflection. Students "own" their portfolios and should have easy access to them.
- Different types of portfolios include showcase, documentation, and evaluation.
- Portfolios integrate assessment with instruction by focusing on improvement and progress.
- Portfolios are adaptable to individual students.
- Scoring is a major limitation of portfolios.
- Portfolios require considerable teacher time for preparation and implementation.
- Portfolios may result in limited generalizability.
- Planning for portfolio assessment includes the identification of learning targets and uses, physical structures, sources of content, guidelines for student self-reflection, and scoring criteria.
- Implementing portfolio assessment includes reviewing with students, supplying content, student self-evaluations, teacher evaluations, and student–teacher conferences.
- Students should be meaningfully involved in the selection of work samples.
- Just enough work samples need to be included to meet the purpose of the portfolio.
- A table of contents should be included in the portfolio.
- Student self-evaluation needs to be taught. Students progress to eventually become skilled at analyzing and critiquing their own and others' works.
- The teacher evaluates checklists of contents, the student's ability to put together the portfolio, individual items, and the content as a whole, among other things, which may include scores from rubrics and written comments.
- Student–teacher conferences should be held throughout the year to review progress and establish plans.

SELF-INSTRUCTIONAL REVIEW EXERCISES

1. Indicate whether each of the following would be considered an advantage (A) or disadvantage (D) of using portfolio assessment.

   a. collaboration between student and teacher
   b. student selection of contents
   c. scoring
   d. continuous monitoring of student progress
   e. training teacher to do portfolios
   f. generalizability
   g. student self-evaluation

2. Indicate whether it would be best to use a showcase (S), documentation (D), or evaluation (E) portfolio for each of the following purposes:

   a. To show examples of all of a student's work
   b. For the student to demonstrate his or her best work
   c. To show what students in a class are capable of doing
   d. To indicate the progress of the class on an important target
   e. For grading
   f. To show a student's progress

3. Evaluate the planning that is illustrated by the teacher in the following example. Is what she has planned consistent with what a portfolio is all about? Why or why not? Is her planning adequate? What else does she need to do?

   Ms. Taylor has decided to implement a mathematics portfolio in her sixth-grade classroom. She believes the portfolios will increase student learning. She provides manila folders for the students and tells them that they will keep all their math worksheets and tests in it. She tells the students that they will be talking to her periodically about what is in the folder.

4. Match the description or example with the appropriate step in implementing portfolio assessment. Each step can be used more than once or may not be used at all.

   _____ **a.** Rubric used to evaluate the   **A.** Review with students
                 sixth writing sample   **B.** Supply content
   _____ **b.** Mr. Lind meets with students   **C.** Student self-reflection
                 once a week   **D.** Teacher evaluation
   _____ **c.** Students ask questions about   **E.** Student-teacher conference
                 how to self-reflect
   _____ **d.** Teacher prepares an overhead
                 that outlines the basics of
                 Portfolio assessment
   _____ **e.** Table of contents is
                 prepared
   _____ **f.** Students select three work
                 samples
   _____ **g.** A checklist includes outline
                 and self-reflection categories

5. The following scenario describes how a middle school social science teacher goes about implementing portfolio assessment in his class. After reading the scenario, review the checklists in Figures 9.4 and 9.6, on pages 237 and 240. Use these checklists as criteria to evaluate how well Mr. Trent does in using portfolios.

   Gary Trent has read a lot lately about portfolios and decides to use them with his seventh-grade social studies classes. He spends the last week before school starts fine-tuning what he hopes his students can learn from doing the portfolios. Although he thinks he must give grades to ensure student motivation, he plans to use the portfolios to demonstrate to other teachers what his students are capable of achieving.

Gary decides to ask his students to bring something to class to hold the materials that will go in the portfolio. He explains to his students that they will be selecting one example each week from their work in his class that shows their best effort. Every month students meet with each other to critique what was included, and after the meeting students complete a self-evaluation worksheet. Throughout the semester Gary plans to talk with each student at least once about the student's portfolio.

Near the end of the semester, Gary collects all the portfolios, grades them, and returns them to his students. He makes sure that each student receives individualized comments with the grade.

ANSWERS TO SELF-INSTRUCTIONAL REVIEW EXERCISES

1. a. A, b. A or D (a disadvantage if students are not provided sufficient direction and supervision), c. D, d. A, e. D, f. D, g. A.

2. a. D, b. S, c. S, d. E, e. E, f. D.

3. This is not really portfolio assessment, at least not in the way portfolios have been discussed in this chapter. Neither the teacher nor the students select anything (everything is included), and there is no indication that any performance-based products are included. There is a lack of specification about the purpose of the portfolio. Folders will be used, but we don't know where they will be placed. There is no indication that student self-reflection guidelines and scoring criteria have been developed.

4. a. D, b. E, c. C, d. A, e. B, f. B, g. D.

5. Gary does something right in using portfolios but needs to be more specific and systematic in a number of areas. It's good that he takes time to plan what he wants to do. However, the stated purpose is not one of the major reasons that portfolios should be used. There is only a brief reference to learning targets, and there is no indication that he has prepared specific scoring criteria or student self-reflection guidelines. Simply asking students to select one example of their work per week is probably too vague. Gary needs to be more specific about what kinds of work should be included and about the physical structure of the portfolio. Because he has several classes, it may not be feasible to store each portfolio in the room. It's not clear that students know enough about portfolios for the procedure to work. It's good that students select the content, and Gary is on target in emphasizing student self-reflection. One problem may be that there will be too many work samples by the end of the semester, making Gary's grading process difficult. It might be better to have students select one work example per week and then at the end of the semester choose a few items from these to demonstrate achievement. Gary's plan to meet with students at least once informally is okay, but there is no provision for a more formal conference near the end of the semester. It's good that he includes individualized written comments.

SUGGESTIONS FOR ACTION RESEARCH

1. Locate two or three examples of portfolios from different teachers. Review the contents of the portfolios carefully, looking for characteristics that have been discussed in this chapter. How are the portfolios alike and how are they different? Are they being used for different purposes? Is the structure and content appropriate for the intended use?

2. Interview students who have had some experience with portfolios. Ask them what they like and don't like about doing portfolios, how much time it takes them to complete their work, and what the teacher does to help them. Focus on student self-reflection. Ask the students how they have self-evaluated themselves and what they think they have learned from the process.

3. Visit two or three classrooms and see how portfolios are organized and stored. If possible, talk with the teachers to get their views about how to organize portfolios so that they are practical.

4. Devise a student portfolio assignment for students. Include each of the steps in Figure 9.3, and include examples where possible. Then ask two or three teachers to review your assignment and give you feedback on how it could be improved, how much time it would take to implement, how realistic it would be, and what students would probably get out of it.

ENDNOTES

1. For example, *Authentic assessment in practice: A collection of portfolios, performances tasks, exhibitions, and documentation*, by Linda Darling-Hammon, Lynne Einbender, Fred Frelow, & Janine Ley-King, New York: NCREST, 1993; Lambdin & Walker; *Portfolio assessment in the reading-writing classroom*, by Robert Tierney, Mark Carter, & Laura Desai, Norwood, MA: Christopher-Gordon Publishers, 1991; *Portfolios in the writing classroom*, by Kathleen Yancey, Urbana, IL: National Council of Teachers of English, 1992.

10

ASSESSING AFFECTIVE TRAITS AND LEARNING TARGETS

The previous four chapters focused on what have traditionally been called *cognitive* learning targets and skills. We now turn to a set of student dispositions and traits that many educators regard as equally important: what have become known as *affective* outcomes. We'll look at how to define affective learning traits and targets and how, practically speaking, to assess these traits and targets in the classroom in

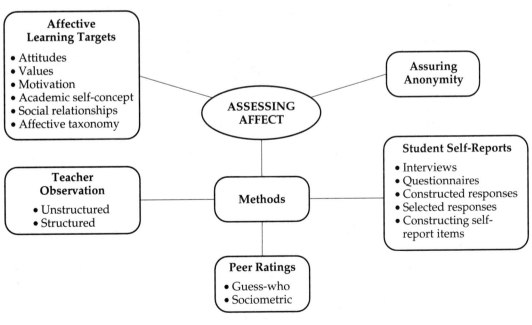

CHAPTER 10   Concept Map

a way that improves instruction and student cognitive learning. I believe these targets, if well-conceptualized and assessed, are essential for providing students with the life skills they need.

ARE AFFECTIVE TARGETS IMPORTANT?

What is interesting about student affect is that while virtually all teachers believe that it is important for students to obtain positive affective traits, there is very little, if any, systematic assessment of affect in the classroom (Stiggins & Conklin, 1992). Teachers know that students who are confident about their ability to learn, who like the school subjects they study, who have a positive attitude toward learning, who respect others, and who show a concern for others are much more likely to be motivated and involved in learning. But, at the same time, most teachers do not rely on any kind of formal affective assessment procedures, nor do they state specific affective learning targets for their students. Why? Three reasons seem plausible. First, especially in the higher grades, schooling is organized and graded by subject matter. Cognitive subject matter targets are relatively agreed upon as desirable for all students. There is a legitimate need to assess and report student attainment of cognitive targets completely separate from affect. This puts affect in a position of being important but still secondary to cognitive learning. It also makes it difficult to come to an agreement about which affective targets are appropriate for all students. That is, it isn't easy to define attitudes, values, and interests, especially because these traits are more private and idiosyncratic.

Second, the assessment of affective targets is fraught with difficulties. There are many potential sources of error in measuring affective traits, which often results in low reliability. Student motivation is a primary concern. They need to take such assessments seriously to provide accurate results, yet many students may be inhibited if their responses are not anonymous. It would be easy to fake responses on self-report instruments if the results are to be used for grading or some other purpose. They may want to please the teacher with positive responses. Another source of error is that some affective traits are easily influenced by momentary or temporary moods. This is especially true for younger students, who may report much more positive affect after a good day or session than is actually the case. Teacher bias can also have a significant influence on what may be recorded or perceived.

Finally, particularly in recent years, there has been a public outcry by some groups against teaching anything other than traditional academic content. These political and religious groups contend that schools have no right to emphasize attitudes, values, or beliefs that may be contrary to what they stand for and want for their children. But many affect-related targets would seem to have universal appeal (e.g., citizenship, positive attitudes toward subjects and learning, and respect for others). Nevertheless, teachers are wary of controversy, so it's easier to avoid affect altogether than to fight parents and special interest groups.

What are the advantages, then, to systematically setting and assessing affective targets? I believe there are several good reasons. Positive affective traits and skills are essential for:

- Being an involved and productive member of our society
- Preparing for occupational and vocational satisfaction and productivity (e.g., work habits, a willingness to learn, interpersonal skills)
- Maximizing the motivation to learn now and in the future
- Preventing students from dropping out of school

Currently, most school and school district mission statements include affective outcomes, and teachers constantly assess affect informally during instruction. The following sections present suggestions and techniques for taking affect to a more serious level. What better way can teachers signal to students that clearly defined positive affect is important than by systematically assessing it? This begins with identifying appropriate affect targets, which we'll consider next.

WHAT ARE AFFECTIVE TRAITS AND LEARNING TARGETS?

The term *affective* has come to refer to a wide variety of traits and dispositions that are different from knowledge, reasoning, and skills (Hohn, 1995). Actually, the term *affect* has a technical meaning that is rather restrictive—the emotions or feelings we have toward someone or something. However, attitudes, values, self-concept, citizenship, and other traits usually considered to be noncognitive involve more than emotion or feelings. In fact, most kinds of student affect involve both emotion and cognitive beliefs. Nevertheless, the literature refers to a range of possible outcomes as affective. I have summarized many of these in Figure 10.1 on page 262. Although there isn't space to consider each of these affective traits in detail, I do want to look at a few of the more commonly used ones. Because of the general nature of the term *affect*, it is best to use these more specific dispositions when developing your learning targets.

Attitude Targets

Attitudes are internal states that influence what students are likely to do. The internal state is some degree of positive/negative or favorable/unfavorable reaction toward an object, situation, person, group of objects, general environment, or group of persons (McMillan, 1980). Attitudes do not refer to behaviors, what a student knows, right or wrong in a moral or ethical sense, or characteristics such as the student's race, age, or socioeconomic status. Thus, we always think about attitudes *toward* something. In schools, that may be learning, subjects, teachers, other

FIGURE 10.1   Affective Traits

Trait	Definition
Attitudes	Predisposition to respond favorably or unfavorably to specified situations, concepts, objects, institutions, or persons
Interests	Personal preference for certain kinds of activities
Values	Importance, worth, or usefulness of modes or conduct and end states of existence
Opinions	Beliefs about specific occurrences and situations
Preferences	Desire or propensity to select one object over another
Motivation	Desire and willingness to be engaged in behavior and intensity of involvement
Academic Self-Concept	Self-perceptions of competence in school and learning
Self-Esteem	Attitudes toward oneself; degree of self-respect, worthiness, or desirability of self-concept
Locus of Control	Self-perception of whether success and failure is controlled by the student or by external influences
Emotional Development	Growth, change, and awareness of emotions and ability to regulate emotional expression
Social Relationships	Nature of interpersonal interactions and functioning in group settings
Altruism	Willingness and propensity to help others
Moral Development	Attainment of ethical principals that guide decision making and behavior
Classroom Environment	Nature of feeling tones in a class

students, homework, and other objects or persons. Usually, then, you can identify the positive or negative attitudes that you want to foster or at least monitor because they are related to current and future behavior. Some examples would include the following:

A Positive *Attitude Toward*

> learning
> school
> math, science, English, and other subjects
> homework
> classroom rules
> teachers
> working with others
> staying on task
> taking responsibility for one's acts

A **Negative** *Attitude Toward*

> cheating
> drug use
> fighting
> skipping school
> dropping out

Another characteristic about attitudes, one that distinguishes them from preferences and opinions, is that they are relatively stable. This means that attitudes are usually consistent over time in situations that are similar. Thus, when a student develops a negative attitude toward math, we think of that internal state as remaining relatively constant for months or even years. In contrast, a student may have a negative opinion about some math homework, or may feel bad about a math test, but that is not the same as a more stable attitude.

Social psychologists, through extensive research, have found that attitudes consist of three elements or contributing factors (McMillan, 1980):

1. an *affective* component of positive or negative feelings
2. a *cognitive* component describing worth or value
3. a *behavioral* component indicating a willingness or desire to engage in specific actions

The *affective* component consists of the emotion or feeling associated with an object or a person (e.g., good or bad feelings, enjoyment, likes, comfort, or anxiety). When we describe a student as liking math or enjoying art, we are focusing on the affective component. The *cognitive* component is an evaluative belief (such as thinking something is valuable, useful, worthless, etc.). In school, students can think history is useless and mathematics is valuable. The *behavioral* component is actually responding in a positive way. A strong and stable attitude is evidenced when all three components are consistent. That is, when Sam likes science, thinks it's important, and reads *Scientific American* at home, he has a very strong positive attitude. But it's likely that for many students these components will contradict one another. Louise may not like English very much but thinks that it's important. What would her attitude be, in a general sense, toward English? That would depend on what components of the attitude you measure. If you only measured the affective component, the attitude would be negative; a measure of the cognitive component would reveal a positive attitude.

This tripartite conceptualization has important implications for identifying attitude targets. Are you interested in feelings, thoughts, or behaviors? If you want to have a learning target like "students will have a positive attitude toward school," you would need to include all three components in your assessment because the general nature of the target would need to be consistent with the assessment. However, if your target is "students will like coming to school," then the assessment should focus on the affective component.

Value Targets

Values generally refer either to end states of existence or to modes of conduct that are desirable or sought (Rokeach, 1973). End states of existence are conditions and aspects of ourselves and our world that we want, such as a safe life, world peace, freedom, happiness, social acceptance, and wisdom. Modes of conduct are reflected in what we believe is appropriate and needed in our everyday existence, such as being, honest, cheerful, ambitious, loving, responsible, and helpful. Each of these values can be placed into categories consistent with different areas of our lives. Thus, you can think about moral, political, social, aesthetic, economic, technological, and religious values.

In school, we are usually restricted to values that are clearly related to academics and what is needed for effective functioning as a citizen and worker. Recently there has been a great deal of debate about developing "character" and the role of schools in moral development (Lickona, 1993). Citizenship is routinely identified as a valuable goal, as are a work ethic and developing aesthetic appreciations. Consider how one national report recently made the argument in relation to citizenship (*National Standards for Civics and Government*, 1994, p. 117):

> *American constitutional democracy cannot accomplish its purposes, however, unless its citizens are inclined to participate thoughtfully in public affairs. Traits of public character such as public spiritedness, civility, respect for law, critical mindedness, and a willingness to negotiate and compromise are indispensable for its vitality.*

But values can be a volatile area. I'd recommend that you stick with values that are relatively noncontroversial and that are clearly related to academic learning and school and district goals. Popham (1994, p. 185) has suggested some values as being sufficiently meritorious and noncontroversial, though with some groups even these will be suspect:

- *Honesty*. Students should learn to value honesty in their dealings with others.
- *Integrity*. Students should firmly adhere to their own code of values (for example, moral or artistic beliefs).
- *Justice*. Students should subscribe to the view that all citizens should be the recipients of equal justice from governmental law enforcement agencies.
- *Freedom*. Students should believe that democratic nations must provide the maximum level of freedom to its citizens.

Other relatively noncontroversial values would include kindness, generosity, perseverance, respect, courage, compassion, and tolerance. Popham also suggests, and I agree with him, that you should limit the number of affective traits targeted and assessed. It is better to do a sound job of assessing a few important traits than to try to assess many traits superficially.

Motivation Targets

In the context of schooling, motivation can be defined as the extent to which students are involved in trying to learn. This includes the students' initiation of learning, their intensity of effort, their commitment, and their persistence. In other words, motivation is the purposeful engagement in learning to master knowledge or skills; students take learning seriously and value opportunities to learn (Ames, 1990; McMillan & Forsyth, 1991). Most of the current research on motivation can be organized according to what is called the *expectancy × value* framework (Feather, 1982). This model suggests that motivation is determined by students' expectations—their beliefs about whether they are likely to be successful—and the value of the outcome. Expectations refer to the *self-efficacy* of the student, which is the student's self-perception of his or her capability to perform successfully. Values are self-perceptions of the importance of the performance. That is, does the student see any value in the activity? Is it intrinsically enjoyable or satisfying? Will it meet some social or psychological need, such as self-worth, competence, or belonging, or will it help the student to attain an important goal? Students who believe that they are capable of achieving success, and that the activity holds value for them, will be highly motivated to learn. If they value the outcome but believe that no matter how hard they try they probably won't be successful, their motivation will be weak. Similarly, we see many very capable students who are unmotivated because the activity holds no importance for them.

I believe your motivation targets should follow from the expectancy × value theory (McMillan, Simonetta, & Singh, 1994). Like attitudes, it is too vague to use the general definition as an outcome, because you are unable to pinpoint the source of the lack of effort and involvement. Thus, I'd suggest that you focus motivation targets on self-efficacy and value, differentiated by academic subject and type of learning (e.g., knowledge, understanding, or reasoning). Here are some examples:

- Students will believe that they are capable of learning how to multiply fractions. (self-efficacy)
- Students will believe that it is important to know how to multiply fractions. (value)
- Students will believe that they are able to learn how bills are passed in the U.S. Senate. (self-efficacy)
- Students will believe that it is important to know how bills are passed in the U.S. Senate. (value)

Academic Self-Concept and Self-Esteem Targets

There is an extensive literature on self-concept and its cousin, self-esteem. Many educators refer to these characteristics when discussing students who have problems with school and learning (e.g., "Sam has a low self-concept" or "Adrianne has a low opinion of herself"). There is no question about the importance of these be-liefs, even though there is controversy over whether self-concept and self-esteem precede or result from academic learning. According to my definition of motiva-tion, some level of positive self-efficacy is needed for achievement. It's also likely that this aspect of self-concept is formed, at least in part, when children experience meaningful success with moderate effort.

For setting targets, it is helpful to remember that self-concept and self-esteem are multidimensional. There is a bodily self, an athletic self, a mathematics self, a social self, and so forth. Each of us has a self-description in each area, which is our self-concept or self-image. In addition, we also have a sense of self-regard, self-affirmation, and self-worth in each area. Thus, a student can have a self-concept that he is tall and thin, but feel very comfortable with that and accept this descrip-tion. Another student can have the same self-concept but feel inferior, inadequate, or have a low self-esteem.

I'd suggest staying away from global self-concept and self-esteem targets, as well as those that do not differentiate between a self-description and an evaluation of that description. Like attitudes and motivation, measuring general self-concept is simply not that helpful. This is because much of what makes up general self-concept comes from areas not directly related to academic learning. By specifying *academic* self-concept, or self-concept of academic ability, you will obtain a more valid indication of what students think about themselves as learners. If you set tar-gets that are specific to subject areas, the resulting information will be more useful. Also, it's helpful to know where students draw the line between descriptions of themselves and whether they like those descriptions. From the standpoint of more serious mental or emotional problems, a general measure may be needed, but it's best to leave that to a school psychologist or counselor.

Social Relationship Targets

Social relationships involve a complex set of interaction skills, including the iden-tification of and appropriate responses to social cues. Peer relations, friendship, functioning in groups, assertiveness, cooperation, prosocial behavior, empathy, taking perspective, and conflict resolution are examples of social relationships that can be specified as targets. Many of these are important at the elementary level as needed skills for academic achievement. At the secondary level, interpersonal abil-ities are becoming more and more important as schools work with the business community to identify and promote the skills needed to be successful in the work-place. For each of these areas, specific targets need to be identified. For example, a target concerned with peer relationships might include showing interest in others, listening to peers, sharing, and contributing to group activities. Cooperative skills could include sharing, listening, volunteering ideas and suggestions, supporting and accepting others' ideas, taking turns, and criticizing constructively. A recent draft of the *National Standards for Civics and Government* (1994) suggests the follow-ing interpersonal targets (p. 119):

- *Civility.* Treating other persons respectfully, regardless of whether or not one agrees with their viewpoints; being willing to listen to other points of view; avoiding hostile, abusive, emotional, and illogical argument.
- *Negotiation and Compromise.* Making an effort to come to agreement with those with whom one may differ, when it is reasonable and morally justifiable to do so.

My recommendation is similar to suggestions about identifying attitude, motivational, and self-concept targets—that it is necessary to be very specific about the target. A general target about "improved social relationships" simply does not provide the level of specificity needed to focus your instruction and assessment. Here are some examples of possible social relationship targets:

- Students will contribute to small group discussions.
- Students will willingly share materials with other students.
- Students will have sustained friendships with two or more other students.
- Students will demonstrate skills in helping other students solve a problem.
- Students will demonstrate that they are able to negotiate with others and compromise.

Classroom Environment Targets

If you have been in very many classrooms, you will understand that each classroom has a unique climate and feel to it; it's as if you can sense the degree to which a class is comfortable, relaxed, and productive, and whether students seem happy, content, and serious. Some classes are warm and supportive, while others seem very cold and rejecting, even hostile. Together, such characteristics make up what is called *classroom environment* or *climate* (Raviv, Raviv, & Reisel, 1990). Obviously, a positive climate promotes learning, so a reasonable affective target would be to establish student feelings, relationships, and beliefs that promote this kind of environment.

Classroom climate is made up of a number of characteristics that can be used as affective targets. These include:

affiliation—the extent to which students like and accept each other

involvement—the extent to which students are interested in and engaged in learning

task orientation—the extent to which classroom activities are focused on the completion of academic tasks

cohesiveness—the extent to which students share norms and expectations

competition—the emphasis on competition between students

favoritism—whether each student enjoys the same privileges

influence—the extent to which each student influences classroom decisions

friction—the extent to which students bicker with one another

> *formality*—the emphasis on enforcing rules
> *communication*—the extent to which communication among students and with
>   teacher is genuine and honest
> *warmth*—the extent to which students care about each other and show empathy

Affective Domain of the Taxonomy of Educational Objectives

One of the earliest treatments of affective objectives was called the *Taxonomy of Educational Objectives, Handbook II: Affective Domain* (Krathwohl, Bloom, & Masia, 1964). It was a companion to Bloom's *Taxonomy* of the cognitive domain. Although the affective taxonomy was developed more than thirty years ago, it was constructed for conceptualizing attitudes, values, and other affective traits in a hierarchy, which is appealing from the standpoint of assessment.

The affective taxonomy arranges affective targets along a five-stage continuum. These stages, with definitions and examples, are summarized in Figure 10.2. Let's look at an example that refers to attitudes toward science. At the most basic

FIGURE 10.2   Affective Taxonomy of Educational Objectives

Category (Level)	Definition	Examples
Receiving (*Attending*)	Develops an awareness, shows a willingness to receive, shows controlled or selected attention.	Student considers reading books for extra credit. Student pays attention to teacher lecture about smoking.
Responding	Shows a willingness to respond and finds some initial level of satisfaction in responding.	Student asks questions about different books. Takes pleasure in playing sports.
Valuing	Shows that the object, person, or situation has worth. Something is perceived as holding a positive value, a commitment is made.	Student reads continually, asks for more books. Asks for further help in improving writing skills. Practices sports all the time.
Organization	Brings together a complex set of values and organizes them in an ordered relationship that is harmonious and internally consistent.	Student develops a plan for integrating reading and sports. Weighs concerns for social justice with governmental size.
Characterization	Organized system of values becomes a person's life outlook and the basis for a philosophy of life.	Student develops a consistent philosophy of life. Reading forms the basis for most everything in the student's life.

Source: Adapted from Krathwohl, D. R., Bloom, B. J., & Masia, B. B. (1964). *Taxonomy of educational objectives, handbook II: Affective domain.* New York: David McKay.

level, *receiving*, students are merely aware of and perceive science. At the next level, students are able to pay attention to the science (*responding*). Next, the students indicate through their voluntary behavior that science has *value*. Once science is valued, it can be organized with other subjects and other values (*organization*). The highest stage is *characterization*, in which science is so highly valued that it becomes a determining tendency and influence on other aspects of the student's life.

The contribution of the affective taxonomy for classroom assessment of affect is that it helps you determine the standard or level of affect that is part of your target. It also provides good suggestions for using student behaviors as indicators of affect at each of the levels. For example, suppose you want your students to develop an appreciation for classical music. At what level do you want your target? Will students simply be aware of what classical music is and what it sounds like (receiving)? Or do you want them to really *like* classical music (valuing)?

METHODS OF ASSESSING AFFECTIVE TARGETS

There are really only three feasible methods of assessing affective targets in the classroom: teacher observation, student self-report, and peer ratings. Because affective traits are not directly observable, they must be inferred from behavior or what students say about themselves and others. There are some very sophisticated psychological measures that can assess many affective traits, but these are rarely used by classroom teachers. As we will see, you need to rely on your own observation skills and some student self-reports.

Keep three considerations in mind whenever you assess affect. First, emotions and feelings (not more stable attitudes) can change quickly, especially for young children and during early adolescence. This suggests that to obtain a valid indication of an individual student's emotion or feeling it is necessary to conduct several assessments over a substantial length of time. What you want to know is what the dominant or prevalent affect is, and if you rely on a single assessment there is a good chance that what you measure is not a good indication of the trait. Measure repeatedly over several weeks.

Second, try to use as many different approaches to measuring the affective trait as possible. Reliance on a single method is problematic because of limitations inherent in that method. For example, if you use only student self-reports, which are subject to social desirability and faking, these limitations may significantly affect the results. However, if student self-reports are consistent with your observations, then a stronger case can be made.

Finally, decide if you need individual student or group results. This is related to purpose and will influence the method that you should use. If your purpose is to use assessment for making reports to parents, then obviously you need information on each student. In this case, you should use multiple methods of collecting data over time, and keep records to verify your judgments. If the assessments will be used to improve instruction, then you need results for the group as a whole. This is the more common and advisable use of affective assessment, primarily because you can rely more on anonymous student self-reports (Popham, 1994).

Teacher Observation

In Chapter 5, teacher observation was discussed as an essential tool for formative assessment. Here the emphasis is on how teachers can make more systematic observations to record student behavior that indicates the presence of targeted affective traits.

The first step in using observation is to determine in advance how specific behaviors relate to the target. This begins with a clear definition of the trait, followed by lists of student behaviors and actions that correspond to positive and negative dimensions of the trait. Let's consider attitudes. We can identify the behaviors and actions initially by considering what students with positive and negative attitudes do and say. If we have two columns, one listing behaviors for positive attitudes and one listing behaviors for negative attitudes, we define what will be observed. Suppose you are interested in attitudes toward learning. What is it that students with a positive attitude toward learning do and say? What are the actions of those with a negative attitude? Figure 10.3 lists some possibilities. These behaviors provide a foundation for developing guidelines, checklists, or rating scales. The ones in the positive column are referred to as *approach* behaviors; those in the negative column *avoidance* behaviors. Approach behaviors result in more direct, frequent, and intense contact; avoidance behaviors are just the opposite, resulting in

FIGURE 10.3 **Student Behaviors Indicating Positive and Negative Attitudes Toward Learning**

Positive	Negative
rarely misses class	is frequently absent
is rarely late to class	is frequently tardy
asks lots of questions	rarely asks questions
helps other students	rarely helps other students
works well independently without supervision	needs constant supervision
is involved in extracurricular activities	is not involved in extracurricular activities
says he or she likes school	says he or she doesn't like school
comes to class early	rarely comes to class early
stays after school	rarely stays after school
volunteers to help	doesn't volunteer
completes homework	often does not complete homework
tries hard to do well	doesn't care about bad grades
completes extra credit work	never does extra credit work
completes assignments before they are due	never completes assignments before the due date
rarely complains	complains
is rarely off task	sleeps in class
rarely bothers other students	bothers other students
	stares out window

less direct, less frequent, or less intense contact. These dimensions—directness, frequency, and intensity—are helpful in describing the behaviors that indicate positive and negative attitudes.

How do you develop these lists of positive and negative behaviors? I have found that the best approach is to find time to brainstorm with other teachers. Published instruments are available that may give you some ideas, but these won't consider the unique characteristics of your school and students. The following characteristics were brainstormed by teachers to indicate a positive student attitude toward school subjects (e.g., mathematics, science, English):

> seeks corrective feedback
> asks questions
> helps other students
> prepares for tests
> reads about the subject outside of class
> asks about careers in the subject
> asks about colleges strong in the subject
> asks other students to be quiet in class
> is concerned with poor performance
> joins clubs
> initiates activities
> stays alert in class and on task

Some behaviors that can be observed for working cooperatively with others in a group include the following:

> stays with the group
> gets physically close to others
> volunteers ideas
> responds to questions
> asks questions
> supports and accepts others' suggestions
> reacts positively to criticism
> encourages others to participate
> seeks clarification from others
> encourages others to do well

Once a fairly complete list of behaviors is developed you will need to decide if you want to use an informal, unstructured observation or one that is more formal and structured. These types differ in preparation and what is recorded.

Unstructured Observation

Unstructured observation is much like what was discussed in Chapter 5. In this case, however, your purpose is to make summative judgments.

An unstructured observation is open-ended; there is no checklist or rating scale for recording what is observed. However, you do know what affective trait you are focused on, and you have at least generated some guidelines and examples of behaviors that indicate the affective trait. In that sense, you have determined in advance what to look for, but you also need to be open to other actions that may reflect on the trait.

You begin by planning the time, date, and place of the observation. During the observation period, or just after it is over, record behaviors that reflect the affective trait. Some of what you record may correspond to the guidelines or a list of possible behaviors, but record other actions also—anything that may have relevance to the target. Keep your interpretations separate from descriptions of the behaviors. Usually the teacher takes brief anecdotal notes and then makes some sense of the notes at a later time. Actually this is what teachers do regularly in their heads in a way that is even less systemic than these unstructured observations. The difference is in whether or not there is any predetermined list of behaviors, and whether the teachers record their observations.

Avoid making conclusions or inferences in what you record. You want to describe what you saw or heard, not what that may mean. Words such as *unhappy, frustrated, sad, motivated,* and *positive* are your interpretations of observed behaviors. It is better to stick to simple descriptions, such as *frowned, asked question, stared out window,* or *kept writing the entire time.* Look for both positive and negative actions. The tendency is to be more influenced by bad or negative behavior, especially if it interferes with other students. Once descriptions from several different times are recorded, then you can look over all of them and come to conclusions about the affective trait. Don't rely on a single observation.

The advantage of unstructured observation is that it is more naturalistic and you are not constrained by what is in a checklist or rating scale. There is no problem if specific behaviors aren't displayed, and behaviors that were not previously listed can be included. A disadvantage is that it is not practical to record much about student behavior on a regular basis. It's hard to find even fifteen or twenty minutes at the end of the day, and it is virtually impossible for most teachers to find any time during the school day.

Structured Observation

A structured observation differs from an unstructured one in the amount of preparation needed and the way you record what is observed. In structured observation, more time is needed to prepare a checklist or rating form that is to be used for recording purposes. This form is generated from the list of positive and negative behaviors to make it easy and convenient for you to make checks quickly and easily.

The format of the checklist is simple and straightforward. The behaviors are listed, and you make a single check next to each behavior to indicate frequency. Frequency can be indicated by answering yes or no, observed or not observed, by the number of times a behavior occurred; or by some kind of rating scale (always, often, sometimes, rarely, never, occasionally, consistently). Rating scales are used to describe behavior over an extended period of time. Two examples are illustrated in Figure 10.4 for assessing attitude toward reading. The first, labeled *frequency approach*, would be used to record the number of times each behavior was observed. The second type is a rating scale. Another example is shown in Figure 10.5 on page 274. In this example, the targeted affective trait is group work and participation. Notice that there is a column to indicate if there was no opportunity to observe the behavior. This allows you to make better sense out of a lack of pos-

FIGURE 10.4   Checklists for Structured Observation of Attitudes Toward Reading

Checklist 1 (Frequency Approach)

Name _____ Date _____ Time _____

Behaviors	*Frequency*
1. Looks at books on table	_____
2. Picks up books on table	_____
3. Reads books	_____
4. Tells others about books read	_____
5. Moves away from books on table	_____
6. Makes faces when looking at books	_____
7. Tells others not to read	_____
8. Expresses dislike for reading	_____

Checklist 2 (Rating Approach)

Name _____ Date _____ Time _____

Behaviors	*Always*	*Often*	*Sometimes*	*Seldom*	*Never*
1. Looks at books on table	—	—	—	—	—
2. Picks up books on table	—	—	—	—	—
3. Reads books	—	—	—	—	—
4. Tells others about books read	—	—	—	—	—
5. Moves away from books on table	—	—	—	—	—
6. Makes faces when looking at books	—	—	—	—	—
7. Tells others not to read	—	—	—	—	—
8. Expresses dislike for reading	—	—	—	—	—

Source: Educational testing and measurement: Classroom application and practice, 4th ed., by Tom Kubiszyn and Gary Borich, p. 175. Copyright © 1993 by HarperCollins College Publishers. Reprinted by permission.

FIGURE 10.5   Checklist for Observing Group Participation

No Opportunity to Observe	Observed	
☑	☐	Shares information
☐	☑	Contributes ideas
☐	☑	Listens to others
☑	☐	Follows instructions
☐	☐	Shows initiative in solving group problems
☐	☐	Gives consideration to viewpoints of others
☑	☐	Accepts and carries out group-determined tasks

Source: Educational testing and measurement: Classroom application and practice, 4th ed., by Tom Kubiszyn and Gary Borich, p. 204. Copyright © 1993 by HarperCollins College Publishers. Reprinted by permission.

itive behavior. If there is no opportunity to do something, students should not be penalized for not getting a check for that behavior. An alternative to the checklist in Figure 10.5 would be to develop a rating scale similar to the one in Figure 10.4 (page 273), in which you could record how often the student shares information, listens to others, and so forth. Your choice of checklist or rating scale depends on the time frame (ratings are better for longer periods of time) and the nature of the behavior. Some behaviors are better suited to a simple checklist, like "follows instructions," and "completes homework." My experience is that a simple scale, with only three descriptors to indicate frequency (e.g., *usually, sometimes, rarely*) is usually sufficient.

With structured observation, it is best to state the descriptions in the positive to avoid confusion. If there is a large number of behaviors, organize them into major categories. This will make it easier to record and draw inferences from the results. Other suggestions are summarized in Figure 10.6.

FIGURE 10.6   Checklist for Using Teacher Observation to Assess Affect

1. Determine behaviors to be observed in advance.
2. Record student, time, date, and place.
3. If unstructured, record brief descriptions of relevant behavior.
4. Keep inferences separate from descriptions.
5. Record both positive and negative behaviors.
6. Make several observations of each student.
7. Avoid personal bias.
8. Record as soon as possible following the observation.
9. Use a simple and efficient system.

Student Self-Report

There are several ways in which students tell us about their affect as a self-report. The most direct way is in the context of a personal conversation or interview. Students can also respond to a written questionnaire or survey about themselves or other students. First, we'll consider interviews.

Student Interview

Teachers can effectively use different types of personal communication with students, such as individual and group interviews, discussions, and casual conversations, to assess affect. In some ways this is like an observation, but because you have an opportunity to be directly involved with the students it is possible to probe and respond to better understand the targeted trait. An important prerequisite for getting students to reveal their true feelings and beliefs is establishing trust. Without a sense of trust, students may not be comfortable expressing their feelings. They will tend to say what they think their teachers want to hear, say what is socially acceptable or desirable, or say very little, if anything. Younger students are usually pretty candid about themselves; older students may be more reserved. You enhance trust by communicating warmth, caring, and respect and by listening attentively to what the students communicate.

An advantage of interviewing is that you can clarify questions, probe where appropriate to clarify responses, and note nonverbal behavior. Students have an opportunity to qualify or expand on previous answers. These procedures help minimize two problems often associated with measuring affect—ambiguity and vagueness.

It is difficult for some students, even when there is a trusting relationship, to articulate their feelings in a one-on-one interview. They may simply be unaccustomed to answering questions about attitudes and values. A group discussion or group interview would be a good alternative for these students. People generally open up more in a group setting, as long as peer pressure and cliques don't interfere. Another advantage of using groups is that it is much more efficient than individual interviews. It would be terribly time-consuming to conduct individual interviews. Also, feelings and beliefs can become more clear as students hear others talk. You can use students as leaders of group interviews. They may be better at probing because they are familiar with the language and lifestyles of their classmates. Respected student leaders will be highly credible.

Be prepared to record student responses and your interpretations. During an interview it is difficult to write very much, and it's not practical to tape record, transcribe, and analyze the transcription. What I suggest is to prepare a brief outline of the major areas that will be covered, leaving space to make brief notes as you interview. As soon as possible after the interview, go back over your notes and fill in enough detail so that what the student said and communicated are clearly indicated. As with observation, be careful to keep your descriptions separate from your interpretations.

Questionnaires and Surveys

You have probably completed many commercial or standardized self-report attitude questionnaires or surveys, so you have a general idea what they are like. However, teachers rarely use such instruments in the classroom (Stiggins & Conklin, 1992). Why is this true when there are literally hundreds of instruments to choose from? I believe that there are several contributing factors. First, most published instruments are not designed to be used by teachers. They are intended more for research than instruction, and usually the affective trait is conceptualized as a general construct that is hard for teachers to make use of in planning or delivering instruction. For example, most self-concept inventories provide a single score for general self-concept, which doesn't provide much help for understanding a student's motivation to learn.

Second, affect is generally not afforded the status of achievement—it just isn't as important—so poorly designed instruments are tolerated. Third, as mentioned previously, measuring affect is risky. Finally, most teachers have not had much training in how to use these instruments, or to develop their own. Whatever the reasons, I hope to show you that these instruments can be very helpful in providing one source of evidence on affect.

According to Stiggins (1994), one key to the successful use of student self-reports is to get students to take the questionnaires seriously. This will happen if students see that what you are asking about is relevant to them and that actions are taken as a result of the findings. You want to help students understand that they have nothing to lose and something to gain by being cooperative. In Stiggins words, enlist "the support of the respondent as an ally, a partner" (Stiggins, 1994, p. 317).

Another key is using questions to which students are willing and able to provide thoughtful responses. This is accomplished if the wording of the questions is precise, if the format is easy to understand and respond to, and if the response options make sense. These and other suggestions are discussed in reviewing the major types of attitude, value, and self-concept self-report instruments.

Constructed-Response Formats

A straightforward approach to asking students about their affect is to have them respond to a simple statement or question. Often, as the following examples illustrate, incomplete sentences can be used.

Examples

> I think mathematics is . . . .
> When I have free time I like to . . . .
> The subject I like most is . . . .
> What I like most about school is . . . .
> What I like least about school is . . . .
> Science is . . . .
> I think I am . . . .

An advantage of the incomplete sentence format is that it taps whatever comes to mind from each student. You are not cuing students about what to think nor suggesting how they should respond, so what you get is what is foremost and most salient in the student's mind. Of course, students need to be able to read and write and take the task seriously. If you use this method, be sure to give students enough time to think and write, and encourage them to write as much as they can think about for each item.

With older students, essay items can also be used. These items provide a more extensive, in-depth response than incomplete sentences. You can ask students for reasons for their attitudes, values, or beliefs.

Examples

Write a paragraph on what subject you like most in school. Tell me why. Comment on what it is about the subject and your experience with it that leads you to like it the most.

Describe yourself as a student. Are you a good student? What are you good at? How hard do you try to get good grades? Does learning come easy or hard for you?

There are two disadvantages to constructed response formats. One is faking. Even if you tell students that their answers are anonymous, they may think you'll recognize their handwriting. Second, scoring the responses takes time and is more subjective than more traditional objective formats. Even with these limitations, this approach offers an excellent way to get a general overview of student perspectives, feelings, and thoughts.

Selected-Response Formats

There are many different types of selected-response formats to choose from when assessing affective targets. We will look at a few commonly used ones. When you decide to create your own instrument and wonder which of these response formats would be best, try to match the format with the trait. There is no single best response format. Some work better with some traits, some work better with others, depending on the wording and the nature of the trait. Your job will be to make the best match.

Most selected-response formats create a scale that is used with statements concerning the trait. A widely used format to assess attitudes, for example, is the *Likert scale*. This scale can be adapted to almost any type of affective trait, so it is very versatile. Students read statements and then record their agreement or disagreement with them according to a five-point scale (*strongly agree, agree, undecided, disagree, strongly disagree*). The statements are generated from your list of positive and negative behaviors or beliefs and are put in a form that makes sense for the response scale. The statements contain some indication of the direction of the attitude, as illustrated in the following examples.

Examples

Mathematics is boring.
It is important to get good grades in school.
It is important to complete homework on time.
Class discussion is better than lectures.
School is fun.
I enjoy reading.
Science is challenging.
Science is difficult.

The agree/disagree response scale indicates intensity.

An advantage of this format is that many such statements can be presented on a page or two to assess a number of different attitudes efficiently. Note that some negatively worded statements are included in the example in Figure 10.7. These should be used sparingly with younger children, with words like *not*, *don't*, or *no* appropriately highlighted or underlined.

The responses to the Likert scale are scored by assigning weights from 1 to 5 for each position on the scale so that 5 reflects the most positive attitude and 1 the most negative attitude. The scores from all the items assessing the same attitude trait are then totaled, though the percentage of responses to each position are probably more important summary indices. In other words, you wouldn't add the scores from items 1, 7, and 8 in Figure 10.7 because they address different traits, though you could add items 3, 9, and 10 that deal with attitudes toward school. The reliability of overall scores is higher if you have several items assessing the

FIGURE 10.7   Likert Scale for School Attitudes

Student Opinion Survey

Directions: Read each statement carefully and indicate how much you agree or disagree with it by circling the appropriate letter(s) to the right.

Key: SA – Strongly Agree
A – Agree
NS – Not Sure
D – Disagree
SD – Strongly Disagree

	SA	A	NS	D	SD
1. Science class is challenging.	SA	A	NS	D	SD
2. Reading is important.	SA	A	NS	D	SD
3. I like coming to school.	SA	A	NS	D	SD
4. I like doing science experiments.	SA	A	NS	D	SD
5. Homework is hard for me.	SA	A	NS	D	SD
6. Cheating is very bad.	SA	A	NS	D	SD
7. Learning about circles and triangles is useless.	SA	A	NS	D	SD
8. I do *not* like to work in small groups.	SA	A	NS	D	SD
9. Doing well in school is important.	SA	A	NS	D	SD
10. I believe that what I learn in school is important.	SA	A	NS	D	SD

same trait that can be added together. This needs to be balanced with the practical limitation on the total number of items in the questionnaire and with the response of students who feel that they don't need to be answering questions that are just about the same as items they have already responded to.

You can use the principle of the Likert scale to construct any number of different response formats. For younger children, for example, the five-point scale is usually truncated to three responses (agree, unsure, disagree), or even two (such as agree or disagree, yes or no, true or not true). Many self-report instruments use a Likert-type scale that asks students to indicate *how often* they have engaged in specific behaviors or had particular thoughts. These scales are easier to respond to because behaviors are more concrete than thoughts. They are best for behaviors and cognitive components of attitudes.

Examples

How often do you believe that most of what you learn in school is important?

a. always
b. frequently
c. sometimes
d. rarely
e. never

How frequently do you *dislike* coming to this class?

a. all the time
b. most of the time
c. sometimes
d. rarely
e. never

How often do you find the classroom activities interesting?

a. almost always
b. often
c. occasionally
d. rarely if ever

Another frequently used variation of the Likert scale is to ask students whether something is true for them. This can be a simple dichotomous item, such as a true/false statement, or you can use a scale.

Examples

How true is each statement for you?

If I want I can get good grades in science.

a. very true
b. somewhat true
c. not at all true

When I really try hard I can do well in school.

a. true
b. untrue

Students try hard to do better than each other in this class.

a. true
b. false

I am a good student.

a. yes
b. no

Scales are mixed in some questionnaires so that there are different scales for different items. In these types of questionnaires, the response formats are dependent on the terminology and intent of each item. Sometimes the nature of the trait is named in the item; then the scale gives students choices. For other items the scale defines the trait being measured.

Examples

How important is it for you to be a good reader?

a. extremely important
b. very important
c. somewhat important
d. not important

Science is:

a. interesting
b. dull
c. difficult

Indicate how you feel about your performance on the test.

_____	_____	_____	_____
immense pride	some pride	some failure	immense failure
_____	_____	_____	_____
very happy	somewhat happy	somewhat sad	very sad

Indicate the extent to which you believe your performance on the project was a success or failure.

a. extreme success
b. somewhat successful

c. failure
d. extreme failure

Circle the statement that best describes your interest in learning *most of the time.*

a. I am pretty interested in what we learn.
b. This class is somewhat interesting, but I find my mind wandering sometimes.
c. I often find this class pretty boring.

For young students the response format is often in the form of faces rather than words.

Examples

Learning about science

Reading books

For classroom climate and value targets, self-report questionnaires often ask students to select from several options. The options refer to different traits or values, rather than showing a range of the same trait.

Examples

I did well on this test because I

a. studied hard.
b. got lucky.

Select one of the following:

a. Students in this class like to help each other out.
b. There is a lot of bickering between students in this class.

Select the statement that you agree with the most.

a. People should be required to volunteer to help those less fortunate.
b. People who find a wallet should give it to the police.

Interests are efficiently measured with checklists, ranking, or simple dichotomous choices.

Examples

Indicate whether you are interested (I) or uninterested (U) in learning about
   each of the historical topics listed.

_____   **a.** Vietnam War
_____   **b.** World War II
_____   **c.** The Holocaust
_____   **d.** The Great Depression
_____   **e.** stock market crash (1929)

Rank the following from most liked (1) to least liked (5).

_____   history
_____   sports
_____   science
_____   music
_____   art

Another common approach to measuring affective traits is to use variations of
the *semantic differential*. These scales use adjective pairs that provide anchors for
feelings or beliefs that are opposite in direction and intensity. The student would
place a check between each pair of adjectives that describes positive or negative aspects of the trait. In the following examples, the traits are attitudes toward a test
and a subject.

Examples

Science Test

fair   _____ _____ _____ _____ _____   unfair
hard   _____ _____ _____ _____ _____   easy

History

boring   _____ _____ _____ _____ _____   interesting
important   _____ _____ _____ _____ _____   useless
like   _____ _____ _____ _____ _____   hate

An advantage of selected-response formats is that they make it easy to assure
anonymity. Anonymity is important when the traits are more personal, such as
values and self-concept. It is also a more efficient way of collecting information.
However, you don't want to ask too many questions. It's best to keep self-report
questionnaires short. Although you need more than a single item to reliably assess
an affective trait, if you have too many items students may lose concentration and

motivation. Select only those traits that you will take action on; don't use items simply because it would be interesting to know what students think. It's also not a good idea to include open-ended items such as "Comments" or "Suggestions" at the end of a selected-response questionnaire.

Constructing Self-Report Items

If you need to develop your own self-report items to assess affect targets, begin by listing the behaviors, thoughts, and feelings that correspond to each affective trait, similar to what I suggested earlier for observations. Once you select a response format, write sentences that are clear and succinct, and write direct statements that students will easily understand. You are not trying to assess knowledge, intelligence, reading ability, or vocabulary, so keep items simple and short. You may find published instruments that will give you some good ideas for how to word items, set up response formats, and in general lay out a questionnaire. Volumes 5 and 6 of the Educational Testing Service Test Collection (Attitude Measures, 5, and Affective Measures and Personality Tests, 6) are excellent sources to identify existing instruments. (The ETS Test Collection can be accessed through Internet and other on-line data retrieval services.) I'd recommend Ruth Wylie's book for self-concept measures (1989), and Anderson (1981) for more information in general on measuring affect. You may find an existing instrument that meets your purpose very well. Now to some specific suggestions, with examples, for constructing items.

In wording the items, avoid the use of negatives, especially double negatives.

Example

> *Poor:* There isn't a student in this class who does not like to work with others.
> *Improved:* Students in this class like to work with each other.

If you are interested in present self-perceptions, which is usually the case, avoid writing in the past tense.

Example

> *Poor:* I have always liked science.
> *Improved:* I like science.

Avoid absolutes such as *always, never, all,* and *every* in the item stem. These terms, because they represent an all-or-none type of judgment, may cause you to miss the more accurate self-perception.

Example

> *Poor:* I never like science.
> *Improved:* I rarely like science.

Avoid items that ask about more than one thing or thought. Double-barrelled items are difficult to interpret because you don't know which of the two thoughts or ideas the student has responded to.

Example

> *Poor:* I like science and mathematics.
> *Improved:* I like science.

These and other suggestions presented in this section are summarized in Figure 10.8, below. I should point out, however, that classroom teachers rarely have an opportunity to develop sophisticated instruments with strong and well-documented technical qualities. Thus, locally developed items and instruments should be used cautiously and in conjunction with other evidence.

Peer Ratings

Peer appraisal is the least common method of assessing affect. This is due to the relatively inefficient nature of conducting, scoring, and interpreting peer ratings. Also, teachers who are tuned in very much at all in a class can accurately observe what is assessed in peer ratings. However, two primary methods of obtaining peer ratings—the guess-who and sociometric techniques—represent approaches that can be used in conjunction with observation and self-reports to strengthen assessment of interpersonal and classroom environment targets.

Guess-Who Approach

In this method, students are asked to list the students they believe best correspond to behavior descriptions. The descriptions may be positive or negative, though usually they are positive to avoid highlighting undesirable behaviors or traits. Typically there are only a few items in this approach so that students can complete it quickly, and scoring is done by simply tallying the number of times each student is listed. One disadvantage is that some shy and withdrawn students may be overlooked, resulting in a lack of information about them. Figure 10.9 illustrates a guess-who format for assessing concern for others.

FIGURE 10.8   Checklist for Using Student Self-Reports to Assess Affect

1. Keep measures focused on specific affective traits.
2. Establish trust with students.
3. Match response format to the trait being assessed.
4. Assure anonymity if possible.
5. Keep questionnaires brief.
6. Keep items short and simple.
7. Avoid negatives and absolutes.
8. Write items in present tense.
9. Avoid double-barrelled items.

FIGURE 10.9   Guess-Who Form for Assessing Students' Concern for Others

Directions

Listed below are descriptions of what some students in this room are like. Read the descriptions and write the names of the students who *best fit* each description. You may write the names of anyone in this room, including those who are absent. Your choices will not be seen by anyone else. Give the student's first name and the initial of the student's last name.

Remember

1. Write the names of students in this room who best fit each description.
2. Write as many names as you wish for each description.
3. The same person may fit more than one description.
4. You should write the student's first name and the initial of the student's last name.
5. Your choices will *not be seen* by anyone else.

Write the Names below Each Description [space would be provided after each description]

1. Who enjoys working and playing with other students?
2. Who is willing to share materials with other students?
3. Who is willing to help other students with their homework?
4. Who makes sure other students are not left out of games?
5. Who encourages other students to do well in school?
6. Who is kind to other students who have a problem?

Source: Linn, R. L., & Gronlund, N. E., *Measurement and assessment in teaching,* 7th Edition, copyright © 1995, p. 276. Adapted by permission of Prentice-Hall, Upper Saddle River, New Jersey.

Sociometric Approach

Sociometric techniques are used to assess the social structure of the class, that is, the interaction patterns among the students. This allows you to learn about the social acceptance and liking patterns of the students. The results can be used for forming small groups of students, targeting interventions with individual students, and identifying cliques, popular students, and social isolates.

Students are asked, in a form similar to what is shown in Figure 10.9, to nominate students they would like to work with or play with. Although this is technically a self-report, the results are used as a way for students to rate each other. The questions would be like the following:

> I choose these students to work with.
> I would like to sit next to _____.
> I would like to have the following students on my team.

It is best to ask about general activities, such as who to work with or sit next to, rather than specific ones (e.g., walking to school or doing a report). It is also advisable to avoid asking negative items (e.g., I would not like to sit next to . . .).

Once the students have made their choices, you need to tabulate the results by listing all the students and indicating the number of times each student was selected. This provides a measure of general social acceptance. Second, create a matrix to identify students who have selected each other. Finally, as illustrated in

Figure 10.10, construct a *sociogram*. This is a diagram that shows the social structure of the group. In this example, the number of times any student was selected is depicted by the concentric circles (students with more than nine choices in the middle, six to nine choices in the second circle, etc.). Not all choices are shown; lines are used for mutual choices and rejections.

Although this is a very interesting and informative technique, constructing the sociogram takes considerable time. However, often teachers are surprised by the results, so if you intend to assess social adjustment and other interpersonal affect targets in depth, a sociogram would be very helpful.

Which Method or Combination of Methods Should I Use?

We have covered three approaches to measuring affect—observation, student self-report, and peer ratings—and each method has advantages and disadvantages (see Figure 10.11 on page 288). Your choice of which of these to use depends on a number of factors. Consider the type of affect you want to assess. You can get a pretty good idea of a student's general reaction to something or someone through observation, but to diagnose attitude components you'll need a self-report of some kind. Observation can be followed by peer ratings to get at socially oriented affect.

If you are interested in group responses and tendencies, which is generally recommended, then a selected-response self-report is probably best because you can assure anonymity and easily score the responses. Finally, you need to take into consideration the use of the information. If you intend to use the results for grading (which I would not recommend), then multiple approaches may be needed, and you'll need to be especially careful about faking on self-reports and even peer judgments. In the end, the choice of method depends most on your context, targets, and level of comfort in using any particular approach.

Assuring Anonymity

Anonymity has been mentioned several times as a desirable feature when assessing affect. Popham (1994) makes the argument that anonymity is not only desirable, but essential to obtaining valid results. He has pointed out that several techniques can be used to enhance perceived anonymity when you are interested in results for the class as a whole:

1. Direct students not to write their names or in any way identify themselves on their self-reports.
2. Inform students that their responses will be anonymous.
3. Position yourself in the class so that students know you cannot see their answers on self-reports.

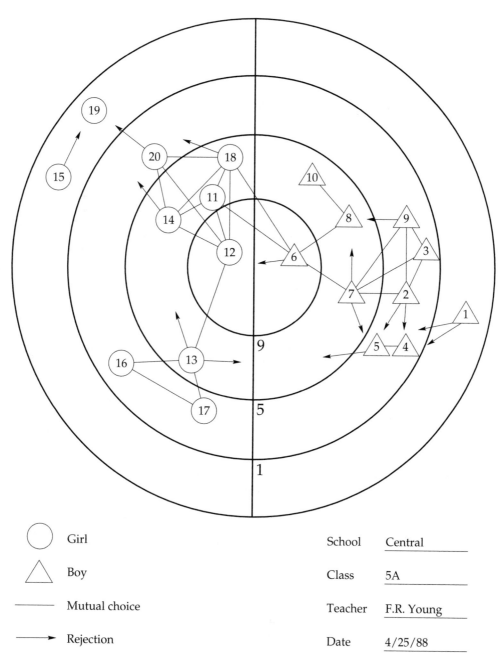

FIGURE 10.10   Example of Sociogram

Source: Linn, R. L., & Gronlund, N.E., *Measurement and assessment in teaching*, 7th Edition, copyright © 1995, p. 282. Adapted by permission of Prentice-Hall, Upper Saddle River, New Jersey.

4. Direct students not to write anything other than checking or circling so that you will not recognize handwriting.
5. Provide a procedure for collecting self-reports so that you won't be able identify responses (e.g., in a container in the back of the room, not on your desk).
6. Tell students why anonymity is important.
7. Use a response format that minimizes the likelihood that responses can be seen by other students.

FIGURE 10.11   Advantages and Disadvantages of Methods to Assess Affect

	Strengths	Weaknesses
Observation	Can observe unobtrusively Can observe nonverbal behavior Can observe natural behavior	Observer bias Not usually anonymous Students unable to explain reasons for behavior Can be time-consuming Absence of behavior doesn't mean absence of affect
Constructed-Response Self-Report	Easy to develop Easy to administer Can be anonymous Elicits uncued responses Reasons for affect can be given Easy to focus on specific affective traits	Time-consuming to score Teacher bias Writing proficiency needed Unable to follow up Students may not understand or follow directions
Selected-Response Self-Report	Easy to administer Easy to score Can be anonymous Easier to compare students Easy to focus on specific affective traits Offers many examples of existing instruments	Reading proficiency needed Reasons for affect not indicated Faking Response set Social desirability
Peer Rating	Easy to administer Focuses on interpersonal targets Students may find it easier to think about others than themselves Provides check on teacher inferences Students perceive that their input is important	Difficult to score and interpret Faking Social desirability Teacher may not follow through on choices

Source: Stiggins, R. J., *Student-centered classroom assessment*, copyright © 1994, p. 315. Adapted by permission of Prentice-Hall, Upper Saddle River, New Jersey.

SUMMARY

This chapter has considered assessing student affect, an important but often neglected area. Sound assessment of affect begins with clear and specific affective targets. Suggestions were made for conceptualizing affective traits that most would consider essential for successful learning. Two methods are used most frequently for measuring affect in the classroom: teacher observation and student self-reports. Observation can be structured or unstructured, and there are many different formats for self-reports. In the end, you'll need to customize the assessment of affect for your students, school, and curriculum. Pick a few most important traits, do a good job of assessing them, and then use the results to improve instruction. Other essential points made in the chapter include the following:

- Positive affective traits impact motivation, involvement, and cognitive learning.
- Although the term *affect* refers to emotions and feelings, affective targets include cognitive and behavioral traits.
- Attitudes are predispositions to respond favorably or unfavorably. They are comprised of cognitive, affective, and behavioral components.
- Values are end states of existence or desired modes of conduct.
- Motivation is the purposeful engagement to learn. It is determined by self-efficacy (the student's beliefs about his or her capability to learn) and the value of learning.
- Academic self-concept is the way students describe themselves as learners. Self-esteem is how students feel about themselves. Both are multidimensional; it's best to avoid general measures of self-concept or self-esteem.
- Social relationship targets involve interpersonal interaction and competence.
- Classroom environment is the climate established through factors such as affiliation, involvement, cohesiveness, formality, friction, and warmth.
- The affective domain of Bloom's taxonomy defines different levels of affect in a hierarchical fashion, from attending to something to using something as a determining factor in one's life.
- Three methods are used to assess student affect: teacher observation, student self-report, and peer ratings.
- Teacher observation can be structured or unstructured. Several observations should be made; recording of behavior should occur as soon as possible after the observation. Inferences are made from what was observed.
- Student self-reports include interviews, questionnaires, and surveys. Trust between the students and the teacher is essential.
- Interviews allow teachers to probe and clarify in order to avoid ambiguity, though they cannot be anonymous and are time-consuming.
- Questionnaires are time-efficient and can be anonymous. Proper student motivation to take the questions seriously is essential.
- Constructed-response questionnaires tap traits without cuing students, which indicates what is most salient to students.
- Selected-response formats, such as the Likert scale, are efficient to score and can be anonymous when assessing groups.

- In constructing questionnaires, keep them brief, write in the present tense, and avoid negative and double-barrelled items.
- Peer ratings can be used to assess interpersonal traits. Frequencies of nominations and sociograms are used to analyze the results.
- Use appropriate techniques for assuring anonymity.

SELF-INSTRUCTIONAL REVIEW EXERCISES

1. What are some reasons why most teachers don't systematically assess affective targets?

2. Match the nature of the learning with the affective target. Each target may be used more than once or not at all.

_____ (1) Cooperation and conflict resolution	a. Attitude
_____ (2) Student expectations and need to do well	b. Value
_____ (3) Honesty and integrity	c. Motivation
_____ (4) Character education	d. Academic self-concept
_____ (5) Cognitive and affective components	e. Social relationships
_____ (6) Responding and organization	f. Classroom Environment
_____ (7) Warmth in the classroom	g. Affective taxonomy
_____ (8) Thinking math is important but not liking it	
_____ (9) Engagement and involvement	
_____ (10) Kindness, respect, tolerance	

3. Critique the efforts of the teachers in the following two scenarios to assess affect. What have they done well and how could they improve?

Scenario 1: Mr. Talbot

Mr. Talbot decided that he wanted to assess his fifth graders on their attitudes toward social studies. He asks students to complete the sentence, "Social studies is . . .". Also, at the end of each week he summarizes how much students have liked the social studies units. He writes a brief description for each student, then gives each a rating of 1 to 5.

Scenario 2: Ms. Headly

Ms. Headly teaches art to middle school students. Because all the students in the school come through her class, she wants to be sure that students leave the class with a positive attitude toward art and strong aesthetic values. She decides to develop and administer a survey of art attitudes and values at the beginning and end of each semester. She consults other teachers to generate a list of thoughts and behaviors that were positive and negative. She uses a response format of "like me" and "not like me" with the fifty items. Ms. Headley instructs the students not to put their names on the surveys.

4. Identify each of the following as a characteristic of observation (O), constructed-response self-report (CRSR), selected-response self-report (SRSR), or peer rating (PR).

a. can take into account nonverbal behaviors
b. relatively easy to administer but difficult to score
c. subject to teacher bias

d. can be anonymous

e. very time-consuming to gather data

f. student explanations for answers can be provided

g. the method of choice for checking which students are leaders

h. can be done without students' knowledge or awareness

ANSWERS TO SELF-INSTRUCTIONAL REVIEW EXERCISES

1. Three reasons were given in the chapter: affect takes second seat to cognitive outcomes; assessing affect is difficult to do well; and teachers do not want to put up with controversy.

2. (1) e, (2) c, (3) b, (4) b, (5) a, (6) g, (7) f, (8) a, (9) c, (10) b or c.

3. *Scenario 1.* On the positive side, Mr. Talbot has used more than one method to assess attitudes, and he has a fairly narrow trait in mind. It's good that he isolates the affective component of attitudes (likes) and that his observation notes are brief. On the negative, though, his sentence is too broad and may not give him much information about attitudes. There is no indication that he has generated examples of approach and avoidance behaviors. Students could easily respond with answers like "short" or "in the morning," which wouldn't be much help. He should try to summarize more frequently than once a week, even though trying to write descriptions for each student will take a lot of time. He records his interpretations rather than student behavior.

   Scenario 2. For the most part, this is an example of good affective assessment. Ms. Headly took the time to first list behaviors, then establish a response format that would work, then develop the items. She assured anonymity, and she looked at attitudes and values before and after her course. However, the survey is pretty long, and she is dependent on a single assessment method. It is possible that her bias would be perceived by students, and it might encourage them to provide positive answers at the end of the semester.

4. a. O and CRSR (interview), b. PR, c. O and CRSR, d. SRSR, e. O and CRSR, f. CRSR, g. PR, h. O.

SUGGESTIONS FOR ACTION RESEARCH

1. Identify some affective targets for students and construct a short questionnaire to assess the targets. If possible, find a group of students who could respond to the questionnaire. After they answer all the questions, ask them about their feelings toward the questions and the clarity of the wording. What do the results look like? Would the teacher agree with the results? How difficult was it to develop the questionnaire?

2. Interview several teachers about affective targets in the classroom. Ask them how they arrived at their targets and whether there is any systematic approach to assessing them. Ask what the advantages and disadvantages would be to using different kinds of assessment techniques, such as observation and student self-reports, and see if their answers match Figure 10.11 on page 288.

11

USING ASSESSMENT FOR GRADING AND REPORTING

In the past few chapters we have seen how teachers can assess students on a variety of learning targets. As was pointed out in the model of classroom assessment presented in Chapter 1, now you need to do something with the assessments. Specifically, you will need to make professional judgments about the quality of student

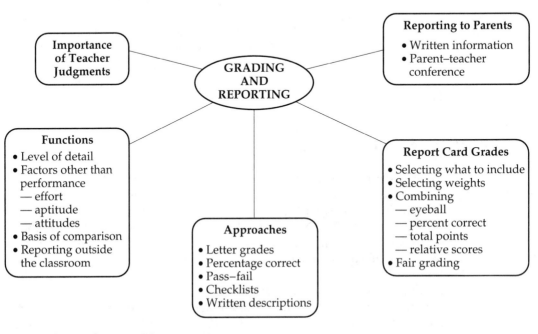

CHAPTER 11   Concept Map

work, then translate that into grades and reports. We'll begin with a discussion of the importance of a teacher's professional judgment in the use of assessment, then we will consider some specific approaches to grading and reporting.

TEACHERS' JUDGMENTS

You are probably aware of several different objective approaches to grading, such as grading on the curve and assigning grades based on the percentage of test items answered correctly. But this doesn't begin to capture the complexity and difficulty of grading. In practice, teachers make a number of professional judgments about how to evaluate and grade students. As I have previously pointed out, judgments are made prior to assessment (e.g., the difficulty of test items, what is covered on the assessment, whether extra credit items will be included), as well as after assessments are completed (e.g., scoring short-answer and essay items). Further judgments are made in combining scores of different assessments to determine grades (e.g., how assessments are weighted, how to handle borderline scores). Here are some typical questions teachers ask that are answered by using their judgment:

Should effort and improvement be included in the grade?
How should different assessments be weighted and combined?
What distribution of grades should I end up with?
What do I do if most of my students fail the test?
Are my grades supposed to mean the same thing as other teachers' grades?
Am I grading students too hard or too easy?
What do I do with students who test well but don't hand in homework?
Should student participation be included in the grade?

There are no straightforward, necessarily correct answers to these questions, and few school districts or schools provide teachers with much more than general guidelines and a grading scale. Consequently, grading practices vary considerably, even within the same school.

Also, unforeseen, unique situations may arise with students. These individual situations will require teachers to use professional judgments. Consider the following scenarios (Brookhart, 1993, pp. 131 & 133):

> *In your seventh grade social studies class, report card grades were based on quizzes, tests, and an out-of-class project which counted as 25% of the grade. Terry obtained an A average on his quizzes and tests but has not turned in the project despite frequent reminders.*
>
> *You are a biology teacher of a high school class which consists of students with varying ability levels. For this class you give two exams in each term. As you compute Bernie's grade for this term, you see that on the first exam, he obtained a score equivalent to a B, and on the second exam, a low A.*

What grades would you give? Should Terry get a low grade even though he scores so high on tests? Should Bernie get an A because he showed improvement?

The evaluating and grading process requires you to make many *professional* decisions. These decisions are based on your personal value system toward a number of different issues. In the end, grading is more a reflection of this value system, of perceived importance or perspective, than a procedure based on following specific correct guidelines or rules. Essentially, you develop a philosophy of grading that translates into what you do. To develop your own personal grading plan, then, you need to consider and answer for yourself the following questions (Frisbie & Waltman, 1992, p. 36):

What meaning should each grade symbol carry?
What should "failure" mean?
What elements of performance should be incorporated in a grade?
How should the grades in a class be distributed?
What should the components be like that go into a final grade?
How should the components of the grade be combined?
What method should be used to assign grades?
Should borderline cases be reviewed?
What other factors can influence the philosophy of grading?

These questions will be answered best if they are based on an understanding of the different purposes or functions grades serve and the types of comparison standards that are used. In the end, you need to utilize methods and comparisons that will best meet your major purpose. As we will see, grades often serve several purposes, which makes matters more complicated.

Let me make one point as clear as I can concerning professional judgments. These are *subjective* and *intuitive* in the sense that there is no single correct procedure or set of rules that take professional decision making out of the process. There is no completely objective procedure, nor should there be. You may use a grading scale, score student tests and performances, then mathematically calculate grades, but this is not a procedure that is necessarily correct because it appears to be objective. Think for a moment about a physician making a decision about whether a patient is sufficiently strong to endure an operation. In a sense, this is like grading. The doctor takes many measures, then examines them *in the light of his or her experience and knowledge* before giving a yes or no judgment. Could two physicians differ in their opinions about whether to operate, given the same information? Absolutely. Likewise, two teachers can differ on the meaning of students' performances. One teacher might look at the tests and conclude that the student has mastered a skill, while another teacher might conclude the opposite. In the end, it is your value system that makes the difference, and to be an effective teacher you need to understand the issues, make some informed judgments, and then be willing to have confidence in your decisions. This is the only way grading and reporting can be valid, fair, and helpful to students.

FUNCTIONS OF GRADING AND REPORTING

Why do teachers mark and grade student performances? The answer to this question is based on how the marks and grades are *used*. Are grades used to improve student learning or report student accomplishment? To rank order students (e.g., class rank) or to motivate students? To inform parents or evaluate curriculum? To evaluate teachers? For guidance and administrative uses? In most schools, marking, grading, and reporting serve a variety of functions. To consider these multiple uses and incorporate your own value system, it is helpful to separate what you do *in* the classroom from uses *outside* your class. That is, you mark papers and give students grades continuously in class, and your use of grades in this context is probably quite different from what others may do with them.

Functions of Grading in the Classroom

What do you want your grades to mean to your students? How do you want them to be affected? Do you want to motivate students to improve? Do you want to point out strengths and weaknesses? How do you want your students to interpret the grades they receive on tests, papers, and projects? The vast majority of teachers want grades to have a positive impact on student learning, motivation, affect, and other outcomes. Yet many use grading practices that do not have that effect. For example, my experience is that the same grading system or approach can be used by two teachers and have quite different meanings to students in each class. Suppose Mr. Wren gives only a few As and Mr. Lanning gives a lot of As. Is a Wren A seen differently by students than a Lanning A? Probably. Do students react differently to As in each class? Probably. This is one of many factors that will determine how grades are interpreted and thus affect students. Some other important influences include the level of detail communicated in the grade about the student performance, whether factors other than performance are included, and the basis of comparison of the grades. We'll consider these with the assumption that the primary use of grades in the classroom is to inform and motivate students.

Level of Detail Communicated

One decision you will make about grading students is how much detail they will receive about their performance. Let me use my daughter as an example. Ryann is in the sixth grade this year and spent several weeks putting together a report on Italy. In looking over the assignment, I thought she did an excellent job (of course there may be just a little bias here!). She got the paper back with a B+ on it and a short comment, "good work." She was somewhat disappointed, but more importantly, didn't know why she did not get a higher grade. There was no information about how the teacher had come to this conclusion. How did this affect her? She was sad and bewildered, in general a negative effect. An alternative could have been for the teacher to provide her with a detailed summary of how each section of the paper was evaluated, so that she could better understand the strengths and weaknesses.

This example demonstrates the importance of level of detail. Whether you use grades or numbers, you have an option of giving a single indication or one that includes enough detail so that students know where they have made mistakes, where to improve, and what they have done well. This more detailed feedback has a positive effect on motivation, and it allows students to make more accurate connections between how they studied or prepared and their performance. At least when returning a conventional test with each item marked correct or incorrect, students can see which questions they missed and figure out their strengths and weaknesses. Unfortunately, for much student work, the level of detail is minimal. What students need is specific information related to the learning targets.

Factors Other Than Performance

It's fairly obvious that the primary determinant of a grade is the performance of the student. The more a student knows and can do, the better the grade. However, it's not as simple as it seems. First, there is the issue of whether *high* means in comparison to other students or in comparison to a well-defined learning target. We'll consider this factor in the next section. Second, when grades are determined solely on performance, there is a tendency to emphasize knowledge and understanding targets, in part because measures for these targets are easier to develop and grades based on such measures are easier to defend. This may mean that reasoning and product targets are deemphasized. Third, what do you do with factors such as student effort, aptitude, improvement, and attitude? These are aspects of student performance that are important for many teachers, particularly when doing whatever they can to encourage and motivate students. A look at each of these traits is warranted.

Let's begin with student effort. There is a common sense logic to why student effort should be considered when grading. Students who try harder are learning more, even if it doesn't show up on a test, paper, or project. More effort suggests more motivation and interest, and shouldn't we reward students when they are motivated and interested? Isn't it good to motivate low-achieving students who try hard? Don't we need to find something to praise low-achieving students for to keep them motivated? Isn't it good to focus students on an internal attributional factor that they can control and use to face subsequent learning tasks with more confidence? Isn't it true that we value effort as a society, so children should learn the importance of effort by seeing it reflected in their grades?

These may be compelling reasons to include effort in determining grades, but there are also some good reasons not to do so. First, different teachers operationalize effort differently, so it is something that would vary from one teacher to another. Second, we don't have a satisfactory way to define and measure effort. It's true that we could define effort as "completing homework" or "participating in class discussion" or "being on task." But each of these definitions is problematic. The one that could be easily and accurately measured, completing homework, is pretty shallow. Participation in class discussion is influenced by many factors, only one of which is controlled by each student. How do you know if a student is on task? Sometimes it seems obvious, though students can fake this pretty well, and most of the time we either can't tell or can't systematically observe and record sufficiently to get a good measure. If students know they will be graded on effort, will they try to make you think that they are trying by how they act, when in fact it's a bluff and they really aren't trying?

Third, does including effort tend to favor more assertive students? What about students who are quiet? Could gender or racial/ethnic characteristics be related to the value of effort or expectations about showing effort? Certainly we would not want our grades to be affected by these characteristics. Fourth, how much would effort count? What amount of a grade or percentage of a score would be reasonable? We really don't know, and how would you keep the level of contribution the same for each student? Finally, are we sending students the wrong message if they learn that they can get by just by trying hard, even if the performance is less than satisfactory?

So what is the resolution? There seem to be some pretty good reasons for and against including effort. This is one of those areas of professional judgment that you'll need to make decisions about. But I do have some suggestions. If you want to include effort, use it for borderline cases. Never allow effort to become a major part of a grade. Second, report effort separately from performance. Do this often and allow students opportunities to disagree with your assessment. Try to define effort as clearly as possible, and stick to your definition. It should be shared with students, with examples. If you include effort for one student, it's only fair to include it for all students.

A second factor that can easily influence grades is student aptitude or ability. This reflects the student's potential or capability for learning. The argument for including aptitude goes something like this. If we can tailor assignments and grading to each student's potential, all students can be motivated and all students can experience success. Rather than grading only on achievement, which favors students who bring a higher aptitude for learning, grades reflect how well each student has achieved in relation to his or her potential. That is, each student is graded by comparing achievement to aptitude. Using this approach, we can better identify when students are over- or under-achieving. High-aptitude students will be challenged, and low-aptitude students will have realistic opportunities for good grades.

However, this argument is based on knowing what aptitude is and being able to assess it. There has never been an agreed upon definition of aptitude, though it often is used synonymously with general intelligence. Recent work by Sternberg (1986) and Gardner (1985) has challenged traditional definitions of intelligence and has shown that we are still a long way from adequately understanding something as complex as aptitude for learning. Furthermore, measuring aptitude is fraught with difficulties, not the least of which concerns cultural bias. Even if we had a proper definition and a good measure, there are insurmountable practical difficulties in trying to assess aptitude for each student and grade each student differently. Then there is the issue of explaining to high-aptitude students and their parents how they can get a higher score than low-aptitude students yet obtain a lower grade. Would you like to explain that? Some teachers essentially adopt two grading systems, one for low-aptitude students that emphasizes improvement, one for high-aptitude students based more on absolute achievement. The problem with this solution is that the meaning of the grades is different.

Thus, while there is no question that students do have different levels of ability, and you need to use this knowledge in instruction and for giving students feedback, you don't want to try to factor it into grades. The only exception might be for borderline situations when giving semester grades. Even then, it would be better to use prior achievement than to use aptitude. Using prior achievement avoids the conceptualization and measurement problems associated with aptitude. This suggests another factor, improvement, that could be used for grading.

Because learning is defined as a change in performance, why not measure how much students know before and then after instruction? Students who show the most improvement, hence learning, would get the highest grades. Again, there are some serious limitations to this approach. What happens when students score high in the beginning, on the pretest, and don't have an opportunity to show improvement? What about student faking, in which students intentionally receive a low score on the pretest to more easily show improvement? Like trying to incorporate aptitude, keeping track of pre- and post-scores for each student would not be very practical. But also like aptitude and effort, improvement can be a positive motivator for borderline situations.

A final factor to consider in classroom grading is student attitudes. Shouldn't students with a positive attitude be rewarded? Suppose two students perform about the same and are between two grades. If one or both students have a very positive attitude, would that mean that they should get the higher grade? Like student effort, attitudes are important, and it would be nice if we could efficiently and accurately include this in grading. The reality is that attitudes are difficult to define and measure, and are susceptible to student faking. So like the other "nonacademic" factors we have considered, it is generally not a good idea to try to use attitudes in grading. It is best if grades are predominately determined by student performance in relation to learning targets. If other factors are included, their influence should be minimal.

Basis of Comparison

A major consideration in determining the meaning and method of grading is whether grades communicate comparisons with other students or to predefined standards or levels of performance. Grading by comparison to the achievement of other students is referred to as *norm-referenced*. In the classroom, this means that the function of each student's grade is to indicate how the student performed in comparison with the other students in the class (or several classes in middle and high school). This method is known popularly as *grading on the curve*. Certain proportions of students are given designated grades, regardless of the level of performance of the students. That is, a certain percent of the class will receive As, Bs, Cs, Ds, and Fs. There is no indication of how much students master or what percentage of test items were answered correctly. A student can answer 70 percent of the items on one test correctly, and if that is the highest score, it will be an A. On another test, a 70 might be relatively low, receiving a C or D. It's also possible for a student to get a C for getting a 95 on a test if others received even higher scores.

In norm-referenced grading, the standard is a relative one that changes, depending on the composition of the class. It is done by rank ordering student performances from highest to lowest, and then assigning grades based on a predetermined curve (e.g., top 10 percent will receive As, next 30 percent Bs, next 40 percent Cs, next 10 percent Ds, bottom 10 percent Fs). If you are in a high-ability class, it's usually more difficult to get a good grade.

Because norm-referenced grading is based on comparing students to each other, its major function is to show which are the highest or best performing students. In this sense, it sorts students, and because this is still a purpose of most schools, some kind of norm-referencing is often incorporated in grading. (Indeed, a definition of grades that includes C as average, and B as above average is a norm-referenced type of comparison.) This could be done by adjusting curves based on student ability (e.g., honors track classes have a higher percentage of As than general track classes), by how difficult teachers make their tests, and how tough teachers are in grading papers, projects, and other products.

One of the myths about norm-referenced grading is that you try to obtain a *curve* of student scores, usually something that looks like a normal curve (Figure 11.1a, page 300). Actually, this type of curve is not what you want, because at each cut point between different grades you have a maximum of students at the borderline between the grades. If your purpose is to conclude that some students clearly know more than others, you would want to obtain a sculpted curve of scores that looks like several waves (in Figure 11.1b). Then each cut point at the bottom of the waves minimizes borderline scores and you will be more accurate in your conclusions. Although you probably won't be able to get scores that look like those in Figure 11.1b, look for naturally occurring breaks. For example, if seven students scored above 80 on a test of knowledge, then the next few students scored between 60 and 70, those two groups of students likely have different amounts of knowledge. However, using this *gap* method of identifying grading categories is fairly arbitrary, and it is likely that the breaks might be at different locations if the data were recollected. Thus, you need to use clear, distinct breaks that are relatively large.

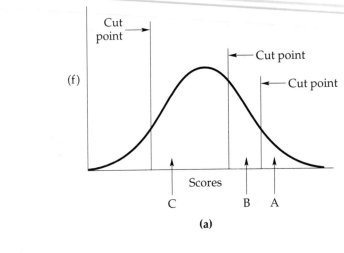

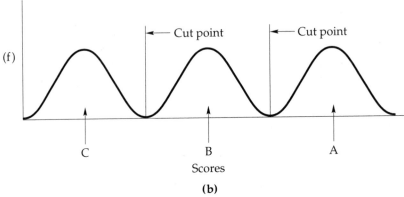

FIGURE 11.1   Normal and Sculpted Grading Curves

Another function of relative grading is to foster student competitiveness. It is clear that when students know that their grade is dependent on how others perform, a very competitive environment is created, which, in turn, usually has a negative impact on student effort, motivation, interpersonal relationships, and teacher communication. The motivation of students who continually score near the bottom is undermined. Student cooperation is reduced. For these reasons, as well as the capriciousness with which some teachers set curves (my son had a teacher who set the curve by the highest score—please don't do that!), most grading is now based on the absolute level of student performance, without any comparison to how others performed.

Grading that is determined by what level of performance is obtained is often called *absolute* or *criterion-referenced*. There is no comparison with other students, so it is theoretically possible for all students to get the same grade. The most common method of using absolute levels of performance is called *percentage-based* grading. This is most typically used for objective tests, when teachers assign a grade to a specific percentage of items answered correctly. Usually the school system establishes the scale, such as the following:

A 94–100   percent correct
B 86–93   percent correct
C 75–85   percent correct
D 65–74   percent correct
F below 65   percent correct

The *standard* is supposedly set by the percent of correct items for each grade. Thus, a scale in which 96–100 is an A is often regarded as more stringent or tough than a scale with an A range of 90–100. I believe this is a myth, due to variation in item difficulty and the reality of needing to sort students. Let's examine item difficulty first.

A score of 70 on a hard test means something different than a 70 on an easy test. Consequently, what is important is not only the percentage correct, but how hard it is to get those items correct. Two teachers, given the same learning target, can easily come up with different assessments that are not the same in terms of difficulty. Suppose you are assessing student knowledge of different regions of the United States. One way to assess the target is to ask which states are in a region; you might say, for example, "Name three plains states." Another approach is to give a multiple–choice question:

Which of the following is a *plains* state?

a. New York
b. Maine
c. Florida
d. North Dakota

The target is the same, but the completion item is more difficult. How do you know how difficult a test is going to be before you give it to your students? This is a common situation that teachers must deal with. Misjudgment about item difficulty is often reflected in test scores that are mostly high (As) or mostly low (Fs). Estimating difficulty prior to the test depends on how others have performed, and the capabilities of those students. For example, if you have a high-aptitude class that works hard to learn the content but then gets a low score on the test, then the test is probably pretty tough. On the other hand, if your low-aptitude class exerts minimum effort and does well, it's probably an easy test.

What happens when you don't have any prior experience, you give a test, and most students get a very low grade? In this circumstance either the students didn't know much or the test was not a fair assessment. Because you don't know which of these is true, you can justifiably make adjustments so that the distribution of scores reflects the range of likely student performance (but I wouldn't advocate adjusting high scores downward). Some teachers do this by using the top score to signify 100 percent and recalculating all the students' scores with this new maximum number of possible correct answers. This is actually too arbitrary because the performance of a single student is too influential, but some adjustment may be needed. Yes, this is *subjective*, but no more so than your choice of item difficulty. Remember, your goal is to fairly evaluate student performance. It's quite possible that a single test or assessment is not fair and that a reliance on the scores would be an injustice to students. In any event, it's not difficult for teachers to tailor item difficulty to their students so that a final distribution of grades meets normative standards or guidelines.

Then there is the reality of needing to sort students. Although theoretically all students can master learning targets and receive As, most teachers simply can't do this. Because we still use school to indicate to others which particular students, from the entire group of students, have performed best, the normative expectation is that teachers (especially middle and high school teachers) will give some As, a lot of Bs and Cs, a few Ds, and even some Fs. To meet this expectation, tests are devised so that not all students will do really well. That is, enough difficulty is built into the test so that not all students will get As. The reality is that most teachers, one way or another, combine absolute performance and sorting in the assigning of grades. This isn't bad or inappropriate, but it needs to be clarified for what it is so that whatever methods are used are fair to students. Recently we have been moving more and more to absolute standards and defining levels of standards in such a way that there is still some sorting of students (some call this setting high standards), but sorting is still a function of schooling we need to deal with.

Another type of criterion-referenced performance standard is to spell out, in some detail, the specific behaviors students must perform to obtain a grade. This is used with performance-based assessments of skills and products. The scoring rubric defines the behaviors, and on the basis of the teacher's observations, a grade is assigned to indicate which behaviors were demonstrated and hence which grade is received. In these systems, students' performances are only compared to the rubrics, not to each other. There may be a grade assigned to different levels of the rubric, but it is more common to simply indicate the level achieved. As we will see in the next section, this leads to a different type of reporting system than the traditional A, B, C, D, and F.

Figure 11.2 summarizes differences between norm- and criterion-referenced approaches to assessment for grading students.

Approaches to Grading

There are several ways you can mark and grade student performance. We will consider the most common types of symbols or scores that are used, including letter grades, percentage correct, pass/fail grades, checklists, written descriptions, and numerical rubric scales. Most teachers use a combination of these in the classroom, even if the nature of final semester or course grades are set by the district.

FIGURE 11.2   Characteristics of Norm- and Criterion-Referenced Assessment

	Norm-Referenced	Criterion-Referenced
Interpretation	Score compared to the performances of other students	Score compared to predetermined standards and criteria
Nature of Score	Percentile rank; standard scores; grading curve	Percentage correct; descriptive performance standards
Difficulty of Test Items	Uses average to difficult items to obtain spread of scores; very easy and very difficult items not used	Uses average to easy items to result in a high percentage of correct answers
Use of Scores	To rank order and sort students	To describe the level of performance obtained
Effect on Motivation	Dependent on comparison group; competitive	Challenges students to meet specified learning target
Strengths	Results in more difficult assessments that challenge students	Matches student performance to clearly defined learning targets; lessens competitiveness
Weaknesses	Grades determined by comparison to other students; some students are always at the bottom	Establishing clearly defined learning targets; setting standards that indicate mastery

Letter Grades

The most common way most teachers mark student performance on products other than objective tests is to give a letter grade. Traditionally, letter grades correspond to different adjectives, such as excellent or outstanding, good, average or acceptable, poor, and unsatisfactory, and often plus and minus symbols are used to provide finer distinctions. Letter grades provide a convenient, concise, and familiar approach to marking. In addition, grades are readily understood by students and parents to provide an overall indication of performance.

The major limitation with grades is that they provide only a general indication of performance. There is nothing wrong with giving students an overall, summary judgment in the form of a grade. However, such a general mark, by itself, does not indicate anything about what was done correctly or incorrectly. Strengths and limitations are not communicated. There is also a tendency for teachers to be influenced by factors other than performance in coming up with a grade on papers, projects, and presentations (e.g., effort, work habits, attitude). Furthermore, because teachers differ in their value systems, the proportion of students getting each grade can vary. In one class, most students can get As and Bs, while in another class, most students receive Bs and Cs.

What you will need to make clear to your students about grades is what each letter means, so that their interpretation is accurate, appropriate, and helpful. Does getting an A mean that I did outstanding work, or does it mean that I did best in the class? Does it mean that the teacher thinks I worked hard on this or that I can do it really well? Does getting a C mean that I did about as well as most students or that I did satisfactory work?

As you can see, there are a number of possible interpretations, depending on how much factors other than performance are included and the basis of comparison (norm- or criterion-referenced). In other words, grades can communicate effort, achievement, improvement, achievement in comparison to aptitude (some teachers grade high-aptitude students tougher), relative standing, or level of mastery. You need to be clear, first to yourself and then to your students, about what each letter grade means. Figure 11.3 presents different interpretations of grades.

Notice that it is possible to combine or mix norm- and criterion-referenced approaches (Terwilliger, 1989). What often occurs is that the higher grades tend to be norm-referenced and the lower ones criterion-referenced. That is, to get an A, students need to perform better than most, while a failure judgment tends to be based on absolute standards. If a purely relative scale was used, and the norming group was the class itself, some students would always fail, despite what might be a high level of performance (a better procedure is to use data from previous classes to set the norm from a larger group). Also, some students would always succeed. It is only with absolute scales that all students can either succeed or fail.

Percentage Correct

For objective tests, the most common approach to reporting performance is to indicate the percentage of items answered correctly. Thus, for example, we often characterize our achievement as getting a 75 or 92 on a test. These numbers refer to the percentage of items or points obtained out of a possible 100. These scores are easy to calculate, record, and combine at the end of the grading period. Usually, letter grades are associated with ranges of scores, so a percentage correct system gives students a finer discrimination in their performance. It is possible, if not very common, to grade everything with percentage correct, even papers and essay items.

One limitation of using percentage correct in grading is that, like a letter grade, only a general indication of performance is communicated. Another disadvantage is that the discriminations that are suggested by a scale from 1 to 100 are much finer that what can be reliably assessed. Because of error in testing, there is no meaningful difference between scores differentiated by one or two points. That is, scores of 92 and 93, or 77 and 78, suggest the same level of student performance. In other words, the degree of precision suggested by percentage correct is not justified given the error that exists.

A third limitation is the tendency to equate percentage of items correct with percent mastered. As I have pointed out, items can differ tremendously in level of difficulty, so when students obtain a high percentage of correct answers, mastery may or may not be demonstrated, dependent on the difficulty level of the test.

FIGURE 11.3   Different Interpretations of Letter Grades

Grade	Criterion-Referenced	Norm-Referenced	Combined Norm- and Criterion-Referenced	Based on Improvement
A	Outstanding or advanced: complete knowledge of all content; mastery of all targets; exceeds standards	Outstanding: among the highest or best performance	Outstanding: very high level of performance	Outstanding: much improvement on most or all targets
B	Very good or proficient: complete knowledge of most content; mastery of most targets; meets most standards	Very good: performs above the class average	Very good: better than average performance	Very good: some improvement on most or all targets
C	Acceptable or basic: command of only basic concepts or skills; mastery of some targets; meets some standards	Average: performs at the class average	Average	Acceptable: some improvement on some targets
D	Making progress or developing: lacks knowledge of most content; mastery of only a few targets; meets only a few standards	Poor: below the class average	Below average or weak: minimum performance for passing	Making progress: minimal progress on most targets
F	Unsatisfactory: lacks knowledge of content; no mastery of targets; does not meet any standards	Unsatisfactory: far below average; among the worst in the class	Unsatisfactory: lacks sufficient knowledge to pass	Unsatisfactory: no improvement on any targets

Thus, it is probably incorrect to conclude that when a student obtains a 100, he or she knows 100 percent of the learning targets, or that a score of 50 corresponds to mastery of half of the targets.

Pass/Fail

The idea of making a simple dichotomous evaluation, such as pass versus fail or satisfactory versus needs improvement, is consistent with mastery learning and objectives-based education. In these approaches to learning and instruction, students are assessed on each learning objective. The judgment is criterion-referenced and results in a mastery/no mastery decision. Typically, students work on each objective until they demonstrate mastery, then move on.

There is a certain appeal to this approach, especially at the early elementary level, but it doesn't reflect very well the actual levels of performance that students demonstrate. Basically, a two-category system is too simple. Most teachers find that at least three categories are needed, something like fail, pass, and excellent, or N (needs improvement), S (satisfactory), and O (outstanding). A related limitation is that when we use a dichotomous system, even less information is being communicated to students than when grades are used. Also, it is difficult to keep standards high with a pass/fail system. The tendency is to "dumb down" the standards so that most students will not fail. This tells students clearly what they need to do to avoid failure, but it doesn't tell them very much about what excellent or outstanding performance is like.

On the other hand, there is now considerable interest in assessing high schools on mastery of skills needed for the workplace, and using the assessments for giving students a "certificate of initial mastery" (Rothman, 1995). In these efforts, there is a conscious effort to keep the standards high.

Checklists

A variation of the pass/fail approach is to give students a checklist of some kind to indicate their performance on each aspect of the learning target. The checklist has two or more categories. In a simple dichotomous checklist, the teacher might prepare a series of statements that describes aspects of the performance that the students need to include and places a check mark next to each one the teacher judges to be demonstrated. To indicate student affect, checks can be placed next to each one demonstrated. This shows both what the student has and has not done.

A more elaborate approach provides students with scales of performance. The teacher makes checks on the scale to indicate the level performance. This is typical when grading performance-based products. The rubric that describes the scoring is used as the checklist. The advantage of this type of grading is that the students receive detailed feedback about what they did well and what needs improvement. The detail in the rubric helps students understand more precisely where they need to improve. Of course the difficulty of this approach is developing the checklists and keeping the system practical. However, once you develop detailed lists, they are fairly efficient because you only make checks. This can be done efficiently, even if there are several such statements for each student product. It is certainly more efficient than writing comments on papers, though some individualized comments are important as well.

A variation of checklists for rubrics is to assign each point on the scale a different number. This allows you to more easily convert the assessment into grades. An example would be the following:

0 no attempt made
1 developing
2 achieving
3 exceeding

Written Descriptions

An alternative to giving a grade or score is to mark students' work with written descriptions. The advantage of this approach is that the comments can be highly individualized, pointing out unique strengths and weaknesses, and can focus attention on important issues. Students appreciate the effort of teachers who take the time to make these comments. Of course, the time needed is a major disadvantage. Most teachers simply do not have sufficient time to give this level of feedback. Then there is the added complication of converting the descriptions into grades or scores for report cards. Here the advantage from one perspective becomes a disadvantage because the uniqueness of the descriptions makes it difficult to grade consistently and fairly.

Recently, assessment experts have focused attention on how grading can improve instruction and student learning (Guskey, 1994). It is clear that from this perspective detailed checklists, narratives, and grading based on prespecified criteria are preferred. To enhance student motivation, the grading needs to be specific. Relative comparisons among students should be avoided. But from a realistic perspective, your grading also must be practical and result in accurate summaries for report cards. The challenge is to incorporate as much detail and reference to learning targets as possible when marking each piece of student work without being overwhelmed. Then you'll need to combine the independent grades into a final grade for the semester. At this point the function of grading is reporting to others. We'll consider this function briefly before looking at some ways to come up with the final grade.

Functions of Grading and Reporting Outside the Classroom

The semester grades you give students are intended much more for audiences other than your students, primarily parents. Indeed, a good reason to give such grades is to keep parents informed of their child's progress and level of performance. Ideally, the format of the report card will be such that parents will find your information helpful in promoting their child's learning, but it is unlikely that you will have much say about format. Typically, a school district sets policy about the nature of report cards and defines what can be communicated. But if there is a way, try to provide as much information and detail as possible. This will help parents provide emotional support and encouragement, know where they need to concentrate their efforts to help their child, make sound educational plans related to course selection, and offer assistance when vocational choices need to be made. We'll look at some procedures for report card grading in the next section.

Grades are also used for administrative and guidance purposes. For determining class rank, graduation, honors, athletic eligibility, transcripts for many colleges, and other administrative uses, a single grade or number is sufficient. These can be easily averaged and combined to make the decisions or provide the information.

Counselors use grades to help students make appropriate vocational and college choices and to help diagnose personal problems that may need attention. In these cases, the function of the grades is to provide more general indicators of student performance, and a single letter grade in each subject or area is adequate.

DETERMINING REPORT CARD GRADES

Unit and semester grades are given by teachers to provide a single indicator of student performance. Recognizing that professional judgment is essential for determining final grades as well as grades for individual assessments, you will need to make some decisions. These decisions can be summarized in the form of three steps:

1. Select what to include in the final grade.
2. Select weights for each individual assessment.
3. Combine weighted scores to determine a single grade.

We will examine each of these steps.

Select What to Include in the Final Grade

This is where you will have a fair amount of leeway. It is up to you to determine which assessments will contribute to the final grade. As I have already suggested, it is best if you base final grades primarily on academic performance. But which performances should be included? Tests? Participation in class? Papers? Quizzes? Homework? Prior to selecting the assessments, think again about your overall learning goals. Your selection of what goes into the final grade should provide the most accurate information in relation to these goals. That is, the assessments selected should be closely aligned with the goals. If you have done a good job of basing your formal assessments on the learning targets, then each of these assessments will contribute meaningfully to the grade. It is less clear if pop quizzes, participation, and homework should be included.

On the one hand, pop quizzes, participation, and homework do focus on student performance, but is their purpose to give students feedback in a formative sense or reward student effort, or can they legitimately serve as documentation of student learning and understanding? If they are primarily formative in nature, to give students practice and feedback, they may be viewed more as instruction than assessment and would not be included in a final grade. Some teachers argue that pop quizzes are not fair to students, and some also contend that homework may reflect parent involvement more than student capabilities. Many teachers realize that participation in class is influenced by group dynamics and personality. Other teachers view pop quizzes, participation, and homework as indicators of how much students are paying attention and learning in class, and will use them to calculate final grades. The choice of whether to include these student performances is yours, and either choice is legitimate. Just be sure to make it clear to students and parents what is going into the grade, and why it is fair.

You will want to be especially careful in considering factors such as attendance, effort, and personal–social characteristics such as cooperativeness, participation, and work habits in determining grades. Specifically, you don't want nonacademic factors, which probably have little relationship to academic learning, to influence the final grade. Suppose a student is absent from school and misses a test? Does that mean a zero is appropriate? Even if the student has been expelled, giving a zero for not being present, and then inferring that the grade ultimately received reflects academic learning, is clearly a mistake. What about a student who, while in a cooperative learning group, doesn't participate very much or contribute to others' learning? Should that student's grade be penalized for displaying weak cooperative skills? Do you evaluate the quality or quantity of the participation? Should a student who continually says silly things be penalized?

I believe the best rule on these matters is this: if a grade is for academic performance in areas such as reading, science, mathematics, history, and the like, then the grade should be determined only by student academic performance. This is essentially a matter of maintaining appropriate validity so that your inferences about academic performance are reasonable. If cooperativeness and participation are important targets, report separate grades for each.

Finally, in planning the assessments that you will include, carefully consider how many are needed to give an accurate overall judgment of each student's performance. Would it be reasonable to base a semester grade on a single exam? How about a nine-week grade—would two tests and a paper be sufficient? Probably most would agree that a single assessment, alone, is definitely not sufficient. Three assessments for a nine-week grade is much better, but even that may not be enough. The rule of thumb with respect to number of assessments needed is the more, the better, as long as assessment time does not interfere significantly with instructional time. So, although one or two assessments would probably be too few, you wouldn't want to give a test every day! Once again, your professional judgment is needed. I have found that at least one fairly major test or other assessment is needed about every two weeks. Most teachers are constrained by a fifty-minute-or-less class period, and it's difficult to sample two weeks of content in anything less than an hour of testing time. Besides, children have limited attention spans. If students lose interest or find it hard to concentrate, error is introduced into the assessment.

Select Weights for Each Assessment

Not only do you need to identify the assessments, you need to decide how much each one will count in the final grade. Obviously, more important assessments are given greater weight. What determines if an assessment is important? You probably guessed it—more professional judgment! The most significant assessments are those that (1) correspond most closely to the learning goals and targets (content-related evidence for validity), (2) reflect instructional time, (3) are most reliable, and (4) are most current.

Because there are multiple learning targets in a unit or semester, you need to break out the percentage that each target contributes to the whole. I have illustrated this in Figure 11.4 in the form of a pie chart for a unit on the animal kingdom. You can see that different percentages correspond to each topic. In this case, the overall goal is determined mostly by vertebrate animal characteristics and behaviors. Now you need to weight your assessments to match these percentages so that the final grade reflects the relative contribution of each topic. This will provide good content-related evidence for validity, which is a primary concern. We'll look at some examples of how to do that in the next section. In this example, about 50 percent of what determines the final grade should be the assessments on vertebrates. This percentage is estimated independent of the length of the book chapters, or assessments, or the instructional time devoted to each topic. What you are determining is solely the value of each of the topics.

Even though instructional time is not a factor in the first consideration of weights, it's still an important barometer of the amount of emphasis given to each topic. For that reason, I think it's only fair to take time devoted to instruction as a factor. As I have already emphasized, students need to know before an assessment is taken what will be covered. Often this includes topics or concepts that have not been discussed in class. Although there is nothing wrong with testing students on material they learn on their own, it's best if the weights reflect instructional focus. If you spent 50 percent of your nine weeks studying simple invertebrates, it probably wouldn't be fair to weight this topic only 15 percent. Similarly, you might de-

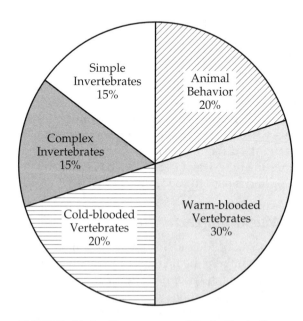

**FIGURE 11.4   Percentage of Each Topic that
Contributes to the Final Grade**

termine that you *intend* to weight vertebrates 50 percent, but when you look back over the weeks you figure that only 25 percent of the students' time was spent learning about vertebrates. This would suggest that a more appropriate weight would be 30–35 percent, at most. Obviously you don't know for sure how much time you take until the instruction is completed. This means that your final determination of weights needs to be finalized close to the end of instruction as well. Weights should not be set in stone at the beginning of the unit.

Reliability is a factor in weighting because, *other things being equal,* especially validity, we want to put more weight on more accurate assessments. This will reduce the overall amount of error that is included in determining the grade. Although most teachers don't get specific numerical reliabilities, generally reliability increases with a greater number of items for each target and for objective items. But it is important to emphasize that the most important concern is validity; highly reliable assessments should never be given more weight than is appropriate, given the validity of the assessment.

If you test the same content more than once, like you would with a cumulative final exam, put more weight on the most current assessment. In fact, a later assessment on the same material might mean that the earlier assessment should be dropped. After all, if your goal is to communicate accurately the nature of a student's current performance, wouldn't the more recent assessment be better? From a practical standpoint, however, you'll find that it's difficult to simply discard an earlier test score. The best compromise is to weight the cumulative exam more than each of the preceding ones so that final performance outweighs what students demonstrate at the beginning or middle of the unit.

Given these considerations you now need to combine the assessments properly to obtain the final grade.

Combining Different Scores and Grades

There are three basic approaches to combining scores and grades: the eyeball method, the percent correct method, and the total points method.

Eyeball Method

The first one is what I call the *eyeball* method because the teacher simply reviews the scores and grades and estimates an average for them, without performing any calculations, to come up with what seems to be the correct grade. This has obvious disadvantages, not the least of which is the lack of objectivity. This method isn't recommended, but it does have one redeeming quality. With eyeballing the teacher asks, "All things considered and looking at the whole as more than the sum of each part, what is the most valid grade for this student?" The notion that it's important to consider everything together has some merit because it recognizes that teacher professional judgment is needed to give grades. At the other extreme, there are teachers who mindlessly calculate averages without any consideration of factors that might be important, such as student absenteeism, improvement, and possible testing error. For example, what would you do if, after working closely with a fourth-grade student for several weeks, she failed a math exam when you knew for certain through classwork that she knew how to do the calculations? Would an F be a fair and accurate grade for this student? Just because the test says it's so, does that mean it *is*?

Percent Correct Method

Because most teachers need to show some objective methods in their grading, scores and grades are typically combined into a single score that converts to a grade. Here you need to be sure that the calculations you use to combine the assessments are done correctly. Because most districts require teachers to use a percent correct scale in grading, we'll focus on combining scores to obtain a composite *percentage correct* score, which is readily converted to a grade.

Consider the example about a unit on animals (Figure 11.4 on page 310). If all you had for the final grade was a test for each of the topics, you would simply multiply the percentage of correct scores obtained by the percentages indicated in the chart, and then add the five products. To make matters simple, let's assume that you gave five 100-point tests, one for each topic. Here are the scores of two students on the five tests:

Test	LaKeith	Dion
1	70	85
2	65	90
3	80	88
4	75	93
5	83	95

You decide to weight each of the tests by the percentage indicated in the pie chart. This can be done by multiplying each test score by percentage expressed as a decimal (e.g., 15 percent, .15; 20 percent, .20) and then adding the resulting products. In this example, LaKeith's composite score would be 75:

$$(70 \times .15) + (65 \times .15) + (80 \times .20) + (75 \times .30) + (83 \times .20) = 75.35.$$

Dion's composite score would be 91:

$$(85 \times .15) + (90 \times .15) + (88 \times .20) + (93 \times .30) + (95 \times .20) = 90.75.$$

These composite scores would then be converted to grades, depending on the grading scale.

In reality, most teachers have a variety of different types of scores and grades, and tests with different numbers of items, so keeping track of these and doing the calculations can get fairly complex. One important principle in doing this is to first *convert each score or grade to the same scale.* If you are using the percent correct scale, this means converting each score or grade to a percent correct score. For a test with 50 items, this means multiplying the raw score obtained by 2. For a test with 10 items, multiply the raw score by 10. What about grades for papers and essay items? Here you need to have a key so each grade is given a percent correct score. For example, an A paper is given a 96, an A– paper a 92, a B+ paper a 90, and so forth. If you are including homework in your grade and using a check, check minus, and check plus system, you need to find a way to convert these to result in a number between 0 and 100. In this case you might decide that each check is an 90, a check plus is 100, and a check minus corresponds to 80.

Let's look at an example of how to do all of this in practice. Figure 11.5 on page 314 illustrates part of a Ms. Lopez's gradebook. The gradebook is a record of student accomplishments and performances throughout the grading period. In this case, you can see that there were two quizzes, a midterm exam, a final exam, a paper, and homework. For each test, Ms. Lopez records the raw score, records grades for papers, and places a checkmark beneath each homework assignment completed. Ms. Lopez has decided that the final grade will be determined as follows:

> final exam, 40%
> midterm exam, 30%
> quizzes, 5% each
> papers, 15 %
> homework, 5%

This means that the unit quizzes, together, will count 10 percent. She has set up her gradebook to efficiently convert the raw scores to the percent correct, weight them, then add them to arrive at composite scores. You will probably find it most convenient to prepare your own gradebook, although computerized gradebooks are available and some teachers find them very useful (see Appendix B for a list of grading software). A good procedure is to use a loose-leaf notebook with graph paper. You can customize the columns to meet your own requirements. Usually attendance and assessment scores and grades are recorded on separate pages.

The first quiz had 25 items, so Ms. Lopez muliplied each raw score by 4 to obtain the percent correct number. The second quiz had 20 items, so she multiplied the raw scores by 5. Each midterm had 50 items, so she multiplied the scores for each by 2. The final exam had 100 points, so it did not need to be converted. She worked out a score for each grade that could be given to the papers, and she gave each completed homework check a 100. To obtain a grade for the homework, she added the scores (either 100 or 0) and then divided by the total number of homework assignments, in this case 2 (this number is small for space reasons; typically much more homework would be recorded). After she has calculated all the weighted scores, she adds them to determine the final unit grade for each student, using a common grading scale (A = 95–100, B = 85–94, C = 75–84, D = 65–74, F= below 65).

Semester: ___Fall 1995___

Unit: ___Plant Biology___

Student	Quiz 1 (5%)			Quiz 2 (5%)			Midterm (30%)			Final Exam (40%)			Paper (15%)		Homework (5%)			Weighted Score	Composite Score	Final Grade
	Raw Score	% Correct	Weighted Score	Raw Score	% Correct	Weighted Score	Raw Score	% Correct	Weighted Score	% Correct	Weighted Score	Grade	% Correct	Weighted Score	#1	#2	Average			
Cross, E.	23	92	4.6	19	95	4.75	47	94	28.2	88	35.2	A-	95	14.25	✓	✓	100	5	92	B+
Elder, C.	20	80	4.0	17	85	4.25	42	84	25.2	92	36.8	B	89	13.35	✓	✓	100	5	88.6	B
Elder, K.	24	96	4.8	16	80	4.00	46	92	27.6	80	32.0	C+	82	12.30		✓	50	2.5	83.2	C+
Knight, M.	18	72	3.6	20	100	5.00	48	96	28.8	75	30.0	B-	86	12.90	✓	✓	100	5	85.3	B-
Marshall, C.	22	88	4.4	18	90	4.50	41	82	24.6	85	34.0	C+	82	12.30	✓	✓	100	5	84.80	C+
McMillan, R.	23	92	4.6	19	95	4.75	43	86	25.8	90	36.0	B	89	13.35	✓	✓	100	5	89.5	B
Orrock, A.	25	100	5.0	18	90	4.50	45	90	27.0	98	39.2	A	98	14.70	✓	✓	100	5	95.4	A-
Williams, J.	19	76	3.8	18	90	4.50	38	76	22.8	78	31.2	B	89	13.35		✓	50	2.5	78.15	C

FIGURE 11.5 Part of Ms. Lopez's Gradebook

In Figure 11.6, the calculations are shown from the scores of two students in Ms. Lopez's class (Figure 11.5), Carrie Elder and Jessica Williams. In these cases, the final unit grades are fairly clear, but what about Christina Marshall? As you can see in Figure 11.5, she is a borderline student, and you will need to be prepared to deal with such cases. In Christina's case, she's so close to a B (84.8), shouldn't the teacher "give" it to her? This is where you would need to think about the strongest information you have about Christina's understanding of plant biology. Her final was an 85, barely a B–, but both her midterm and paper grades were in the C range. Normally these would be your best indicators of understanding the content, so from one perspective it would justifiable to leave her final grade as a C+. On the other hand, if she had gotten only a couple more questions correct on any of the exams, her composite score would have been over 85. Isn't there enough error in those tests to justify giving her the benefit of the doubt and raising her grade to a B–? This is also a reasonable response. What will help in such cases is to think about your classroom interaction with Christina and other students who obtained a B as a final grade. Was she as knowledgeable as the B students? If so, it would be reasonable to raise her grade. Were there any extenuating circumstances that would have influenced her work? Another approach I have found to work well is to grade hard for each test and assignment, then give borderline students the higher final grade. What you want to be able to say with confidence is that the final grade is a fair and accurate indication of student performance on the learning goal.

Total Points Method

If you don't like to calculate percentages, you can use the same approach by giving each assessment a number of points and adding the points obtained for all the assessments to get a total. The points should be assigned to each assessment to reflect their weight in determining the total. For example, we could use points for Ms. Lopez rather than percentages. If the final is to count as 40 percent of the grade, then 40 percent of the total number of points should be allocated to the final exam. If the final had 100 questions, and each item counted for one point, then there would need to be a grand total of 250 points possible. The remaining points could be allocated to each assessment based on the percentage times 250. Thus, each quiz

FIGURE 11.6   Calculation of Unit Final Grades

	Quiz 1	Quiz 2	Midterm	Final	Paper	Homework	Composite
C. Elder	20×4=80	17×5=85	42×2=84	92	B (89)	✓✓(100)	
	80×.05=4.0	85×.05=4.25	84×.3=25.2	92×.4=36.8	89×.15=13.35	100×.05=5	
	4.0 +	4.25 +	25.2 +	36.8 +	13.35 +	5 =	88.6
J. Williams	19×4=76	18×5=90	38×2=76	78	B (89)	✓ (50)	
	76×.05=3.8	90×.05=4.5	76×.3=22.8	78×.4=31.2	89×.15=13.35	50×.05=2.5	
	3.8 +	4.5 +	22.8 +	31.2 +	13.35 +	2.5 =	78.15

would have 12.5 points, the midterm would have 75 points, and the paper would have 37.5 points.

You can see the disadvantage of this approach. Either you have to adjust the number of items to equal the points each assessment should provide, or you have to change the score of an assessment to reflect the points. This means that each quiz, in this case, would have a maximum of 12.5 points, regardless of the number of items. Obviously this is pretty cumbersome, so if the total points method is used, the assessments are carefully designed to avoid the recalculation of any individual assessment so that they can simply be added. However, this tends to constrain the nature of the assessments. Rather than have the method of combining scores drive the assessments, let each assessment be constructed to provide the best measure of student performance, and then combine. The percent correct approach is much better than total points for this reason.

Combining Relative Scores and Grades

If you happen to be one of a small percentage of teachers who grade using a norm-referenced approach, you have an additional step to take when combining scores. Because the emphasis is on relative standing, you need to take into account the degree or amount of difference between students on each assessment. This is because the contribution of each assessment is a function of the difference between students as well as the score. To illustrate with a simple example, suppose I give a midterm and all students obtain the same score. On the final, the scores are pretty well distributed. I want the midterm to count for 50 percent, so I weight it appropriately, multiply by the score, and then add the product to the final exam. This is, in reality, weighting the final exam 100 percent. Because all students obtained the same score on the midterm, what is added to the final is the same for each student. Thus, the only variability I can get is what is provided by the final exam. Although you are unlikely to have a situation in which all students scored the same on a test, differences in variation will affect the actual contribution of each assessment to the total.

There isn't space here to go into detail, with examples, of how to combine relative scores into a final grade. The suggested approach is to calculate linear transformations of each raw score to a standard score. You first figure the standard scores, then weight them, then add them together. The final determination of grades is made on the basis of what percentage of students should receive each grade. I'd suggest treatments by Carey (1994), Kubiszyn and Borich (1993), and Oosterhof (1987) for more detail on combining relative grades.

Suggestions for Fair Grading

Teachers have an overriding concern for grading students fairly (Brookhart, 1993). This is good, and we have discussed many factors teachers need to consider to achieve fair grading practices. These suggestions, and some new ones, are summarized in Figure 11.7 as do's and don'ts. A couple of issues deserve some additional attention.

One issue that many teachers will disagree about is how to handle the zeros that students obtain when they do not hand in an assignment or are absent from

FIGURE 11.7 Do's and Don'ts of Effective Grading

Do	Don't
Use well thought out professional judgments	Depend entirely on number crunching
Try everything you can to score and grade fairly	Allow personal bias to affect grades
Grade according to preestablished learning targets and standards	Grade on the curve using the class as the norm group
Clearly inform students and parents of grading procedures at the beginning of the semester	Keep grading procedures secret
Base grades on student performance	Base grades on intelligence, effort, attitudes, or motivation
Rely most on current information	Penalize poorly-performing students early in the semester
Grade, and return assessments to students as soon as possible and with as much feedback as possible	Return assessments weeks later with little or no feedback
Review borderline cases carefully; when in doubt, assign the higher grade	Be inflexible with borderline cases
Convert scores to the same scale before combining	Use zero scores indiscriminately when averaging grades
Weight scores before combining	Include extra credit assignments that are not related to the learning targets
Use a sufficient number of assessments	Rely on one or two assessments for a semester grade
Be willing to change grades when warranted	Lower grades for cheating, misbehaving, tardiness, or absence

class for some reason. To clarify the issue, you need to consider the effect of a zero on an average. If I have a zero for 20 percent of my grade because I didn't hand in any homework, I could have a 80 percent average on all the tests and flunk the class ($80 \times .80 = 64$; $20 \times 0 = 0$; $64 + 0 = 64$). Would this grade be a fair representation of what I knew, of how I performed? I think not! If you average zeros in this way you actually weight them more than other grades because the range between 0 and D is so much greater than ranges between other grades.

One of the worst offenses in grading is the indiscriminant use of zeros. It seems to me that you need to record a failure in the above situation, but not give it a zero. Perhaps a 65 would be appropriate, but not completing an assignment does not mean zero achievement or learning. You may react by thinking that a score of 65 would encourage students not to do their work, because the penalty is not very severe. However, this is a motivational problem, and it shouldn't be solved by grading practices. Grades should reflect only performance in relation to learning targets. Another problem of averaging zeros is that student motivation may be quite negatively affected if it becomes impossible to achieve a passing grade. The likely result in this circumstance is that the student simply will not try to learn any more.

A second approach to zeros is to use them only for assessments that have a minuscule effect on the final grade. This is done by weighting the assessment very little. However, a better policy, from my perspective, is to avoid zeros altogether.

Another issue is the lowering of grades in response to student cheating. Obviously cheating is a very serious offense, and appropriate disciplinary action is warranted. However, lowering grades is not appropriate discipline because of the extreme negative impact this may have on the grade. Suppose you give a zero to a student when he or she is caught cheating on a test. Does this score accurately represent the student's knowledge and performance? Here you are using grades to punish the student. It would be better to find another kind of punishment and retest the student.

Finally, it's important to be willing to change grades when justified. In the first place, mistakes are made in calculating grades. A possible hint of this occurs when a final grade for a student doesn't seem right. In this circumstance, go back over the calculations to be sure there are no mistakes. Second, students sometimes have legitimate arguments about a grade. It is possible to overlook things. In fact, this is probable when you grade a lot of assessments. So, be willing to admit that you were wrong and record the best, most accurate score or grade.

REPORTING STUDENT PROGRESS TO PARENTS

An important function of grades is to provide information that can be shared with parents. We know that parents are critical to student learning, and effectively reporting student progress can help parents better understand their children and know what they can do to provide appropriate support and motivation. Reporting to parents can take many forms, including weekly or monthly reports, phone calls, letters, newsletters, conferences, and, of course, report cards. Although grades are the most common way by which parents keep abreast of student progress, what those grades communicate is usually quite limited. Most report cards only indicate current status in different subjects, and they do not provide the detail needed for parents to know what to *do* with the information (see Guskey, 1996, and Azwell & Schmar, 1995, for alternatives to traditional report cards). Consequently, you'll probably need to supplement report cards with other forms of communication.

Written Information

One approach to reporting student progress is to provide some type of written report. This could be done weekly, biweekly, or monthly. In the progress report, include learning targets for the period, student performances on individual assessments, descriptions of student motivation and affect, suggestions for helping the student, and grades if possible. Because this will take some time, it's best to have a standard form on which you can quickly record information. Older students can be taught to calculate their current grade average in the class. You will want to be sure to include some positive comments. It may be helpful to identify two or three areas that the parents could focus on until the next report. If possible, provide specific expectations for what you want parents to do at home to help. Be clear in asserting that parents need to be partners in the learning process. If these expectations can be individualized for each student, so much the better, but even a standard list of expectations is good.

Another type of written communication is the informal note or letter. Taking only a minute or two to write a personal note to parents about their child is much appreciated. It shows concern and caring. Begin such a note with something positive, then summarize progress and suggest an expectation or two.

Parent–Teacher Conferences

The parent–teacher conference is the most common way teachers communicate with parents about student progress. This is typically a face-to-face discussion, though phone conferences and calls can also be used. In fact, brief phone calls by the teacher to talk with parents, like informal notes, are very well received and appreciated, especially when the calls are about positive progress and suggestions rather than for disciplinary or other problems.

Parent–teacher conferences are required in most elementary schools. Middle and high school teachers find conferences much more difficult to conduct because of the number of students. But even if the conference is in the context of a back-to-school night, most of the suggestions in Figure 11.8 apply.

It is essential to plan the conference and to be prepared. This means having all the information well-organized in advance and knowing what you hope to achieve from the conference. This will probably include a list of areas you want to cover

FIGURE 11.8   Checklist for Conducting Parent–Teacher Conferences

1. Plan each conference in advance.
2. Conduct the conference in a private, quiet, comfortable setting.
3. Begin with a discussion of positive student performances.
4. Establish an informal, professional tone.
5. Encourage parent participation in the conference.
6. Be frank in reviewing student strengths and weaknesses.
7. Review language skills.
8. Review learning targets with examples of student performances that show progress.
9. Avoid discussing other students and teachers.
10. Avoid bluffing.
11. Identify two or three areas to work on in a plan of action.

and some questions to ask parents. If possible, you may be able to find out what parents would like to review prior to the conference. Examples of student work should be organized to show progress and performance in relation to learning targets. The conference is an ideal time for pointing out specific areas of strength and weakness that report card grades cannot communicate.

You want the conference to be a conversation, not a lecture. Listening to parents will help you understand their child better. Even though it is natural to feel anxious about meeting with parents, it's important to take a strong, professional stance. Rather than being timid, take charge. This should be done with a friendly and informal tone that encourages parents to participate. You'll want to be positive, but you need to be direct and honest about areas that need improvement. Keep the focus on academic progress rather than student behavior. I think it's always important to discuss student performance in reading, writing, and speaking. These language skills are essential and should be reviewed. Avoid discussing other students or teachers, and be willing to admit that you don't know an answer to a question. By the end of the conference you should identify, in consultation with the parents, a course of action or steps to be taken at home and at school.

SUMMARY

This chapter stressed the importance of a teacher's professional judgment when implementing a grading and reporting system. There is no completely objective procedure for grading. Grading is professional decision making that depends on the teacher's values and beliefs, experience, and best subjective judgments. We reviewed the different functions of grading and took a close look at how factors other than academic performance affect grades. The chapter examined the basis of comparison used in grading, as well as approaches to grading. Approaches to combine assessments were presented, along with reporting procedures to parents. Important points include the following:

- In the classroom, the major function of grading is to provide students with feedback about their performance.
- Teachers need to provide a sufficient level of detail for grading to be informative for students.
- Generally, use effort, student aptitude, improvement, and attitudes as factors affecting grades only in borderline cases.
- Grades communicate comparison between student performance and the performance of other students (norm-referenced) or between student performance and predetermined standards (criterion-referenced).
- The major function of norm-referenced systems is to rank and sort students. Student competitiveness is fostered; most teachers find they must do some kind of sorting.

- The major function of criterion-referenced systems is to judge students in relation to absolute levels of performance.
- Percentage-based correct is the most common type of criterion-referenced grading. Percentage correct depends on student understanding of content, and on skills, as well as item difficulty.
- The goal in grading is to provide a fair and accurate record of student performance in relation to learning targets.
- Approaches to grading include using letters, percent correct measures, pass/fail tests, checklists, and written descriptions.
- Determining report card grades requires professional decisions about what to include, how to weight each assessment, and how weighted assessments are combined.
- It is important to clarify the role homework may play in determining grades; nonacademic factors should not be included.
- Provide a sufficient number of assessments to obtain a fair and accurate portrait of the student.
- Weight each assessment by the contribution to the goal, instructional time, reliability, and recency. Give more recent, comprehensive assessments more weight.
- Put all assessments on the same scale before weighting and combining. Weight before combining.
- Consider variation of each assessment if combining relative comparisons.
- Be flexible with borderline cases; don't let numbers make what should be professional into subjective decisions.
- Do not use zeros indiscriminately when averaging scores.
- Grades should not be affected by inappropriate student behavior or cheating.
- Grades should be changed when warranted to reflect the most fair and accurate record of student performance.
- Reporting student progress to parents can be done by phone, with written materials, and in teacher–parent conferences.
- Reports to parents should be well prepared with samples of student work to illustrate progress and areas that need further attention.
- Teacher–parent conferences are informal, professional meetings where teachers discuss progress with parents and determine action steps to be taken.

SELF-INSTRUCTIONAL REVIEW EXERCISES

1. Indicate whether each of the following refers to norm-referenced (NR) or criterion-referenced (CR) grading.

   a. used to show which students are the worst in a group
   b. average test scores are typically lower
   c. easily adapted from scoring rubrics
   d. uses percentile rank

e. uses percentage correct
f. items tend to be easier
g. determination of standards is subjective
h. fosters student competitiveness

2. In what ways is teacher professional judgment important in determining the actual standard employed in grading students?

3. What major limitation do most approaches to grading have in common? What can teachers do to avoid this limitation?

4. From the following scenario, summarize what Ms. Gallagher did wrong when she determined her report card grades.

   Ms. Gallagher calculated semester grades on the basis of a midterm, a comprehensive final exam, and student participation, which consisted of homework, class participation, and effort. Each component was worth 100 points; they were added and then divided by three to obtain the composite score, which was then translated to a grade.

5. Using the following grading scale and scores, what percent correct grade would Ralph and Sally receive?

   90–100 A, 80–89 B, 70–79 C, 60–69 D, <60 F

   Midterm # 1, 20%
   Midterm # 2, 20%
   Final exam, 30%
   Paper, 20% (A=100, A–=92, B+=88, B=85, B–=82, C+=78, C=75, C–=72)
   Participation, 10% (same scale as paper)

	Ralph	*Sally*
Midterm #1, 40 possible points	30 points	35 points
Midterm #2, 50 possible points	40 points	35 points
Final exam, 200 possible points	170 points	140 points
Paper	B+	C
Participation	A–	A

6. Shaunda is a sixth grader. She is the youngest in a low-income family of six. Because her parents are not home very much, Shaunda takes on responsibilities with her brothers and sisters. The family lives in a small home, so it's hard for Shaunda to get the privacy she needs to do her homework. Consequently she often does not hand in any homework. She has a very positive attitude toward school; she is very attentive in class and tries hard to do well. Your class uses the following grading policy: in-class work accounts for 25 percent of the final grade; homework, 25 percent; and 50 percent for tests and quizzes. The grading scale in the school is 95–100, A; 85–94, B; 75–84, C; 65–74, D; < 65, F. Shaunda's averages are in-class work, 85 percent; homework, 30 percent; and tests and quizzes, 70 percent. What overall composite percent correct would Shaunda have? What grade would you give her? Does the grade reflect her academic performance? Should the grading policy be changed?

7. Suppose you have a very capable student who does very well on tests (e.g., 95s) but very poorly on homework. He just doesn't want to do work he sees as boring. His homework scores pull his test scores down so that the overall average is B-. What final grade would you give?

ANSWERS TO SELF-INSTRUCTIONAL REVIEW EXERCISES

1. a. NR, b. NR, c. CR, d., NR, e. CR, f. CR, g. CR, h. NR.

2. The standard is set by how difficult the teacher: makes the assessment items; scores essay, short-answer, and performance-based assessments; and sets the criterion level (e.g., the percentage correct).

3. The major limitation of letter grades, percent correct, and pass/fail approaches is that they provide only a general overview of performance. Supplemental information that details the strengths and weaknesses of the students is needed.

4. I hope you noticed immediately that Ms. Gallagher made several significant errors. First, there are too few assessments to determine a semester grade; many more are needed. Second, the three components should not be weighted equally. Because the final is comprehensive, it should count the most. The participation grade is weighted too heavily and should not combine academic work (homework) with nonacademic factors. The weighting makes it possible for students who have poor performance to do satisfactorily in the course. There is no indication how much each of the separate participation components is counted. This example is pretty bad!

5. First, convert all scores to the same 100-point scale. Because the first midterm is worth 40 points, the score would be multiplied by 2.5, the second midterm score by 2, and the final exam divided by 2. Each of these scores is multiplied by the appropriate weight and then added.

   Ralph: $(30 \times 2.5 \times .2) + (40 \times 2 \times .2) + (170/2 \times .3) + (88 \times .2) + (92 \times .1) = 15 + 16 + 25.5 + 17.6 + 9.2 = 83.3 = B$

   Sally: $(35 \times 2.5 \times .2) + (35 \times 2 \times .2) + (140/2 \times .3) + (75 \times .2) + (100 \times .1) = 17.5 + 14 + 21 + 15 + 10 = 77.5 = C+$

6. Shaunda's composite score would be figured as $(85 \times .25) + (30 \times .25) + (70 \times .5) = 21.25 + 7.5 + 35 = 63.75$. According to the grading scale, she would receive an F. This reflects the relatively high contribution of homework and the fact that she was not able to get much of it finished. However, her classwork and performance on tests tell a different story, and a more accurate grade would be a D. Suppose homework was 10 percent instead of 25 percent and classwork was 40 percent. Then her composite would be a 72, almost 10 points higher. Given her home situation, she certainly should not fail, and the grading scale needs to be changed to put more weight on academic performance. The relatively high percentage for in-class work, 25 percent, is subject to teacher bias and should be reduced.

7. Actual test performance should not be affected negatively by nonacademic factors such as effort and compliance. I'd use a policy that homework won't hurt a grade, but could improve it, and give the student an A. Obviously, the student did not really need the homework, which suggests a change in homework assignments.

SUGGESTIONS FOR ACTION RESEARCH

1. Create a grading plan that would make sense for a class you plan to teach. Include a statement of purpose and explain what would be included, how weights would be established, and the final grading scale. Then give the plan to other students and ask them to critique it. If possible, give the plan to a classroom teacher and see how realistic it is.

2. Interview teachers on the subject of grading. Do they use a norm-referenced or criterion-referenced approach, or a combination? Ask them about the areas that require professional judgments, like what to do with borderline students, how zeros are used, how to apply extra credit, and the like. Ask them how they use grades to motivate students.

3. Observe a class when graded tests or papers are returned to students. What is their reaction? What do they seem to do with the information?

4. Conduct an experiment by giving some students just grades and other students grades with comments and suggestions for improvement. See if the students react differently. Interview the students to determine if the nature of the feedback affected their motivation.

5. Talk with some parents about their experiences with parent–teacher conferences. What did they get out of it? How could it have been improved? Were the suggestions in Figure 11.8 on page 319 followed?

12

ASSESSING MAINSTREAMED STUDENTS

One of most significant changes for teachers in the last decade has been accommodating exceptional students who have been mainstreamed into regular classrooms. Students with mild disabilities are now routinely included with other students in the same class, and the regular classroom teacher is responsible for both instructing and evaluating these students. Teachers are also responsible for using assessment information to identify those students who may be eligible for special education services. In this chapter, we review the role of the regular teacher in

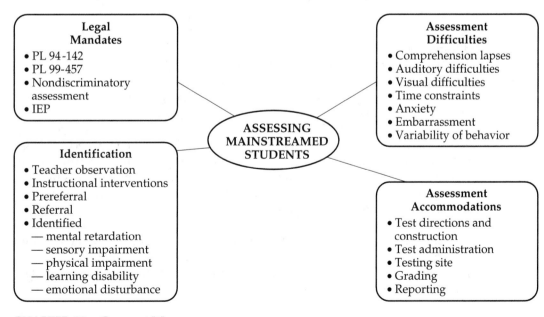

CHAPTER 12   Concept Map

identifying and adapting assessment practices so that they are fair and unbiased for mainstreamed students. First, we'll look briefly at the implications of the legal mandates in this area.

LEGAL MANDATES

In 1975, the Education for All Handicapped Children Act, Public Law 94-142, was passed to provide free appropriate public education for school-aged individuals with disabilities (not "disabled individuals") in the least restrictive environment. The act required states to establish procedures to assure that students with disabilities are educated, to the maximum extent possible, with students who are not disabled; that is, in the least restrictive environment. The most common procedure for meeting this mandate has been to mainstream students with disabilities by placing them in regular education classes with appropriate instructional support. In fact, students can only be removed from regular classes when the severity of the disability prevents satisfactory instruction and learning progress. As a result, most classroom teachers must now be familiar with how students are identified as having "special needs," and how assessment procedures used in the course of regular classroom instruction need to be modified to ensure that these students are evaluated fairly.

Another important law was passed in 1986 to extend all rights and protections of PL 94-142 to preschoolers aged three to five. This law is referred to as PL 99-457. The effect of this law has been to encourage states to provide services for individuals from birth through kindergarten, with required services for three- to five-year-olds. More recently, The Americans with Disabilities Act, PL 101-336, and the Education of the Handicapped Act Amendments of 1990, PL 101-476, indicate further assurances for persons with disabilities, although these are not focused on schooling. Thus, the trend is toward increasing governmental involvement in protecting the rights of individuals with disabilities, and you will be responsible for adhering to these regulations with students who are mainstreamed.

According to PL 94-142, classroom teachers are responsible for gathering and providing the information used to identify students who may become eligible for special education services and for developing and implementing an individualized education program (IEP). Assessments used by teachers provide the information necessary to determine if students are making satisfactory progress toward meeting learning targets as specified in the IEP. For both of these responsibilities the act specifies that all testing and evaluation must be *nondiscriminatory*. For identification purposes, the law requires that the selection and administration of materials and procedures used for evaluation and placement must not be racially or culturally discriminatory. At a minimum, the law requires that (Wood, 1992, p. 10):

1. *Trained personnel administer validated tests and other evaluation materials and provide and administer such materials in the child's native language or other mode of communication.*
2. *Tests and other evaluation materials include those tailored to assess specific areas of educational need and not merely those designed to provide a single general intelligence quotient.*
3. *Trained personnel select and administer tests to reflect accurately the child's aptitude or achievement level without discriminating against the child's disability.*
4. *Trained personnel use no single procedure as the sole criterion for determining an appropriate educational program for a child.*
5. *A multidisciplinary team assess the child in all areas related to the suspected disability.*

Essentially, these provisions mean that assessment must be planned and conducted so that the disability does not contribute to the score or result. That is, it would be unfair to use a test written in English to determine that a student whose primary language is Spanish has mental retardation, just as it would be unfair to conclude that a student with a fine motor disability did not know the answer to an essay question because there was insufficient time to write the answer. In other words, it is illegal for the attribute being measured to be influenced by the disability.

With respect to writing and implementing the IEP, teachers have several responsibilities. As a member of a selected committee that writes the IEP, the regular classroom teacher provides important information, because the plan must be based on a clear and accurate documentation of the present level of educational functioning. This includes identification of a student's deficits and weaknesses, as well as the student's strengths. Although standardized test scores are used to establish levels of functioning, these scores need to be supplemented and corroborated by teacher observation and the student's classroom performance. Because parents (and sometimes the students) are on the committee, you will need to translate technical measurement terms, such as *stanine* and *percentile*, into familiar language.

Another teacher responsibility is setting short- and long-term learning targets and specifying the criteria and evaluation procedures that will be used to monitor progress toward meeting the targets. Here, it is important to set truly *individualized* targets. Every student needs a customized set of realistic targets that take into account identified strengths and weaknesses and preferred learning modes and styles. Appropriately delineated evaluation criteria and procedures need to reflect the degree of difficulty in the tasks, the variety of methods that should be employed, and a reasonable timetable. For example, if all the criteria are based simply on whether or not the teacher made the test, or if the students achieved an 85 percent accuracy rate, or if a goal is reached by the end of the year, then there is probably inadequate specificity. Rather, it should be clear in the plan that there are exemplars of the targeted performance, that multiple methods of assessment are used, and that the timetable for expected progress includes intermediate checkpoints.

Finally, teachers are responsible for assuring that the student will participate in regular classroom activities to the maximum extent possible. This includes both formal and informal classroom assessments. Here, your understanding of what is required with each type of assessment will be used with your knowledge of the specific disabilities of the students to ensure that, whenever possible, assessment procedures are modified only when necessary.

ASSESSING STUDENTS FOR IDENTIFICATION

The steps leading to identifying a student as having one or more of the disabilities that qualifies the student to receive special education services are summarized in Figure 12.1. To examine your role in this process, as related to assessment, we'll consider two major categories of steps: those done prior to identification and the actual identification of various characteristics of disabilities.

Steps Prior to Identification

Initially, students are observed and evaluated by the classroom teacher, who then tries intervention strategies to see if these changes are sufficient for improving student performance. In effect, you need to be certain that relatively simple changes in teaching methods or materials are not sufficient to improve the student's performance.

If the student continues to have difficulties after you make these instructional interventions, the next step is to more closely analyze the student's ability to perform as expected. This usually includes the diagnostic assessment of specific learn-

---

**FIGURE 12.1   Steps in Identifying Students
for Special Education Services**

Step 1: Initial teacher assessment of student
Step 2: Instructional interventions
Step 3: Diagnostic assessment of specific difficulties
Step 4: Prereferral group review
Step 5: Instructional interventions
Step 6: Referral
Step 7: Formal assessment
Step 8: Identification

Source: Adapted from Wood, Judith, *Adapting instruction for mainstreamed and at-risk students*, 2nd ed., copyright © 1992, p. 41. Adapted by permission of Prentice-Hall, Upper Saddle River, New Jersey.

ing difficulties or deficits using routine, teacher-made assessments. An analysis of errors may pinpoint these difficulties and suggest specific remediation strategies.

For students with continuing difficulties, some schools have a formal process of prereferral review. This may be called the prereferral committee or the child study team. In other schools, you will need to form your own small committee. Either way, the purpose of this group is to provide an external review of your tentative diagnosis and feedback concerning instructional interventions that have been tried. The group usually includes other teachers, school administrators, the school counselor, and special education teachers. Sometimes members of the committee may observe the student in class or conduct individual assessments. Often the committee will recommend additional interventions that may effectively address the problem, or a specific plan will be developed. In the event that the student still struggles, despite this fairly extensive review and implementation of different instructional strategies, then you will need to refer the student for a comprehensive educational assessment.

Formal referral is a serious step, because it suggests that the student may be eligible for special education services. Consequently, you will need to have specific documentation of the learning or behavior difficulties, interventions that have been tried, and the results of these interventions. It would be inadequate to simple say, for example, "Derek is always causing trouble in class. He likes to bother other students by poking and provoking them. We have tried several different approaches with Derek, each with limited success. He has a lot of trouble with mathematics." Rather, the information needs to be specific, for example:

> *Derek physically touched, hit, or poked other students an average of fifteen times per day in a way that disturbed or bothered the students. He talks without raising his hand in class discussions 75 percent of the time. Time out, individual contracts, and sessions with the counselor have been used with limited success that soon dissipates. Derek has turned in homework only 20 percent of the time. In class, he is unable to complete mathematics assignments that deal with the addition and subtraction of complex fractions. He is off task with mathematics assignments 50 percent of the time.*

A screening committee will review the written referral, and parents will be contacted. Suggestions for additional instructional interventions may be made. If the committee concludes that a formal assessment is needed, parental permission is secured and a comprehensive evaluation begins. This process includes the assessment of all areas of suspected disability, which is administered and interpreted by specialists in different areas (e.g., a school psychologist to administer intelligence, personality, and projective tests; a physical therapist to evaluate gross motor skills; and an audiologist to evaluate hearing acuity). Students are tested by a variety of methods, which may include additional informal observation by the regular classroom teacher. In any event, identification is confirmed when classroom teacher evaluations and those of the specialists coincide.

Identification

Following formal assessment, the student may be identified as having one or more specific educational disabilities. Each of the disabling conditions is confirmed by applying specific criteria. We will examine the assessment criteria and implications of several common mild learning deficits, because students with these deficits are the ones most likely to be mainstreamed into regular classes.

Mental Retardation

Students are identified as having mental retardation, or educational disabilities, on the basis of low scores on a standardized intelligence test and consistent deficits of what are termed *adaptive behaviors* that adversely affect educational performance. *Adaptive behaviors* are those that are needed for normal functioning in daily living situations, for example, expressive and receptive communication, daily living skills such as personal hygiene and eating habits, coping skills, and motor skills. The severity of the retardation is indicated in degrees: severe, moderate, and mild.

Although school psychologists will take care of the IQ testing, it may be up to you to provide much of the information regarding adaptive behaviors. Often, you accomplish this with the help of established adaptive behavior scales, such as the Vineland Adaptive Behavior Scale, the Adaptive Behavior Scale, and the Adaptive Behavior Inventory for Children. Teachers, as well as primary caregivers, are interviewed with these types of instruments to document the student's behavioral competence. In addition, it is important for you to confirm findings from these instruments with more informal observations. Thus, you will contribute critical information on adaptive behaviors.

You need to keep two cautions in mind when assessing adaptive behavior. First, there is no single adaptive behavior instrument that covers all areas of behavior, and the data for these instruments are gathered from third-party observers. Thus, it is important to select the instrument that will provide the most valid inferences for the situation and to keep in mind that third parties may be biased. Second, you need to be careful that a student's cultural or linguistic background does not cause the student to be inappropriately labeled as having inadequate adaptive behavior. Some students who are perfectly capable of functioning in their day-to-day living environments may have difficulty functioning in the classroom because of the cultural or language differences.

Sensory Impairment

Students who have deficits with vision, hearing, or speech may be identified as sensory impaired. This could include a communication disorder, such as stuttering or impaired articulation; visual difficulties, even with correction, including eye-hand coordination; or a hearing problem that interferes with educational performance. One of the first things you should do with students experiencing difficulty in learning is to check for visual and hearing acuity. Obviously, students who have trouble seeing or hearing will have trouble academically. Your close and careful observation of students will provide clues to these types of impairments.

Physical Impairment

Other physical disabilities are not sensory, such as an orthopedic impairment (cerebral palsy, amputations) or a physical illness like epilepsy, diabetes, or muscular dystrophy. Generally, these conditions will be obvious, and resources will be provided to make appropriate accommodations.

Learning Disability

A learning disability is identified when there is a processing deficit that manifests itself in a severe discrepancy between performance and ability. This includes perceptual handicaps such as dyslexia, but not sensory or physical impairment, mental retardation, or environmental, cultural, or economic disadvantage. These students have average or above average intelligence, but they are functioning at low levels (at least one standard deviation below ability scores) due to physiological, psychological, or cognitive processes involved in understanding and using language or mathematical reasoning. You may be called upon to administer a standardized test to document the discrepancy, and you will surely be needed to comment on data from the student's cumulative folder and classroom performance and behavior. As before, the process is dependent on your careful observation and evaluation of the student.

It is important to be able to distinguish between a learning disability and slow learning. A slow learner may also have a discrepancy between ability and achievement and may need remedial education, but the reason for the low performance is not an impairment in intellectual functioning. It may well be due to emotional problems or economic disadvantage, but these types of deficiencies are not sufficient to identify a student as learning disabled.

Emotional Disturbance

Also called an emotional disability, a behavioral disorder, or serious emotional disturbance, a student identified as emotionally disturbed consistently, over a long period, exhibits one or more of the following characteristics: poor academic performance not due to other disabilities; poor interpersonal relationships; inappropriate behaviors or feelings in normal circumstances; unhappiness, melancholy, or depression; or unfounded physical symptoms or fears associated with school or personal problems. Often students who are emotionally disturbed will become withdrawn.

You will need to make systematic observations of a student who may be classified under the category of emotional disturbance. This could include, for example, noting each time the student displays inappropriate behavior, such as crying or yelling, in normal circumstances for no apparent reason. When the inappropriate

FIGURE 12.2   Classroom Teacher's Role in the Assessment Process

Steps in the Assessment Process	Regular Classroom Teacher's Role
Prior to referral	Use informal assessment methods to monitor daily progress, curriculum-based assessment, and behavioral observations; consult with committee members Implement educational interventions
Diagnosis of specific disability	Recognize behaviors and characteristics of specific disabilities so that students can be identified, evaluated, and served if appropriate Recognize behaviors and characteristics that indicate cultural or linguistic differences and that do not warrant special education services
Referral	Document through data collection of student work samples, behavioral observations, teacher-made tests, and other informal measures to identify educational strengths and weaknesses Consult with committee members Consult with parents Complete necessary referral forms Attend child study committee meeting and present appropriate data collected on student progress and behaviors Participate during development and implementation of identification and IEP for students in the regular class setting

Source: Adapted from Wood, Judith, *Adapting instruction for mainstreamed and at-risk students,* 2nd ed., copyright © 1992, p. 41. Adapted by permission of Prentice-Hall, Upper Saddle River, New Jersey.

behavior continues for an extended time, under different conditions, a serious emotional problem may be found. However, final diagnosis will require consultation with a specialist, such as a counselor or school psychologist.

Figures 12.2 and 12.3 summarize the teacher's role in the assessment and identification processes. Figure 12.2 summarizes responsibilities for different steps in the assessment process, and Figure 12.3 shows a teacher's responsibilities for identification in major categories. Generally, your observations of the student are used to corroborate the specialists' findings.

ASSESSMENT PROBLEMS ENCOUNTERED BY STUDENTS WITH DISABILITIES

Your goal in assessing student learning is to obtain a fair and accurate indication of performance. Because disabilities may affect test-taking ability, you will need to make accommodations, or changes, in assessments when needed to ensure valid inferences and consequences. There are many justifiable ways to alter assessments for students with disabilities. Before we consider these, it will be helpful to review the problems encountered by students with disabilities in testing situations. These difficulties are summarized in Figure 12.4.

FIGURE 12.3   Classroom Teacher's Role in the Identification Process

Disability	Teacher's Role	Questions
Mental retardation	Document adaptive behaviors; meet with child study committee	How well does the student function with daily life skills? Do deficits in daily living skills affect academic performance? Does cultural or linguistic background contribute to deficits in daily living skills?
Sensory impairment	Document visual, auditory, or speech impairments; meet with child study committee	Can the student see well enough? Is there adequate eye/hand coordination? Is there a problem with the student's hearing? Is there a speech problem of some kind?
Physical disability	Observe effect of disability on academic performance; meet with the child study committee	Does the disability adversely affect academic performance?
Learning disability	Document learning problems and achievement; interpret information in the cumulative folder; meet with the child study committee	Is there a large discrepancy between ability and achievement? Are sensory, physical, and mental disabilities ruled out? Does the student have average or above-average intelligence?
Emotional disturbance	Document inappropriate behaviors and feelings; meet with child study committee	Is the behavior extreme for the circumstances? Is the behavior fleeting or consistent? Are any other disabilities responsible for the poor performance? How well does the student interact with others? Is the student unhappy, depressed, or withdrawn much of the time?

FIGURE 12.4   Problems Encountered by Students with Disabilities That Impact Classroom Assessment

Problem	Impact on Assessment
Comprehension difficulties	Understanding directions; completing assessments requiring reasoning skills
Auditory difficulties	Understanding oral directions and test items; distracted by noises
Visual difficulties	Understanding written directions and test items; decoding symbols and letters; visual distractions
Time constraint difficulties	Completing assessments
Anxiety	Completing assessments; providing correct information
Embarrassment	Understanding directions; completing assessments
Variability of behavior	Completing assessments; demonstrating best work

Comprehension Difficulties

Many students with mild disabilities have difficulty with comprehension. This means that they may not understand verbal or written directions very well. If there is a sequence of steps in the directions, they may not be able to remember the sequence or all the steps, particularly if the directions are verbal. Lengthy written directions may be too complicated, and the reading level may be too high. There may be words or phrases that the student does not understand. If the directions include several different operations, the student may be confused about what to do. Obviously, without a clear understanding of how to proceed it will be difficult for these students to demonstrate their knowledge or skills.

Students with mild disabilities will have even more difficulty understanding directions or test items that require reasoning skills. These students may respond well to knowledge and understanding questions and deal well with concrete ideas, but they may not respond very well to abstractions. For example, it would be relatively easy for such students to respond to a straightforward short-answer question such as "What are the characteristics of a democratic government?" but much harder to respond to a more abstract question such as "How is the government of the United States different from a socialistic government?"

Auditory Difficulties

Students with auditory disabilities will have trouble processing information they hear quickly and accurately. Although they can hear, they will have difficulty processing the information easily. This makes it especially hard for these students to follow and understand verbal directions. Thus, their responses to oral tests and quizzes may be minimal, not because they haven't mastered the content, but because they don't fully understand the question. It is easy for teachers simply to read or talk too fast, but this does not allow sufficient time for students with auditory disabilities to process the information.

These students may also be sensitive to auditory distractions in the classroom. Such distractions are common in most classrooms, and it is easy to become accustomed to some background noise. This could include sound from the hallway or an adjoining classroom, talking among students, outside noise, desk movement, pencil sharpening, questions asked by students, teacher reprimands, school announcements, and so on. Although these sounds will seem "normal" and will not bother most students, those with auditory disabilities will be distracted and their attention will be diverted from the task at hand. This is a particular problem if the noise accompanies oral directions from the teacher, because the student will find it difficult to focus on the directions. It's not that these students are not paying attention or need to concentrate more. They have a disability that makes it difficult to discriminate sounds and keep focused.

Visual Difficulties

Students with visual disabilities have difficulty processing what they see. These students may copy homework assignments or test questions from the board incorrectly by transposing numbers or interchanging letters. Often the student has difficulty transferring information to paper. A cluttered board that requires visual discrimination may also cause problems. Visual disabilities also become a handicap on some handwritten tests if the test is not legible and clearly organized. The printing and cursive writing of most teachers is fine, but the handwriting of some teachers is not very legible for students with visual disabilities. Some students with a visual disability have difficulty decoding certain symbols, letters, and abbreviations, such as +, −, *b* and *d*, < and >, and *n* and *m*. One symbol may be confused with another, and test problems with many symbols may take a long time for these students to understand.

Some types of objective test items will be a problem because of visual perceptual difficulties. For example, lengthy matching items pose particular problems because the student may take a long time to peruse the columns, searching for answers and identifying the correct letters to use. Multiple-choice items that run responses together on the same line make it hard to discriminate among the possible answers.

Visual distractions can also interfere with test taking. For some students, a single visual cue—such as students moving in the classroom when getting up to turn in papers, student gestures, teacher motions, or something or someone outside—will disrupt their present visual focus and make it difficult to keep their concentration.

Time Constraint Difficulties

Time can pose a major problem for many students with disabilities. Frequently visual, auditory, motor coordination, and reading difficulties make it hard for some students to complete tests in the same time frame as other students. It's not that the students are lazy or intentionally slow. It simply takes them longer due to their disability. Thus, students should not be penalized for being unable to complete a test, especially timed tests that are constructed to reward speed in decoding and understanding questions and writing answers.

Anxiety

Although most students experience some degree of anxiety when completing tests, students with disabilities may be especially affected by feelings of anxiety due to fear that their disability will make it difficult to complete the test. Some students are simply unable to function very well in a traditional test setting, because the length or format of the test will overwhelm them. It is not because they don't have the knowledge; they may think their disability will affect their work.

One general strategy to reduce unhealthy anxiety is to make sure that students have learned appropriate test-taking skills. They need to know what to do if they do not fully understand the directions and how to proceed in answering different types of items (e.g., looking for clue words in multiple-choice items, true/false items, and completion items; crossing out incorrect alternatives in multiple-choice items; crossing out answers used in matching items). They also need to know to skip difficult items and come back to them when they have answered all other questions.

Embarrassment

Students with disabilities may be more sensitive than other students to feelings of embarrassment. They often want to hide or disguise their problems so that they are not singled out or labeled by their peers. As a result, they may want to appear to be "normal" when taking a test by not asking questions about directions and handing in the test at the same time as other students do, whether or not they are finished. They don't want to risk embarrassment by being the only one to have a question or by being the last one to complete their work. Students who are mainstreamed may also be embarrassed if they take a different test than others.

Variability of Behavior

The behavior of students with disabilities may vary greatly. This means that their disabilities may affect their behavior one day and not the next, and it may be impossible to predict this variability. This is especially true for students with emotional disturbances. For example, a student with a conduct disorder may be very disruptive one day and seem normal the next. Consequently, you will need to be tolerant and flexible in your assessments, realizing that on a particular day the disability may pose extreme difficulties for the student.

ASSESSMENT ACCOMMODATIONS

Once you understand how disabilities can interfere with valid assessment, you can take steps to adapt the test or other type of assessment to accommodate the disability. These accommodations lessen the impact of the disability on the answers students provide. They can be grouped into three major categories: adaptations in test construction, test administration, and testing site (Wood, 1992).

Adaptations in Test Directions and Construction

The first component to adapt is the test directions. You can do this for all students, or you can provide a separate set of directions for students with disabilities. Here are some ways to modify test directions:

1. Read written directions aloud, slowly, and give students ample opportunity to ask questions about the directions. Reread directions for each page of questions.
2. Keep directions short and simple.
3. Give examples of how to answer questions.
4. Focus attention by underlining verbs.
5. Provide separate directions for each section of the test.
6. Provide one direction for each sentence (list sentences vertically).

7. Check the students' understanding of the directions.
8. During the test, check student answers to be sure that the students understand the directions.

The general format of the test should be designed to simplify the amount of information that is processed at one time. Accomplish this by leaving plenty of white space on each page so that students are not overwhelmed. The printing should be large, with adequate space between items; this results in a smaller number of items per page. The test should be separated into clearly distinguished short sections, and only one type of question should be on each page. The printing should be dark and clear. If bubble sheets are used for objective items, use larger bubbles. Be sure multiple-choice items list the alternatives vertically, and do not run questions or answers across two pages. Number each page of the test. Some students may be aided by a large sheet of construction paper that they can place under the test or cut out to allow a greater focus on a particular section of the test. If possible, design the format of an adapted test to look as much like the test for other students as possible.

Other accommodations to the format of the test will depend on the type of item, as illustrated in the following examples.

Short-Answer and Essay Items

Students with disabilities may have extreme difficulty with short-answer items because of the organization, reasoning, and writing skills required. For these reasons, complicated essay questions requiring long responses should be avoided. If you use an essay question, be sure students understand terms like *compare, contrast,* and *discuss.* Use a limited number of essay questions, and allow students to use outlines for their answers. Some students may need to record their answer rather than writing it; all students will need to have sufficient time.

Example

>   *Poor:* Compare and contrast the Canadian and United States governments.
>
>   *Improved: Compare* and *contrast* the Canadian and United States governments.
>   **I.** *Compare* by telling how the governments are *alike.* Give two examples.
>   **II.** *Contrast* by telling how the governments are *different.* Give two examples.

If the short-answer question focuses on recall, you can adapt them in ways that will help students to organize their thoughts and not be overwhelmed.

Example (adapted from *Creating a Learning Community at Fowler High School,* 1993)

>   *Poor:*
>   Directions: On your own paper, identify the following quotations. Tell (1) who said it, (2) to whom it was said or if it was a soliloquy, (3) when it was said, and (4) what it means.

But soft, what light through yonder window breaks?
It is the east, and Juliet is the sun.
Arise, fair sun, and kill the envious moon.
(Include a series of several more quotes.)

Improved:
Directions: In the space provided, identify the following for each quotation.

Tell   **1.** Who said it
          2. To whom it was said or if it was a soliloquy
          3. When it was said
          4. What it means

Who said it; to whom it was said   *When it was said*

Juliet   When Tybalt kills Mercutio
Romeo   When Juliet waits for news from Romeo
Paris
Mercutio   The balcony scene
The Prince   When Paris discusses his marriage with Friar

1. But soft, what light through yonder window breaks?
      It is the east, and Juliet is the sun.
      Arise, fair sun, and kill the envious moon.

Who said it   *To whom*   *When*   *What it means*

_____   _____   _____   _____

                              _____   _____

                              _____   _____

Multiple-Choice Items

If the test contains multiple-choice questions, have students circle the correct answer rather than writing the letter of the correct response next to the item or transferring the answer to a separate sheet. Arrange response alternatives vertically, and include no more than four alternatives for each question. Keep the language simple and concise, and avoid wording such as "a and b but not d," or "either a or c," or "none of the above" that weights the item more heavily for reasoning skills. Limit the number of multiple-choice items, and give students with disabilities plenty of time to complete the test. Other students may easily be able to answer one item per minute, but it will take exceptional students longer. Basically, you need to follow the suggestions listed in Chapter 6 and realize that poorly constructed and formatted items are likely to be more detrimental to students with disabilities.

Binary-Choice Items
True/false and other binary-choice items need to be stated clearly and concisely. Answers should be circled. Negatively stated items should be avoided. Sometimes students are asked to change false items to make them true, but this is not recommended for students with disabilities. Limit the number of items to from ten to fifteen.

Completion Items
These items can be modified to reduce the student's dependence on structured recall by providing word banks that accompany the items. The word bank is a list of possible answers that reduces dependence on memory. The list can be printed on a separate sheet of paper so that the student can move it up and down on the right side of the page. Also, provide large blanks for students with motor control difficulties.

Performance-Based Assessments
The first accommodation to performance-based assessments may need to be in the directions. Students with disabilities need directions that clearly specify what is expected, with examples, and a reasonable time frame. Because these assessments involve thinking and application skills, it is important to be certain that students with disabilities are able to perform the skills required. The steps may need to be clearly delineated. Obviously, if some aspect of the performance requires physical skills or coordination that the disability prevents or makes difficult, assistance will need to be provided. If the performance requires group participation, you will need to closely monitor the interactions.

Portfolios
In some ways this type of assessment is ideal for students with disabilities because the assignments and products can be individualized to show progress. This means that you may need to adapt the portfolio requirements to fit well with what the student is capable of doing. In the portfolio you could include your reflection of how the student made progress despite the presence of the disability to demonstrate how the student was responsible for success.

Adaptations in Test Administration

Adaptations during test administration involve changes in procedures that lessen the negative effect of disabilities while the student is taking the test. Most of these procedural accommodations depend on the nature of the disability or difficulty, as summarized in Figure 12.5 on page 340, and are based on common sense. For example, if the student has a visual problem, you need to give directions orally and check carefully to determine if students have understood the questions. For students who are hindered by time constraints, provide breaks and make sure students have sufficient time to complete the test.

FIGURE 12.5   Adaptations in Test Administration

Disability or Problem	Adaptations
Poor comprehension	1. Give test directions both orally and in written form. 2. Double check student understanding. 3. Avoid long talks before the test. 4. Allow students to tape-record responses to essay questions or the entire test. 5. Correct open-ended responses for content only and not for spelling or grammar. 6. Provide examples of expected correct responses. 7. Remind students to check for unanswered questions. 8. Allow the use of multiplication tables or calculators for math tests. 9. Read the test aloud for students with reading comprehension difficulties. 10. Give an outline for essay question responses. 11. Give students an audio recording of instructions and questions. 12. Use objective items.
Auditory difficulties	1. Use written rather than oral questions. 2. Go slowly for oral tests, enunciating and sounding out distinctly. 3. Seat students in a quiet place for testing. 4. Stress the importance of being quiet to all students.
Visual difficulties	1. Give directions orally as well as in written form. 2. Give exam orally or tape-recorded on audiocassette. 3. Allow students to take the test orally. 4. Seat the student away from visual distractions (e.g., windows and doors). Use a carrel or place desk facing wall. 5. Avoid having other students turn in papers during the test. 6. Meet classroom visitors at the door and talk in the hallway.
Time constraint difficulties	1. Allow more than enough time to complete the test. 2. Provide breaks during lengthy tests. 3. Give half the test one day, half the second day. 4. Avoid timed tests. 5. Give students with slow writing skills oral or tape-recorded tests.
Anxiety	1. Avoid adding pressure by admonishing students to "Hurry and get finished" or by saying "This test will determine your final grade." 2. Do not threaten to use test results to punish students. 3. Do not threaten to use tests to punish students for poor behavior. 4. Give a practice test or practice items. 5. Allow students to retest if needed. 6. Do not threaten dire consequences if students do not do well. 7. Emphasize internal attributions for previous work. 8. Avoid having a few major tests; give many smaller tests. 9. Avoid norm-referenced testing; use criterion-referenced tests.
Embarrassment	1. Make the modified test closely resemble the regular test; use the same cover sheet. 2. Avoid calling attention to mainstreamed students as you help them. 3. Monitor all students the same way. 4. Do not give mainstreamed students special attention when handing out the test. 5. Confer with students privately to work out accommodations for testing. 6. Do not single out mainstreamed students when returning tests.
Variability of behavior	1. Allow retesting. 2. Allow student to reschedule testing for another day. 3. Monitor closely to determine if behavior is preventing best work.

Source: Adapted from Wood, Judith, *Adapting instruction for mainstreamed and at-risk students*, 2nd ed., copyright © 1992, pp. 333–334. Adapted by permisison of Prentice-Hall, Upper Saddle River, New Jersey.

In general, it is best to place a Testing—Do Not Disturb sign on your classroom door to discourage visitors and other distractions. You will need to monitor these students closely as they take the test, and encourage them to ask questions. It is also helpful to encourage them to use dark paper to underline the items they are currently working on (Lazzari & Wood, 1994).

Adaptations in Testing Site

You may find it necessary to allow students with disabilities to take the test in a different location than the regular classroom. This alternative test site is often the resource room in the school or some other room that is quiet with fewer distractions. As long as someone can monitor the testing, the student will have more opportunities to ask questions and feel less embarrassed when asking for clarification or further explanation. You will want to work out the details of using an alternate testing site with the special education teacher.

If you are unsure about how you should accommodate students who are mainstreamed for assessment, check with the special education teacher in your school. This individual can help you more fully understand the strengths and limitations of each student, as well as the appropriateness of specific adaptations.

GRADING AND REPORTING ACCOMMODATIONS

The purpose of grading is to provide an accurate indication of what students have learned. For students who are mainstreamed, it is necessary to consider some adaptations to the grading procedures used for all students to make sure that student disabilities do not unduly influence the determination of the grade. This may present a dilemma for teachers. On the one hand, is it fair to use different grading standards and procedures for some students? On the other hand, is it fair to possibly penalize students by forcing an existing grading scheme on them that may have detrimental impacts? The ideal solution would be to keep the grading system for mainstreamed students the same as what is used for other students, and be sure that appropriate accommodations have been made in the assessment strategies to ensure that the information on which the grade is determined is not adversely affected by the disability. However, depending on the student's IEP, it may be necessary to adapt the grading system that is used.

Grading Accommodations

Several types of grading accommodations are appropriate for mainstreamed students (Mehring, 1995). These include IEP grading, shared grading, and contract grading.

IEP Grading

The IEP grading system bases grades on the achievement of the goals and objectives stated in the student's IEP. The criteria needed to obtain satisfactory progress are stated in the IEP. It is problematic, however, to translate success in reaching IEP objectives to grades. One approach is to use the school district's performance standards to determine grades. For example, if the student has performed at the 90 percent proficiency level, as required by the IEP to demonstrate competence, and 90 percent translates to a B letter grade, then the student is assigned a B for that assessment. Another approach is to review the criteria in the IEP and match levels of performance with what other students need to demonstrate for different grades. If you decide, for instance, that the level of mastery a mainstreamed student demonstrates by achieving but not exceeding all IEP objectives is about the same level as that demonstrated by other students receiving Cs, then the grade for the mainstreamed student would also be a C. If the student exceeded stated IEP objectives, then a B or A may be appropriate.

Because the goal of mainstreaming is to make the educational experience of students with disabilities like other students, it is best if the grading procedures reflect the same criteria. You should avoid a process whereby the grade is determined merely on the percentage of IEP objectives obtained because there is a tendency to inadvertently set low or easier objectives to help students obtain good grades (Cohen, 1983).

Shared Grading

In shared grading, the regular classroom and special education or resource room teachers determine the grade together. The weight that each teacher provides for the grade should be agreed on at the beginning of the marking period. This usually reflects the extent to which each teacher is responsible for different areas of learning. Typically, the classroom teacher will have the most influence on the grades of a mainstreamed student.

One advantage to this type of grading is that the special education or resource room teacher may be able to provide some insight that would explain some bad grades and other mitigating circumstances related to the student's disability. Using this team approach also helps the classroom teacher determine appropriate criteria and standards for grading.

Contracting

A contract is a written agreement between the regular classroom teacher and the student that specifies the nature of the work that the student must complet to achieve a particular grade. Teachers frequently use contracts for mainstreamed students because they can integrate IEP objectives and clearly state for the student and parents the type and quality of work to be completed. For older students, the contract should include options for achieving different grades. Contracts for elementary level students should be simpler, with more general outcomes at a single level, as illustrated in Figure 12.6. Several components should be included in a contract, such as the following:

- A description of the work to be completed
- A description of criteria by which work will be evaluated
- Signatures of the student, teacher, and other involved parties
- A time line for completion of the work

FIGURE 12.6   Sample Contract for Elementary-Level Students

My Contract

If I . . .

- take my belongings from my backpack and put them in my desk without being asked,
- come to my reading group the first time it is called,
- clean off my desk after snack and put all the garbage in the trash can,
- raise my hand each time I want to answer, and
- put all my finished papers in the "done" basket before lunch

. . . then I will receive a "plus" for the morning's work.

If I . . .

- line up on the playground the first time the whistle is blown,
- put all the classroom supplies back in the supply boxes after project time,
- put all my finished papers in the "done" basket before I go home,
- put my homework papers in my portfolio to take home, and
- put my belongings in my backpack, get my coat from the cubby, and line up before my bus is called

. . . then I will receive a "plus" for the afternoon's work.

_____   _____
Student   Teacher

                              _____
                              Date

Source: Wood, Judith, *Adapting instruction for mainstreamed and at-risk students*, 2nd ed., copyright © 1992, p. 356. Adapted by permission of Prentice-Hall, Upper Saddle River, New Jersey.

Reporting Accommodations

Regardless of the grading system that you employ, it will probably be necessary to supplement the regular progress report with additional information. This is typically done as a checklist or a narrative summary that interprets achievement in light of the student's disability. A checklist is convenient for showing progress in developmentally sequenced courses and can easily integrate IEP with course objectives to give a more complete report. The checklist states the objectives and the teacher indicates if each has been mastered or needs further work.

A narrative summary helps you to give the student a still more personalized evaluation. Although such a report takes some time, it more fully explains why the teacher believes the student demonstrated certain skills, which skills were not mastered, and which need special attention. The narrative can also be used to report on behavioral performance, emotions, and interpersonal skills, as well as academic performance. Specific incidents or examples can be described. The following is an example of a progress report for an eighth-grade student with a learning disability (Mehring, 1995, p. 17). Notice that the teacher has indicated areas of improvement, accommodations (typing), and areas that will be stressed in the future.

> *Alphonso has improved his ability to recognize and correct spelling errors. He has mastered the recognition and capitalization of proper nouns, names, titles, and buildings. He is not yet consistent in his capitalization of cities. Punctuation, especially the use of commas, is also an area in which Alphonso needs improvement. He has been using the computer to prepare drafts of his written products. This has made it easier for him to edit since his handwriting is laborious and illegible at times. The overall quality and length of his creative writings has improved significantly since the last reporting period. We will continue to focus on capitalization and punctuation throughout the next grading period. In addition, we will begin working on recognizing and correcting sentence problems (fragments, run-ons, unclear pronoun reference, and awkward sentences).*

By focusing a supplemental progress report on the learning process, students will have a better idea how they need to change to improve their performance. Students and parents need to know if a specific approach to learning needs to be modified or if there is something that needs to be further investigated.

SUMMARY

The purpose of this chapter was to introduce you to the assessment adaptations needed to accommodate mainstreamed students who have a disability. Overall, suggestions made in other chapters apply to mainstreamed students, but you need to keep some additional considerations in mind. In general, it is important to make sure that a student's disability does not influence his or her performance on tests and other types of assessments. Major points in the chapter include the following:

- Legal mandates in PL 94-142 require educational experiences, including assessment, to take place in the least restrictive environment.
- Regular classroom teachers are responsible for gathering information to identify students for special education services.
- The evaluation of students for identification must be nondiscriminatory—in the student's native language and not racially or culturally biased.
- Teacher observation is a major component in identification and writing the student's IEP.
- Teachers are responsible for setting individualized learning targets with appropriate assessments.
- Teachers are responsible for providing specific assessment information for referral and possible identification.
- Procedures are implemented to make it difficult to identify a student for special education services.
- Students are identified as having one or more educational disabilities, based in part on careful teacher observation.
- Teachers are responsible for assessing the adaptive behaviors of students referred and identified as having mental retardation.

- Comprehension difficulties require adaptations in test directions.
- Auditory and visual difficulties require a minimum of distractions.
- Time constraint difficulties require longer testing time and frequent breaks in testing.
- Anxiety and embarrassment need to be minimized for mainstreamed students.
- The behavior of students with disabilities varies from day to day; this variation needs to be considered when observing and evaluating student behavior.
- Adaptations may need to be made to test directions, the format of the test, and the construction of different types of items.
- Adaptations may be needed during test administration and to the testing site.
- Grading students who are mainstreamed needs to include consideration of IEP objectives, opinions of other teachers working with the student, and contracting.
- Supplemental reports and feedback are helpful for focusing attention on IEP and learning process objectives.

SELF-INSTRUCTIONAL REVIEW EXERCISES

1. According to PL 94-142, what are the two essential responsibilities of regular classroom teachers concerning the assessment of students who are mainstreamed?

2. Indicate whether each of the following statements represents nondiscriminatory assessment (Y for yes, N for no):

   a. A single procedure may be used for identification.
   b. Assessment is conducted by a multidisciplinary team.
   c. Assessments are conducted in English.
   d. The disability may not affect the scores students receive.
   e. Racial and cultural discrimination must be avoided.

3. Read the following scenario and indicate whether the teacher has properly followed the steps necessary to refer a student for identification.

   Mrs. Albert was immediately suspicious of Jane, thinking that she might have a learning disability. Jane did not achieve very well on written tests and seemed to have trouble concentrating. She was also distracted very easily. Mrs. Albert tried Jane in another reading group, but this did not seem to help. After looking at Jane's previous test scores, Mrs. Albert decided to refer her for identification.

4. Indicate whether each of the descriptions listed is characteristic of students with mental retardation (MR), emotional disturbance (ED), sensory impairment (SI), physical impairment (PI), or learning disability (LD).

   a. diabetes
   b. language deficit
   c. discrepancy between ability and achievement
   d. poor adaptive behaviors
   e. poor eyesight
   f. slow learning

5. Indicate whether each of the difficulties listed is characteristic of students with comprehension difficulties (CD), sensory difficulties (SD), time constraint difficulties (TCD), anxiety (A), embarrassment (E), or variability of behavior (VB).

   a. gets sequence of steps wrong
   b. worries excessively about performance
   c. hands in an incomplete test with other students
   d. has trouble one day finishing a test, no trouble the next day
   e. takes longer to complete the test

6. Indicate whether each of the following test administration adaptations would be considered good practice (Y for yes, N for no).

   a. making tests with fewer items
   b. closely monitoring students while they are taking a test
   c. modifying the test
   d. giving special attention when handing out the test
   e. using norm-referenced testing
   f. emphasizing internal attributions
   g. giving practice tests
   h. allowing students to take a written test orally
   i. using objective rather than essay items
   j. using normal seating arrangements
   k. checking student understanding of directions

7. Read the following scenario and indicate what was correct and what was incorrect or lacking in the teacher's assessment accommodations.

   Mr. Parvin was careful to read all the directions aloud, and he gave examples of how the students should answer each item. He prepared a separate set of directions for his mainstreamed students. He designed the test to make sure as many questions as possible were included on each page. He underlined key words in the short-answer questions and wrote objective items so that the students corrected wrong answers. Mr. Parvin did not permit questions once students began the test. He told students that they had to complete the test in thirty minutes, and he placed a sign on the door indicating that testing was taking place.

8. Ms. Rameriz has a student with a learning disability in her classroom. His name is Tyron. Ms. Rameriz has decided to use a contract grading procedure, and she wants to be able to report progress on the contract to Tyron's parents. How would Ms. Rameriz begin to develop her contract, and how would she report progress to his parents?

ANSWERS TO SELF-INSTRUCTIONAL REVIEW EXERCISES

1. Gathering information for identification and implementing the IEP.

2. a. N, b. Y, c. N, d. Y, e. Y.

3. Mrs. Albert did some things right but in general did not do enough to justify formal referral. She seems to have targeted behaviors that are characteristic of students with a learning disability, and she did try one instructional intervention. However, more instructional interventions are needed to be sure that the problems could not be ameliorated in the class without referral. There is no indication that the teacher made any more structured, diagnostic assessments, and there is no evidence of any type of prereferral review. A serious oversight is that Mrs. Albert has not requested that outsiders review the situation.

4. a. PI, b. LD, c. LD, d. MR, e. SI, f. none.

5. a. CD, b. A, c. E, d. VB, e. TCD.

6. a. N, b. Y, c. Y, d. N, e. N, f. Y, g. Y, h. Y, i. Y, j. N, k. Y.

7. Correct procedures included reading the directions aloud, giving examples, underlining key words, and placing a sign on the door. Incorrect procedures, from an adaptation perspective, included giving students with disabilities a separate set of directions (which may cause embarrassment), putting too much on each page of the test, asking students to correct wrong answers for objective items, not permitting questions during the test, and giving students what seems like a short time limit.

8. It would be best to begin with a clear indication of the work to be completed and how different grades will be assigned. A specific time line for completing the work should be included. Signatures of the student and parents are needed to assure that all understand the contract. The teacher's report should not simply indicate what grades are achieved, but it should include some personalized comments and suggestions.

SUGGESTIONS FOR ACTION RESEARCH

1. Interview two or three regular classroom teachers about the accommodations they make for students who are mainstreamed in the classes. Ask about their experience in gathering information for identification and setting learning targets, as well as about the assessment accommodations they have made. Compare their responses to suggestions in the chapter.
2. Interview two special education teachers. Ask them what they believe regular classroom teachers need to know to accommodate students who are mainstreamed. In their work with regular classroom teachers, what do they see as the teachers' greatest weaknesses when making assessment accommodations?
3. Interview school division central office personnel who are responsible for mainstreamed students. What is the district's approach toward mainstreaming? What kind of support is provided for the teachers?
4. In a team with one or two other students, devise a plan for how you would accommodate the assessment of one or two actual students who have been mainstreamed. You will need as much information about the students as possible, and it would be best if you could observe the students. Once the plan is complete, review it with the students' teacher(s) for feedback and suggestions.

13

ADMINISTERING AND INTERPRETING STANDARDIZED TESTS

Standardized testing was considered in Chapter 4 in the context of instructional planning. In that chapter, we reviewed different types of standardized tests and scores to better understand students' initial levels of achievement and aptitude, strengths and weaknesses, and deficiencies, in order to establish learning targets

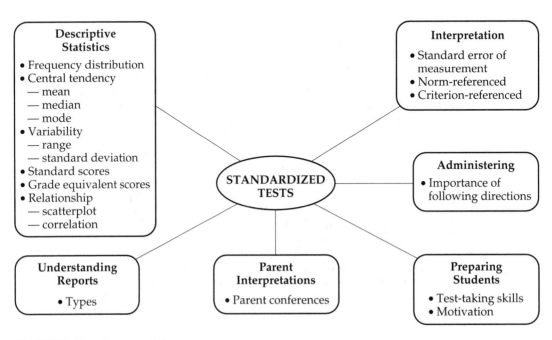

CHAPTER 13   Concept Map

and plan an effective instructional program. In this chapter, we are concerned with other important uses of standardized tests by classroom teachers, including year-to-year program evaluation and interpreting standardized test scores to parents. We will also discuss your role in administering standardized tests. First, however, we need to review the statistical terms and numerical indices that are commonly used in creating and reporting standardized test scores. Although the term *statistics* may create some anxiety, we will deal with a conceptual understanding that does not require advanced mathematical calculations.

FUNDAMENTAL DESCRIPTIVE STATISTICS

Descriptive statistics are used to describe or summarize a larger number of scores. The nature of the description can be in the form of a single number, like an average score, a table of scores, or a graph. You have seen and read many of these kinds of descriptions (e.g., the average rainfall for a month, the median price of new homes, a baseball batting average). Descriptive statistics efficiently portray important features of a group of scores to convey information that is essential for understanding what the scores mean. For standardized tests, descriptive statistics are used as the basis for establishing, reporting, and interpreting scores.

Frequency Distributions

The first step in understanding important characteristics of a large set of scores is to organize the scores into a frequency distribution. This distribution simply indicates the number of students who obtained different scores on the test. In a *simple frequency distribution*, the scores are ranked, from highest to lowest, and the number of students obtaining each score is indicated. If the scores are organized into intervals, a *grouped frequency distribution* is used. Suppose, for example, that a test had eighty items. Figure 13.1 on page 350 illustrates the scores received by twenty students, as well as simple and grouped frequency distributions that show the number of students obtaining each score or interval of scores.

Often the scores are presented graphically as a frequency polygon or histogram to more easily explain important features (Figures 13.2a and 13.2b on page 351). The *frequency polygon* is a line graph, which is formed by connecting the highest frequencies of each score. The *histogram* is a bar graph, which is formed by using rectangular columns.

For a relatively small number of scores, a frequency polygon will usually be jagged, as shown in Figure 13.2a. For a large number of scores and test items, the line will look more like a smooth curve. The nature of the curve can usually be described as being *normal, positively skewed, negatively skewed*, or *flat*. Typically, for standardized tests, the curve will very closely approximate a normal distribution (a symmetrical, bell-shaped curve) for a large group of students (e.g., for the norming group). If the distribution is *positively skewed*, most of the scores are

FIGURE 13.1   Frequency Distributions of Test Scores

Student	Score	Simple Frequency Distribution		Grouped Frequency Distribution	
		Score	*f*	Interval	*f*
Austin	96				
Tyler	94	96	1	92–96	3
Tracey	92	94	1	86–91	4
Karon	90	92	1	80–85	7
Hannah	90	90	2	74–79	3
Lanie	86	86	2	68–73	3
Allyson	86	84	3		
Felix	84	80	4		
Tryon	84	78	1		
Freya	84	74	2		
Mike	80	70	2		
Mark	80	68	1		
Ann	80				
Kristen	80				
Laura	78				
Megan	74				
Michelle	74				
Kathryn	70				
Don	70				
Jim	68				

piled up at the lower end and there are just a few high scores. For a *negatively skewed* distribution it is just the opposite—most of the scores are high with few low scores. In a flat distribution, each score is obtained with about the same frequency. Figures 13.3a–13.3d on page 352 illustrate each of these types of curves.

Measures of Central Tendency

A measure of central tendency is a single number that is calculated to represent the average or typical score in the distribution. There are three measures of central tendency commonly used in education: the mean, median, and mode. The *mean* is the arithmetic average. It is calculated by adding all the scores in the distribution and then dividing that sum by the number of scores. It is represented by $\overline{X}$ or M. For the distribution of scores in Figure 13.1 the mean is 82.

$$\overline{X} \;=\; \frac{\Sigma X}{N}$$

where

$\overline{X}$ = the mean
Σ = the sum of (indicates that all scores are added)
X = each individual score
N = total number of scores

for Figure 13.1:

$$\overline{X} \;=\; \frac{1,640}{20}$$

$$\overline{X} \;=\; 82$$

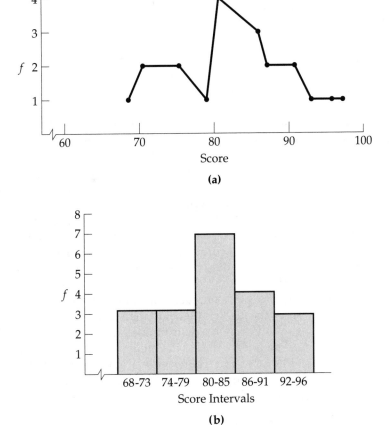

(a)

(b)

FIGURE 13.2   Frequency Polygon (a) and Histogram (b) of Scores from Figure 13.1

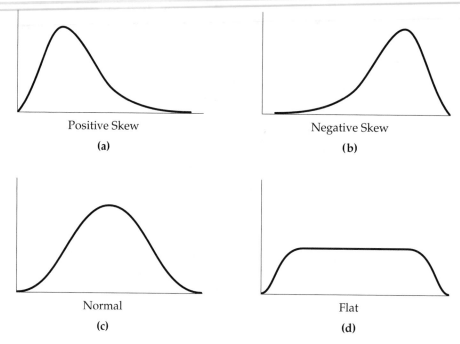

Positive Skew

(a)

Negative Skew

(b)

Normal

(c)

Flat

(d)

FIGURE 13.3   Types of Frequency Distributions

The *median*, represented by *mdn*, is the midpoint, or middle, of a distribution of scores. In other words, 50 percent of the scores are below the median, and 50 percent of the scores are above the median. Thus, the median score is at the 50th percentile. The median is found by rank ordering all the scores, including each score even if it occurs more than once, and locating the score that has the same number of scores above and below it. For our hypothetical distribution, the median is 82 (84 + 80/2; for an uneven number of scores it will be a single existing score).

The *mode* is simply the score in the distribution that occurs most frequently. In our distribution, more students scored an 80 than any other score, so 80 is the mode. It is possible to have more than one mode; in fact, in education, *bimodal distributions* are fairly common.

In a normal distribution, the mean, median, and mode are the same. In a positively skewed distribution, the mean is higher than the median (hence skewed positively), and in a negatively skewed distribution, the mean is lower than the median. This is because the mean, unlike the median, is calculated by taking the value of every score into account. Therefore extreme values affect the mean, whereas the median is not affected by an unusual high or low score.

Measures of Variability

A second type of statistic that is essential in describing a set of scores is a measure of variability. Measures of variability, or dispersion, indicate how much the scores spread out from the mean. If the scores are bunched together close to the mean, then there is little or a small amount of variability. A large or great amount of variability is characteristic of a distribution in which the scores are spread way out from the mean. Two distributions with the same mean can have very different variability, as illustrated in Figure 13.4.

To more precisely indicate the variability, two measures are typically used, the range and standard deviation. The *range* is simply the difference between the highest and lowest score in the distribution (in our example 28; 96 – 68). This is an easily calculated but crude index of variability, primarily because extreme high or low scores result in a range that indicates more variability than is actually present.

A more complicated but much more precise measure of variability is standard deviation. The *standard deviation (SD)* is a number that indicates the *average* deviation of the scores from the mean. It is calculated by employing a formula that looks difficult but is relatively straightforward. These are the essential steps:

1. Calculate the mean of the distribution.
2. Calculate the difference each score is from the mean (these are called deviation scores).
3. Square each difference score (this makes all the deviation scores positive).
4. Add the squared difference scores.
5. Divide by the total number of scores in the distribution.
6. Calculate the square root of the result of step 5.

These steps are illustrated with our hypothetical set of test scores in Figure 13.5 on page 354. Essentially, you simply calculate the squared deviation scores, find the *average* squared deviation score, and then take the square root to return to the original unit of measurement. In this distribution, one standard deviation is equal to 7.92. Unless you are using a normative grading procedure, standard deviation is not very helpful for classroom testing. However, because of the relationship between standard deviation and the normal curve, it is fundamental to understanding standardized test scores.

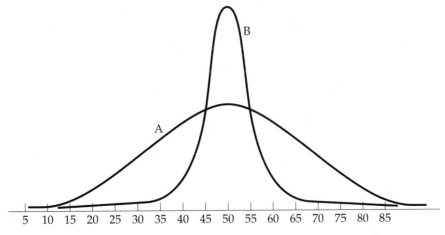

FIGURE 13.4 Distributions with the Same Mean, Different Variability

FIGURE 13.5   Steps in Calculating Standard Deviation

Score	(1) Deviation Score	(2) Deviation Score Squared	(3) Squared Deviation Scores Added	(4) Added Scores Divided by N	(5) Square Root
96	96–82=14	14×14=196	196		
94	94–82=12	12×12=144	+144		
92	92–82=10	10×10=100	+100		
90	90–82=8	8×8=64	+ 64		
90	90–82=8	8×8=64	+ 64		
86	86–82=4	4×4=16	+ 16		
86	86–82=4	4×4=16	+ 16		
84	84–82=2	2×2=4	+ 4		
84	84–82=2	2×2=4	+ 4		
84	84–82=2	2×2=4	+ 4		
80	80–82=–2	–2×–2=4	+ 4		
80	80–82=–2	–2×–2=4	+ 4		
80	80–82=–2	–2×–2=4	+ 4		
80	80–82=–2	–2×–2=4	+ 4		
78	78–82=–4	–4×–4=16	+ 16		
74	74–82=–8	–8×–8=64	+ 64		
74	74–82=–8	–8×–8=64	+ 64		
70	70–82=–12	–12×–12=144	+144		
70	70–82=–12	–12×–12=144	+144		
68	68–82=–14	–14×–14=196	$\underline{+196}$ = 1,256	1,256/20=62.8	$\sqrt{62.8}$=7.92

With a standardized test, the frequency distribution of raw scores for the norming group will usually be distributed in an approximately normal fashion. In a normal distribution, the meaning of the term *one standard deviation* is the same in regard to percentile rank, regardless of the actual value of standard deviation for that distribution. Thus, $+1SD$ is always at the 84th percentile, $+2SD$ is at the 98th percentile, $-1SD$ is at the 16th percentile, and $-2SD$ is at the 2nd percentile in every normal distribution. This property makes it possible to compare student scores to the norm group distribution in terms of percentile rank and to compare relative standing on different tests. For instance, suppose a norm group took a standardized test, and on the basis of their performance a raw score of 26 items answered correctly was one standard deviation above the mean for the norm group (84th percentile). When a student in your class gets the same number of items correct (26), the percentile reported is the 84th. Obviously, if the norm group was different and 26 items turned out to be at $+2SD$, then the student's score would be reported at the 98th percentile. You would also know that a score at one standard deviation on one test is the same in terms of relative standing as one standard deviation on another test. Most importantly for standardized tests, standard deviation is used to compute standard scores and other statistics that are used for interpretation and analysis.

Standard and Grade Equivalent Scores

Standard scores were introduced in Chapter 4; we will now look at how these scores are determined. Because standardized tests typically report both raw and standard scores, you will need this knowledge to understand and accurately interpret the meaning of the reports. The term *standard* does not mean a specific level of performance or expectation. Rather, it refers to the standard normal curve as the basis for interpretation.

z-Score

The simplest and most easily calculated standard score is the z-score, which indicates how far a score lies above or below the mean in standard deviation units. Since $1SD = 1$, a z-score of 1 is one standard deviation unit above the mean. The formula for computing z-scores is relatively straightforward if you know the value of one standard deviation:

$$z\text{-score} = \frac{X - \overline{X}}{SD}$$

where

$$
\begin{aligned}
X &= \text{any raw score} \\
\overline{X} &= \text{mean of the raw scores} \\
SD &= \text{standard deviation of the raw score distribution}
\end{aligned}
$$

For example, a z-score for 90 in our hypothetical distribution would be 1.01 (90 – 82/7.92). If the raw score is less than the mean, the z-score will be negative (e.g., the z-score for 70 in our distribution of twenty students would be –1.01 (70 – 82/7.92).

Using the z-score formula with a set of raw scores from a test will result in what is called a *linear transformation*. This means that the distribution of z-scores will be identical to the distribution of raw scores. It is also possible to *normalize* the raw score distribution when converting to z-scores. This transforms the distribution to a normal one, regardless of what the raw score distribution looked like. If the raw score distribution is normal, then using the formula will also result in a normal distribution of z-scores. For most standardized tests, the standard scores are normalized. Thus, a z-score of 1 is at the 84th percentile, a z-score of 2 is at the 98th percentile, and so forth.

Because the z-score distribution has a standard deviation equal to 1, these scores can easily be transformed to other standard scores that will only have positive values (e.g., T-scores, NCEs, stanines, SAT scores).

T-Score

T-scores are the same as z-scores except the T-score distribution has a different mean, 50, and a different standard deviation, 10. T-scores are obtained by using a simple formula to convert from z-scores:

$$T\text{-score} = 50 + 10(z)$$

Thus, a T-score of 60 is the same as a z-score of 1; both are at the 84th percentile. Like z-scores, T-scores may be straight linear transformations from the raw score distribution, or normalized.

Normal Curve Equivalent

The normal curve equivalent (NCE) is a normalized standard score that has a mean of 50 and a standard deviation of 21.06. The reason for selecting 50 for the mean and 21.06 for the standard deviation was so that NCE scores, like percentiles, would range from 1 to 99. The percentiles of 1, 50, and 99 are equivalent to NCEs of 1, 50, and 99. However, at other points on the scale, NCEs are not the same as percentiles. For example:

NCE	Percentile
90	97
75	88
25	12
10	3

It is fairly easy to confuse NCEs with percentiles because they convert to the same range of scores (1–99), especially for someone who is not familiar with measurement principles. Thus, you will need to be careful when explaining what NCEs mean to parents. So why are NCEs used at all? Because they are standard scores (percentiles are not), they can, like other standard scores, be used for research and evaluation purposes. For example, Chapter 1 programs have frequently used NCEs to report growth and improvement.

Stanines

These types of standard scores were discussed in Chapter 4. The term *stanine* is derived from the fact that the normal curve is divided into nine parts (standard nines). The parts are constructed so that each stanine, except 1 and 9, has a width equal to one half a standard deviation. Each stanine covers a specific area of the normal curve in terms of percentiles:

Stanine	Percentile Rank
9	96 or higher
8	89 to 95
7	77 to 88
6	60 to 76
5	40 to 59
4	23 to 39
3	11 to 22
2	4 to 10
1	Below 4

Notice that there is a different percentage of scores in stanines 5, 6, 7, 8, and 9. This is because the width of the stanine is the same in relation to the curve of the normal distribution. Another way you can think about stanines is that they have a mean of 5, with a standard deviation of 2. Because they are normalized, stanines from conceptually similar but different tests can be compared, such as aptitude and achievement tests. Remember that meaningful differences in performance are indicated when the scores differ by at least two stanines.

Developmental Standard Score

Most standardized tests use what is called a *developmental standard score* (also called the *level*, *scale*, or *growth* score) to show year-to-year progress in achievement and to compare different levels of the same test. Each test publisher uses a different scale, ranging between 0 and 999. Higher scores are associated with higher grade levels. For example, the Iowa Test of Basic Skills uses a score of 200 to indicate the median performance of students in the fourth grade, 150 as the median for first graders, and 250 as the median for eighth graders. The complete scale, across grade levels, is as follows:

Grade:	K	1	2	3	4	5	6	7	8	9
SS:	130	150	168	185	200	214	227	239	250	260

Thus, the median performance for third graders is assigned a score of 185, and so on. *The Comprehensive Tests of Basic Skills*, Fourth Edition, uses a mean score of 707 for fourth-grade reading and 722 for fifth-grade reading. These median and mean scores, and associated standard deviations, provide anchors against which a student's progress can be compared. This makes it possible to use developmental standard scores to plot performance from year to year. However, because they are more abstract than other scores, they are relatively difficult to interpret.

Deviation IQ and Standard Age Scores

For many years, the results of IQ and general ability testing have been reported on a scale that has a mean of 100 and a standard deviation of 15 or 16. Originally, IQ scores were actual intelligent quotients, calculated by dividing mental age by chronological age and multiplying this ratio by 100. Today, IQ scores are determined like other derived standard scores. For each age group in a norming sample, the raw scores are converted to z-scores, then to deviation IQ scores by multiplying the z-score by 15 or 16 and adding that product to 100. Most test publishers refer to the student's "ability," "aptitude," or to "standard age" scores rather than IQ because *intelligence* today refers to many other traits besides academic ability or reasoning. Some of these tests have a standard deviation as small as 12 or as large as 20. This is one reason that it is inappropriate to compare the scores of two individuals who have taken different tests.

Other Standard Scores

The advantage of standard scores—being able to convert raw scores to scores directly related to the normal curve and percentile rank—is also a disadvantage from the standpoint that there are so many different standard scores. Some test publishers use unique standard scores. Once you understand the nature of the scores, you can readily interpret the results. But you may need to look in the technical manual of the test to know what the publisher has assigned as the mean and standard deviation.

Grade Equivalents

Grade equivalents (GEs) were also introduced in Chapter 4. These scores are much like developmental scale scores, except that the unit is expressed in grade levels and months. As pointed out earlier, GEs are only useful in indicating growth or progress; they should not be used for grade placement. In addition, most GEs are determined by interpolation. That is, a test may be given to beginning fourth graders, and the median score for that group will be assigned a grade equivalent of 4.0. The same test might be given to a beginning group of fifth graders, with the median score given a GE of 5.0. No other tests are given, but scores are still reported in months (e.g., 4.2 or 4.8). If the students in grades 4, month 2, and month 8 were not given the test, how was the *median* of each group determined? The answer is that the medians were interpolated, estimated, from existing scores. This means that the reported scores of, say, 4.1 or 4.6, are only estimates. For some tests, GEs are extrapolated beyond the grade levels actually tested. Thus, a test may be given to students in grades 3, 4, and 5, but GEs may range from 2.0 to 7.0 and beyond. Extrapolated scores are less accurate than interpolated ones, and they should be interpreted cautiously.

Figure 13.6 shows a normal distribution with the corresponding standard deviation units, percentiles, and selected standard scores.

Measures of Relationship

It is often helpful, even necessary, to know the degree to which two scores from different measures are related. Typically, this degree of relationship is estimated by what is called a *correlation coefficient*. Correlations are reported in standardized test technical manuals for validity and reliability. Also, an important principle in interpreting test scores, standard error of measurement, is determined from correlation.

Scatterplot

The *scatterplot*, or *scattergram*, is a graphic representation of relationship. When used in education, a scatterplot can give you a descriptive picture of relationship by forming a visual array of the intersections of students' scores on two measures. As illustrated in Figure 13.7 on page 360, each measure is rank-ordered from lowest to highest on a different axis. The two scores from each student are used to establish a point of intersection. When this is completed for all students, a pattern is formed that provides a general indication of the direction and strength of the relationship. The direction of the pattern indicates whether there is a positive, a negative, a curvilinear, or no relationship. It is positive if scores on one variable increase with increases in the other scores, and it is negative (inverse) if scores on one variable increase as scores on the other measure decrease. If the pattern looks like a U shape, it is curvilinear; and if it is a straight line or no particular pattern at all, there is little if any relationship.

Scatterplots help to identify intersections that are not typical, which lower the correlation coefficient, and to identify curvilinear relationships. However, these scatterplots are rarely reported in standardized test manuals. Typically, these manuals report the correlation coefficients.

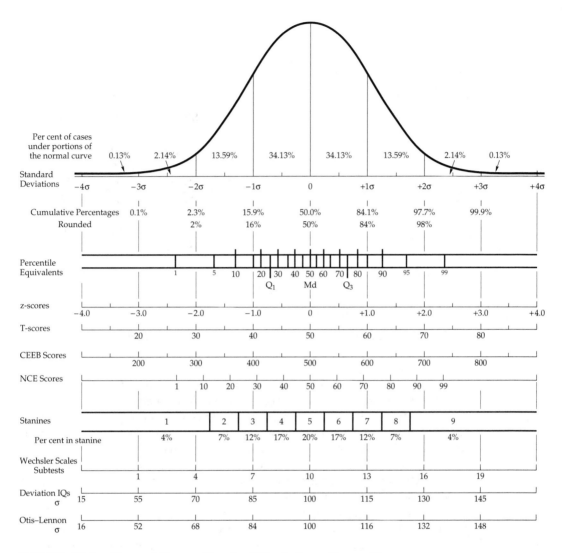

FIGURE 13.6   Normal Curve, Standard Deviations, Percentiles, and Selected Standard Scores.

Source: Test Service Notebook No. 148, p. 2. Used courtesy of The Psychological Corporation. Harcourt Brace Jovanovich, Publishers.

Correlation Coefficients

The *correlation coefficient* is a number that is calculated to represent the direction and strength of the relationship. The number ranges between –1 and +1. A high positive value (e.g., +.85 or +.90) indicates a high positive relationship, a low negative correlation (e.g., –.10 or –.25) represents a low negative relationship, and so forth. The *strength* of the relationship is independent from the *direction*. Thus, a positive or neg-

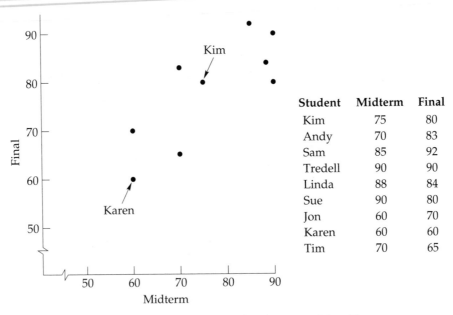

Student	Midterm	Final
Kim	75	80
Andy	70	83
Sam	85	92
Tredell	90	90
Linda	88	84
Sue	90	80
Jon	60	70
Karen	60	60
Tim	70	65

FIGURE 13.7   Scatterplot of Relationship between Two Tests

ative value indicates direction, while the value of the correlation, from 0 to 1 or from 0 to – 1, determines strength. A perfect correlation is designated by either +1 or –1. As the value approaches these perfect correlations it becomes stronger, or higher. That is, a correlation is stronger as it changes from .2 to .5 to .6, and also as it changes from –.2 to –.5 to –.6. A correlation of –.8 is stronger (higher) than a correlation of +.7.

There are several different types of correlation coefficients. The most common one is the Pearson product-moment correlation coefficient. This is the one most likely to be used in test manuals. It is represented by r.

Four cautions need to be emphasized when interpreting correlations. First, correlation does not imply causation. Just because two measures are related, it does not mean that one *caused* the other. There may be other factors involved in causation, and the direction of the cause is probably not clear. Second, be alert for curvilinear relationships, because most correlation coefficients, such as the Pearson, assume that the relationship is linear. Third, also be alert to what is called *restricted range*. If the values of one measure are truncated, with a small range, it will in all likelihood result in a low correlation. Given a full range of scores, the correlation would be higher. Fourth, relationships expressed as correlation coefficients generally are less precise than the number would suggest. That is, a very high correlation of .80 does not mean that 80 percent of the relationship is accounted for. If you think of correlation as predicting one score from another score, you will see how relatively imprecise this can be. Examine the scatterplots of various correlations in Figure 13.8. You will see that in a moderate relationship (e), if you try to predict the value of score on the y axis, say, from a score of 8 on the x axis, a range of 4 to 9 is predicted.

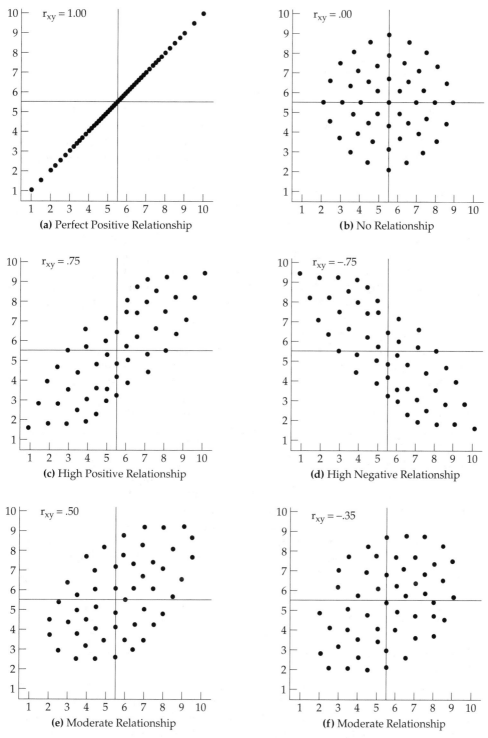

FIGURE 13.8   Scatterplots of Various Correlations

Source: Mehrens, W. A., & Lehmann, I. J., *Using standardized tests in education* (4th ed.), p. 49. Copyright © 1987. New York: Longman.

INTERPRETING STANDARDIZED TESTS

Armed with a basic knowledge of important descriptive statistics, you can now better understand how to interpret and use your students' standardized test scores. We will begin our discussion with one more technical issue, standard error of measurement, then we will look at issues involved in norm- and criterion-referenced interpretation, before examining some actual standardized test score reports.

Standard Error of Measurement

As I have stressed throughout this book, every test has some degree of error. Chapter 3 introduced the relationship between error and reliability. Basically, as error increases, reliability decreases. But we can only directly measure reliability in a test; we cannot know what type or amount of error has influenced a student's score. Therefore we estimate the degree of error that is probable, given the reliability of the test. This degree of error is estimated mathematically and is reported as the *standard error of measurement* (SEM).

SEM is determined by a formula that takes into account the reliability and standard deviation of the test. If a student took a test many times, the resulting scores would look like a normal distribution. That is, sometimes the student would get "good" error and get a higher score, and sometimes the student would get "bad" error, resulting in a lower score. If we assume that the student's *true* score is the mean of this hypothetical distribution, then we can use this as a starting point for estimating the *actual* true score. From what we know about the normal curve and standard deviation, 68 percent of the time the actual true score would be between one standard deviation of the student's normal curve of many testings, and 96 percent of the time the actual true score would fall within two standard deviations of this distribution. We call the standard deviation of this hypothetical normal distribution the standard error of measurement.

For example, if a student's GE score on a test was 3.4, and the test had a standard error of measurement of .2, then we would interpret the student's true performance, with 68 percent confidence, to be 3.4 +/−.2; and with 96 percent confidence, we would interpret the student's true score to be 3.4 +/−.4. In other words, the standard error of measurement creates an interval, and it is within this interval that we can be confident that the student's true score lies. Different degrees of confidence are related to the number of standard errors of measurement included (these intervals can be thought of as *confidence bands*). Of course, we do not know *where* in the interval the score lies, so we are most accurate in interpreting the performance in terms of the interval, not as a single score.

The idea of interpreting single scores as bands or intervals has important implications. If you are drawing a conclusion about the performance of a single student, your thinking should be something like this: "Trevor's performance in mathematics places him between the 86th and 94th percentiles," rather than, "Trevor's score is at the 90th percentile." This will give you a more realistic and accurate basis for judging Trevor's real or actual level of performance. When comparing two scores from the same test battery, a meaningful difference in performance is indicated only when the intervals, as established by one standard error of measurement, do not overlap. Thus, it would be wrong to conclude that a student's language achievement score of 72 is *higher* than the reading score of 70 if the standard error is two or more. The same logic is needed for comparing ability with achievement or for comparing the scores of different individuals on the same test. That is, if the bands do not overlap, then you should conclude that there is no difference between the scores.

Fortunately, test publishers report standard errors of measurement to help you interpret the scores properly, and often they are displayed visually in the form of a shaded band surrounding the score. Unfortunately, there is usually a slightly different standard error of measurement for each subtest and for different ranges of scores. Thus, in the technical manual, there are tables of standard errors of measurement (isn't that exciting!). I don't want to suggest that you consult these tables for each student and for each score. However, it may be helpful to use this information in decisions regarding referral for identification for special education, and for placement into special programs. Many standardized test reporting formats display the appropriate standard error of measurement on each student's report, although you will need to look at a key to know the exact nature of the band. Some tests use one SEM, others use the middle 50 percent.

Interpretation of Norm-Referenced Standardized Tests

Most standardized tests are designed to provide norm-referenced interpretations. This allows you to compare performance to a well-defined *norming* or reference group and to determine relative strengths and weaknesses of students. When comparing an individual's performance to the norm group, the overall competence of this group is critical in determining relative position. Ranking high with a low-performing group may indicate, in an absolute sense, less competence than ranking low in a high-performing group. Thus, the exact nature of the norming group is important, and several types of norms can be used.

Types of Standardized Test Norms

Norms are sets of scores. Each type of norm differs with respect to the characteristics of the students who comprise the norm group. The most commonly used type are *national norms*. These norms are based on a nationally representative sample of students. Generally, testing companies do a good job of obtaining national samples, but there is still variation from one test to another based on school cooperation and the cost of sampling. Also, most testing companies oversample minorities and other under-represented groups. Thus, one reason that national norms from different tests are not comparable is that the sampling procedures do not result in equivalent norm groups. For example, you should never conclude that one student has greater knowledge or skill than another because her reading score on the Stanford Achievement Test was at the 90th percentile, compared to another student who scored at the 80th percentile on the Metropolitan Achievement Test (there would also be differences in the content of the items). One the other hand, most testing companies use the same norm group for both achievement and aptitude batteries, which allows direct achievement/aptitude and subtest score comparisons.

There are also many different *special group norms*. These types of norms are comprised of subgroups from the national sample. For example, special norms are typically available for large cities, high- or low-socioeconomic status school districts, suburban areas, special grade levels, norms for tests given at different times of the year (usually fall or spring), and other specific subgroups. Whenever a special group norm is used, the basis for comparison changes, and the same raw score on a test will probably be reported as a different percentile rank. For instance, because both achievement and aptitude are related to socioeconomic status (higher socioeconomic status, higher achievement), school districts that contain a larger percentage of high-socioeconomic-status students than is true for the population as a whole (and hence the national norm group) almost always score above the mean with national norms. Conversely, districts with a high percentage of low-socioeconomic-status students typically have difficulty scoring above the mean. However, if the high-socioeconomic-status district is compared to suburban norms, the percentile ranks of the scores will be lower; for low-socioeconomic-status districts, the percentiles will be higher if the norm group is low-socioeconomic-status districts. Understandably, then, suburban districts almost always want to use national norms.

One common misconception is that students who test in the spring of the year will obtain a higher percentile rank than students who test in the fall. This is not the case because each of these testing times has a separate norm group, so that a student is compared only to those in the norming group who took the test at the same time during the year. However, a grade equivalency or developmental score would be higher for students taking the spring test because they would, in fact, have greater knowledge than students in the same grade level in the fall.

Another type of norm is one that is for a single school district. These are called *local norms*. Local norms are helpful in making intraschool comparisons and in providing information that is useful for student placement in appropriate classes. These different types of norms make it very important for you to examine standardized test reports and know the type of norm that is used to determine percentile rank and standard scores.

Using Test Norms

Once you understand clearly the type of norm group that is used, you will be in a position to interpret the scores of your students accurately. In making these interpretations and using the norms correctly, you should adhere to the following suggestions (Figure 13.9).

FIGURE 13.9   Checklist for Using Norm-Referenced Test Scores

1. Are norms differentiated from standards and expectations?
2. Is the type of norm matched with intended use?
3. Is the norm group sampling representative and well described?
4. Are the test norms current?

1. Remember That Norms Are Not Standards or Expectations. Norm-referenced test scores show how a student compares to a reference group. The scores do not tell you how much the student knows in terms of specific learning targets, nor how much students should know. Students who score below the norm (that is, below the mean score) may or may not be meeting your learning targets. That determination is criterion-referenced.

2. Match Your Intended Use of the Scores with the Appropriate Norm Group. As we have discussed, there are many different types of norms. You need to determine your intended use and then use the norm group that will provide you with the most valid comparison. For determining general strengths and weaknesses and aptitude/achievement discrepancies, national norms are appropriate. If you want to use the scores to select students for a special class, local norms are probably best. When you counsel a student regarding a career, national norms will not be as helpful as norms more specific to the field.

3. Sampling for the Norm Group Should Be Representative and Well Described. You should supplement the test publisher's description of the norming group with an examination of the specific nature of the sampling that was used. This can be found in the technical manual for the test. Often, we need to be sure that specific subgroups are represented in the proper proportion. This determination will only be possible if the sampling procedures are clearly described and relevant characteristics of the sample are provided, such as gender, age, race, socioeconomic status, and geographic location.

4. If Possible, Use the Most Recently Developed Test Norms. Standardized test norms are developed on the basis of sampling one year, and this serves as the reference group for several more years. Thus, you may well use the same test that was normed in, say, 1990, with your students in 1996. This means that the performance of your students in 1996 is compared to how well students performed on the test in 1990. Over the years between the norming and current testing, the curriculum can change to be more consistent with the test, and there can be changes in your student population. These factors affect the current scores, and make it possible for all school divisions to be rated above average. For the norming group, 50 percent of the students are below average. This distribution is set so that in the future more than 50 percent of the students could obtain a raw score higher than the mean raw score of the norming group. In general, the most current norms provide the most accurate information. You should be wary of using old test norms that have not been updated.

The Scholastic Assessment Test (SAT—previously the Scholastic Achievement Test) provides an interesting illustration of how the date of the norming group makes an impact. Until 1995, the norming group for the SAT consisted of 10,000 college-bound students tested in 1941. Every year since then, each student who has taken the SAT has been compared to this 1941 norm group. This has resulted in a decline in SAT averages because the population of students taking the SAT recently has a much larger percentage of lower ability students. Thus, this decline is a function of a population of students taking the SAT, which is different from the original norming group. Today, the SAT has been *renormed* to more adequately reflect the population of students who take the test.

Criterion-Referenced Interpretations

As we previously discussed, criterion-referenced interpretations compare student performance to established standards rather than to other students. Some standardized tests are only criterion-referenced (they may also be called objectives based, domain-referenced, or content-referenced). These tests are designed to provide a valid measure of skills and knowledge in specific areas. Most norm-referenced tests also provide criterion-referenced information by indicating the number of items answered correctly in specific areas, but because the primary purpose of these tests is to compare individuals, they typically do not provide as meaningful information as what criterion-referenced tests provide. Thus, you need to keep in mind that there is a difference between a criterion-referenced standardized test and criterion-referenced interpretations.

Whether the test is norm- or criterion-referenced, it is important for each skill or area for which a score is reported to be described in detail. With delimited and well-defined learning targets, the score can more easily be interpreted to suggest some degree of mastery. Without a clearly defined target, such interpretation is questionable at best. Typically, criterion-referenced tests do the best job of this because it is essential to their primary purpose.

Your judgment concerning the degree of a student's mastery is usually based on the percentage of correctly answered items that measure a specific target. The meaning that is given to the percentage of correct answers is generally made by the teacher, based on a review of the definition of the target and the difficulty of the items. This involves your professional judgment; in some districts standards may be set by a team, a group of educators, or parents. An important aspect of making this decision is having a sufficient number of items to adequately measure the target. Criterion-referenced tests are designed to have enough items for each score, while norm-referenced tests may or may not have enough items. Generally you need at least six items for each score.

Although results are not reported as percentile ranks or standard scores, there may be information in the technical manual about the difficulty of items or average scores of various groups. This information is helpful when deciding the correspondence between the percentage of items answered correctly and mastery of the skill or content area. One approach to doing this is to set in your mind a group of "minimally competent" students in reference to the target, then see how many items these students answer correctly. If the mean number of correct answers is, say, seven of ten, then your "standard" becomes 70 percent of the items. It may be that the level is set in relation to a goal for students by the end of the year, or you may set standards on how others have performed in the past. Regardless of the approach, the interpretation is largely a matter of your professional judgment, so think carefully about the criteria you use.

With these recommendations, keep the following suggestions in mind when making criterion-referenced interpretations from standardized tests (summarized in Figure 13.10).

1. Determine the Primary Purpose of the Test—Is It Norm- or Criterion-Referenced? Criterion-referenced tests are designed for criterion-referenced interpretations. As long as the descriptions of the knowledge and skills match your learning targets, these types of tests will provided the best information. Be wary of using norm-referenced tests.

2. Examine the Definitions of Knowledge and Skills Measured for Clarity and Specificity. For each score that is reported there needs to be an adequate definition of what is being measured. Norm-referenced tests tend to define what is measured more broadly; criterion-referenced tests more specifically. You may need to consult the technical manual to get sufficient detail of the definition to make a valid judgment about the match between what the tests says it is measuring and what you want measured. There should be good content-related evidence of validity to demonstrate an adequate sampling of content or skills from a larger domain.

3. Be Sure There Is a Sufficient Number of Items to Make a Valid Decision. The general rule is to have at least six to eight different test items for each target. For learning targets that are less specific, more than ten items may be needed. In some norm-referenced tests you may see skills listed with as few as three or four items. This is too few for making reasonable conclusions, especially if the items are objective, but it may suggest a need for further investigation.

4. Examine the Difficulty of Items and Match This to Your Standards. Norm-referenced tests may not use easy items because they do not discriminate among students, while criterion-referenced tests tend to have easy items so that most students will do reasonably well. This means that the difficulty of the items may differ considerably with the same definition for the target. Inspect the items carefully and use your knowledge of their difficulty in setting standards.

FIGURE 13.10   Checklist for Using Criterion-Referenced Test Scores

1. Is the primary purpose of the test norm- or criterion-referenced?
2. Are measured targets delimited and clearly defined?
3. Are there enough items to measure each target adequately?
4. Is the difficulty level of the items matched with the learning targets?

UNDERSTANDING STANDARDIZED TEST SCORE REPORTS

When you first look at some standardized test score reports, they may seem to be very complicated and difficult to understand (you may have even had that reaction to the examples in Chapter 4). This is because they are designed to provide as much information as possible on a single page, and often the results are presented as numerical scores and in the form of graphs. For a comprehensive battery, scores are often reported for each skill as well as each subskill. The best approach for understanding a report is to consult the test manual and find examples that are explained. Most test publishers do a very good job of showing you what each part of the report means.

There are also many different types of reports. Each test publisher will have a unique format for reporting results and will usually include different kinds of scores. In addition, there are typically different formats to report the same scores. Thus, the same battery may be reported as a list of students in your class, the class as a whole, a skills analysis for the class or individual student, individual profiles, profile charts, growth scale profiles, and other formats. Some reports include only scores for major tests, others include subskill scores and item scores. Different norms may be used. All of this means that each report contains somewhat different information, organized and presented in dissimilar ways. You need to first identify what type of report you are dealing with, then find an explanation for it in an interpretive guide. After you have become acquainted with the types of standardized tests and reports used in your school, you will be in a position to routinely interpret them in accurate and helpful ways.

Chapter 4 presented examples of several types of individual reports. Figures 13.11 and 13.12, pages 369–371 illustrate class reports for two different standardized tests. For the Iowa Test of Basic Skills, an item analysis provides information on the performance of the class, building, and district for each skill. Figure 13.11 shows that for Ms. Olson's class of twenty-one students, the average percent correct for the nine questions measuring number systems and numeration, was 76. For the school and the district the average was 68, and for the national norming group the average was 65. The bar graph shows how much the class score differed from the national average. By examining all the math scores you get a good sense of where the strengths and weaknesses were for the entire class. For example, this class is relatively strong in number systems and numeration, fractions and money, problem-solving strategies, and interpreting relationships, and it is relatively weak with estimation, and single-step and multiple-step addition and subtraction problems. If this were a spring testing, it would help you evaluate the effectiveness of instruction in these areas. If the test were given in the fall, it would help you diagnose student weaknesses for instructional planning.

Figure 13.12 on page 371 uses a different format for reporting results for an entire class. In the California Achievement Tests Class Record Sheet, the scores of individual students are listed, with a class average at the end. This report gives you results for different skills, but not for individual items as does the report in Figure 13.11. Notice that several types of scores are presented for each skill area, but no building or district comparisons are made. This type of report provides an overview of all skill areas, while the report in Figure 13.11 provides more detail about skills in a single area.

FIGURE 13.11   Sample, Iowa Test of Basic Skills Group Item Analysis Report

Iowa Tests of Basic Skills

Service 6: Group Item Analysis

Class Report: Diff=Class Minus National   All Diff's Are Printed

Class/Group:	Ms Olson	Building:	Linden	Grade:	1
System:	Dalen Community	Bldg. Code:	303	Level:	7
Norms:	Spring 1992	Test Date:	03/93	Form:	K
Order No.:	000-A33-73804-00-001	Page:	358		

Item No.	Math Concepts	Item Count	Class Avg %C N=21	Building Avg %C N=139	System Avg %C N=247	Nat'l Avg %C	Diff Class Minus Nat'l	Difference (Class Minus Nat'l) −20 0 +20
	Number Systems & Numeration	9	76	68	68	65	+11	
1	Compare & order		95	89	91	86	+9	
5	Compare & order		90	83	80	72	+18	
7	Compare & order		86	72	75	74	+12	
12	Place value		90	90	89	88	+2	
15	Compare & order		76	68	67	67	+9	
17	Place value		90	83	84	71	+19	
22	Compare & order		38	31	30	30	+8	
26	Properties		48	35	34	32	+16	
29	Compare & order		67	65	62	62	+5	
	Whole Numbers	3	84	85	83	82	+2	
2	Reading & writing		81	82	84	85	−4	
6	Reading & writing		100	93	89	93	+7	
11	Relative values		71	79	75	68	+3	
	Geometry	4	82	86	84	80	+2	
3	Geometric figures		90	93	92	91	−1	
14	Properties, patterns & relationships		76	82	78	72	+4	
19	Geometric figures		67	74	73	67	0	
25	Properties, patterns & relationships		95	95	93	89	+6	
	Measurement	4	88	88	88	82	+6	
9	Appropriate units		100	98	97	95	+5	
13	Estimate measurements		81	80	81	72	+9	
16	Length, distance, temp, wt, vol		95	97	95	81	+14	
21	Estimate measurements		76	76	78	79	−3	

(continued)

FIGURE 13.11 *(Continued)*

Item No.	Math Concepts	Item Count	Class Avg %C N=21	Building Avg %C N=139	System Avg %C N=247	Nat'l Avg %C	Diff Class Minus Nat'l	Difference (Class Minus Nat'l) −20 0 +20
	Fractions & Money	4	79	63	63	57	+22	+
10	Representation		90	71	72	68	+22	+
23	Representation		38	24	27	22	+16	
24	Representation		95	82	79	85	+10	
27	Relative values		90	76	74	54	+36	+
	Number Sentences	4	75	71	67	67	+8	
4	Solving sentences		95	86	84	79	+16	
8	Symbols		86	89	88	91	−5	
18	Variables		57	51	47	48	+9	
20	Variables		62	58	49	51	+11	
	Estimation	1	29	46	49	47	−18	
28	Standard rounding in context		29	46	49	47	−18	
	Single-Step: +/−	6	62	68	65	66	−4	
1	Whole numbers: +		86	88	85	87	−1	
2	Whole numbers: −		38	47	44	46	−8	
3	Whole numbers: +		67	73	71	65	+2	
4	Whole numbers: +		76	83	79	82	−5	
6	Whole numbers: −		52	58	56	60	−8	
7	Whole numbers: +		52	60	57	57	−5	
	Single-Step: ×/+	3	57	56	49	51	+6	
5	Whole numbers: ×		71	70	63	53	+18	
10	Whole numbers: ÷		48	50	42	48	0	
12	Whole numbers: ÷		52	48	43	51	+1	
	Multiple-Step	2	50	53	49	55	−5	
8	Whole numbers: +/−		52	56	53	60	−8	
11	Whole numbers: +/−		48	50	45	49	−1	
	Prob Solv Strategy	5	73	61	57	58	+15	
9	Extraneous info: +		52	35	33	34	+18	
13	Solution method: +		90	81	76	79	+11	
14	Solution method: −		81	72	68	72	+9	
15	Solution method: ×		62	50	45	41	+21	+
16	Solution method: −		81	69	65	66	+15	
	Read Amounts	3	76	79	80	74	+2	
17	Circle graph		76	81	83	79	−3	
20	Bar/Line Graph		86	82	82	79	+7	
24	Table	67	73	74	63		+4	
	Compare Quantities	6	46	49	49	46	0	
18	Compare: diffs		57	60	58	51	+6	
19	Compare: ratios		38	41	40	40	−2	
21	Compare: ratios		38	37	42	42	−4	
23	Compare: rank		43	47	46	47	−4	
26	Compare: rank		48	53	52	49	−1	
27	Compare: diffs		52	55	57	47	+5	
	Interpret Relationships	2	67	53	56	50	+17	
22	Relationships		71	62	61	48	+23	+
25	Relationships		62	44	51	51	+11	

CAT/5

CALIFORNIA ACHIEVEMENT TESTS, FIFTH EDITION

PAGE 1

CLASS RECORD SHEET
CLASS: POLK   GRADE: 5.7

A

STUDENTS	Scores	READING			LANGUAGE				MATHEMATICS				SPELL	STUDY SKILLS	SCI	SOC ST
		VOCAB	COMPR	TOTAL	MECH	EXPR	TOTAL	COMPU	C&A	TOTAL	TOTAL BATTERY					

Column headers: VOCAB, COMPR, TOTAL (READING); MECH, EXPR, TOTAL (LANGUAGE); COMPU, C&A, TOTAL, TOTAL BATTERY (MATHEMATICS); SPELL, STUDY SKILLS, SCI, SOC ST

ALLEN   KEN
BIRTH DATE: 7/15/80
CODES:
FORM: A   LEVEL: 15

	READING			LANGUAGE			MATH			TB	SPELL	STUDY	SCI	SOC ST
NP	47	68	57	49	37	44	37	76	59	53	41	6	60	65
NS	5	6	5	5	5	5	4	6	5	5	5	6	6	6
NCE	48	60	54	49	43	47	43	65	55	52	45	60	56	58
SS	713	745	729	717	719	718	716	754	735	727	710	744	743	750

ARNOLD   STEPHAN
BIRTH DATE: 2/5/80
CODES:
FORM: A   LEVEL: 15

NP	61	66	64	73	56	66	32	63	49	61	6	49	81	70
NS	6	6	6	6	5	6	4	6	5	6	2	5	7	6
NCE	56	58	58	63	53	59	40	57	50	56	18	50	68	61
SS	728	743	736	743	738	741	710	739	725	734	639	719	766	755

BROWN   SUSAN
BIRTH DATE: 11/30/79
CODES:
FORM: A   LEVEL: 15

NP	70	65	68	83	69	77	12	51	28	59	87	44	62	83
NS	6	6	6	7	6	6	3	5	4	5	7	5	6	7
NCE	61	58	60	70	60	66	26	50	38	55	74	47	56	70
SS	737	742	740	756	750	753	679	726	703	732	766	712	745	771

B   **C**

CLASS SUMMARY

D

STUDENTS	Scores	READING			LANGUAGE			MATHEMATICS			TOTAL BATTERY	SPELL	STUDY SKILLS	SCI	SOC ST
		VOCAB	COMPR	TOTAL	MECH	EXPR	TOTAL	COMPU	C&A	TOTAL					
	MDNP	47.5	63.0	56.5	65.5	49.0	58.7	28.3	42.5	32.0	51.7	44.0	45.7	45.5	55.5
	MNS	4.9	5.2	5.1	5.6	4.8	5.3	3.9	5.0	4.5	5.1	4.6	4.6	4.8	4.9
	MNCE	49.2	53.6	51.6	56.5	48.6	53.2	38.9	50.1	44.9	49.8	46.4	46.7	47.6	47.7
	MSS	714.1	733.3	723.9	729.4	726.4	728.1	706.5	724.3	715.7	722.4	709.7	709.1	724.4	726.3

NUMBER OF STUDENTS =

NP-   NATIONAL PERCENTILE
NS-   NATIONAL STANINE
NCE-   NORMAL CURVE EQUIVALENT
SS-   SCALE SCORE

Total Battery includes Total Reading, Total Language, and Total Mathematics.

SCHOOL: TAFT ELEM
DISTRICT: WINFIELD
CITY: WINFIELD
STATE:

FORM-LEVEL: A-15
NORMS FROM: 1991
TEST DATE: 4/24/92
SCORING   PATTERN (IRT)
QUARTER MONTH: 31

CTBID: 9120T94477-0001-03-0000-1-000042

MACMILLAN
McGRAW-HILL

FIGURE 13.12   Sample, California Achievement Tests, Fifth Edition, Class Record Sheet

Source: CTB/McGraw-Hill, California Achievement Tests. Copyright © 1992. Reprinted with permisson of The McGraw-Hill Companies.

INTERPRETING TEST REPORTS FOR PARENTS

Most teachers interpret the results of standardized tests for parents, although recent research found that nearly half of our teachers feel unprepared to do this (Nolen, Haladyna, & Haas, 1989). Because you are in contact with the student daily and are aware of the student's classroom performance, you are in the best position to communicate with parents regarding the results of standardized tests. You can determine what level of detail to report and how the results coincide with classroom performance. This is done most effectively face to face in the context of a teacher–parent conference, though many schools send written reports home without scheduling a conference. In such a conference, you can point out important cautions and discuss the results in a way that will make sense. Prior to the conference, you should review available information and have it prepared to show student progress and areas of strength and weakness that may need specific action at home and school. This should include other examples of student work, in addition to the test results, to lessen the tendency to place too much value in test scores.

In preparing for the conference, keep in mind that most parents will be interested in particular types of information. These include some indication of relative standing, growth since earlier testing, weaknesses, and strengths. For each of these areas you should present the relevant numbers, but be sure to include a clear and easy-to-understand narrative—using plain, everyday language—that explains the numbers. You should always include some explanation of norms and the standard error of measurement. It is important for parents to realize that, for most reports, the scores do not represent comparisons with other students in the class. Parents obviously don't need an extended explanation of error, but it's important for them to understand that the results represent *approximate* and not absolute or precise performance.

Of the different types of scores to report to parents, percentiles are most easily understood, even though some parents will confuse percentile with percentage correct. They may also think that percentile scores below 70 are poor because they are accustomed to grading systems in which 70 or below may mean failure. In fact, for most standardized tests, students will score in the average range if they answer 60 to 70 percent of the items correctly. Grade equivalents are commonly reported but easily misunderstood. Often parents think that GEs indicate in which grade a student should be placed. You will need to be diligent in pointing out that GEs are only another way of comparing performance to the norm group.

Some standardized tests have special reports that are prepared for parents. Although these are very informative, it is still important to supplement the scores with a note from the teacher indicating a willingness to confer with the parents, by phone or in person, to answer any questions and clarify the meaning of the results.

In summary, the following suggestions will help you interpret standardized test reports confidently and in a way that will accurately inform parents and help the student.

1. Understand the Meaning of Every Score Reported to Parents.   It is embarrassing, not to mention unprofessional, not to know how to interpret each score on the report.

2. Examine Individual Student Reports Comprehensively Prior to a Conference with Parents.   This will prevent you from trying to understand and explain at the same time.

3. Gather Evidence of Student Performance in the Classroom That Can Supplement the Test Scores.   This demonstrates your commitment to the preparation and careful analysis of each student's performance, and it provides more concrete examples of performance that parents can easily understand.

4. Be Prepared to Address Areas of Concern Most Parents Have, Such as Standing, Progress, Strengths and Weaknesses.   This may require you to review the student's previous performance on other standardized tests.

5. Be Prepared to Distinguish between Ability and Achievement.   Many parents will want to know if their child is performing "up to their ability." You might even have a short written description of the difference to supplement your verbal explanation.

6. Explain the Importance of Norms and Error in Testing for Proper Interpretation.   This could include your knowledge of any extenuating circumstances that may have affected the student's performance.

7. Summarize Clearly What the Scores Mean.   Don't simply show the numbers and expect the parents to be able to understand. You will need to summarize in language that the parents can comprehend.

8. Try to Create a Discussion with Parents, Rather Than Making a Presentation to Them.   Ask questions to involve parents in the conference and to enhance your ability to determine if they in fact understand the meaning of the scores.

PREPARING STUDENTS FOR TAKING STANDARDIZED TESTS

You want your students to perform as well as possible on standardized tests, and with high-stakes testing accompanying increased demands for accountability, it is important for every student to have a fair opportunity to do his or her best work. This is accomplished if students are properly prepared prior to taking the test, and this preparation will probably be your responsibility.

One area to address is making sure that students have good test-taking skills. These skills help to familiarize the students with item formats and gives them strategies so that the validity of the results is improved. You don't want a student to get a low score because he or she lacks test-taking skills. Students should be proficient with the test-taking skills listed in Figure 13.13.

You will also want to set an appropriate classroom climate or environment for taking the test. This begins with your attitude toward the test. If you convey to students that you believe the test is a burden, an unnecessary or even unfair imposition, then students will also adopt such an attitude and may not try their best. Be happy with the test, convey an attitude of challenge and opportunity. Discuss with your students the purpose and nature of the test. Emphasize that it is most important for students to try to do their best, not just to obtain a high score. Tell the students how the tests will be used in conjunction with other information; this will reduce anxiety. You want to enhance student confidence by giving them short practice tests. These tests help to acquaint students with the directions and the types of items they will answer.

Student motivation is an important factor. Motivate your students to put forth their best effort by helping them understand how the results from the test will benefit them. Show how results can be used to improve learning and essential life skills, their knowledge of themselves, and planning for the future. Avoid comments that might make students concerned or anxious.

Some of your students may be so anxious about the test that their anxiety seriously interferes with their performance. If you suspect that a student's performance is adversely affected by test anxiety after you have done all you can to alleviate the fears, then you may want to have the student examined by a counselor to determine the extent of the problem. If necessary, appropriate counseling

---

FIGURE 13.13   Important Test-Taking Skills

---

1. Listening to or reading directions carefully.
2. Listening to or reading test items carefully.
3. Setting a pace that will allow time to complete the test.
4. Bypassing difficult items and returning to them later.
5. Making informed guesses rather than omitting items.
6. Eliminating as many alternatives as possible on multiple-choice items before guessing.
7. Following directions carefully in marking the answer sheet (e.g., darken the entire space).
8. Checking to be sure the item number and answer number match when marking an answer.
9. Checking to be sure that the appropriate response was marked on the answer sheet.
10. Going back and checking the answers if time permits.

Source: Linn, R. L., & Gronlund, N. E., *Measurement and assessment in teaching,* 7th Edition, copyright © 1995, p. 430. Adapted by permission of Prentice-Hall, Upper Saddle River, New Jersey.

FIGURE 13.14   Do's and Don'ts of Test-Preparation

Do	Don't
Improve student test-taking skills	Use the standardized test format for classroom tests
Establish a suitable environment	Characterize tests as an extra burden
Motivate students to do their best	Tell students important decisions are made solely on the test scores
Explain why tests are given and how results will be used	Use previous forms of the same test
Give practice tests	Teach the test
Tell students they probably won't know all the answers	Have a negative attitude about the test
Tell students not to give up	
Allay student anxiety	
Have a positive attitude about the test	

and desensitization exercises can be explored. At the very least, incorporate your awareness of the anxiety when interpreting the results of the test.

Of course, be sure that the physical environment for taking the test is appropriate. There should be adequate work space and lighting as well as good ventilation. The room should be quiet, without distractions, and the test should be scheduled to avoid events that may disturb the students. Students should be seated to avoid distractions and cheating. Morning testing is preferred. It is best to remove any visual aids that could assist students and to place a sign on the outside of the door, such as Testing—Do Not Disturb.

Figure 13.14 lists some do's and don'ts regarding test preparation.

ADMINISTERING STANDARDIZED TESTS

Because most standardized tests are given in the classroom, you will most likely be responsible for administering them to your students. The most important part of administering these tests is to *follow the directions carefully and explicitly.* This point cannot be overstated. You must adhere strictly to the instructions that are given by the test publisher. The procedures are set to assure standardization in the conditions under which students in different classes and schools take the test. The directions will indicate what to say, how to respond to student questions, and what to do as students are working on the test. Familiarize yourself with the directions before you read them to your students, word for word as specified. Don't try to paraphrase directions or recite them from memory, even if you have given the test many times.

During the test you may answer student questions about the directions or procedures for answering items, but you should not help students in any way with an answer or what is meant by a question on the test. Although you may be tempted to give students hints or tell them to "answer more quickly" or "slow down and think more," these responses are inappropriate and should be avoided. It's as if you need to suspend your role as classroom teacher for a while and assume the role of test administrator. This isn't easy, and you may well catch yourself making minor changes when giving the directions.

While observing students as they take the test, you may see some unusual behavior or events that could affect the students' performance. It is best to record these behaviors and events for use in subsequent interpretation of the results. Interruptions should also be recorded.

The test directions will contain time limits for subtests. You must follow these strictly, including the instruction to collect completed answer sheets and tests promptly. Once the test is over, you will need to account for all copies to ensure test security. Some tests will require that you write down the exact beginning and ending times.

SUMMARY

The purpose of this chapter was to introduce you to the principles of standardized testing to enable you to administer such tests and interpret your students' scores. Although standardized testing may not directly influence your day-to-day teaching, you have a professional responsibility to interpret the scores from these types of tests accurately for yourself, students, and parents. The results of standardized tests, when used correctly, will provide helpful information concerning the effectiveness of your instruction and progress of your students. Important points in the chapter include the following:

- Frequency distributions show you how scores are arrayed: normal, positively skewed, negatively skewed, flat.
- Measures of central tendency include the mean, median, and mode.
- Measures of variability, such as the range and standard deviation, provide numerical values for the degree of dispersion of scores from the mean.
- Standard scores, such as z, T, NCE, the developmental scale, and deviation IQ scores, are converted from raw scores into units of standard deviation.
- Grade equivalency scores indicate performance related to norming groups and should be cautiously interpreted.
- Scatterplots show relationships graphically as being positive, negative, or curvilinear.
- Correlation coefficients are numbers from –1 to 1 that indicate direction and strength of the relationship.
- Correlation does not imply causation.

- Standard error of measurement (SEM) expresses mathematically the degree of error to be expected with individual test scores; test results are best interpreted as intervals defined by the SEM.
- Percentile rank, standard scores, and grade equivalents for students are based on comparisons with the norming group.
- Norm-referenced test scores provide external measures and help identify relative strengths and weaknesses.
- Different types of norms, such as national norms, special group norms, or local norms, influence the reported percentile ranks and other comparative scores.
- Norms are not standards or expectations; they should be recent, appropriate to your use, and based on good sampling.
- Criterion-referenced interpretations depend on the difficulty of the items and professional judgments to set standards.
- Good criterion-referenced judgments depend on well-defined targets and a sufficient number of test items to provide a reliable result.
- Standardized test reports vary in format and organization; consult the interpretive guide to aid in understanding.
- Adequate interpreting of standardized test scores to parents depends on your preparation, your full understanding of the meaning of the scores, your ability to translate the numerical results into plain language, and placing the scores in the context of classroom performance.
- Prepare your students for taking standardized tests by establishing a good environment, lessening test anxiety, motivating students to do their best, avoiding distractions, and giving students practice tests and exercises.

SELF-INSTRUCTIONAL REVIEW EXERCISES

1. For the following set of numbers, calculate the mean, median, and standard deviation. Also, determine linear z and T scores for 18, 20, and 11.

   10, 17, 18, 15, 20, 16, 15, 21, 12, 11, 22.

2. If you have a normal distribution of scores with a mean of 80 and a standard deviation of 6, what is the approximate percentile rank of the following scores: 86, 68, 83, and 71.

3. Given the following standardized test scores for Mary, an eighth grader, her mother believes that Mary is in the wrong grade. She believes Mary would be better off in the ninth grade. She also believes that the test scores seem to indicate that Mary is stronger in science than in language arts, mathematics, or social science. How would you respond to Mary's mother?

Test	NATL PR	Stanine	GE
Mathematics	75	6	9.2
Science	87	7	9.7
Social studies	80	7	9.4
Language arts	63	6	8.5
Study skills	72	6	9.0

4. Refer back to Figure 4.4 on pages 85–86. For this student, indicate what you believe are his strengths and weaknesses on the basis of the reported standardized test scores. Assume a standard error of measurement of 8.

5. Indicate whether each of the following suggested activities would help or hinder student performance on a standardized test.

   a. Tell students their futures depend on their scores.
   b. To avoid making students anxious, do not tell them very much about the test.
   c. Make sure the room temperature is about right.
   d. Arrange desks so that students face each other in groups of four.
   e. Give students a practice test that is very similar in format.
   f. Tell students they probably won't be able to answer many of the questions.
   g. Teach to the test.
   h. Tell students you think the test is taking away from class time and student learning.

ANSWERS TO SELF-INSTRUCTIONAL REVIEW EXERCISES

1. $\overline{X} = 161/11 = 16.09$; $mdn = 16$. Rounding the mean to 16, the SD is 3.83. The z and T-scores are as follows: 18: $z = 18 - 16/3.83 = .53$; $T = 50 + 10(.53) = 55.3$; 20: $20 - 16/3.83 = 1.05$; $T = 50 + 10(1.05) = 60.5$; 11: $11 - 16/3.83 = -1.31$; $T = 50 + 10(-1.31) = 36.9$.

2. The score of 86 is one standard deviation above the mean, so the percentile is the 84th; 68 is two standard deviations below the mean, so the percentile is the 2nd; 83 is one half of a standard deviation above the mean, so the percentile rank is between 50 (mean) and 84 (one SD); because 34 percent of the scores lie in this range, one half of 34 is 17, so 83 is at about the 67th percentile (50 + 17) (actually it would be a little greater than 17 because of the curve of the distribution, but 67 is a good approximation); using the same logic, 71, which is one and one half standard deviations below the mean, would be at approximately the 8th percentile (50 – 34 + 8).

3. Mary's mother is probably looking at the GEs and thinking that this means Mary should be in the ninth grade. This is not true. It's very possible that most of the students in the eighth grade have GEs of 9 or higher. It's true that Mary's science score is her highest, but, given a normal standard error of measurement that is about 6 percentile points, the confidence interval overlaps suggest that there is no meaningful difference between science (81–93) and social studies (74–86), but it could be concluded that the science score is definitely higher than the language arts (57–69). The stanines give you the impression that the scores on all the tests are about the same, which is somewhat misleading. Yes, they are all well above the norm, but the science percentile score is at the top of stanine 7, while the language arts percentile is at the bottom of stanine 6. Refer to examples of reports in Chapter 4 for interpretation. Give example of some test scores.

4. The first step would be to create the confidence bands for each of the tests. Vocabulary would be 55–75, reading comprehension would be 40–58, reading total would be 48–62, and so forth. The two reading subscales show no difference; the language total, relatively, shows a weakness in comparison to the reading and math totals and to science.

Science is clearly a strength. Social studies is weak. Word analysis and reading comprehension appear to be above average. Michael is strong across the board in math, with the possible exception of single-step addition and subtracting whole numbers (but there were only a few items for each subskill, so this would be very tentative).

5. a. hinder, b. hinder, c. help, d. hinder, e. help, f. hinder, g. help, h. hinder.

SUGGESTIONS FOR ACTION RESEARCH

1. Observe a class in which students take a standardized test. If possible, take a copy of the test administration guidelines with you and determine how closely the teacher followed the directions. What has the teacher done to motivate the students and set a proper environment? Observe the students as they are taking the test. Do they seem motivated and serious? How quickly do they work?

2. Sit in on two or three teacher–parent conferences that review the results of standardized tests. Compare what occurs with the suggestions in the chapter. How well, in your opinion, does the teacher interpret the scores? Is the teacher accurate?

3. Interview some parents about standardized tests. What did they get from the reports? Which types of scores were most meaningful? Did the results surprise them? Were the results consistent with other performance, such as grades?

4. Interview some teachers about standardized testing. Ask them how they use the results of standardized tests to improve their instruction. Ask them to recall situations where parents did not seem to understand the results of the test very well. Looking back, what could the teacher have done differently to enhance parent understanding?

REFERENCES

Airasian, P. W. (1994). *Classroom assessment* (2nd ed.). New York: McGraw-Hill, Inc.

Ames, C. A. (1990). Motivation: What teachers need to know. *Teachers College Record, 91*, 409–421.

Anderson, L. W. (1981). *Assessing affective characteristics in the schools*. Boston: Allyn & Bacon.

Arter, J., & Spandel, V. (1992). Using portfolios of student work in instruction and assessment. *Educational Measurement: Issues and Practice, 11*, 36–44.

Azwell, T., & Schmar, E. (1995). *Report card on report cards: Alternatives to consider*. Portsmouth, NH: Heineman.

Bacon, M. (1993). *Restructuring curriculum, instruction, and assessment in the Littleton Public Schools*. Littleton, CO: Littleton Public Schools.

Beyer, A., & others (1993). *Alternative assessment: Evaluating student performance in elementary mathematics*. Ann Arbor Public Schools. Palo Alto, CA: Dale Seymour Publications.

Beyer, B. K. (1985). Critical thinking: What is it? *Social Education, 22*, 270–276.

Billups, L. H., & Rauth, M. (1987). Teachers and research. In V. Richardson-Koehler (Ed.), *Educator's handbook*. White Plains, NY: Longman.

Bloom, B. S. (Ed.) (1956). *Taxonomy of educational objectives: The classification of educational goals. Handbook 1. Cognitive Domain*. New York: David McKay Co.

Braun, C. (1976). Teacher expectation: Sociopsychological dynamics. *Review of Educational Research, 46*, 185–213.

Brookhart, S. M. (1993). Teachers' grading practices: Meaning and values. *Journal of Educational Measurement, 30*, 123–142.

Brophy, J. (1981). Teacher praise: A functional analysis. *Review of Educational Research, 51*, 5–32.

Brophy, J. E., & Alleman, J. (1991). Activities as instructional tools: A framework for analysis and evaluation. *Educational Researcher, 20*, 9–23.

Camp, R. (1992). Portfolio reflections in middle and secondary school classrooms. In K. B. Yancey (Ed.), *Portfolios in the writing classroom*. Urbana, IL: National Council of Teachers of English. Copyright © 1992 by the National Council of Teachers of English. Reprinted with permission.

Carey, L. M. (1994). *Measuring and evaluating school learning* (2nd ed.). Boston: Allyn & Bacon.

Cohen, S. B. (1983). Assigning report card grades to the mainstreamed child. *Teaching Exceptional Students, 15*, 86–89.

Collins, A., & Dana, T. M. (1993). Using portfolios with middle grades students. *Middle School Journal, 25*, 14–19.

Creating a learning environment at Fowler High School. (1993). Syracuse, NY: Inclusive Education Project, Syracuse University.

Davis, M. M. D. (1995). *The nature of data sources that inform decision making in reading by experienced second grade teachers.* Doctoral dissertation, Old Dominion University.

Doyle, W. (1986). Classroom organization and management. In M. C. Wittrock (Ed.), *Handbook of research on teaching* (3rd ed.). New York: Macmillan.

Ekman, P., & Friesen, W. V. (1969). The repertoire of nonverbal behavior: Categories, origins, usage, and coding. *Semiotica, 69,* 49–97.

Elawar, M C., & Corno, L. (1985). A factorial experiment in teachers' written feedback on student homework: Changing teacher behavior a little rather than a lot. *Journal of Educational Psychology, 77,* 162–173.

Ennis, R. H. (1987). A taxonomy of critical thinking dispositions and abilities. In J. B. Baron and R. J. Sternberg (Eds.), *Teaching thinking skills: Theory and practice.* New York: W. H. Freeman.

Evertson, C., & Green, J. (1986). Observation as inquiry and method. In M. C. Wittrock (Ed.), *Handbook of research on teaching* (3rd ed.), pp. 162–213. New York: Macmillan.

Feather, N. (Ed.). (1982). *Expectations and actions.* Hillsdale, NJ: Erlbaum.

Frisbie, D. A., & Waltman, K. K. (1992). Developing a personal grading plan. *Educational Measurement: Issues and Practice, 11,* 35–42.

Gagne, E. D., Yekovich, C. W., & Yekovich, F. R. (1993). *The cognitive psychology of school learning* (2nd ed.). New York: HarperCollins College Publishers.

Gardner, H., (1985). *Frames of mind: The theory of multiple intelligences.* New York: Basic Books.

Gold, S. E. (1992). Increasing student autonomy through portfolios. In K. B. Yancey (Ed.), *Portfolios in the writing classroom.* Urbana, IL: National Council of Teachers of English.

Good, T. L., & Brophy, J. E. (1994). *Looking in classrooms.* New York: HarperCollins.

Gordon, M., (1987). *Nursing diagnosis: Process and application.* New York: McGraw-Hill.

Gronlund, N. E. (1993). *How to make achievement tests and assessments* (5th ed.). Boston: Allyn & Bacon.

Gronlund, N. E. (1991). *How to write and use instructional objectives* (4th ed.). New York: Macmillan.

Guskey, T. R. (Ed.). (1996). *Communicating student learning: 1996 ASCD Yearbook.* Alexandria, VA: Association for Supervision and Curriculum Development.

Guskey, T. R. (1994). Making the grade: What benefits students? *Educational Leadership, 52,* 14–20.

Haertel, E. (1990). From expert opinions to reliable scores: Psychometrics for judgement-based teacher assessment. Paper presented at the annual meeting of the American Educational Research Association, Boston, MA.

Hanna, G. S. (1993). *Better teaching through better measurement.* Orlando, FL: Harcourt Brace Jovanovich, Inc.

Hein, G. E., & Price, S. (1994). *Active assessment for active science: A guide for elementary school teachers.* Portsmouth, NH: Heinemann.

Herman, J. L., Aschbacher, P. R., & Winters, L. (1992). *A practical guide to alternative assessment.* Alexandria, VA: Association for Supervision and Curriculum.

Hohn, R. L. (1995). *Classroom learning & teaching.* White Plains, NY: Longman.

Jackson, P. W. (1968). *Life in classrooms.* New York: Holt, Rinehart, and Winston.

Jamentz, K. (1994). Making sure that assessment improves performance. *Educational Leadership, 51,* 55–57.

Kindsvatter, R., Wilen, W., & Ishler, M. (1992). *Dynamics of effective teaching* (2nd ed.). White Plains, NY: Longman.

Kissock, C., & Iyortsuun, P. T. (1982). *A guide to questioning: Classroom procedures for teachers.* London: The Macmillan Press, Ltd.

Knapp, M. L. (1978). *Nonverbal communication in human interaction* (2nd ed.). New York: Holt.

Koretz, D., McCaffrey, D., Klein, S., Bell, R., & Stecher, B. (1993). *The reliability of scores from the 1992 Vermont portfolio assessment program.* (CSE Technical Report 355). Los Angeles: University of California, Center for Research on Evaluation, Standards, and Student Testing.

Krathwohl, D. R., Bloom, B. S., & Masia, B. B. (1964). *Taxonomy of educational objectives, handbook II: Affective domain.* New York: David McKay.

Kubiszyn, T., & Borich, G. (1993). *Educational testing and measurement: Classroom application and practice* (4th ed.). New York: HarperCollins College Publishers.

Lambdin, D. V., & Walker, V. L. (1994). Planning for classroom portfolio assessment. *The Arithmetic Teacher, 41,* 318–324.

Lane, S., Parke, C., & Moskal, B. (1992). Principles for developing performance assessments. Paper presented at the 1992 Annual Meeting of the American Educational Research Association.

Lazzari, A. M., & Wood, J. W. (1994). *Test right: Strategies and exercises to improve test performance.* East Moline, IL: LinguiSystems, Inc.

Leathers, D. G. (1986). *Successful nonverbal communication: Principles and applications.* New York: Macmillan.

Lickona, T. (1993). The return of character education. *Educational Leadership, 51,* 6–11.

Linn, R. L., & Gronlund, N. E. (1995). *Measurement and assessment in teaching* (7th ed.). Englewood Cliffs, NJ: Prentice-Hall.

Marzano, R. J. (1992). *A different kind of classroom: Teaching with dimensions of learning.* Alexandria, VA: Association for Supervision and Curriculum Development.

Marzano, R. J., Brandt, R., & Hughes, C. S. (1988). *Dimensions of thinking: A framework for curriculum and instruction.* Alexandria, VA: Association for Supervision and Curriculum Development.

Marzano, R. J., Pickering, D., & McTighe, J. (1993). *Assessing student outcomes: Performance assessment using the dimensions of learning model.* Alexandria, VA: Association for Supervision and Curriculum Development.

McMillan, J. H. (1980). Attitude development and measurement. In J. H. McMillan (Ed.), *The social psychology of school learning.* New York: Academic Press.

McMillan, J. H. & Forsyth, D. R. (1991). What theories of motivation say about why learners learn. In R. J. Menges and M. D. Svinicki (Eds.), *College teaching: From theory to practice.* San Francisco: Jossey-Bass.

McMillan, J. H., Simonetta, L. G., & Singh, J. (1994). Student opinion survey: Development of measures of student motivation. *Educational and Psychological Measurement, 54,* 496–505.

Mehrabian, A. (1971). *Silent messages.* Belmont, CA: Wadsworth.

Mehrens, W. A., & Lehmann, I. J. (1987). *Using standardized tests in education* (4th ed.). New York: Longman.

Mehring, T. A. (1995). Report card options for students with disabilities in general education. In T. Azwell & E. Schmar (Eds.), *Report card on report cards: Alternatives to consider.* Portsmouth, NH: Heinemann.

Morgan, N., & Saxton, J. (1991). *Teaching, questioning, and learning.* New York: Routledge.

National standards for civics and government. (1994). Calabasas, CA: Center for Civic Education.

Nolen, S. B., Haladyna, T. M., & Haas, N. S. (1989). A survey of Arizona teachers and administrators on the uses and effects of state-mandated standardized achievement testing (Tech. Rep. No. 89–2). Phoenix, AZ: Arizona State University, West Campus.

Norris, S. P., & Ennis, R. H. (1989). *Evaluating critical thinking.* Pacific Grove, CA: Midwest Publications.

Oosterhof, A. C. (1987). Obtaining intended weights when combining students' scores. *Educational Measurement: Issues and Practices, 6,* 29–37.

Popham, W. J. (1994). Anonymity-enhancement procedures for classroom affective assessment. Paper presented at the Annual Meeting of the American Educational Research Association, New Orleans, LA.

Popham, W. J. (1995). *Classroom assessment: What teachers need to know.* Boston: Allyn & Bacon.

Porter, C., & Cleland, J. (1995). *The portfolio as a learning strategy*. Portsmouth, NH: Boynton/Cook Publishers, Inc.

Quellmalz, E. (1987). Developing reasoning skills. In J. B. Baron & R. J. Sternberg (Eds.), *Teaching thinking skills: Theory and practice*. New York: W. H. Freeman.

Raviv, A., Raviv, A., & Reisel, E. (1990). Teachers and students: Two different perspectives?! Measuring social climate in the classroom. *American Educational Research Journal, 27*, 141–157.

Rokeach, M. (1973). *The nature of human values*. New York: The Free Press.

Rothman, R. (1995). The certificate of initial mastery. *Educational Leadership, 52*, 41–45.

Simpson, E J. (1972). The classification of educational objectives in the psychomotor domain. *The psychomotor domain* (Vol. 3). Washington, DC: Gryphon House.

Stenmark, J. K. (1991). *Mathematics assessment: Myths, models, good questions, and practical suggestions*. Reston, VA: The National Council of Teachers of Mathematics, Inc.

Sternberg, R. J. (1986). The future of intelligence testing. *Educational measurement: Issues and practice, 5*, 19–22.

Stiggins, R. J. (1994). *Student-centered classroom assessment*. New York: Merrill.

Stiggins, R. J., & Conklin, N. F. (1992). *In teachers' hands: Investigating the practices of classroom assessment*. Albany, NY: State University of New York Press.

Terwilliger, J. S. (1989). Classroom standard setting and grading practices. *Educational Measurement: Issues and Practice, 8*, 15–19.

Tittle, C. K., Hecht, D., & Moore, P. (1993). Assessment theory and research for classrooms: From *Taxonomies* to constructing meaning in context. *Educational Measurement: Issues and Practices, 12*, 13–19.

Valencia, S. W., & Calfee, R. (1991). The development and use of literacy portfolios for students, classes, and teachers. *Applied Measurement in Education, 4*, 333–345.

Wiggins, G. P. (1993). *Assessing student performance: Exploring the purpose and limits of testing*. San Francisco: Jossey-Bass.

Wolf, D. P. (1989). Portfolio assessment: Sampling student work. *Educational Leadership, 46*, 35–39.

Wolf, D. P. (1993). Assessment as an episode of learning. In R. Bennett & W. Ward (Eds.), *Construction vs. choice in cognitive measurement* (pp. 213–240). Hillsdale, NJ: Lawrence Erlbaum Associates.

Wood, J. W., (1992). *Adapting instruction for mainstreamed and at-risk students* (2nd ed.). New York: Merrill/Macmillan.

Wurtz, E. (1993). Promises to keep: Creating high standards for American students. Report on the Review of Education Standards from the Goals 3 and 4 Technical Planning Group to the National Education Goals Panel, Washington, DC.

Wylie, R. C. (1989). *Measures of self-concept*. Lincoln, NE: University of Nebraska Press.

APPENDIX A

NATIONAL CONTENT STANDARDS PROJECTS

Subject	Developers	Order Information
Arts	The Consortium of National Arts Education Associations	*National Standards for Arts Education*, write MENC Publication Sales, 1806 Robert Fulton Dr., Reston, VA 22091, or call (703) 860-4000
Civics	The Center for Civic Education	*National Standards for Civics and Government*, write Center for Civic Education, 5146 Douglas Fir Rd., Calabasas CA 91302-1467, or call (818) 591-9321
Economics	The National Council on Economic Education, the Foundation for Teaching Economics, the American Economics Association Committee on Economic Education, and the National Association of Economics Education	Write National Council of Economic Education, 1140 Avenue of the Americas, New York NY 10036, or call (212) 730-7007
English	National Council of Teachers of English and the International Reading Association	*Standards for the Assessment of Reading and Writing*, write to International Reading Association, 800 Barksdale Rd., P.O. Box 8139, Newark, DE 19714-8139, or call (302) 731-1600
Foreign languages	The American Council on the Teaching of Foreign Languages, the American Association of Teachers of German, the American Association of Teachers of French, and the American Association of Teachers of Spanish and Portuguese	Write to the American Council on the Teaching of Foreign Languages, or call (914) 963-8830.

Subject	Developers	Order Information
Geography	The National Council for Geographic Education, the National Geographic Society, the Association of American Geographers, and the American Geographical Society	*Geography for Life: National Geographic Standards 1994*, write to National Geographic, P.O. Box 1640, Washington, DC 20013-1640, or call (202) 775-7832
Health	The American Cancer Society, the Association for the Advancement of Health Education, the American School Health Association, the Society of State Directors of Health, Physical Education, and Recreation, and the School Health Education and Services section of the American Public Health Association	Call (703) 476-3441
History	The National Center for History in the Schools at the University of California at Los Angeles	*National Standards for World History*, *National Standards for United States History*, and *National Standards for History for Grades K–4*, write the National Center for History in the Schools, 10880 Wilshire Blvd., Suite 761, Los Angeles, CA 90024-4108, or call (310) 825-4702
Mathematics	The National Council of Teachers of Mathematics	*Curriculum and Evaluation Standards for School Mathematics*, *Professional Standards for Teaching Mathematics*, and *Assessment Standards for School Mathematics*, write N.C.T.M., 1906 Association Dr., Reston, VA 22091-1593, or call (800) 235-7566
Physical education	The National Association for Sport and Physical Education	*Content Standards*, and *Assessment Guide for School Physical Education*, write N.A.S.P.E., 1900 Association Dr., Reston VA 22091, or call (800) 321-0789
Science	The National Research Council, drawn from the National Academy of Sciences, the National Academy of Engineering, and the Institute of Medicine	*National Science Education Standards*, call (202) 334-1399
Social studies	The National Council for the Social Studies	*Expectations of Excellence: Curriculum Standards for Social Studies*, write Whitehurst & Clark, 100 Newfield Ave., Raritan Center, Edison, NJ 08837, or call (800) 683-0812

APPENDIX B

SOFTWARE PACKAGES FOR GRADING AND ITEM BANKING

The following list of software programs can be used for computerized grading and item banking. You will want to check on the hardware requirements. Yearly updates can be obtained from Data Pro Research Corporation, Delran, NJ 08075. See Kubiszyn & Borich (1993) and Hanna (1993) for descriptions of most of these programs. Of course, updates and new versions are available on a regular basis.

Apple Grader, available from AV Systems, Inc., 1445 Estrella, Santa Barbara, CA 93110.

Authorware Professional, Micrograde 2.0, and Microtest III, and Oyster, available from Chariot Software, 3659 India St., San Diego, CA 92103.

Cactus Grade Book, available from Cactusplot Company, 1422 North McAllister, Tempe, AZ 85281.

Classmate, Gradebook Deluxe, Test It! Deluxe, and TestWriter, available from BrainTrain, 1915 Huguenot Rd., Richmond, VA 23235.

Compu-Mark, available from Chautauqua Computer Systems, Box 1161, High River, Alberta, Canada T0L 1B0.

EA Gradebook, available from Educational Activities, Inc., 1937 Grand Ave., Baldwin, NY 11510.

Electronic Grade Book and Test Generator, available from Queue, Inc., 338 Commerce Dr., Fairfield, CT 06430.

Exam in a Can, available from Tom Snyder Productions, Inc., 90 Sherman St., Cambridge, MA 02140.

E-Z Grade, available from Cambridge Career Products, P.O. Box 2153, Charleston, WV 25328.

Grade Book 1.2, available from Bobbing Software, 67 Country Oaks Dr., Buda, TX 78610.

Grade Machine, The, Misty City Software, 10921 129th Pl. NE, Kirkland, WA 98033.

Grade Manager, available from MECC, 3490 Lexington Ave., St. Paul, MN 55112.

Grade Reporter, available from Cross Educational Software, Inc., 504 East Kentucky Ave., P. O. Box 1536, Ruston, LA 71270.

Grade 2, available from IBM Direct, PC Software Department, One Culver Rd., Dayton, NJ 08810.

Gradebook, available from K and G Software, 1314 3rd St., East Wenatchee, WA 98801.

Gradebook Plus, available from Scholastic, Inc., 1290 Wall St. West, Lyndhurst, NJ 07071.

Grading System and Grading System Programs PC, available from CMA Micro Computer, 558888 Yucca Trail, Unit 6, P.O. Box 2080, Yucca Valley, CA 92286-2080.

MicroCAT Computerized Testing System, available from Assessment Systems Corporation, 2233 University Ave., Suite 200, St. Paul, MN 55114-1629.

LXR-Test 4.1, available from Logic Extension Resources, 9651 Business Center Dr., Suite C, Rancho Cucamonga, CA 91730.

Report Card II, available from Sensible Software, 20200 G. 9 Mile Rd., Suite 150, St. Clair Shores, MI 48080.

SRA Micro Test Administration System, available from Science Research Associates, 155 N. Wacker Dr., Chicago, IL 60606.

INDEX